SCIENCE
HORIZONS

Silver Burdett Ginn

MORRISTOWN, NJ ■ NEEDHAM, MA

Atlanta, GA ■ Dallas, TX ■ Deerfield, IL ■ Menlo Park, CA

SCIENCE HORIZONS

Sterling Edition

George G. Mallinson
Distinguished Professor
of Science Education
Western Michigan University

Jacqueline B. Mallinson
Associate Professor of Science
Western Michigan University

Linda Froschauer
Science Senior Teacher
Central Middle School
Greenwich, CT

James A. Harris
Principal, D.C. Everest
Area School District
Schofield, Wisconsin

Melanie C. Lewis
Professor, Department of Biology
Southwest Texas State University
San Marcos, Texas

Catherine Valentino
Former Director of Instruction
North Kingstown School Department
North Kingstown, Rhode Island

Acknowledgments appear on pages 568–571, which constitute an extension of this copyright page.

Dear Students,

What do roller coasters, rockets, race cars, and robots have in common? Science is one thing they have in common. Without science, none of them would exist.

Science is a part of everything around you. Take a look at some of the objects in your classroom. Can you explain the scientific ideas represented by a pair of scissors or a stapler? Do you understand how a light bulb works? Understanding how parts of your world work is one of the goals we have for you in science this year.

Imagine joining a group of people who are starting a colony on a distant planet. You can take along only a few small items on the voyage. How would you decide what to take? This year you will learn how to think and how to solve problems such as this.

Some problems, such as How can I avoid abusing drugs? affect you directly. Other problems, such as What can be done to reduce air pollution? affect the world you live in. Science can help you to solve these kinds of problems.

We have still another goal for you this year — to have fun in science. Can you imagine jewelry with ancient flies trapped inside? You will see how the insects got there. Does riding on a roller coaster sound like fun? Then turn to the chapter called "Reaching New Horizons" to meet people who have spent their lives designing roller coasters, solving scientific problems, and having fun!

With our best wishes,
The Authors

Contents

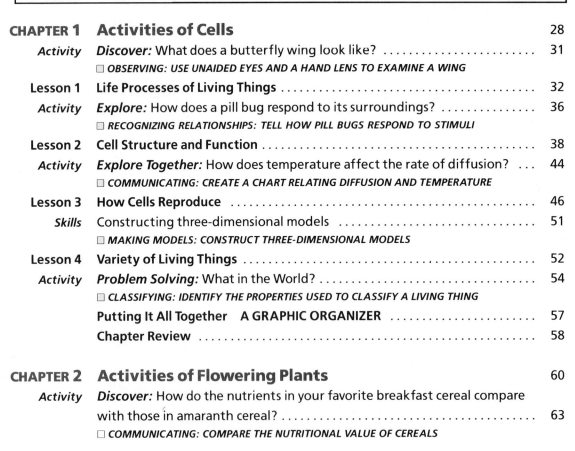

UNIT TWO
PHYSICAL SCIENCE

UNIT THREE
EARTH SCIENCE

UNIT FOUR
HUMAN BODY

Coaster Crazy

Oh-h-h-h-h-h-h No-o-o-o-o-o! We were headed for the loop, and we were in the lead car. Just ahead of us, two metal tracks glinted in the afternoon sun. Up and up they rose. Closer and closer they loomed. We were going straight up. We were upside down! In an instant a valley of tracks flew up to meet us. My white knuckles sank deeper into the padded safety bar in front of us.

Up the next hill we flew. My throat was dry. I felt heavier and heavier. I saw nothing but sky. Then my stomach seemed to float up to my throat. And down and down we plunged. Just ahead lay the black, yawning entrance of a tunnel. It gulped us up. In the darkness we swerved to the right. Then we swerved to the left and raced toward a circle of light that got larger and larger.

We escaped from the tunnel. Squinting in the brightness, I held my arms up and floated down the last long hill. A screeching halt bounced me forward and then back. The car sat still. But my heart pounded on.

Have you ever been on a roller coaster? You might describe your ride in much the same way. Descriptions like this one may explain how certain roller coasters got their names. Some of their names are Iron Dragon, Cyclone, King Cobra, and Shock Wave.

Roller coasters roar through amusement parks all over the world. There are over 250 roller coasters in North America alone. There is even a club for people who like roller coasters.

There are many different kinds of roller coasters. But the one thing that roller coasters have in common is that they are all made for thrills. One called the

Great American Scream Machine has seven loops. Another, Magnum XL-200, goes faster than the speed limit on most highways. Ninja (NIHN juh) hangs below a rail and swings while it is in motion. On some coasters people are allowed to ride standing up through a loop-the-loop.

What makes a roller coaster work? The trick is in the height of the hills. The speed that is built up going down one hill must be enough to carry you up and over the top of the next hill. A force pulls you down a roller coaster hill. The same force has pulled you toward the earth all your life. Gravity is its name.

Explore Together

ACTIVITY

How does the height of a ramp affect the distance a marble can push an object?

Gravity makes a roller coaster work, but teamwork builds it. Some people plan and design it. Some make materials for it. Some do the actual building. Teamwork gets the job done. In science, activities called **Explore Together** are done by teamwork. Each team, or group, has five members.

Each member has a part in finding the answer to a question. The Organizer gathers and organizes materials and then directs the cleanup when the activity is finished. The Investigator handles materials as the procedure steps direct. The Manager makes sure the activity gets done. The Manager assists the Investigator, keeps time, performs math, and acts as the safety officer.

The Recorder makes drawings and writes down ideas, observations, and answers. The Reporter shares the results and conclusions with the class. All members perform roles assigned to the Group.

Materials

scissors · milk carton · plastic ruler with groove · meterstick · file card · masking tape · marble · calculator

Procedure

Manager A. Use scissors to cut four slots in the side of a milk carton. The slots should be 4 cm, 8 cm, 12 cm, and 16 cm from the bottom of the carton.

Investigator B. Make a ramp by placing a plastic ruler in the 4-cm slot. Adjust the ruler so that the distance from the bottom of the carton to the lower end of the ruler is 24 cm.

Manager C. Fold a file card in half. Place the card, as shown, 5 cm from the lower end of the ruler. Mark this spot with a piece of masking tape.

Investigator D. Place a marble at the top of the ramp. Release the marble so that it rolls down the ramp and into the folded card.

Recorder E. Measure the distance that the card moved. Record this measurement in a table.

F. Repeat steps **D** and **E** four times.

Manager G. Use a calculator to find the average distance the card moved and record this number in your table.

H. Repeat steps **B** through **G** for each slot in the carton.

Writing and Sharing Results and Conclusions

Recorder 1. Make a graph of the average distance the card moved at each height of the ramp.

Group, Recorder 2. How did the ramp height affect the distance the marble pushed the card?

Reporter 3. How do your results and conclusions compare with those of your classmates?

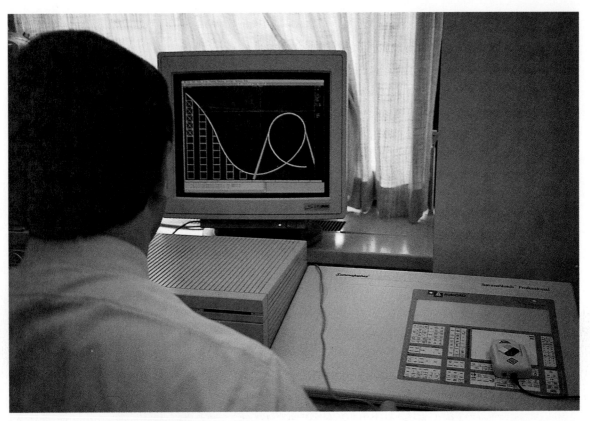

▲ Computer image of a roller coaster loop.

Have you ever felt afraid on a roller coaster? Perhaps you felt that you might fly out into space. Or maybe you felt that you had to duck at the entrance to a tunnel. Many people are afraid to ride a roller coaster. But the truth is that, although rides have become scarier, they have become safer.

The use of computers has made roller coasters safer. Many of today's roller coasters use computers to control braking systems and keep the cars safely separated. Computers can let work crews know if a wheel needs repair. Rides are even designed with the help of computers. And they are designed to be safe. Tunnels are made high enough for a tall basketball player to ride through safely.

Computers, however, cannot control the riders. One of the most important ways to make roller coasters safe is for riders to observe the safety rules.

Besides being designed with safety in mind, roller coasters, of course, are designed to give the rider thrills. Sometimes the thrills are too thrilling even for the designer.

Ron Toomer is one of the leading designers of roller coasters. He has designed many of them. But he had never ridden a roller coaster before he started designing rides. Even now he avoids riding them because he gets motion sickness.

Designers of roller coasters plan a ride so that the thrills come rapidly one after the other. The rider is recovering from one thrill when he or she realizes that another lies just ahead. Designers know that the most successful roller coasters keep the riders screaming from the beginning of the ride to the end.

People who design roller coasters have a difficult job. They must be very creative. But they must also know science. They must know about safety concerns. Roller coaster designers must learn many skills.

Roller coaster loop ▶

THINKING

Skills

Finding the data to use

In science you will learn a variety of skills through **Skills** lessons. In each lesson you will **practice** the skill, **think** about how the skill is used, and then **apply,** or use, the new skill.

Suppose you need to use the data from a table to answer a question about roller coasters. Usually a table is arranged so that you can find certain data easily. Often a table will have more data than you need to answer one question. You must find the data that you need.

Practicing the skill

1. Look at the table below. It gives data for several roller coasters. The *lift* is the height of the first hill. The first hill on a roller coaster is the highest.

2. Think about this question. Does a longer roller coaster always have a higher lift than a shorter roller coaster? Find the data that will help you answer the question.

3. Write the title of each column that gives you the data you need.

Name	Time (minutes)	Total length (meters)	Lift (meters)
Ninja	3.5	824	18
Magnum XL-200	2.5	1557	61
Shock Wave	2.3	1220	50
Great American Scream Machine	2.3	1159	53
Iron Dragon	2	854	23

Thinking about the skill

This data is arranged so that the times required to complete the rides are in order. How could you arrange the data so that it would help you compare lift with length more easily?

Applying the skill

1. Suppose you want to find the average speed of each roller coaster. Find the data you would use.

2. Write the title of each column that gives you the data you need.

Roller coasters are designed to give thrills. Because their designs have become more and more exciting, roller coasters have become more and more popular. There are people who ride roller coasters just to give the coasters thrill ratings.

The new roller coasters can cost millions of dollars to build. But money collected from the people riding them will pay for their building cost by the end of the first or second year.

One skill required to design roller coasters is math. William Cobb is another leading designer of roller coasters. Mr. Cobb uses math to determine the speed and action of the car at every point along the ride. The results tell the designer how the car needs to be sloped on a turn.

There are many problems to solve in designing roller coasters. Three problems that designers have solved concerned wind, wheels, and loops.

Problem Solving

It Has Its Ups and Downs

Loops in a roller-coaster ride are exciting. Finding how to use the loops in a design involves problem solving. This book has activities that give you practice in problem solving. There are four steps to follow.

First, **think** about the problem to be solved. List facts about the problem that you already know. Gather any other information you might need. Second, use the information to **plan** a way to solve the problem. List the things you will need to carry out your plan. Third, gather the things that you need and **do,** or carry out, what you planned. Record your results and conclusions. Fourth, **share** your results and conclusions with your classmates.

Now use these steps to solve this problem.

High winds off Lake Erie caused the cars of Magnum XL-200 to slow down. The picture here shows how the problem was solved. A wind gauge was mounted at the top of the first hill. A wind gauge measures wind speed. Sometimes the wind decreased the speed of the cars too much. The brakes, which are used to control the speed of the ride, were then released. The wind became the coaster's brake.

There was another problem with the Magnum XL-200. The wheels were not lasting as long as expected. Replacing the wheels became costly. The problem was solved by making the diameter

How can you design a wire roller coaster that has one loop?

Think Think of what you know about roller coasters.

Plan Design a plan for a roller coaster. Your plan must include at least one loop. Use a flexible wire 2 m long for the track and a bead or hexnut for the car. The wire must stand by itself. Draw the plan.

Do Try your plan. Tape one end of the wire to the floor. Bend the wire into the shape you planned. On top of the first hill, place the "car" and then release it. It must travel to the end of the wire. If it does not, change your plan.

Share Explain your plan to your classmates. If you had to change the plan, tell how and why you changed it.

of the wheels larger. The wheels then turned more slowly, and there was less wear on them.

The big breakthrough in modern coasters came in solving the problem of the loop. At first, designers planned a track that made a perfect circle. But then they realized that there would be problems. As the car reached the top of the circle, the speed of the car would decrease. The riders, upside down, would be in danger of falling out. As the car reached the bottom of the circle, the speed of the car would increase. Riders would be forced down hard enough to cause injury.

The solution was found by changing the shape of the loop. Instead of forming a circle, the new design formed the shape of a teardrop. The teardrop shape decreases the speed of the cars at the bottom of the loop and increases their speed at the top.

Next season, when the roller coasters begin crawling up those first big hills, will you go coaster crazy? Will you, as one person did, ride the same coaster over 8,000 times? Will you spend, as another person did, about 3 months just waiting in line?

What does the future hold for roller coaster riders? Designers are already dreaming up more of these screaming machines. Will they someday go twice the speed of automobiles? Perhaps some designer will dream up a roller coaster with cars that do jumps or float over magnets. Perhaps future roller coasters will be made so that the design of the tracks can be changed every week. Could roller coasters one day be powered by rockets?

You cannot know what the future holds for roller coaster design. But you can be sure that science will be an important part of that future. Science is a way to ask and answer questions. In this book you will discover many answers to questions about the world of today. Perhaps in its pages you will also discover answers to questions about the future world.

SCIENCE
HORIZONS

Unit One

LIFE SCIENCE

Activities of Cells

Taking a Closer Look

Look at the pictures. Can you guess what is shown in each one? The images have been enlarged by a device called a scanning electron microscope, or SEM. In school you may have used one kind of microscope, called a light microscope. This device uses lenses and light to produce an enlarged image of an object.

Many details are too small to be seen through a light microscope. An SEM uses a beam of electrons instead of a beam of light. Because an SEM uses electrons, it can show many more details.

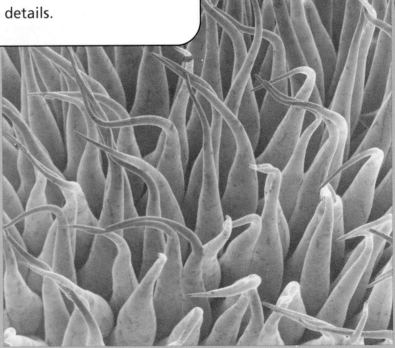

▲ Hibiscus's feathery stigma hairs 600X

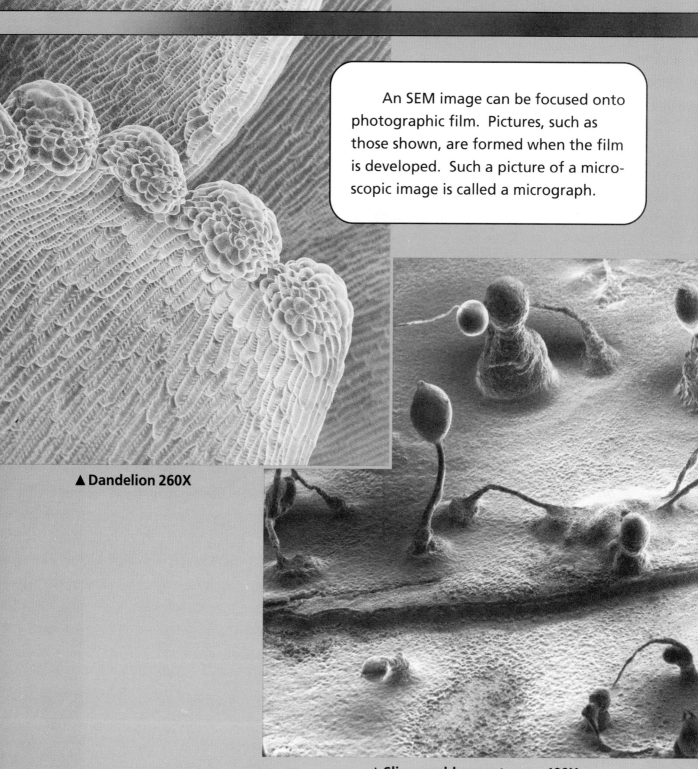

An SEM image can be focused onto photographic film. Pictures, such as those shown, are formed when the film is developed. Such a picture of a microscopic image is called a micrograph.

▲ Dandelion 260X

▲ Slime mold spore towers 100X

▲ Mustard white butterfly

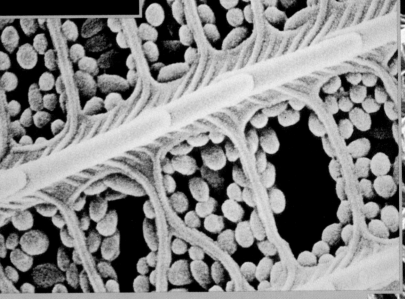

▲ Butterfly wing 6190X

Notice that all of the SEM micrographs shown are in color. But images produced by the SEM are black and white. A computer was used to add color to the SEM images. For example, an image of a blue fiber can be colored blue, red, green, or any other color.

Look again at the pictures and read the captions. How many of the micrographs did you guess correctly?

Discover

What does a butterfly wing look like?

Materials hand lens · microscope · microscope slide · cover slip · butterfly wing

Procedure

The SEM image below shows the wing of a butterfly. The picture shows the tiny scales that cover the wing. These scales make the wing of a butterfly seem dusty.

To see the scales, rub some dust from a butterfly wing onto a slide. Then look at the slide with a hand lens. Finally, look at the scales with a microscope. Use each power of the microscope to study the scales. Draw what you see at each power. How does what you see change as you increase the power of the microscope?

In this chapter you will learn about the main traits of living things. You will read about the structure of cells and how cells divide. You will also find out how scientists group all living things.

▲ Butterfly wing 1010X

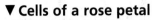
▼ Cells of a rose petal

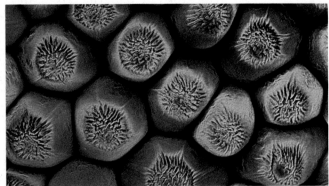

1. Life Processes of Living Things

Words to Know
cell
life processes
metabolism
reproduction

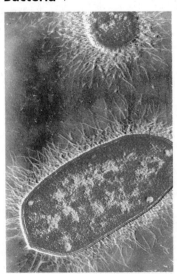

Bacteria ▼

What are the main traits of living things?

There are many different kinds of living things. All living things are made up of the same basic building blocks—cells. The **cell** is the basic unit of all living things. The pictures on this page and the next show all or part of different kinds of living things as seen through a microscope. What do the pictures have in common? They all show cells. Some of the pictures, such as those of bacteria, show one-celled organisms. Others show groups of cells from many-celled organisms.

All organisms carry out certain activities to

survive. For example, all organisms grow. They respond to things around them. They produce more living things like themselves. All the activities that enable organisms to survive are called **life processes.**

In a one-celled organism, all the life processes are carried out by the one cell. In a many-celled organism, the life processes are carried out by groups of cells. For example, some groups of cells working together cause movement. Muscle cells cause the hand to move. Nerve cells receive and transmit the message to the muscle cells.

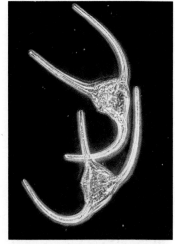
▲ One-celled organisms from the ocean

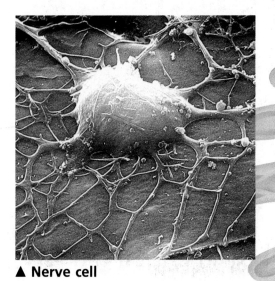
▲ Nerve cell

What are the life processes?

GROWING All living things grow. In a many-celled organism, growth occurs in two ways. One way growth occurs is by an increase in the number of cells. Another way is by an increase in the size of cells.

RESPONDING TO SURROUNDINGS All living things respond to their surroundings. For example, a moth will fly toward a light. A lion will chase a zebra. The roots of a plant will grow toward a source of water.

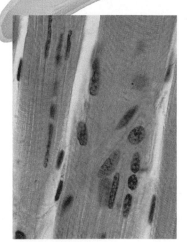
▲ Muscle cells

▲ A bobcat chasing a
snowshoe rabbit

The picture above shows a bobcat chasing a rabbit, a
source of food. What are some other ways that living
things respond to their surroundings?

OBTAINING ENERGY All living things need energy
to carry on their life processes. Some organisms get
energy from food they gather. Other organisms
produce their own food. Living things obtain energy
by breaking down food, which contains stored energy. Substances that make up food are broken
down through chemical changes in the cells. All the
chemical changes that take place in a living thing
are called its **metabolism** (muh TAB uh lihz um).

RELEASING AND USING ENERGY One very important chemical process that takes place in cells is
respiration (res puh RAY shun). Respiration is a
process in which oxygen combines with food, releasing energy. Most of the living things you know about
release energy from food by respiration. Some simple organisms, such as certain bacteria, carry on a

process that is somewhat like respiration. This process does not use oxygen. But the end result of the process is also the release of energy from food.

RELEASING WASTES The chemical changes that take place in an organism produce wastes. These wastes may be in the form of gases, liquids, or solids. The wastes must be removed from the organism or it will die. In one-celled living things, wastes pass through the cell membrane to the outside of the cell. In many-celled living things, the removal of wastes is more complex. Waste removal is often through a system of tubes.

PRODUCING NEW ORGANISMS All living things can produce more living things of their own kind. The process by which organisms produce more of their own kind is **reproduction** (ree pruh DUK shun). Living things produce offspring that are like themselves. For example, orangutans, which are many-celled, produce only orangutans. And amebas, which are one-celled, produce only amebas. Reproduction is the life process that ensures that a certain kind of living thing will continue to exist.

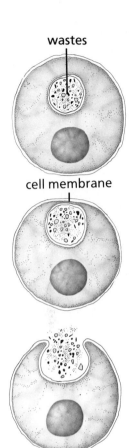

wastes

cell membrane

▲ **A cell releasing wastes**

An orangutan mother and baby ▼

35

Explore

ACTIVITY

How does a pill bug respond to its surroundings?

Have you ever picked up a rock and found pill bugs underneath? Pill bugs are small land animals that are related to crabs and lobsters. How will they behave in your classroom?

Materials
5 pill bugs · shoebox with lid · 2 cotton swabs · dropper bottle of vinegar · paper towels · water

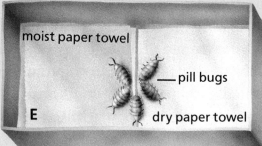

shoebox

moist paper towel

pill bugs

E

dry paper towel

Procedure

A. Place a pill bug in a shoebox lid. Observe the pill bug.

B. Carefully touch the pill bug with a cotton swab.
   1. How does the pill bug respond?

C. Place a few drops of vinegar on the cotton swab. Carefully move the cotton swab near the pill bug, but do not touch the bug.
   2. How does the pill bug respond to the vinegar?

D. Fold a paper towel and put it on one side of the bottom of the shoebox. Fold a second paper towel, moisten it, and put it on the other side of the shoebox.

E. Place five pill bugs in the center of the bottom of the shoebox. Draw a picture of the location of the pill bugs. Cover the box and wait 15 minutes.

F. Remove the lid of the shoebox. Draw a picture of the location of each pill bug now.
   3. Have the pill bugs moved?

Writing and Sharing Results and Conclusions

1. Describe how pill bugs respond to touch, to vinegar, and to moisture.

2. Why are pill bugs often found under rocks?

3. How do your results and conclusions compare with those of your classmates?

How do living and nonliving things differ?

Some nonliving things may seem to carry out life processes. Here you see a picture of icicles. Icicles can increase in length. But are icicles alive? Do they grow, as a living thing grows?

Look at the picture of soap bubbles. Then look at the picture of the many-celled organism. Compare the two pictures. The soap bubbles and the organism look a lot alike. But are the soap bubbles alive? No. Soap bubbles and icicles are nonliving things. They do not carry out life processes. Only living things can carry out life processes.

▲ "Growth" of icicles

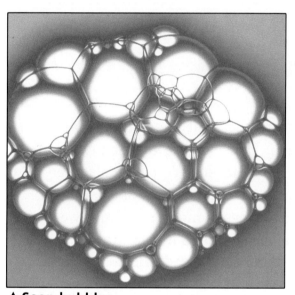

▲ Soap bubbles

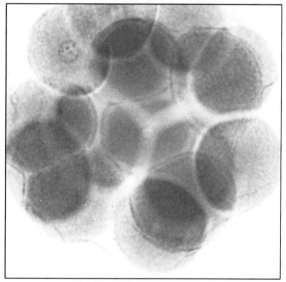

▲ Many-celled organism

Lesson Review

1. Define the term *life processes.*
2. Name four life processes and explain how each enables a living thing to survive.
3. Give an example of one living thing and one nonliving thing. Explain the main way in which they differ from each other.

Think! Suppose that you found an unfamiliar object that may be living. How can you find out whether it is living or nonliving?

Physical Science
CONNECTION

The energy used by living things is called chemical energy. This form of energy can be changed into other forms, like mechanical energy when a muscle moves.

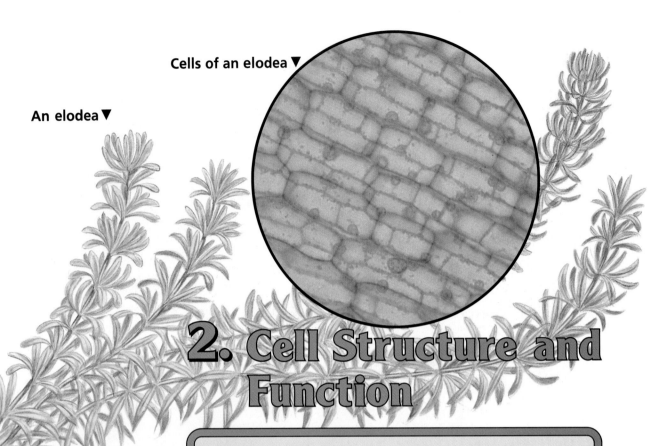

An elodea ▼

Cells of an elodea ▼

2. Cell Structure and Function

Getting Started Look at the pictures at the top of this page. You can see a common plant often found in fish tanks. You can also see a close-up of the surface of a leaf of that plant. Notice that the surface is made up of many cells. What do all these cells have in common?

What are the main parts of a cell?

Recall that all living things are made of the same basic building blocks, cells. The cells of all living things—from whales to amebas—are alike in certain ways. For example, each cell has a membrane, or thin covering, surrounding the cell. Inside this membrane is a jellylike substance that contains most of the cell parts.

Look at the animal cells and plant cells on this page and the next. Find a dark, round structure inside each of the cells. This structure is the nucleus

(NOO klee us). The **nucleus** is the control center of the cell.

The nucleus contains parts that sometimes look like threads. Each of the threadlike parts in a cell nucleus is called a **chromosome** (KROH muh sohm). Look at the chromosomes in the picture at the right. Chromosomes contain a code, or set of directions, that controls all cell functions. This code controls the traits of the organism. It also controls how the traits are passed on to new cells that form when a cell reproduces.

Single chromosomes usually cannot be seen clearly. They can be seen best during the reproduction of a cell.

The nucleus is surrounded by a thin covering called the nuclear (NOO klee ur) membrane. Find this structure in the drawing of the animal cells on the next page. The nuclear membrane helps control the movement of materials into and out of the nucleus. This membrane allows some things to enter and some things to leave the nucleus.

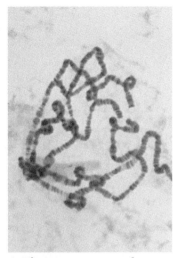

▲ Chromosomes of a fruit fly

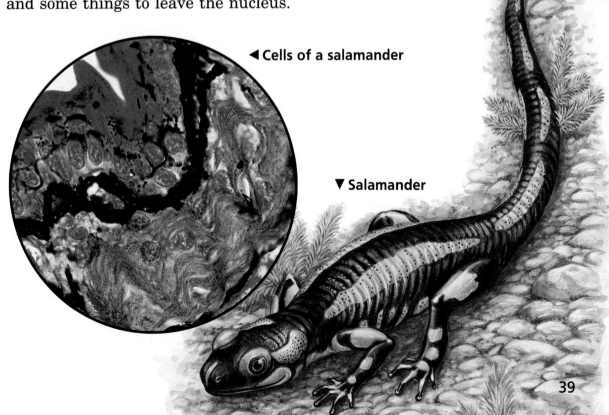

◄ Cells of a salamander

▼ Salamander

39

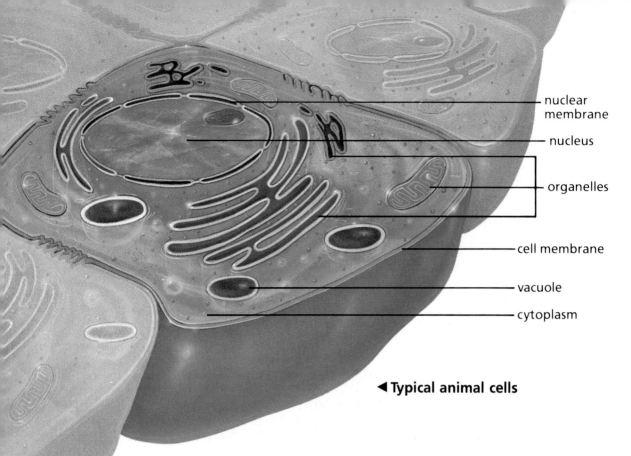

nuclear membrane

nucleus

organelles

cell membrane

vacuole

cytoplasm

◀ **Typical animal cells**

Not every cell has a nucleus and a nuclear membrane. Some cells have nuclear material scattered throughout their jellylike part. You will read more about such cells on page 55.

Cytoplasm (SYT oh plaz um) is the thick, jellylike substance that surrounds the nucleus and forms most of the cell. All cells contain cytoplasm. Most of the life processes of a cell take place in structures that float in the cytoplasm.

Look again at the drawing of the animal cells, above. Notice that the cytoplasm contains many small structures. These structures are called organelles (or guh NELZ), or "small organs." They carry out activities that keep the cell alive.

In some cells there are structures that look like air bubbles. These structures are vacuoles (VAK yoo-ohlz). A **vacuole** is a fluid-filled sac in the cell. The vacuole may contain stored food and water that will be used by the cell. Or it may contain waste gases that will leave the cell. Some vacuoles contain chemicals that help digest food. The vacuoles of some cells are very large. In the plant cells shown below, the vacuoles nearly fill the cells.

Every cell is enclosed by a cell membrane. A **cell membrane** is a structure that surrounds and protects the cell. It also controls the movement of materials into and out of the cell. The cell membrane acts somewhat like a screen. It allows only certain materials to enter and to leave the cell. Why is this "screening" action of the cell membrane important to the cell?

Besides a cell membrane, some cells have a cell wall. A **cell wall** is a rigid structure that surrounds the cell membrane. Plant cells have a cell wall. Animal cells do not. Look for the cell walls in the drawing of plant cells. The cell walls protect the cells and give them shape.

Typical plant cells ▼

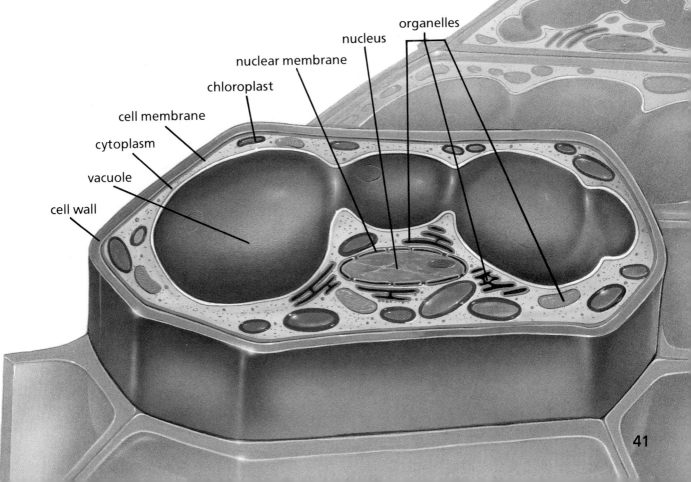

organelles

nucleus

nuclear membrane

chloroplast

cell membrane

cytoplasm

vacuole

cell wall

How do plant and animal cells compare?

Plant cells are like animal cells in many ways. Plant cells have a nucleus, a cell membrane, vacuoles, and organelles. But plant cells have some parts that animal cells do not have.

As you know, every plant cell has a cell wall. Nearly all plant cells have chloroplasts (KLOR uh-plasts). A chloroplast is a structure that contains green-colored matter used in food making in plants. The green matter in the chloroplasts is called chlorophyll (KLOR uh fihl). It is chlorophyll that gives plants their green color. Find the chloroplasts in the picture below.

Chloroplasts are the food factories of plants. Inside the chloroplasts, energy from the sun is used in the food-making process. In the presence of chlorophyll and sunlight, water and carbon dioxide are combined. A chemical change occurs, producing food in the form of sugar. Oxygen is given off as another product of the process.

▼ **Chloroplasts in plant cells**

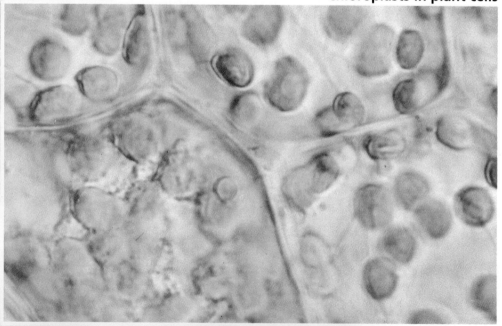

How do materials move into and out of cells?

Did you ever burn toast in your kitchen? After a while, the burned toast could probably be smelled in other rooms. How can the odor move from the kitchen to the living room?

Particles of gas from the burned toast enter the air all around the toast. These particles bump into other particles in the air. They move in all directions, away from the toast. In time the particles move from the air in the kitchen to the air in the living room. Someone standing in the living room can then smell the odor of the burned toast. You can see this process in the drawing of the house, shown below. Where else could someone smell the burned toast?

Diffusion of particles from burned toast ▼   **Diffusion of particles several hours later ▼**

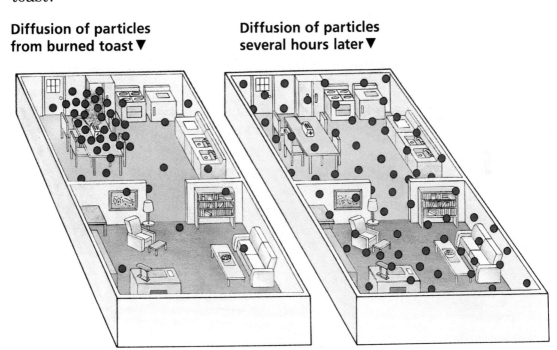

The process by which particles move from one region to another is called **diffusion** (dih FYOO-zhun). In diffusion, particles move from a region where there is a large amount of a substance to one where there is a small amount.

Explore Together

How does temperature affect the rate of diffusion?

Materials

Organizer   masking tape · 3 500-mL beakers · marking pencil · water · 3 thermometers · food coloring · clock

Procedure

Recorder, Investigator

A. Tape a strip of masking tape to each of three 500-mL beakers. Using a marking pencil, label the beakers *Cold Water, Room-Temperature Water,* and *Hot Water.*

Investigator

B. Fill the first beaker with refrigerated water. Fill the second beaker with room-temperature water. Fill the third beaker with hot water. **Caution:** *Let water from the tap run until it is hot, but not scalding hot.*

Manager, Recorder

C. Place a thermometer in each of the beakers. Record the temperature of the water in each beaker.

Investigator

D. Now place 1 drop of food coloring in the center of each beaker on the surface of the water.

Group, Recorder

E. Observe and record what has happened in each beaker after 5 minutes, 15 minutes, 30 minutes, and 60 minutes.

Writing and Sharing Results and Conclusions

Group, Reporter

1. How long did it take for food coloring to diffuse throughout the water in each beaker?

2. How was the diffusion of food coloring affected by the temperature of the water?

3. How do your results and conclusions compare with those of your classmates?

In time there are equal amounts of the particles in all parts of the house. Why would the smell of burned toast be faint hours later?

Substances also move by diffusion inside the cells of living things. Diffusion is one of the main ways that materials move back and forth across the cell membrane. Materials such as water, oxygen, and wastes move between cells. Look at drawing *A* on this page. It shows a large amount of oxygen outside a cell. Inside the cell there is a small amount of oxygen. In which direction does the oxygen diffuse? Look at drawing *B*. Under what conditions do wastes diffuse out of a cell?

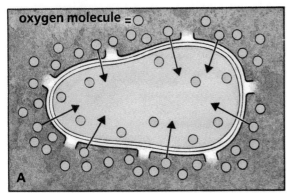

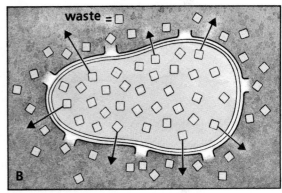

▲ Diffusion of oxygen and wastes across a cell membrane

Lesson Review

1. Identify each part of the cell shown here. Describe the functions of parts *b* and *e*.
2. Name the control center of a cell. Describe the main structures in the control center.
3. Describe the roles of the vacuole, cell membrane, and cell wall.
4. State two ways that plant and animal cells differ.
5. Describe the main process by which materials move into and out of cells.

Think! Some cells have nuclear material but no nucleus. Predict what would happen if a cell had neither nuclear material nor a nucleus.

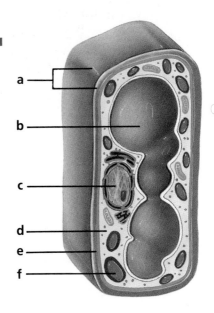

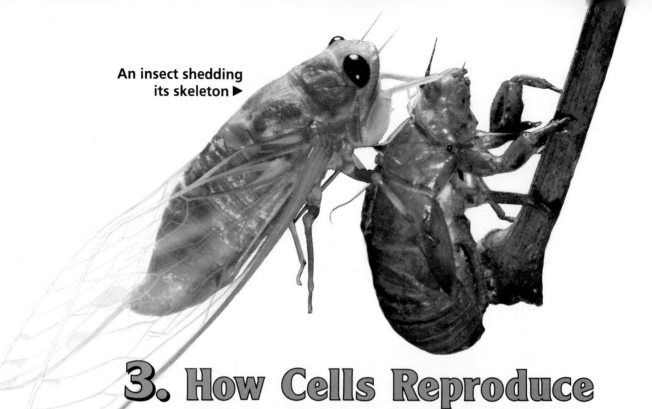

An insect shedding its skeleton ▶

3. How Cells Reproduce

Getting Started Do the shoes you wore two years ago still fit you today? Probably your feet are a size or two larger now than they were then. What changes taking place in your body cells could have caused your feet to grow?

Words to Know
mitosis

▲ Cells of developing frogs

How do living things grow?

All living things produce new cells. Growth in living things occurs mainly by the production of new cells. The picture at the left shows three frogs when they had only eight cells. The frogs increase in size by the addition of new cells. When fully grown, these frogs will have trillions of cells. Growth also occurs by an increase in the size of older cells. For example, plant roots lengthen when certain cells get larger.

New cells replace cells that wear out or die. For example, the cells that form the outer layer of your skin are completely replaced in 28 days. Blood cells also wear out and are replaced by new cells. At certain times in their lives, the bodies of some insects grow too large for their outer skeletons. Then the insects shed their entire skeletons, as shown on page 46. Some animals, such as sea stars, can regrow injured body parts. The two pictures show a sea star before and after a regrowth. Find the regrown arms of the sea star in the second picture.

▼ A sea star with injured arms

▼ Regrowth of the injured arms

How does a cell reproduce?

How are new cells formed? New cells are formed by the process of cell division. This process is called mitosis (mye TOH sihs). **Mitosis** is the process by which one cell divides, forming two new cells. The cell that divides is called the parent cell. The two new cells that are formed are called the daughter cells.

In mitosis, the chromosomes in the nucleus of the parent cell divide into two identical sets. Each daughter cell receives a set of chromosomes. So the daughter cells contain the same number and same kinds of chromosomes as did their parent cell.

Mitosis is a continuous process. But the process is often described in phases to make it easier to understand.

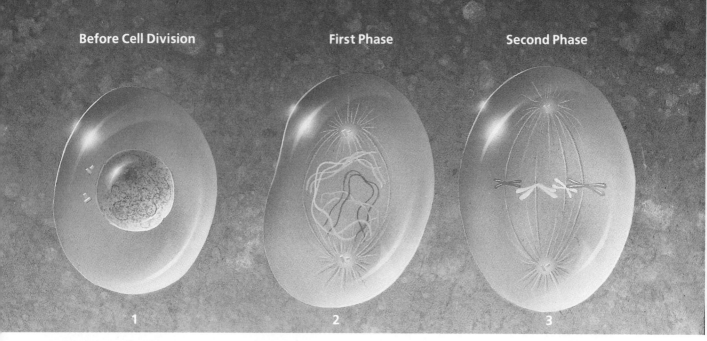

▲ **Stages of mitosis in an animal cell**

At the top of this and the next page are drawings of the phases of mitosis in an animal cell. The cell shown here has four pairs of chromosomes in each nucleus. On page 49 are pictures of mitosis in a whitefish cell. As you read, refer to the drawings of mitosis, shown above.

BEFORE CELL DIVISION Before mitosis begins, the cell is very active. It is growing, and it is storing material. Look at drawing *1*, above. Notice that the chromosomes cannot be seen clearly in the nucleus. Just before mitosis begins, the chromosomes double by splitting lengthwise.

FIRST PHASE Look at drawing *2*, which shows the early part of this phase. The chromosomes are seen as a tangle of threads inside the nucleus. The nuclear membrane begins to dissolve. A football-shaped structure made of very fine fibers forms. Toward the end of this phase, the doubled chromosomes thicken. They look like two pieces of yarn knotted together. Some of the fibers become attached to the chromosomes. The fibers then begin to pull the chromosomes apart.

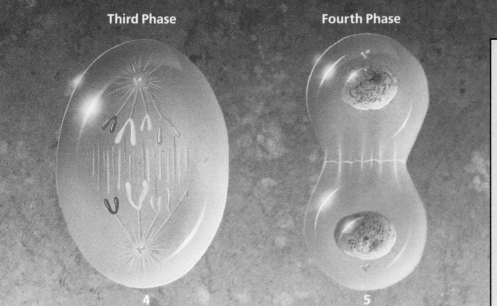

Third Phase   **Fourth Phase**

4   5

SECOND PHASE The fibers in the nucleus continue to pull on the pairs of chromosomes. By the end of this phase, the doubled chromosomes are lined up along the middle of the cell. Notice that the nuclear membrane has completely dissolved.

THIRD PHASE The fibers pull the doubled chromosomes apart. The chromosomes in each pair move toward opposite parts of the parent cell.

FOURTH PHASE The cell now contains two identical sets of chromosomes. Notice that the sets are at opposite parts of the parent cell. A new nuclear membrane begins to form around each set of chromosomes. The fibers that pulled the chromosomes apart disappear. The middle of the cell pinches inward, and the cytoplasm is divided in half. Two new daughter cells are formed.

Each daughter cell has the same number and kinds of chromosomes as the parent cell. Each has the same set of instructions for controlling cell activities as the parent cell. But the daughter cells may be smaller than the parent cell. After mitosis is complete, most cells begin to increase in size.

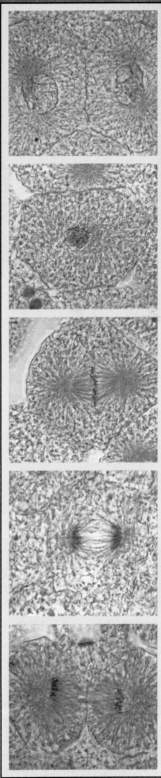

▲ **Stages of mitosis in a whitefish cell**

In one-celled organisms, mitosis results in two new organisms. So in some one-celled organisms, mitosis is a form of reproduction. The picture below shows a one-celled organism reproducing. You can see that the daughter cells look just like the parent cell. Two new organisms have formed.

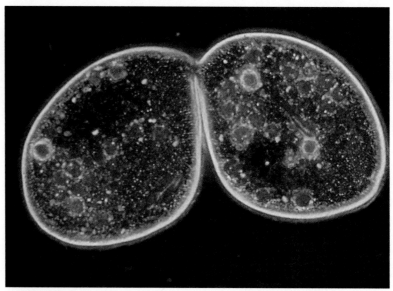

▲ Mitosis in a paramecium, a one-celled organism

In many-celled organisms, mitosis is the process by which cells increase in number. This increase in cells can provide new cells to replace old cells. It can also be the process by which the organism increases in size.

Lesson Review

1. Define the term *mitosis*.
2. Describe what happens to the chromosomes during mitosis.
3. Compare the number and kinds of chromosomes in the parent cell and the daughter cells.

Think! Suppose the chromosomes did not double before mitosis began. How would the number of chromosomes in the daughter cells compare with the number of chromosomes in the parent cell?

Skills

THINKING

Constructing three-dimensional models

How is a battery-run model car like a real car? Like a real car, a model is three-dimensional. It also has the same shape as a real car, and it moves. However, there are many differences between a model and an actual car. For example, the model and actual car are different sizes. The model does not run on gasoline. A model can tell you a lot about the thing it represents. But a model is never exactly like the real thing.

Practicing the skill

1. Make a model of one-celled organisms that live in water. You can do this by putting some water in a dish. Then sprinkle pepper grains on the water.

2. Observe the pepper grains. Describe how they behave on the water.

3. Drop one drop of soap solution on the surface of the water. What happens to the pepper grains? How is the action of the pepper grains like that of living things?

4. In what ways is a floating pepper grain a good model of a one-celled organism? In what ways is it not like the real thing?

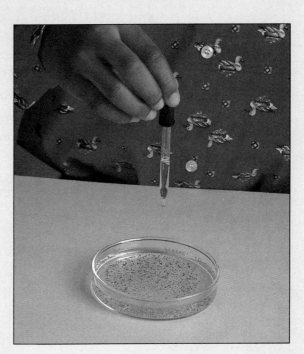

Thinking about the skill

What materials would you use to make a three-dimensional model of one-celled organisms? Describe how the model would look. How is it like a one-celled organism? How is it different?

Applying the skill

Put some seltzer water in a beaker. Drop a raisin in the seltzer water. What do you observe? Drop four more raisins in the seltzer water, one at a time. How are the raisins good models of living things? How are they not like the real thing?

4. Variety of Living Things

Getting Started Suppose you had a collection of records. How would you organize your records? You might arrange them by type of music, such as "rock" and "folk." How else could you group the records?

▲ A beetle

How do scientists group living things?

Grouping records is a little like classifying, or grouping, living things. Living things are grouped by the traits they share. In the past, living things were grouped by the traits that could be observed with the unaided eye. Today, scientists use instruments to help them group living things.

The microscope has shown scientists many differences among cells. Chemical studies have shown scientists that living things differ in the ways they obtain energy. Such studies have helped scientists to classify certain living things.

In 1959, R. H. Whittaker, an American scientist, suggested that all living things be placed into five main kingdoms, or groups. A **kingdom** is the largest unit of classification of living things. Most scientists today use Whittaker's system.

What organisms are in the five kingdoms?

ANIMALS Animals make up one kingdom of living things, the animal kingdom. The organisms on page 52 are animals. How are those animals different from each other? How are they alike?

All animals have certain traits in common. They are made up of many cells. Animal cells lack a cell wall. Animals cannot make their own food. They get energy by eating other living things. Most animals can move on their own from place to place. Which of the animals shown cannot move around?

PLANTS Plants make up the plant kingdom. Like animals, most plants are made up of many cells. Unlike animals, plants can make their own food. Most plants cannot move on their own from place to place. Turn back to page 42 to review some of the ways that plant and animal cells differ from each other. Remember that plant cells contain structures with chlorophyll. What are these structures called? What is another important way that plant cells and animal cells differ?

▼ Young ferns

▼ A cactus tree

Problem Solving

What in the World?

Have all the plants and animals on the earth been discovered? No! Scientists keep finding and classifying new living things. Certain scientists have been studying the living things on a mountaintop in Venezuela. They have discovered more than 20,000 new kinds of plants and animals there!

How might you classify the living thing shown here?

This picture shows one of the living things found by the scientists in Venezuela. What is this organism? Suppose you were one of the scientists studying it. What kinds of things would you need to know to classify the organism?

▼ Mushrooms

▼ Mold on an orange

FUNGI (FUN jye; *singular*, fungus [FUNG gus]) Fungi make up the fungus kingdom. **Fungi** are one-celled or many-celled living things that look somewhat like plants but do not have chlorophyll. Like plants, cells of fungi have a cell wall. Most fungi cannot move from place to place. Unlike plants, fungi cannot make their own food. Fungi get energy from other living things or from things that were once alive. Some fungi, such as mushrooms and molds, are shown. Where might you find fungi growing?

PROTISTS (PROH tihsts) Protists make up the protist kingdom. A **protist** is a one-celled organism that lives in water or in moist places. Most protists can be observed only with a hand lens or microscope. On page 29 an SEM shows details of a protist called a slime mold. A few protists can be seen with the unaided eye.

Some protists, such as amebas, are animallike. Others, such as the diatoms shown, are plantlike and have a cell wall. Other protists, such as a euglena (yoo GLEE nuh), are both plantlike and animallike.

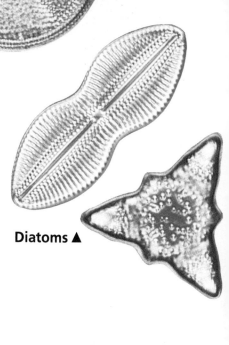

Diatoms ▲

MONERANS (moh NER unz) The moneran kingdom is made up of living things called monerans. A **moneran** is a one-celled organism that lacks a nucleus but has nuclear material throughout the cytoplasm. Monerans can be seen only with a microscope. They have a cell wall but lack many of the organelles found in cells of members of the other kingdoms.

Bacteria (bak TIHR ee uh) are the most common monerans. Many kinds of bacteria cannot make their own food. They live on other living or once-living things. Bacteria can be found in the air, soil, and water. They are one of the main causes of disease in humans. Some bacteria, such as the blue-green bacteria shown below, make their own food.

A bacterium ▼

▼ Sulfur springs covered with blue-green bacteria

Are viruses living or nonliving?

Scientists are still trying to find a way to classify a virus (VYE rus). A **virus** is something that does not fit into any of the five kingdoms. Viruses do not have all the traits of living things. Viruses are not cells. Nor are they made up of cells. Most scientists do not consider viruses to be living things.

Viruses do have one trait of living things. They can reproduce. But to reproduce, a virus must first enter a living cell and take control of it. Viruses can cause disease in living things. In humans, viruses cause such diseases as chickenpox, mumps, flu, and the common cold. One type of virus causes acquired immune deficiency syndrome (AIDS).

▼ **Boy with chickenpox**

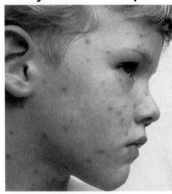

The virus that
causes chickenpox ▶

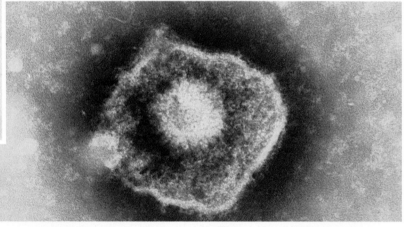

Lesson Review

1. Describe the system of classification of living things used today.
2. List the names of the five kingdoms. Give an example of one organism from each kingdom.
3. List at least three main traits of organisms of each of the five kingdoms.
4. What is a virus? Name three diseases caused by viruses.

Think! What might cause scientists to use a classification system that has more kingdoms than found in the present system?

Chapter 1 Putting It All Together

Chapter Connections

Work with a partner. Choose one of the shapes in the graphic organizer. Explain to your partner how the terms or phrases in one shape are related to one another. Then have your partner do the same thing with a different shape.

LIFE PROCESSES

Growing
Responding to
   surroundings
Obtaining energy
Releasing and using
   energy
Releasing wastes
Producing new
   organisms

CELL STRUCTURE

Nucleus
Nuclear membrane
Chromosomes
Cytoplasm
Organelles
Vacuole
Cell membrane
Cell wall
Chloroplasts

REPRODUCTION

Mitosis
   Before cell division
   First phase
   Second phase
   Third phase
   Fourth phase

CLASSIFICATION

Five Kingdoms
   Animals
   Plants
   Fungi
   Protists
   Monerans
      Viruses?

Writing About Science • Persuade

Find out more about viruses. Then decide whether you think they are living or nonliving things. Using facts you have learned, write a paragraph that supports your opinion.

Science Terms

A. Write the letter of the term that best matches the definition.

1. Threadlike part of a cell nucleus
2. Thick, jellylike substance that surrounds the nucleus and gives the cell its shape
3. Fluid-filled sac in the cell
4. Control center of the cell
5. Largest unit of classification of living things
6. Something that does not fit into any of the five kingdoms of living things
7. Rigid structure that surrounds the cell membrane
8. Basic unit of all living things
9. Structure that surrounds the cell and controls movement into and out of the cell

a. cell
b. cell membrane
c. cell wall
d. chromosome
e. cytoplasm
f. kingdom
g. nucleus
h. vacuole
i. virus

B. Copy the sentences below. Use the terms listed to complete the sentences correctly.

fungi   diffusion   life processes   metabolism
mitosis   moneran   protist   reproduction

1. The process by which living things produce more living things of their own kind is _____.
2. A one-celled organism that lacks a nucleus is a _____.
3. A one-celled organism that lives in moist places, has a nucleus, and has a cell membrane is a _____.
4. All the chemical activities needed for the growth of a living thing are called its _____.
5. The process by which particles move from one region to another is called _____.
6. The name for all the things that organisms do to survive is _____.
7. Many-celled living things that look somewhat like plants but do not contain chlorophyll are _____.
8. The process by which one cell divides to form two new cells is called _____.

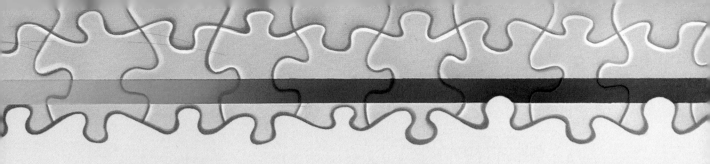

Science Ideas

Use complete sentences to answer the following.

1. List four major life processes. Explain how each process helps in the survival of living things.

2. Identify parts *a–f* in the drawing of the plant cell. Describe the function of each part.

3. Copy the chart below on a separate sheet of paper. Across the top of the chart are questions. On your paper, write the answer in each box.

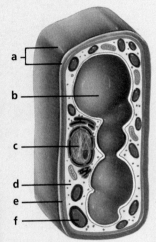

Cell Part	Found in animal cells?	Found in plant cells?
nucleus		
cytoplasm		
cell membrane		
cell wall		
chloroplasts		

4. Drawings *A–D* show some stages in cell division. List the drawings in the right order. Describe what is happening in each drawing.

5. What are the main groups into which organisms are classified? List an organism from each group.

6. List two main ways in which the cells of animals differ from those of monerans.

Applying Science Ideas

A 1950s biology book shows a classification system with four kingdoms: animals, plants, monerans, and protists. Explain whether this system was right or wrong.

Using Science Skills

Think about an electrical appliance, such as a vacuum cleaner, a clothes washer, or a blender. How might one of these appliances be a model of a living thing? In what ways is it not like a living thing?

A

B

C

D

2

Activities of Flowering Plants

Getting a Good Thing Growing

Some day you may see fields filled with plants that have red, orange, purple, and gold flowers. But the plants, called amaranth (AM uh ranth), will not be grown for their flowers. They will be grown for their many uses to people.

Hundreds of years ago, amaranth was grown as a food crop in Mexico. Amaranth seeds are grain. The Aztecs and Incas ground amaranth seeds and made flour for baking bread. Whole seeds were cooked as a snack, similar to popcorn.

For centuries, amaranth was an important part of Aztec food and culture. Then suddenly, in the early 1500s, it almost disappeared. At that time, Mexico was invaded by Spanish soldiers led by Hernando Cortes (hur NAN-doh kor TEZ). Cortes knew that to conquer the Aztec people, he would have to destroy their culture. For this reason, he made it against the law to grow amaranth.

Amaranth was forgotten for over 400 years. But in the early 1970s, people again became interested in amaranth grain. Unlike grains such as wheat, rice, and corn, amaranth has a high-quality protein. When amaranth is combined with other, more common grains, it provides complete proteins. Complete proteins contain everything needed for building new cells in the body.

The most common sources of complete proteins are meat and dairy products. But compared to grains, those foods are costly. They are also in short supply in many parts of the world. For these reasons, many people do not get enough protein in their diets.

Fortunately, amaranth is also easy to grow. It can survive in places where other grain crops do poorly. Also, it needs little water and can grow in various kinds of soil. Because amaranth is an inexpensive source of protein and is easy to grow, it could be an important crop in many poor countries. Amaranth could improve the diet of Americans as well. Some farmers in the United States are already growing it. Look at the picture of amaranth cereals. In the future you might eat a breakfast of amaranth cereal and snack on popped amaranth seeds. If you do, remember the Aztecs. They knew the importance of amaranth a long time ago.

Discover

How do the nutrients in your favorite breakfast cereal compare with those in amaranth cereal?

Materials empty boxes of various cereals

Procedure

You can find amaranth in a breakfast cereal found in health food stores. The chart shown lists the nutritional information for amaranth cereal.

Compare the nutritional information on the side of your cereal box with that for amaranth cereal. How does your favorite cereal compare with amaranth? Which cereal do you think is better for you?

NUTRITIONAL INFORMATION FOR AMARANTH FLAKES (for a 1–oz serving)	
Calories	100
Protein	4 g
Fat	1 g
Carbohydrates	21 g
Sodium	5 mg
Potassium	65 mg

In this chapter you will learn how seeds are produced by flowering plants and how the seeds form new plants. You will also learn how flowering plants make food, get energy, and move materials throughout the plant.

1. Transporting Materials

Words to Know
root hair
xylem
phloem
stomates

Getting Started Think about the system of pipes that carry water through your home. Pipes carry water to different rooms. Draw what you think might be the arrangement of these pipes. In some ways, this system of pipes is like the system of tubes that carry water throughout a plant.

◀ Geranium

stem

flower

leaf

root

What are the parts of a flowering plant?

A plant is a living thing that makes its own food. One type of plant is a seed plant. A seed plant is one that produces new plants by forming seeds. A flowering plant is a seed plant that produces seeds in flowers. Roots, stems, leaves, and flowers are the organs of a flowering plant. Find each of these organs in the drawing of the plant.

Roots anchor a plant in soil and take in water and minerals. Stems support the leaves and flowers. Leaves are the main food-making organs of a plant. Roots, stems, and leaves also transport, or move, materials throughout a plant.

How are materials moved through a plant?

Materials enter the roots of a plant through root hairs. A **root hair** is a threadlike structure that grows from the surface of a root. Root hairs grow in tiny spaces in the soil. These spaces hold water and minerals, which the root hairs absorb.

The plant in the picture is a radish seedling. A seedling is a young plant that develops from a seed. Find the part of the seedling's root that looks fuzzy. It looks fuzzy because it is covered with thousands of tiny root hairs. Each root hair is part of a single cell, as you can see in the drawing of cells in a root.

A tissue is a group of like cells that work together. A plant has two kinds of tissue made of tubes that carry materials through the plant. Water and minerals move from the root hairs to the tissue called xylem (ZYE lum). **Xylem** is a kind of tissue made of tubes that carry water and minerals upward through a plant. In the drawing, notice how these materials move from root hairs into xylem tubes.

▲ Radish seedling

California poppy ▼

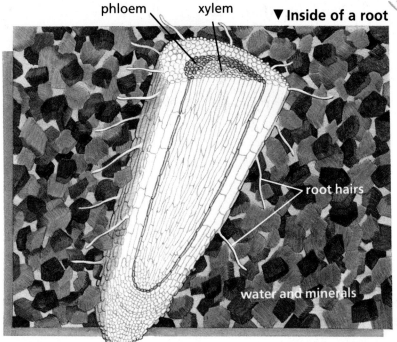

phloem   xylem   ▼ Inside of a root

root hairs

water and minerals

65

Phloem (FLOH em) is a kind of tissue made of tubes that carry food through a plant. Food is made in leaves and in other green parts of the plant, such as some stems. Phloem carries the food to all parts of the plant. Phloem also carries food that is stored in roots and stems to other parts of the plant.

Look at the drawing below of the inside of the stem of a sunflower plant. Find the xylem and phloem in the stem. Notice that these tubes are arranged in bundles. The veins of leaves are also bundles of xylem and phloem. Now look at the drawing at the left of the whole plant. Trace the path of the xylem and phloem from the roots, to the stem, and then to the leaves. The xylem and phloem extend from the tips of the roots to the tips of the leaves.

The arrows in the drawing show the directions in which materials move through a plant. In which tissue, xylem or phloem, do materials move only upward through the plant? In which tissue do materials move both upward and downward?

Flow of materials in a plant ▼

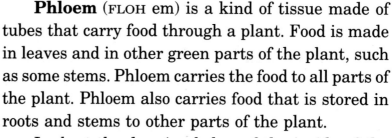

◄ **Inside of a stem ▼**

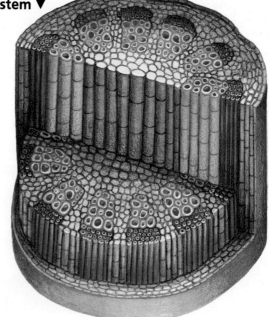

▢ xylem
▮ phloem

66

How does water leave a plant?

You have learned that water travels up a plant from the roots to the leaves. Some water is used in making food. But the plant takes in much more water than it needs for making food. What happens to this water? Some water, in the form of water vapor, is given off by the leaves through the stomates. **Stomates** are small openings usually found on the bottom surface of leaves. Look at the picture of the underside of a leaf. Notice that many stomates are found in a very small area of the leaf.

▼ Zebrina

▲ Stomates in a Zebrina leaf

Water vapor, a gas, moves through the stomates of a plant into the air. Carbon dioxide and oxygen are other gases that move into and out of the plant. These gases also pass through the stomates. Later in this chapter you will learn how these gases are used by the plant.

Sometimes during very dry weather, a plant may lose too much water vapor through its stomates. When a plant loses too much water, it may wilt and die. The stomates can control the amount of

Explore Together

When do the stomates in a leaf open?

ACTIVITY

Materials

Organizer

well-watered and wilted leaves · 2 cards with a hole in the center · 4 clear plastic cups · water · petroleum jelly · clear nail polish · microscope slide · microscope

B

A

Procedure

Investigator, Manager

A. Push the stalk of a leaf from a well-watered plant through a hole in a card. Seal around the hole with petroleum jelly. Place the stem in a cup of water and place another cup over the leaf, as shown.

B. Repeat step **A**, using a leaf from a wilted plant. Let both setups stand in a warm, sunny place for several hours.

Investigator, Group

C. Look at the inside of each top cup.
   1. In which cup do drops of water appear?
   2. Where did the drops come from?

D. Coat the bottom surface of another leaf from each plant with clear nail polish. Let the polish dry. Remove the sheet of dried polish, place it on a microscope slide, and look at the sheet under a microscope.

Investigator, Recorder

   3. Count the number of open stomates on the nail polish sheet from each of the two plants.

Writing and Sharing Results and Conclusions

Group, Reporter

1. Which releases more water into the air, a well-watered leaf or a dry leaf?

2. How do the stomates on the two leaves differ?

3. When do the stomates of a plant open?

4. How do your results and conclusions compare with those of your classmates?

68

water a plant loses. When only a little water is available to the plant, the stomates close. Very little water is lost through stomates that are closed.

Look at picture A of a magnified stomate. Notice that two cells called guard cells surround the stomate. When the guard cells fill with water, they swell. The swelling causes the guard cells to bulge outward, opening the stomate. Picture B shows what happens when a plant does not receive enough water. In this case, water moves out of the guard cells. The guard cells become limp, causing the stomate to close.

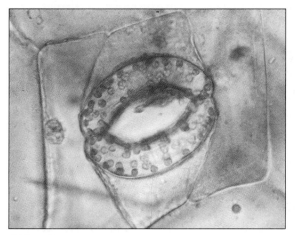

(A) Open stomate

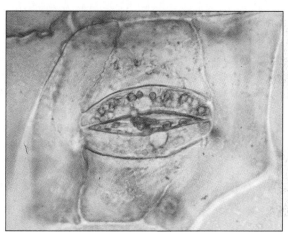

(B) Closed stomate

Lesson Review

1. What is a root hair and what does it do?
2. Trace the movement of water and minerals through a plant.
3. What are two ways in which phloem differs from xylem?
4. Explain how guard cells cause a stomate to close.

Think! Suppose one plant is dug up with a ball of soil around its roots and another plant is simply pulled out of the ground. Which plant is likely to grow better when it is replanted? Explain why.

Physical Science
CONNECTION

One reason water moves up through tubes in a plant is that water molecules attract each other. To show this, sprinkle water onto a sheet of wax paper. Use a toothpick to move one drop around the sheet, pulling along other drops.

2. Making and Using Food

Getting Started Many words contain the root word *photo* (FOHT oh). Think of the words *photograph* and *photocopy*. *Photo* means "light." The word *synthesis* (SIHN thuh sihs) comes from a Greek word that means "to put together." Using this information, write a definition of the word *photosynthesis* (foht oh SIHN thuh sihs).

Words to Know
photosynthesis
chloroplast
chlorophyll
respiration

How do plants make food?

When you define the word *photosynthesis* by its parts it means "put together with light." Scientists define **photosynthesis** as the process by which plants make food. In this process, carbon dioxide and water combine in the presence of light to form sugar, a food.

Most photosynthesis in plants takes place in the cells of leaves. A waxy covering coats the surfaces of leaves. Some leaves, such as those shown, have thicker coats of wax than others. How might this coating help protect the inner parts of the leaf?

The drawing on the next page shows a leaf as it would look under a microscope. Beneath both the top and bottom waxy surfaces of the leaf is a tissue made of a single layer of cells. These cells also help protect the inner part of the leaf.

▲ Waxy coating on leaf

70

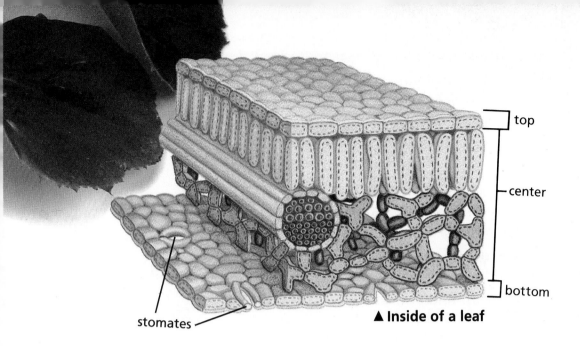

top

center

bottom

stomates

▲ Inside of a leaf

Notice that stomates are found in the layers of protective cells on the surfaces of the leaf. You know that gases move into and out of the leaf through the stomates. These openings connect to large air spaces in the middle layer of the leaf. Carbon dioxide in this layer is available to the food-making cells of the leaf.

Now find a vein in the drawing of the leaf. Remember that veins are made of bundles of xylem and phloem tissue. Xylem in the vein carries water to the food-making cells. What other materials move through the vein?

Most photosynthesis takes place within cells in the middle layer of the leaf. These cells contain many chloroplasts (KLOR uh plasts). A **chloroplast** is a green structure in plant cells where food is made. Look at the picture of a magnified leaf. Chloroplasts are also found in cells of other parts of the plant that are green.

A chloroplast is green because it contains a pigment, or coloring material, called chlorophyll (KLOR uh fihl). **Chlorophyll** is a green pigment that absorbs energy from sunlight. This energy is then used in the process of making food.

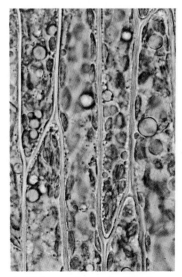

▲ Chloroplasts in leaf cells

71

Problem Solving

Show Your Colors

Have you ever seen a rainbow? Or have you ever passed sunlight through a prism? Then you know that sunlight is a mixture of many colors of light.

How do different colors of light affect the growth of plants?

Plan an experiment to find out. Use grass seeds and red, green, blue, and clear cellophane. What other materials might be useful? What will be your control? What differences in plant growth might you look for? Show your plan to your teacher. Then try it.

You can think of a chloroplast as a food factory. Carbon dioxide and water are the raw materials that go into the factory. Sunlight is the energy that changes the raw materials into the product—food in the form of sugar. Oxygen is given off as another product of the process.

Photosynthesis is a complex process. A series of chemical reactions change the raw materials to the food product. But the process can be shown simply by the starting materials and end products.

water + carbon dioxide + energy → sugar + oxygen

Refer to the numbers in the drawing of the leaf as you read about the steps that describe photosynthesis.

1. Water is taken in by the roots and moves through the xylem to food-making cells.

2. Sunlight strikes the leaf, passes through the top layers of cells, and is captured by the chlorophyll, which is in the chloroplast. Energy from sunlight is stored in the chloroplast.

3. Stored energy in the chloroplast breaks water into two gases, hydrogen (HYE droh jun) and oxygen. Oxygen is given off and moves out of the leaf through the stomates.

4. Air enters the leaf through the stomates. Carbon dioxide from the air combines with hydrogen, forming a type of sugar.

5. The sugar moves through the phloem to other parts of the plant. Some of the sugar is used by the plant as soon as it is made, and some of the sugar is stored. The rest of the sugar may be changed into other foods, namely, starches, proteins, or fats.

*Use what you know about how plants make food and you can save a space colony. Try **Investigating Plant Growth**.*

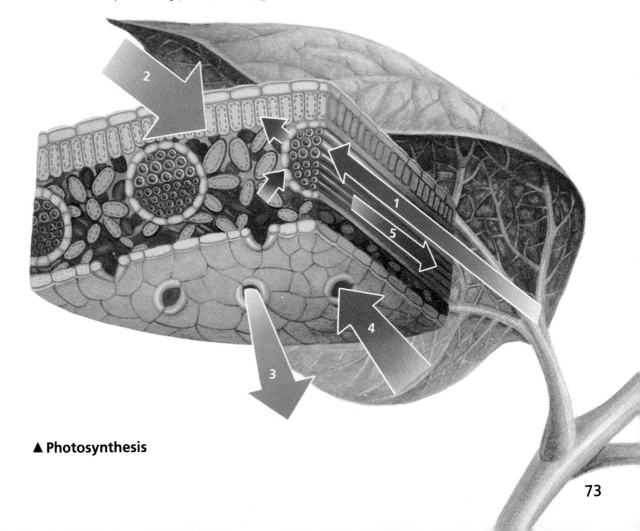

▲ **Photosynthesis**

How does a plant get energy from food?

Plants need energy to grow, to replace worn out cells, to get rid of wastes, and to reproduce. All living things get energy from food. The stored energy in food must be changed into a form that cells can use. **Respiration** (res puh RAY shun) is a process in living things in which oxygen combines with food, releasing energy.

Energy stored in food is released when the food is combined with oxygen. Respiration is a complex process, but it can be shown simply by the starting materials and end products.

food + oxygen → energy + carbon dioxide + water

Refer to the numbers in the drawing of the leaf as you read about the steps that describe respiration.

1. Sugar, which is made in the leaf, is carried through the phloem to cells in all parts of the plant. Sugar that is not used at once may be stored.

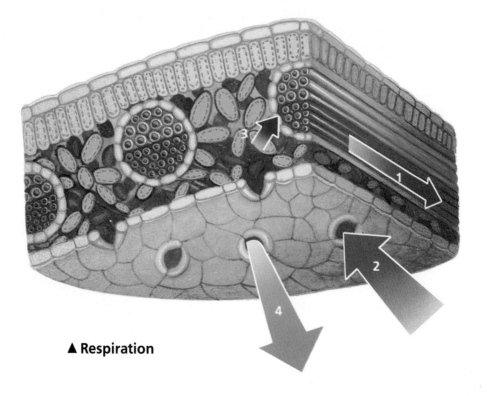

▲ Respiration

74

2. Air enters the plant through the stomates. Oxygen from the air enters the cells where it combines with sugar.

3. Oxygen combines with sugar. The sugar breaks down into the gases carbon dioxide and water vapor. During this process, energy is released.

4. Carbon dioxide and water vapor leave the plant through the stomates.

Remember that energy is used to combine carbon dioxide and water to make food and oxygen in the process of photosynthesis. Respiration is the opposite of photosynthesis. Food is combined with oxygen, energy is released, and carbon dioxide and water are given off. Look at the table to compare respiration and photosynthesis.

COMPARISON OF PHOTOSYNTHESIS AND RESPIRATION	
Photosynthesis	Respiration
Takes place only in cells with chlorophyll Food (sugar) is made Sun's energy is stored in sugar Carbon dioxide is taken in Water is taken in Oxygen is given off	Takes place in all cells Food (sugar) is broken down Energy stored in sugar is released Carbon dioxide is produced and given off Water is produced and given off Oxygen is used

Lesson Review

1. Write an equation that shows the starting materials and end products of photosynthesis.
2. Describe the steps of photosynthesis.
3. Write an equation that shows the starting materials and end products of respiration.
4. Describe the steps of respiration.
5. Compare photosynthesis and respiration.

Think! Certain plants can be grown in rich, moist soil in a sealed glass jar. A plant grown in this way does not need to be watered. How can a plant carry on both photosynthesis and respiration in a closed jar?

Physical Science
CONNECTION

Photosynthesis can be shown by using a chemical equation. In such an equation, symbols are used to show chemicals, such as water (H_2O) and oxygen (O). Use a reference book to find the chemical equation for photosynthesis.

3. Producing Seeds

Words to Know
stamen
sperm
pistil
ovary
pollination
fertilization

Getting Started Think about the many kinds of seeds people eat. Earlier, you read about the value of amaranth seeds as a food. Pepper and mustard are made from ground seeds. What are some other seeds that people eat? How are seeds important to a plant?

What are the parts of a flower?

You know that reproduction is the process by which living things produce new living things of the same kind. Many seed plants form seeds inside flowers. The flower is the reproductive organ of a flowering plant.

Look at the picture of a lily. Like most of the flowers you know, the lily has colored petals. Leaf-like parts called sepals are found at the base of flowers. In some flowers, the sepals are green. But the sepals of a lily are the same color as its petals. Sepals protect the flower while it is developing.

Parts of a flower ▼

pistil

stamens

petal

ovary

Inside the petals is a ring of stalklike parts called stamens (STAY munz). A **stamen** is the male reproductive part of a flower. How many stamens are shown in the picture on page 76? Notice the small orange sac at the top of each stamen. These sacs produce and contain pollen grains, as shown. Each pollen grain contains a male reproductive cell. The male reproductive cell is the **sperm.**

In the picture, find the pistil. The **pistil** is the female reproductive part of the flower. It has a sticky top. The large base of the pistil is the **ovary** (OH vuh ree). Find the ovary in the picture. Within the ovary are one or more ovules (AHV yoolz). An ovule is a body that contains a female reproductive cell, called an egg cell.

*Before Matt could help his grandfather, he had to learn all about orchids. You, too, can learn more about these beautiful plants as you read **Grandfather's Orchids** in Horizons Plus.*

How do flowers produce seeds?

For reproduction to take place, pollen grains from the male stamen must be carried to the female part of the flower, the pistil. **Pollination** (pahl uh-NAY shun) is the process by which pollen grains move from a stamen to a pistil. Pollen grains that land on the pistil cling to its sticky top.

▼ Pollination

Explore

How does a flower help a plant reproduce?

Years ago, ranchers in New Zealand wanted to grow clover for hay to feed their sheep. They brought clover seeds from Europe and planted them. The seeds grew into plants with purple flowers. But the flowers produced no seeds. The ranchers had forgotten something—there were no bumblebees in New Zealand! So the clover could not be pollinated. You can guess how the ranchers solved their problem.

Materials
flower · hand lens · white paper · straight pin

Procedure
A. Use a hand lens to examine a flower, as shown in the picture.
   1. Which parts of the flower can you identify?

B. Gently remove the sepals and petals. Then remove one stamen and look at the top part with a hand lens. Shake some pollen from the stamen onto paper and look at it with the hand lens.
   2. Draw some pollen grains.

C. Remove the rest of the stamens. Touch the tip of the pistil.
   3. How does the pistil feel?

D. Place the pistil on the paper. Use a straight pin to pick apart the ovary. Use the hand lens to look at the ovules.
   4. Draw what you see.

A

Writing and Sharing Results and Conclusions
1. Why does pollen that lands on a pistil not blow away?
2. How does the location of the ovules help the plant reproduce?
3. How do your results and conclusions compare with those of your classmates?

Two main ways in which flowers are pollinated are by insects and by wind. Insects, such as bees, are attracted to the bright petals and sweet odors of some flowers. Bees land on the flower to drink a sweet liquid called nectar. When a bee brushes against a stamen, pollen grains cling to the bee. As the bee moves about the flower, some pollen is transferred to the pistil.

The pollen of some types of flowers is scattered by wind. When the wind blows, it may carry pollen from the stamen to the pistil. Grasses and some trees are pollinated by the wind.

Pollination leads to the formation of one or more seeds in a flower. Refer to the numbers in the drawing of a peach flower as you read about the steps that describe what happens after pollination.

Growth of pollen tube and fertilization ▼

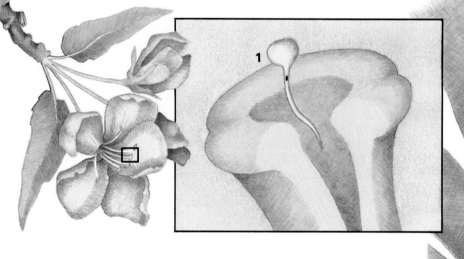

1. When a pollen grain sticks to the top of the pistil, the pollen grain forms a tube.
2. The tube, called a pollen tube, grows down through the pistil to the ovary.
3. The sperm inside the pollen grain travels down the pollen tube to an ovule. In the ovule, a sperm joins an egg cell. The joining of a sperm and an egg cell is **fertilization** (fur tul ih ZAY shun).

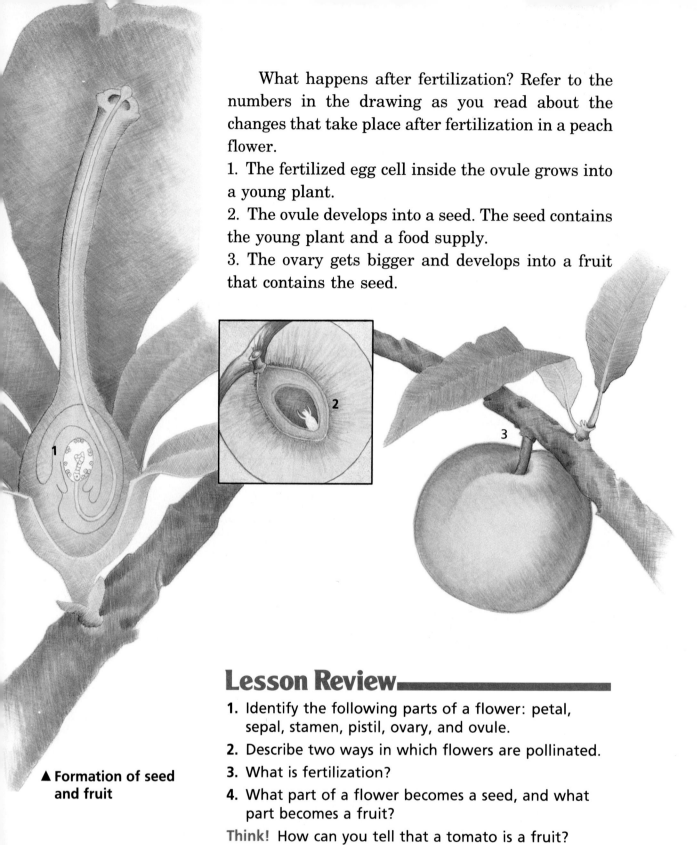

What happens after fertilization? Refer to the numbers in the drawing as you read about the changes that take place after fertilization in a peach flower.

1. The fertilized egg cell inside the ovule grows into a young plant.

2. The ovule develops into a seed. The seed contains the young plant and a food supply.

3. The ovary gets bigger and develops into a fruit that contains the seed.

▲ Formation of seed and fruit

Lesson Review

1. Identify the following parts of a flower: petal, sepal, stamen, pistil, ovary, and ovule.

2. Describe two ways in which flowers are pollinated.

3. What is fertilization?

4. What part of a flower becomes a seed, and what part becomes a fruit?

Think! How can you tell that a tomato is a fruit? What are some other foods that are often called "vegetables" but are really fruits?

THINKING

Skills

Using numbers to record data from observations

If you were making observations about plants, you might measure the stem and count the leaves. Measuring and counting are useful ways of gathering data. You can record such data with numbers and compare them to other data.

Practicing the skill

1. The pictures show several flowers. All are monocots. Monocots are one of the two main groups of flowering plants.

2. How many petals does each flower have?

3. Are these numbers related in any way? Look for a number other than 1 that can be divided into all these numbers.

▲ Spiderwort   ▲ Day Lily   ▲ Trillium   ▲ Canada Lily

Thinking about the skill

Making observations that include numbers helps scientists see patterns. What do the observations about the flowers suggest about other monocots?

Applying the skill

Find a picture of a plant. Make several observations about the plant that can be recorded as numbers. Have a classmate draw the plant using your observations. Compare the drawing to your picture. What numbers were helpful?

4. Growth of New Plants

Getting Started How long can a seed stay alive? It depends on the kind of seed. In 1982, a lotus seed found in China sprouted. The seed was known to be 466 years old! What part of a seed might make it possible for it to live for a long time?

Words to Know
embryo
seed coat
germination

How do seeds travel?

Seeds need enough space in which to grow. Seeds usually travel some distance away from the parent plant. Look at the pictures. Some seeds, such as those of cocklebur, have stickers. How do the stickers help the seeds to travel? Milkweed seeds are very light and maple seeds are "winged." What helps milkweed and maple seeds to travel?

Many seeds are hidden in fruits. Animals may eat the fruits and either discard or eat the seeds. A fruit such as a cherry may be carried for some distance before the animal eats it and drops the

▲ Cocklebur seeds

Milkweed seeds ▶

82

▲ Cherry seed

▲ Bird carrying berries

seed. The seeds of some fruits may be eaten but not digested. They pass out of the animal and into the soil. How might the bird shown above spread the seeds of the berry?

Under what conditions do seeds germinate?

Look at the picture and the drawing of the parts of a seed. The **embryo** is the part of the seed that develops into the young plant. A seed also contains stored food. The **seed coat** is a tough covering that protects the seed. Notice that the seed coat encloses the embryo and its food supply.

Germination (jur muh NAY shun) is the development of the embryo into a young plant. The length of time that a seed can live before it starts to germinate (JUR muh nayt), or develop, depends on the kind of seed. Some seed coats are much harder than others. The toughness of the seed coat helps determine how long a seed can live. Think back to the story of the old lotus seed. Lotus seeds have very hard seed coats.

For a seed to germinate, conditions must be suitable for growth to start. One condition is the presence of water. All seeds need water in order to germinate. Many seeds begin to germinate when water soaks through the seed coat.

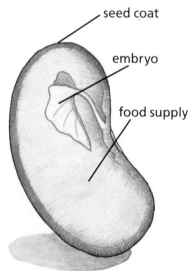

seed coat

embryo

food supply

▲ Parts of a seed

▲ Ash berries

A second condition necessary for germination is temperature. The temperature needed depends on the type of seed. Some seeds must stay cold for a period of time before germination can begin. An example is the seed of an ash tree. Seeds of this tree are found in the ash berries shown.

The seeds of some plants must get very hot before they can germinate. These plants are found in areas that often burn. When the mature plants are killed by fire, the seeds are ready to germinate. Because the mature plants are dead, the seedlings have the space in which to grow. If the seeds could germinate at all times, there would be few if any seeds available after a fire.

The embryo in a seed needs energy to grow. As it develops, the embryo uses up its stored food. The seed becomes a seedling. Once the food stored in the seed is used up, the seedling will die unless it has begun to make its own food. So the seedling needs light to carry out photosynthesis. Like all plants, the seedling also needs water and minerals from the soil in which it grows.

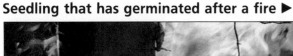

Seedling that has germinated after a fire ▶

▲ **Germination of a bean seed**

Refer to the numbers in the drawing as you read about the steps that describe the germination of a bean seed.

1. Water enters the seed, causing it to swell. The seed coat splits open as a root begins to grow.

2. The root continues to grow and a stem pushes up through the soil. The seed coat falls off.

3. Young leaves grow and open. The leaves begin to make food.

4. The roots and leaves continue to develop as the stored food is used. The seed has become a seedling.

How can new plants be grown without seeds?

You have learned how flowering plants reproduce with seeds. Many flowering plants can also be reproduced without seeds. For example, you can grow a new geranium plant from a stem cutting, which is a piece of cut-off stem with leaves.

Another way that people often reproduce plants is by grafting. In grafting, a stem cutting from one plant is joined to the rooted stem of another plant. Look at the numbered drawings as you read about one kind of grafting. (1) A stem cutting is taken from a tree that has produced seedless oranges. (2) This cutting is joined to the cut-off rooted stem of another kind of tree. (3) The cutting and the rooted stem are bound together. (4) The grafted tree grows and eventually produces seedless oranges. What is one advantage of grafting to fruit growers?

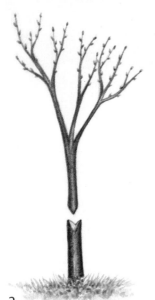

▲ Grafting

Physical Science
CONNECTION

Some popular products were developed by studying things in nature. Research how the study of seeds led to the development of velcro.

Lesson Review

1. Identify the parts of a seed.
2. Name two things that seeds need to germinate and two things that seedlings need for growth.
3. Describe four steps of germination.
4. What are two ways a flowering plant can reproduce without seeds?

Think! It is possible to produce a tree with plums on one branch, apricots on another branch, and peaches on a third branch. How can such a tree be grown?

Chapter Connections

Each of the rectangles in this graphic organizer could become the main idea of another graphic organizer. Choose one rectangle. Use information from the chapter to make a graphic organizer from that box.

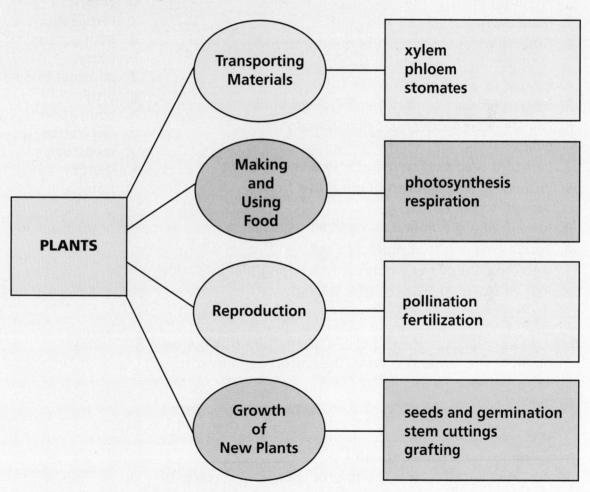

Writing About Science • Inform

Some flowering plants, such as tulips, daffodils, and onions, grow from bulbs. They also grow from seeds. What is a bulb? How do bulbs grow and reproduce? Find out about bulbs and write a report.

Science Terms

A. Write the letter of the term that best matches the definition.

1. Process in which oxygen combines with food, releasing energy
2. Male reproductive cell
3. Green pigment that absorbs energy from sunlight
4. Process in which plants make food
5. Male reproductive part that produces pollen
6. Female reproductive part that contains the ovary
7. Part of a seed that develops into a young plant
8. Process by which pollen grains move from a stamen to a pistil
9. Joining of a sperm and an egg cell
10. Tough covering that protects a seed
11. Development of the embryo into a young plant
12. Part of the pistil that contains ovules

a. chlorophyll
b. embryo
c. fertilization
d. germination
e. ovary
f. photosynthesis
g. pistil
h. pollination
i. respiration
j. seed coat
k. sperm
l. stamen

B. Number your paper from **1** to **5**. Use the terms below to complete the sentences. Write the correct term next to each number.

chloroplast   phloem   root hair   stomates   xylem

1. A kind of tissue called _____ makes up tubes that carry water and minerals through a plant.
2. Small openings usually found on the bottom surfaces of leaves are _____.
3. A green structure found in many plant cells and in which food is made is a _____.
4. A kind of tissue called _____ makes up tubes that carry food through a plant.
5. A threadlike structure that grows out from the surface of a root is a _____.

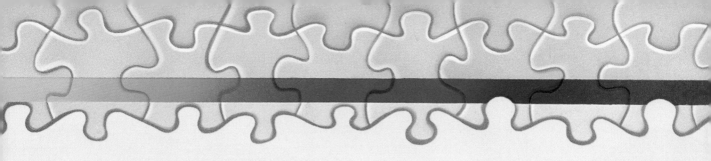

Science Ideas

Use complete sentences to answer the following.

1. How does a plant take in water and minerals?
2. How are xylem and phloem alike, and how are they different?
3. What causes guard cells to swell, and how does this swelling affect stomates?
4. In which process, photosynthesis or respiration, is oxygen used up and in which process is it released?
5. In which process, photosynthesis or respiration, is energy stored and in which process is it released?
6. Look at drawing A of a flower. Write the number of each of these parts: petal, ovary, stamen, pistil.
7. Describe the steps by which a sperm cell in a pollen grain unites with an egg cell in an ovule.
8. Look at drawing B of a seed. Write the number of each of these parts: stored food, seed coat, embryo.
9. What conditions are usually necessary for germination?
10. What happens to each part of drawing B after germination?
11. Describe the steps of one kind of grafting used to reproduce a plant.

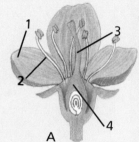

A

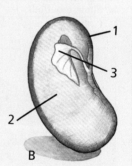

B

Applying Science Ideas

1. Gardeners sometimes dig around the base of a plant to loosen the soil. How does this benefit the plant?
2. Many flowering plants, such as water lilies, grow in water. How are these plants similar to land plants? What is the advantage to a water plant of having leaves that float?

C

Using Science Skills

Remove the seeds from an apple. Count the seeds. How can you find out if all apples have the same number of seeds?

Chapter 3

How Living Things Interact

▲ Guam broadbill

▲ Bridled white-eye

▲ Rufous-fronted fantail

Gone Forever

Far away in the Pacific Ocean is a tiny island called Guam. In the past the forests there were filled with rare and beautiful birds. Only 30 years ago the Guam broadbill, the bridled white-eye, and the rufous-fronted fantail lived on Guam. These birds were found nowhere else on the earth.

Now all three kinds of birds are gone. Scientists have been eager to find out what killed off these birds. Finding out the cause of their death might help the scientists save other kinds of birds found only on Guam.

There were several possible killers. One suspect was DDT, a chemical used to kill insects. Birds exposed to DDT lay eggs that have thin, fragile shells. Often the baby birds in these eggs die before they hatch. But scientists later found that there was too little DDT on Guam to have killed so many birds.

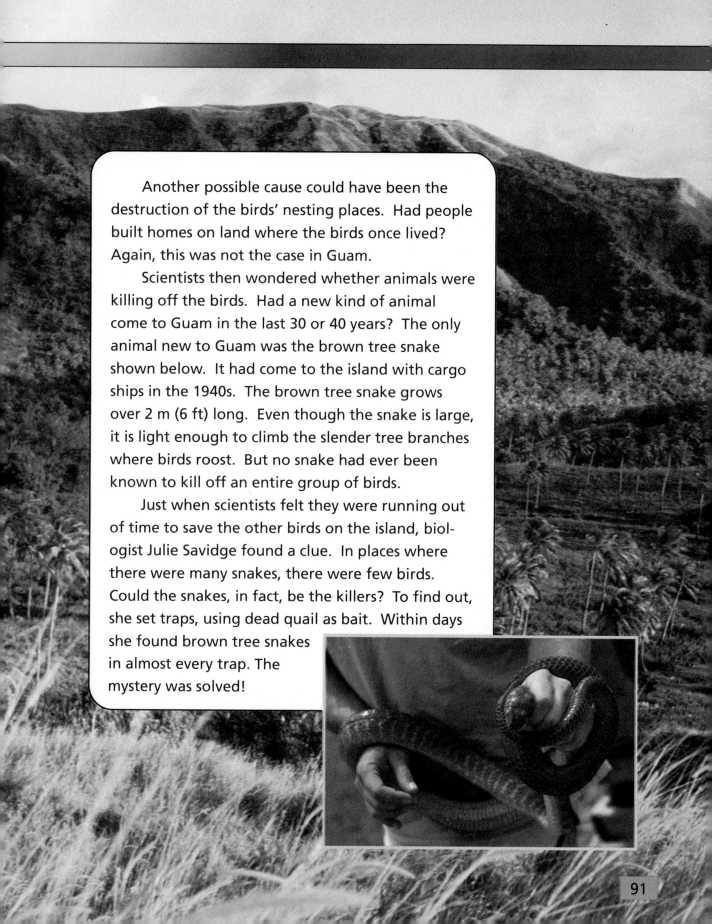

Another possible cause could have been the destruction of the birds' nesting places. Had people built homes on land where the birds once lived? Again, this was not the case in Guam.

Scientists then wondered whether animals were killing off the birds. Had a new kind of animal come to Guam in the last 30 or 40 years? The only animal new to Guam was the brown tree snake shown below. It had come to the island with cargo ships in the 1940s. The brown tree snake grows over 2 m (6 ft) long. Even though the snake is large, it is light enough to climb the slender tree branches where birds roost. But no snake had ever been known to kill off an entire group of birds.

Just when scientists felt they were running out of time to save the other birds on the island, biologist Julie Savidge found a clue. In places where there were many snakes, there were few birds. Could the snakes, in fact, be the killers? To find out, she set traps, using dead quail as bait. Within days she found brown tree snakes in almost every trap. The mystery was solved!

Unfortunately, solving the mystery did not solve the problem. Two more bird species, the Micronesian kingfisher and the Guam rail, were now in danger of dying out. In 1984, scientists rescued 31 kingfishers and 19 rails. They sent them to zoos where they would be safe and could breed. By 1988 their numbers had grown to 55 kingfishers and 125 rails. One day Guam may have an area that is safe for these rare birds. In the meantime, scientists will release some of the birds on a nearby island that is free of snakes. Will the birds be able to find food on their own? Will they mate and increase in number? Only time will tell.

Guam rail

ACTIVITY

Discover

What would happen if a hermit crab lived in a vegetable garden?

Materials   hermit crab · variety of vegetables

Procedure

Problems often occur when people bring plants or animals into a new environment. For example, plants new to an area may crowd out native plants. Or new animals may eat all the food of native animals. This can also happen on a small scale in an aquarium or a terrarium.

Understanding how living things interact can prevent these problems. What would happen if a hermit crab were set loose in a vegetable garden? To help you make your prediction, test various vegetables to find out which ones a hermit crab will eat.

In this chapter you will learn more about the effects of animals on other living things and on their environment. You will also learn how energy is transferred from one living thing to another.

1. Living Things and Energy

Words to Know
ecosystem
producer
consumer
decomposer
herbivore
carnivore
omnivore

Getting Started Suppose you were the only person on a small tropical island. What would you need to live? What things would be easy to find? What things would be difficult to find?

▲ The tropical rain forest— a large ecosystem

What is an ecosystem?

Think again about being on a small tropical island. All the living things and nonliving things on the island affect one another. Living and nonliving things together form an ecosystem (EK oh sihs tum). An **ecosystem** is all the living and nonliving things in an environment and the ways that they affect one another. Living and nonliving things in an ecosystem exchange energy and materials.

Ecosystems can vary in size and in the number of living and nonliving things they contain. For example, an ecosystem can be as large as a forest or as small as a puddle of water. The pictures on these pages show two ecosystems. One ecosystem shown is very large. It is a tropical rain forest. The other ecosystem shown is small. It consists of the living and nonliving things under a rock. What small ecosystems can you find in and around your school?

Look closely at the two ecosystems. Tall trees, vines, and lizards are some living things in the rain forest ecosystem. What are some living things in the small ecosystem under the rock? Soil and water are two of the nonliving things that make up these two ecosystems. What are some other nonliving things in the ecosystems?

Ecosystems can differ in several ways besides size. They can differ in the kinds of organisms they contain. They can also differ in climate. Climate is the average weather of a region over a long period of time. But all ecosystems have one thing in common: energy is transferred from one part to another.

*How could you help to save a salt marsh? Find out when you read **A Delicate Balance** in Horizons Plus.*

▼ **A small ecosystem**

Carnivores (KAHR nuh vorz) form another group of consumers. A **carnivore** is an organism that eats only animals. Cats, owls, skunks, seals, and some spiders are carnivores. What are some other carnivores?

A third group of consumers includes omnivores (AHM nih vorz). An **omnivore** is an organism that eats both plants and animals. Monkeys and raccoons are omnivores. Look at the pictures on this page. What kinds of consumers are shown? To which group of consumers do you belong?

▲ Raccoon eating an apple

▲ Raccoon eating a fish

Lesson Review

1. What is an ecosystem? Give an example of a large ecosystem and a small ecosystem.
2. In an ecosystem, what is the main source of energy to which all energy can be traced?
3. Compare the ways in which a producer and a consumer obtain energy.
4. Name and describe the three main kinds of consumers and give an example of each.

Think! A Venus' flytrap is a small plant that traps and digests insects. If living things are grouped according to the way they obtain energy, how is the Venus' flytrap grouped? Explain your answer.

THINKING

Skills

Using what you observe to draw conclusions

When you want to learn about an object, you can observe it.
You can use what you observe to draw conclusions.

Practicing the skill

1. Observe the animal jawbones in the drawings. Horses and goats are plant-eating animals. Notice the broad, flat molars that help them to grind plant material.

2. Observe the teeth of the house cat and the lion. These animals are meat-eating animals that tear their food. Compare the teeth of a meat-eating animal with the teeth of a plant-eating animal.

3. Compare the teeth in the unlabeled jawbone with the teeth of plant-eating and meat-eating animals. Use what you observe to conclude whether this kind of animal eats meat or plants.

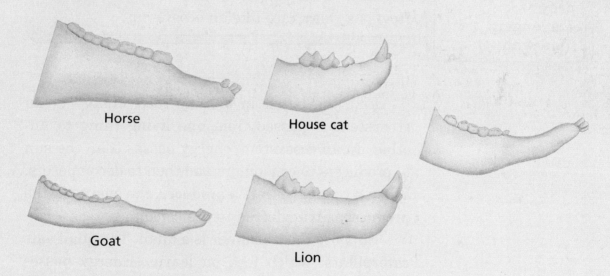

Horse

House cat

Goat

Lion

Thinking about the skill

What did you observe about the teeth in the unlabeled jawbone that helped you to draw a conclusion about what the animal ate?

Applying the skill

Use what you observed to draw conclusions that might fit all meat-eating animals. Write your conclusions.

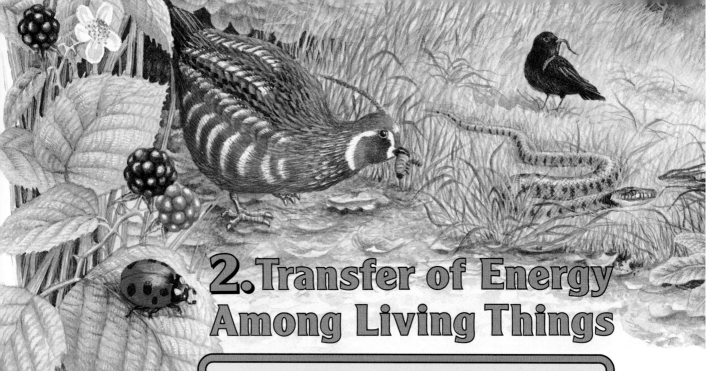

2. Transfer of Energy Among Living Things

Getting Started Have you been in a relay race? If you have, then you know that a runner on each team carries a baton, or stick. The baton is passed from runner to runner on the team. How is a relay race like an ecosystem?

Words to Know
food chain
predator
prey
scavenger
food web

How does energy move in an ecosystem?

Like the baton in a relay race, energy in an ecosystem is passed from one living thing to another. In an ecosystem, energy passes from the sun to producers to consumers and then to decomposers. When a consumer eats a producer, the energy in the producer is transferred to the consumer.

Suppose the consumer is a quail. The quail eats caterpillars, which feed on leaves. Energy passes from the leaves to the caterpillar to the quail. The caterpillar eats leaves, which contain stored chemical energy. When the quail eats the caterpillar, the stored chemical energy passes to the bird's body. The quail uses some of the energy to carry out its life processes. It also stores some of the energy in its body cells, such as muscle and fat cells.

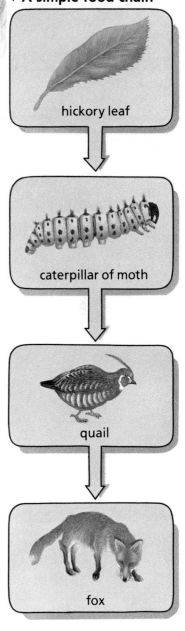

▼ A simple food chain

hickory leaf

caterpillar of moth

quail

fox

What is a food chain?

The path by which energy is transferred from one organism to another is called a **food chain**. A food chain shows which organisms are consumed by which other organisms. It also shows the transfer of energy from producer to consumer.

Look at the drawing of the food chain shown at the right. Notice that it begins with a plant. Remember that the plant contains energy stored during photosynthesis. In this food chain, the plant is the producer. Energy, shown by arrows, passes from the producer to a consumer, a caterpillar. When a quail eats the caterpillar, the energy in the caterpillar is passed on to the quail. An arrow shows the energy passing from the caterpillar to the quail. In this food chain, what is the source of the fox's energy?

Look at the drawing at the top of this and the opposite page. You will notice that several living things eat other living things shown. What other food chains might exist among the living things in the drawing?

▲ Bear preying on a fish

In a food chain some animals eat other animals. An animal that hunts and kills another animal for food is called a **predator** (PRED uh tur). An animal that is hunted by another animal is called the **prey** (pray). For example, a fox may eat a toad. The fox is the predator, and the toad is the prey. Which predator is shown on this page? Which predators can you find at the top of pages 100–101?

The picture below shows birds called vultures eating the remains of a zebra. Vultures are known as scavengers (SKAV ihn jurz). A **scavenger** is an animal that eats a dead or dying animal it finds. It does not hunt or kill the animal.

▲ Scavengers feeding

What is a food web?

Many ecosystems are very large. In such ecosystems the transfer of energy may be complex. Like the strands of a spider's web, the parts of an ecosystem are linked to one another. Several food chains may be linked. These links may be shown in a food web. A **food web** is overlapping, or linking, food chains in an ecosystem. Look at the drawing of the food web. Which producers do you see? Which consumers depend directly on these producers?

▼ A food web

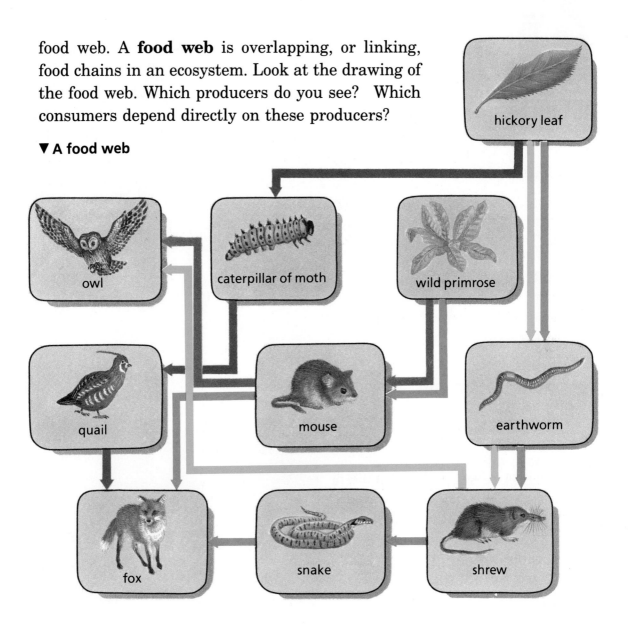

Is any stored energy "lost" in an ecosystem?

In an ecosystem, consumers do not always eat all the food available to them. A bird may crack open a seed but leave some small part of the seed uneaten. What becomes of the remaining seed?

Some of the food not eaten by consumers becomes food for scavengers. The rest, including wastes, provides food for decomposers. Remember, a decomposer is an organism that breaks down the

Explore

On what animals does an owl prey?

Owls are predators that hunt at night. They eat small animals but cannot digest the bones. The bones are rolled into a pellet, or ball, in the owl's stomach. Later the owl spits out the pellet.

Materials

owl pellet · paper towel · hand lens · tweezers · toothpick

Procedure

A. Remove the foil from an owl pellet. Place the pellet on a white paper towel. Look at the outside of the pellet with a hand lens.

B. Use your fingers, tweezers, and a toothpick to carefully separate the contents of the pellet.

C. Sort all the bones you find on a paper towel. Group the bones to form all or part of a skeleton.

Writing and Sharing Results and Conclusions

1. How many bones did you find in the pellet?

2. Compare your results with those of your classmates.

3. How might you find out what kinds of animals an owl eats?

remains of once-living things. This breakdown releases energy and substances needed by living
things. Any energy that is not used by a decomposer
is given off as heat. So, no energy is really "lost." You
can see in the drawings below that the energy that
began with the sun is always found somewhere in
the ecosystem.

▼ **Energy relationships in an ecosystem**

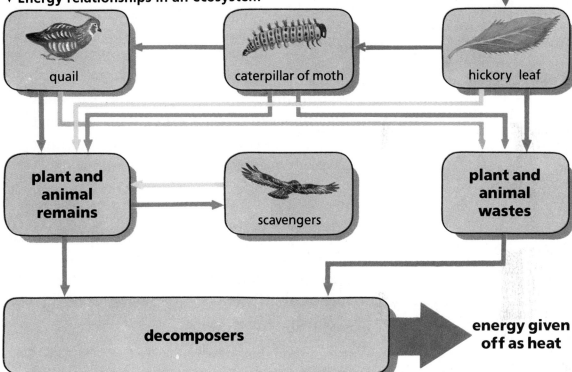

Lesson Review

1. What is a food chain? Give an example of a food chain and trace the flow of energy in that chain.
2. Describe how a predator, a prey, and a scavenger differ from each other. Give an example of each.
3. What is a food web? How are food chains and a food web related?
4. Briefly describe the role of decomposers in an ecosystem.

Think! Draw and label a simple food web that might be found in your neighborhood.

Physical Science
CONNECTION

The unit commonly used to measure the energy value of food is the Calorie. Find out how many Calories are found in an apple, a candy bar, and a hamburger. Which contains the most Calories?

3. Cycles in an Ecosystem

Getting Started   Have you eaten food that was cooked in boiling water? Some of that same water might have once been ice at the South Pole! How can water used today be the same water that was once at the South Pole?

How is water cycled through an ecosystem?

Think of the earth as a giant ecosystem formed of living and nonliving things. Water, carbon, oxygen, and nitrogen are four nonliving things that cycle through this ecosystem. All the living things in an ecosystem need these nonliving materials.

The movement of water through an ecosystem is called the **water cycle.** During this cycle, water may pass through several physical states. At different times it may be a solid, a liquid, or a gas. These changes in the state of water are caused by changes in its temperature. Refer to the drawing below as you read about the water cycle.

1. Water in the lake absorbs energy from the sun. The energy is changed to heat, warming the water.

▼ The water cycle

1   energy from sun

4   formation of clouds

3   cooling of water vapor

2   evaporation

9   water returns to lake

106

2. Liquid water at the surface of the lake evaporates, or changes to a gas called water vapor.

3. As it rises into the air, the water vapor cools.

4. High above the earth, the water vapor condenses, or changes from a gas to droplets of liquid water. These water droplets form clouds.

5. The water in the clouds falls to the earth as a liquid or as a solid. Precipitation (pree sihp uh TAY-shun) is the process by which moisture falls to the earth as rain, snow, sleet, or hail.

6. Some of the water that falls enters the ground and is absorbed by the roots of plants.

7. Some water is used by plants during photo-synthesis. Excess water is given off by the plants through their leaves.

8. Much of the water that enters the ground collects there as ground water.

9. Much of the ground water ends up in larger bodies of water, such as lakes, streams, and rivers. The cycle continues with evaporation from these bodies of water.

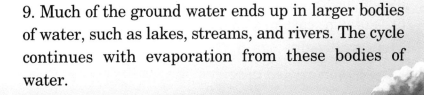

5 precipitation

7 use of water in photosynthesis

6 water enters roots

8 ground water

How are carbon and oxygen cycled?

Like water, carbon and oxygen are also needed by living things. The movement of carbon and oxygen through an ecosystem is called the **carbon-oxygen cycle.** Refer to the drawing below as you read about the carbon-oxygen cycle.

1. Plants take in carbon dioxide gas from the air.

2. Plants use carbon dioxide in photosynthesis. Carbon compounds, such as sugars and starches, are produced. Oxygen is given off as a waste product of photosynthesis.

3. Respiration is a process that occurs in both plants and animals. In this process, oxygen combines with the food stored as carbon compounds and energy is released. Carbon dioxide is given off as a waste product of respiration.

4. When an animal eats a plant, it takes in carbon compounds stored in the plant.

5. When plants, animals, and other organisms die, decomposers break down their remains. During this breakdown, carbon dioxide is released into the air. The cycle begins again.

▼ The carbon-oxygen cycle

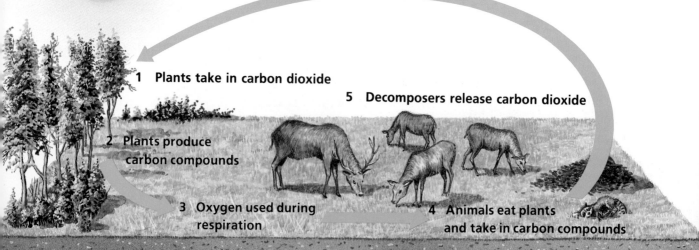

1 Plants take in carbon dioxide

5 Decomposers release carbon dioxide

2 Plants produce carbon compounds

3 Oxygen used during respiration

4 Animals eat plants and take in carbon compounds

Explore Together

What role does an elodea play in the carbon-oxygen cycle?

Organizer

Materials
jar · water · dropper · bromothymol blue
indicator (BTB) · drinking straw · elodea · watch

Procedure

Investigator

A. Half fill a jar with water. Use the dropper to add enough BTB to turn the water light blue.

Investigator

B. Breathe out into the water through a straw. You will be breathing out carbon dioxide gas. Continue to do this until the water changes color. BTB changes color when carbon dioxide gas is present in water. It will change from blue to yellow.

Caution: Do not suck on the straw. If you do, by accident, suck in any water, rinse your mouth out several times with tap water.

Group, Recorder

1. What color was the water after you blew into it?

2. What caused the water to change color?

Manager

C. Place an elodea plant in the jar of water with the BTB. Place the jar in direct sunlight for 1 hour.

Investigator
Group, Recorder

D. After 1 hour observe the color of the water.

3. What color is the water in the jar?

4. What caused the water to change color?

Writing and Sharing Results and Conclusions

Group, Reporter

1. What gas did the elodea use that caused a color change in the water?

2. What process was taking place in the elodea that used this gas?

How is nitrogen cycled through an ecosystem?

Living things need nitrogen to form substances called proteins. Nitrogen gas makes up about 79 percent of the air. But the nitrogen in proteins does not come directly from nitrogen gas in air.

As nitrogen cycles through an ecosystem, it is used by living things. The movement of nitrogen through an ecosystem is called the **nitrogen cycle.**

1. Plants such as clover contain certain kinds of bacteria in their roots. These bacteria take nitrogen gas from the air and change it to nitrates. Nitrates are substances that contain nitrogen and oxygen. Nitrates are used by plants to make plant proteins.

2. Some of the nitrates produced by the bacteria pass out of plant roots into the soil. Other plants growing in the soil can then absorb these nitrates.

3. When plants and animals die, decomposers break down their remains, releasing nitrates into the soil. These nitrates are also used by plants.

▼ The nitrogen cycle

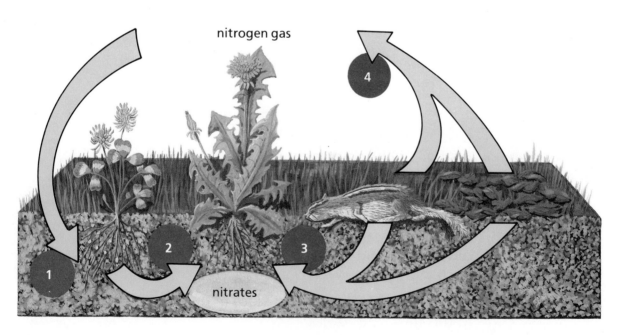

4. Certain bacteria break down nitrates, releasing nitrogen gas. The nitrogen gas is returned to the air. The nitrogen cycle continues.

What other nonliving things cycle?

Besides water, carbon, oxygen, and nitrogen, there are other nonliving substances cycling in an ecosystem. Some of these substances have been added by human activity. For example, when humans burn fossil fuels, they add oxides of sulfur and nitrogen to the air. Oxides are substances formed of oxygen and other elements. These oxides combine with water vapor, forming acids. The result is called acid rain. As water travels throughout the earth's ecosystem, it also carries acids. These acids can harm living things, such as the plants and animals in lakes and rivers.

Industries produce many other chemicals that also cycle through the ecosystem. On the next two pages you will read about chemicals called CFCs. You will find out how these chemicals are affecting an ecosystem at the South Pole.

▲ Tree damaged by acid rain

Lesson Review ━━━━━

1. Trace the path of a drop of water in the water cycle. Begin the cycle at the surface of a lake.
2. Describe the role of respiration and photosynthesis in the carbon-oxygen cycle.
3. Which important substance in plant and animal bodies contains nitrogen? How do plants obtain the nitrogen for this substance?
4. Describe three things bacteria do in the nitrogen cycle.

Think! What might happen to change the three cycles just described? Describe an event that could change the cycles and the effect of the change.

Earth Science
CONNECTION

Lightning can cause a great deal of damage. However, lightning is one of the sources of ammonia, which is used in the nitrogen cycle.

How can a hole in the ozone layer threaten the ocean's food chain?

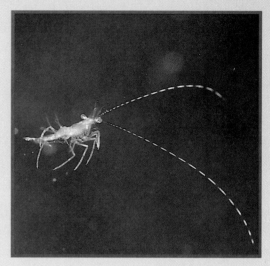

The sun's energy gives life to plants and animals. But a part of the sun's energy can do harm. The sun's ultraviolet (ul truh VYE uh liht) rays damage living things. Many of those rays, also called UV light, never reach the earth. They are blocked by the earth's ozone layer. The ozone layer is a layer of gas far above the clouds. But pollution is damaging the ozone layer. Some scientists think this damage could let in enough UV light to hurt life in the ocean.

The most serious ozone damage is over the poles. A small hole has appeared over the North Pole. But a much larger hole in the ozone opens over the South Pole each winter. This hole is now as big as the contiguous United States. Some scientists fear that the ocean food chain of the Antarctic could be in danger.

Too much UV light reduces photo-synthesis in plants. This causes many plants to die. Tiny floating ocean plants are at the bottom of the Antarctic food chain. They are eaten by tiny shrimplike animals, called krill. If too much UV light kills the plants, the krill would also die. Many whales and penguins eat krill. They too would starve. Small fish and squid that eat krill would probably die. And the penguins that eat those fish and squid would die, too. Perhaps other food chains would also be affected.

Chemicals called chlorofluorocarbons (klor oh floor oh KAHR buns) cause the problem. These chemicals, known as CFCs, are made and used in many countries.

and Society

STS

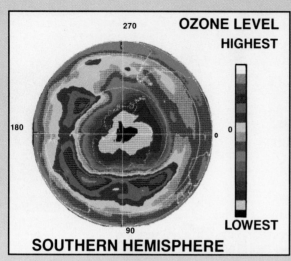

OZONE LEVEL
HIGHEST

270

180

0

0

90

LOWEST

SOUTHERN HEMISPHERE

CFCs keep the food in your refrigerator cool. They are used to clean tiny computer chips. They are even used in frozen yogurt machines.

Sometimes CFCs leak out of machines. They rise high into the atmosphere. There they are broken down by UV light. When CFCs break down they release chlorine gas. It is the chlorine that breaks down ozone. This results in holes in the ozone layer.

Many countries have agreed to reduce the amount of CFCs they make by the end of the century. But CFCs will still be made for many years. Using other chemicals instead of CFCs is expensive. Some of these other chemicals do not work as well as CFCs. So CFC makers say they cannot switch right away.

In many countries, people are urging their governments to speed up a ban on CFCs. Meanwhile the chlorine that is already in the atmosphere continues to destroy ozone. Will banning CFCs be too little, too late?

Critical thinking

1. Suppose a CFC maker is discussing the ozone problem with someone who insists on a CFC ban by all countries. What view might each take?
2. Explain why the destruction of the Antarctic food chain is important to the rest of the world.

Using what you learned

Look at a globe. Turn it to the South Pole. Cup your hand over the South Pole. This represents the hole in the ozone. Now spread your hand out. Do your fingers come close to any land? What other living things on the earth would be threatened if the hole in the ozone layer got larger?

blue jay

sparrow

grackle

4. Populations

Words to Know
population
community
extinct organism

Getting Started Think about playing Musical Chairs. In this game, players compete for a chair to sit on. What happens when there are more players than chairs? Now think about a group of animals looking for food. How is looking for food like Musical Chairs?

What is a population?

Imagine that you fill a bird feeder with seed. Then you hang the feeder on a tree. A sparrow, a bluejay, and a grackle are nearby. Each approaches the feeder. The three birds compete with each other for the food. Which bird, do you think, will get food from the feeder first? Why? As in Musical Chairs, in which people compete for a place to sit, organisms also compete for food.

Think again about the birds at the bird feeder. A sparrow is one kind of bird. It is one of many sparrows that live in the region near the feeder.

A group of the same kind of organism living together in the same region is called a **population** (pahp yoo-LAY shun). All the sparrows in a region make up the sparrow population. The squirrels living in a park make up the squirrel population. All the daisies growing in a field make up a daisy population.

Many different populations may live in the same region. For example, in a field of daisies there may also be populations of grasses, dandelions, crickets, earthworms, and spiders. The populations in a region affect one another. All the populations living together in a region form a **community** (kuh-MYOO nuh tee). What are some of the living things in the community shown?

Living things in a community ▼

How can the size of a population be measured?

Scientists can find out the size of a population without counting every member. Suppose they want to know the size of the grass population in a lawn. They divide the lawn into many small sections of the same size. They count the number of grass plants growing in one section. Then they multiply this number by the number of sections in the lawn. The answer provides a good guess about the size of the grass population in the whole lawn.

▲ Penguins

Look at the picture of the penguins. The region has been divided into four equal sections. Count the number of penguins in one section. What is the size of the penguin population shown?

What controls the size of a population?

The size of a population is affected by the conditions of the ecosystem. An organism can live only if basic needs are met. It must have enough food, air, water, space, and the right temperature. The organism must be safe from predators. Remember the birds in Guam that were killed by the tree snakes.

Food supply can also affect the size of a population. Consider a population of foxes in a forest. A fox is a carnivore. It preys on birds, snakes, toads, and other forest animals. For a fox to survive, it must eat a large number of other animals. Suppose some of the animals on which the fox feeds die in a forest fire. Members of the fox population will compete with one another for the remaining animals. Some of the foxes will die because they cannot find enough food. In time the fox population will get smaller.

People can cause changes in the size of populations of living things. For example, people build

Problem Solving
Population Explosion!

The size of a population is affected by such things as the kinds of food and the amount of space available. A population will increase or decrease as these conditions change.

What affects the size of a duckweed population?

Duckweed is a tiny plant that grows very quickly on the surface of fresh water. For example, it grows on the surface of lakes and ponds. Design an experiment that tests the effects of changing conditions in a duckweed's environment. Compare your design with that of other students. If possible, test your experiment. Then make a list of the ideal conditions for the growth of duckweed.

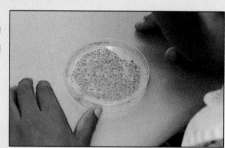

homes and highways where plants and animals once lived. Sometimes the plant and animal populations are destroyed. At other times, the organisms survive by moving to another region.

Disease can affect the size of a population. For example, most of the elm trees in the eastern United States have died. They died because of Dutch elm disease, which is caused by a fungus.

Sometimes human activity can endanger a population of plants or animals. Today African elephants are a population in danger of being killed off. For centuries African elephants have been prized for the ivory in their tusks. Ivory is carved into such things as jewelry. Often elephants have been killed for their tusks. The size of the elephant population today is about half that of what it was a dozen years ago. African elephants are in great danger unless efforts are made to stop the killing.

▼ **African elephants**

Suppose all of the members of a population die. Then that kind of organism is extinct. An **extinct organism** is one that was once alive but no longer exists anywhere on the earth.

Plants and animals can become extinct for many reasons. Their ecosystems may be destroyed. They may die of disease. They may be killed by humans. The dodo was a gentle, flightless bird that lived on an island in the Indian Ocean. These birds were all killed within 100 years by sailors looking for food on the island. The dodo became extinct in 1680.

▼ **The extinct dodo**

Lesson Review

1. What is a population? Give two examples of populations.
2. Describe a way to find out the size of a population without counting every member.
3. List three conditions that might cause a population to change in size.
4. Name an extinct organism and explain how it became extinct.

Think! Suppose an animal in your region were in danger of becoming extinct. Propose a way to prevent its extinction.

118

Chapter Connections

Make a list of the main ideas in this chapter. Use the graphic organizer to help you.

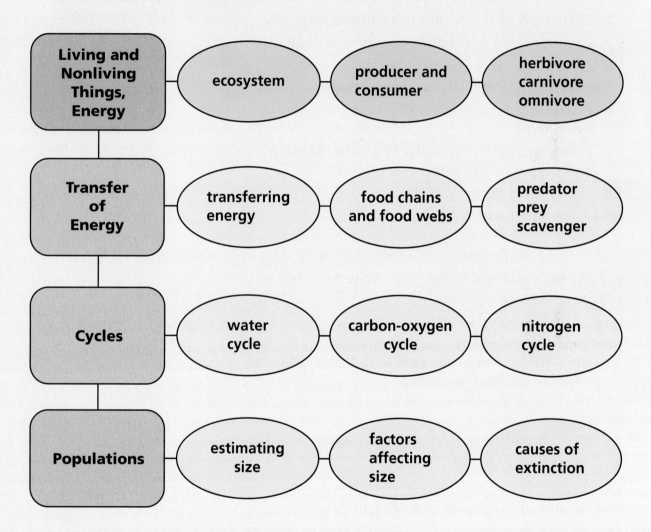

Living and Nonliving Things, Energy	ecosystem	producer and consumer	herbivore carnivore omnivore
Transfer of Energy	transferring energy	food chains and food webs	predator prey scavenger
Cycles	water cycle	carbon-oxygen cycle	nitrogen cycle
Populations	estimating size	factors affecting size	causes of extinction

Writing About Science • Imagine

Choose an animal in your environment. Draw and label a food web that includes that animal. Identify two things that might happen to upset that food web. How might the parts of the web be changed? Write a paragraph about your ideas.

Science Terms

A. Write the letter of the term that best matches the definition.

1. Animal hunted by another animal
2. Movement of water through an ecosystem
3. Organism that eats both plants and animals
4. All the populations living together in a region
5. Overlapping food chains in an ecosystem
6. Organism that breaks down remains of once-living things
7. Living and nonliving things in an environment and the ways they affect one another
8. Living thing that makes its own food
9. Animal that eats a dead animal it finds

a. community
b. decomposer
c. ecosystem
d. food web
e. omnivore
f. prey
g. producer
h. scavenger
i. water cycle

B. Copy the sentences below. Use the terms listed to complete the sentences.

carbon-oxygen cycle   carnivore   consumer   extinct organism
food chain   herbivore   nitrogen cycle   population   predator

1. The path by which energy is transferred from one organism to another is called a _____.
2. The movement of nitrogen through an ecosystem is the _____.
3. A group of the same kind of organisms living together in the same region is a _____.
4. An animal that eats only animals is a _____.
5. An animal that hunts another animal is a _____.
6. An organism that was once alive but no longer exists anywhere on the earth is an _____.
7. The movement of carbon and oxygen through an ecosystem is the _____.
8. An animal that eats only plants is a _____.
9. An organism that gets its energy from other living things is a _____.

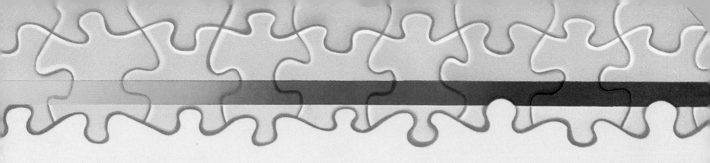

Science Ideas

Use complete sentences to answer the following.

1. List at least ten things in a large ecosystem that could be found within your region of the country.
2. Explain the role of the sun in an ecosystem.
3. Name and describe the three main groups of consumers. Give an example of an organism from each group.
4. Describe what a food chain is. Draw and label a simple food chain.
5. Explain the difference between a predator and a prey. In what way does a scavenger benefit from a predator?
6. What is a food web? Draw and label a food web that includes a human being.
7. Trace the path of a drop of water from a cloud back to a cloud as the drop passes through the water cycle.
8. Trace the path of carbon as it is used by a plant in photosynthesis. Explain what happens to carbon during respiration in the plant.
9. What is the main source of nitrogen that plants use in building up protein? What is one way that nitrogen gas is returned to the air after it passes through the nitrogen cycle?
10. Describe two conditions that could lead to the extinction of a population of animals.

Applying Science Ideas

1. Look at the food chain on page 101. Predict what would happen to the food chain if a disease killed off 25 percent of the quails in the region.
2. Explain how CFCs are related to the death of penguins at the South Pole.

Using Science Skills

Imagine that you are walking to school. You pass a small pond and observe tadpoles swimming in the water. You also see a dam built of tree trunks and sticks. Then you notice a nest in the fork of a tree. What animals, besides tadpoles, are probably nearby?

Life in the Ocean

Living Lights

When Christopher Columbus first sailed on the Caribbean Sea, he wrote of seeing "candles moving in the sea" at night. On some nights, modern sailors can also see a glow on dark ocean waters. Waves breaking on a beach at night sometimes have a soft blue shine. Boats that move quickly through the water sometimes leave a faint glowing trail behind them.

The light from the ocean is caused by bioluminescence (bye oh loo muh NES uns). Bioluminescence is the production of light by a living thing. If you have seen fireflies flashing, you have seen one example of this living light. Chemical reactions in some cells of the firefly give off light.

There are many kinds of bioluminescent living things in the sea. Some kinds of squids, like the one shown here, give off light. The "candles" that Columbus saw were probably Bermuda fireworms. And the glow of dark crashing waves comes from tiny one-celled organisms. When the water is disturbed, these organisms give off blue-green light.

Many fish that give off light use the light to help them catch food. The anglerfish in the picture seems to have a fishing pole sticking out from its head. This part of the fish lights up. Other fish are attracted to the light. When they come near the light, the anglerfish eats them.

The saber-toothed viperfish also uses light to catch food. This fish has a long lighted whisker under its chin. It also has lights behind its teeth. Ocean animals that move toward the lights will swim right into the viperfish's mouth.

The lantern fish, shown below, uses light in two ways. This fish has rows of lights on its belly. The lantern fish swims near the surface of the water at night. The light on the underside of the fish blends in with moonlight shining into the water. Larger fish that might eat the lantern fish cannot see it from below. So the lantern fish is using light as a way to avoid being seen by an enemy.

The lantern fish also uses light for mating. Each species of lantern fish has its own pattern of light. Male and female patterns are different, too. The light helps these fish find other fish with which they can mate.

Discover

How can you make an ocean creature?

ACTIVITY

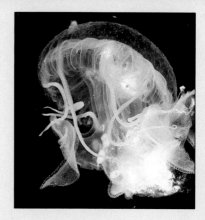

Materials   construction paper · clay · marking pens · paste · pipe cleaners · string

Procedure

You have seen that ocean creatures have unusual ways of getting food and avoiding enemies. Some ocean creatures hide from enemies by blending in. Other ocean creatures have ways to scare enemies away.

Think about the things an ocean creature must do to survive. Then think about ways its body design could help it survive. Design an ocean creature with an unusual body. Then construct your animal. Be prepared to explain to the class how the animal uses the characteristics you have given it.

In this chapter you will learn about organisms that live in the oceans. You will discover that each part of the ocean is different and has different living things in it.

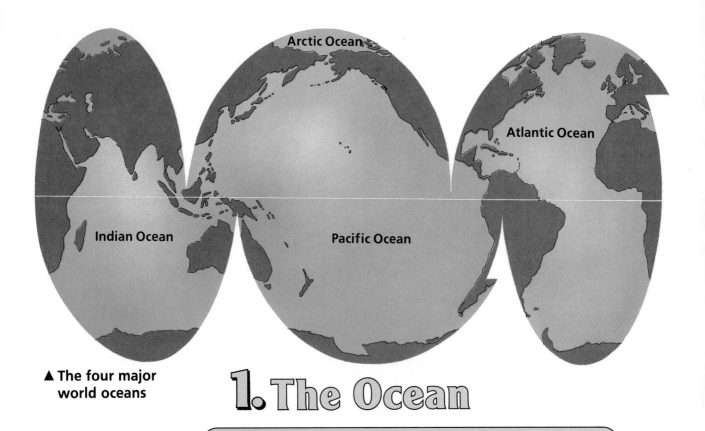

Arctic Ocean

Atlantic Ocean

Indian Ocean

Pacific Ocean

▲ The four major
world oceans

1. The Ocean

Words to Know
plankton
intertidal zone
shallow-ocean
 zone
open-ocean zone

Getting Started Fold a sheet of paper into four equal sections. One section represents the part of the earth's surface that is not covered with water. The other three sections represent the part that is covered with water. What percentage of the earth's surface is covered with water?

Where is life found in the ocean?

Look at the map of the earth. Notice that one large body of water covers much of the earth's surface. This large body of water is usually divided into four major oceans. Find the four major oceans on the map. What are the names of the oceans? Find the places on the map where water can flow from one ocean to another.

The ocean contains billions of animals and plants of every size and shape. But living things are

126

found in much greater numbers in some parts of the ocean than in other parts. Why are there more organisms in some parts of the ocean?

Just as on land, all life in the ocean depends on producers. Producers are living things that make food. Most producers in the ocean are microscopic plants. Remember that plants need light in order to make food. But light cannot reach great depths in water. So most ocean producers are found in the upper, well-lighted regions of the ocean.

All animals depend on producers for their food. Because of this, most animals are found where there are large numbers of producers. Since producers are found in regions of the ocean that receive much sunlight, most of the ocean's animal life is found there, too.

Plankton (PLANGK tun) are tiny plants and animals that float in the ocean. Most ocean food chains begin with microscopic plant plankton. A food chain is the path through which energy is transferred from one organism to another. Follow the drawing showing an ocean food chain beginning with plant plankton and ending with a killer whale.

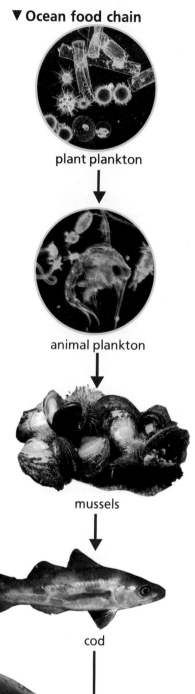

▼ Ocean food chain

plant plankton

animal plankton

mussels

cod

killer whale

Problem Solving

A Salty Problem

Have you ever thought about what might happen to a freshwater plant if it were placed in salt water? Salt water causes certain changes in the cells of freshwater plants. These changes do not occur when the plants are in fresh water.

How are freshwater plants affected by salt water?

Plan an experiment to test the effect of salt water on the cells of a plant that does not live in salt water. Use a potato in your experiment. How does the potato look and feel before the experiment? What does the potato look and feel like after it has been in salt water?

What are the zones of the ocean?

Scientists divide the ocean into three major zones. These zones are based on two factors. They are the depth of the water and the amount of sunlight that reaches different depths. Look at the drawing that shows the three ocean zones.

The **intertidal** (ihn tur TYD ul) **zone** is the area of shoreline that is under water during some parts of the day and above water during other parts of the day. The organisms that survive in this zone live under very harsh conditions.

The **shallow-ocean zone** is the area of the ocean that starts at the low-tide line and ends where the ocean bottom drops off sharply. The water in this zone extends to a depth of about 200 m (656 feet). Most of the life in the ocean is found in the shallow-ocean zone.

Beyond the shallow-ocean zone, the ocean becomes very deep. The **open-ocean zone** is the area of the ocean with the greatest depth. This zone has an average depth of 4,720 m (14,000 feet). Most of the ocean is open ocean. There are fewer producers here than in the other two zones. How do you think this affects the numbers of animals in the open-ocean zone?

Notice that the three zones are different distances from the shore. As the ocean bottom slopes down from the shore, the water gets deeper. The zones are further divided according to the amount of light that passes through the water. Find the light zone and the dark zone in the drawing.

intertidal zone

shallow-ocean zone

open-ocean zone

▼ Zones of the ocean

light zone

dark zone

Lesson Review

1. Why can the four major oceans be considered part of one world ocean?
2. How does the amount of light affect where life is found in the ocean?
3. Describe how plant plankton fits into an ocean food chain.
4. Describe the three zones of the ocean.

Think! Suppose that a great deal of very fine mud was mixed with the ocean water near the shoreline. How might this affect the growth of plants there?

Earth Science
CONNECTION

The oceans greatly affect the long-term weather, or climate, on the earth. Use reference books to find out about the Gulf Stream and the Japan Current and how they affect the weather in North America.

129

Are the drugs of tomorrow out at sea?

Imagine yourself swimming in a warm blue ocean. The beauty of the scene might be of great interest to you. But to some scientists the scene might be more like a peek into a drugstore of the future.

Nearly half of the drugs people take today contain substances first found in nature. Many people take the drug called aspirin. It was first found in the bark of the willow tree. Digitalis is a heart medicine. This drug was first made from the foxglove flower. Now scientists are looking for new drugs from new sources. Scientists have turned to the sea as a possible source of future drugs.

From tiny submarines, scientists are studying life on the ocean floor. Thousands of samples of ocean life are collected. Each sample is tested carefully. Some of the samples contain soft, colorful sponges. Bacteria grow in the sponges. Scientists have found that some of these bacteria produce chemicals that fight cancer cells.

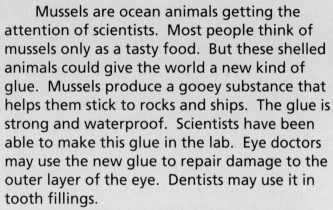

Mussels are ocean animals getting the attention of scientists. Most people think of mussels only as a tasty food. But these shelled animals could give the world a new kind of glue. Mussels produce a gooey substance that helps them stick to rocks and ships. The glue is strong and waterproof. Scientists have been able to make this glue in the lab. Eye doctors may use the new glue to repair damage to the outer layer of the eye. Dentists may use it in tooth fillings.

Finding new sources of drugs and other medical treatments is difficult. It can take many years and millions of dollars to find just one new drug. Finding new treatments for diseases is worth the effort.

Critical thinking

1. Blue-green bacteria from the ocean make a useful substance. The substance strengthens the immune system of animals. The immune system helps the body fight disease caused by infection. Suppose this substance was made into a drug. What effect could it have on people suffering from diseases?

2. Suppose a sea sponge becomes a source of a powerful cancer-fighting drug. The sea sponge would probably be gathered in great numbers. What could be done to prevent sea sponges from quickly disappearing?

Using what you learned

Find out about other plants and animals that help produce drugs and other medical treatments. Research where they live and how they are used. Write facts about the use of each in drugs and medical treatments.

131

2. Living Things of the Intertidal Zone

Getting Started Imagine living in a place where you are first pounded by waves. Then you are left to dry in the air. Living things in the intertidal zone must withstand harsh conditions like these.

What are the conditions of the intertidal zone?

The intertidal zone is a zone of great change. The conditions of the intertidal zone change because of tides. It is **high tide** when the water reaches the highest point on land. During high tide, most of the intertidal zone is under water. At **low tide** the water is at its lowest point on land. Then, most of

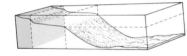

▼ Low tide

▼ Sea gull feeding

132

the intertidal zone is out of water. Look at the pictures. How do you think conditions change in the intertidal zone during high and low tides?

Low tide is a time of harsh conditions for intertidal plants and animals. At low tide, living things in the intertidal zone are exposed to air. The air may dry and overheat them in hot weather. Or the air may cause them to freeze during cold weather. They may have to adjust to changes in the amount of salt in the water. This happens if it rains or snows during low tide. How would rain affect the amount of salt in this zone? Also at low tide, intertidal organisms may be eaten by land animals.

Gooseneck barnacles feeding ▼

When the tide comes in, the plants and animals are again covered with water. The water contains oxygen that they need. It also carries food that the animals need. But high tide brings another harsh condition. Many of the organisms are now pounded by waves that crash against them.

▼ High tide

How do organisms survive in the intertidal zone?

Any body part or behavior that helps an organism survive is called an adaptation (ad up TAY shun). Organisms living in the intertidal zone have a variety of adaptations that help them survive.

Animals that live on sandy beaches, such as the mole crab and the clams in the drawing, burrow into the sand during low tide. By burrowing at low tide, the bodies of the mole crab and clams do not dry out. The mole crab uses its legs and the clams use their strong foot to dig into the sand. These animals feed on plankton when they are covered by water.

Many tiny animals, such as worms, live in the spaces between sand grains. These spaces are filled with water. So these animals also do not dry out. Look at the drawing that shows some animals that live in the spaces between sand grains. How do you think their body shapes help them survive here?

Animals that live between sand grains ▼

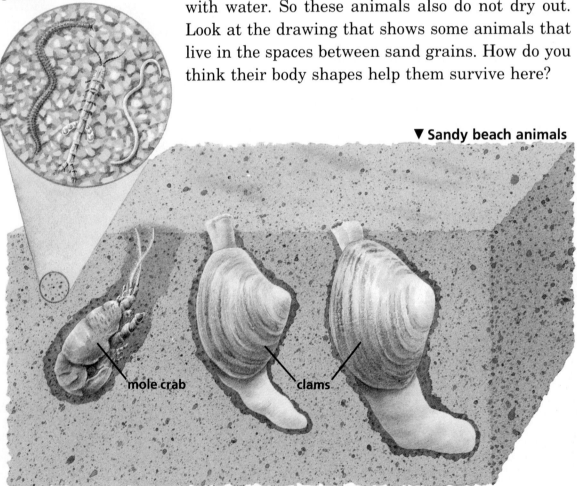

▼ Sandy beach animals

mole crab

clams

Explore Together

What does a hermit crab look like?

Organizer

Materials

hermit crab · large jar or aquarium · sand · twig · pieces of coral or clean rocks · small dish · water · lettuce · apple · raw fish · uncooked oatmeal

Procedure

Investigator, Recorder

A. Examine the hermit crab's borrowed shell first. **Caution:** *When holding hermit crabs keep your hands flat so you do not get pinched. Wash hands when you are finished handling the crabs.*
   1. How large is the shell?

Manager

B. Set the hermit crab on a moist sponge or in a shallow dish with water. Place a piece of food near the shell. This will make the crab move its head and claws out of the shell.

Investigator, Recorder

C. Examine and draw the body parts that you can observe.
   2. How many legs do you see?

Investigator, Recorder

D. Examine and draw the head of the crab.
   3. What type of structures are found on the head?

E. Examine and draw the front claws of the crab.
   4. How do the claws compare in size and structure?

Group, Reporter

Writing and Sharing Results and Conclusions

1. What are the names of all the body parts that you saw?

Reporter

2. How does your drawing of a hermit crab compare to those of your classmates?

135

Animals living on rocky shores must withstand the force of strong waves. Many rocky shore organisms attach themselves to the rocks. Because they are firmly attached, they are not knocked off the rocks by the crashing waves. Barnacles give off a glue that cements them to the rocks. Limpets clamp down with their strong foot. Mussels attach themselves to the rocks by a group of threads. During low tide, all these animals close their shells. This protects them from drying out and from being eaten.

Other animals survive the changing tides because they are hidden in the seaweed that clings to the rocks. Look at the animals shown in the drawing and pictures. These delicate animals attach to seaweed. At high tide the seaweed helps cushion these animals from the crashing waves. At low tide the seaweed remains moist and keeps the animals from drying out. Certain crabs, slugs, snails, and sea stars also survive low tide in this way.

▲ Limpet attached to rock

Animals attached to seaweed ▼

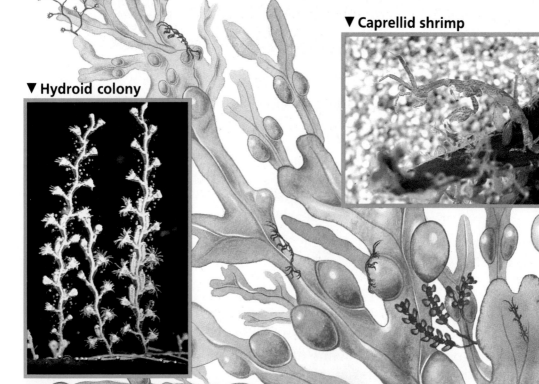

▼ Hydroid colony

▼ Caprellid shrimp

Sea anemones and snail ▼

▲ Tide pool   ▲ Tide pool ▶

An ideal place to find intertidal organisms is in tide pools. A **tide pool** is a depression in rock that is filled with ocean water. The picture shows some organisms you might find in a tide pool. Some of these organisms are normally found below the low-tide line. They can survive in tide pools because they are covered by water at all times.

▲ Observing tide pool organisms

Lesson Review

1. How are conditions in the intertidal zone different during low and high tides?
2. Choose one intertidal animal of the sandy beach and one intertidal animal of the rocky shore. Describe the adaptations that help each animal survive in the intertidal zone.

Think! Imagine a tide pool on a hot summer day. During the day, there is a rainstorm. List the conditions that the tide-pool organisms have to adjust to on this summer day.

Earth Science
CONNECTION

The intertidal zone is a zone that is greatly affected by oil spills. Use magazines and newspapers to find out about the damage caused by the Alaskan oil spill in 1989.

137

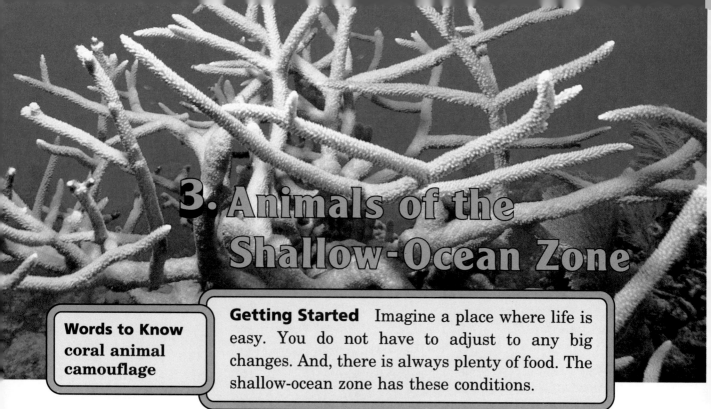

3. Animals of the Shallow-Ocean Zone

Words to Know
coral animal
camouflage

Getting Started Imagine a place where life is easy. You do not have to adjust to any big changes. And, there is always plenty of food. The shallow-ocean zone has these conditions.

What are the conditions of the shallow-ocean zone?

The shallow-ocean zone extends from the end of the intertidal zone to a depth of about 200 m (656 feet). Because it is close to land, nutrients from the land enter the water in this zone. Nutrients are substances that organisms need to live and grow. Rainwater washes nutrients from the land into streams and rivers. Rivers empty into the ocean. Nutrients that settle to the bottom of the shallow-ocean zone are churned up by wave action and mixed with water. Plants in the shallow-ocean zone use these nutrients in their life processes.

Recall that most of the life in the ocean is in the shallow-ocean zone. Since this zone is fairly shallow, light reaches most parts of the bottom. So producers have nutrients and they have light needed for photosynthesis. Since there are many plants in this zone, there are many animals as well. The world's major fishing areas are in this zone.

What is a coral reef?

The rocklike structures in the picture on page 138 have been produced by groups of small ocean animals. The picture shows part of a coral reef. The small ocean animals that built the reef are coral animals. A **coral animal** is an animal that forms a limestone skeleton.

Coral reefs grow in shallow, clear water that has a temperature of at least 18°C (65°F). Coral reefs are formed by billions of coral animals, each producing a hard skeleton. Only the thin top layer of the reef is made of live coral. The layers of reef under this living layer are the skeletons of dead coral animals. Over many years the skeletons pile up and a reef is formed.

If you were to observe a coral reef during the day, you would see only the skeletons that the coral animals produce. But if you observed it at night, you would see the coral animals. The coral animals feed at night. Look at the picture of coral animals feeding. Find the fingerlike tentacles (TEN tuh kulz) that they use to catch floating plankton.

*Have you ever eaten octopus? It is a delicacy that should not be missed. Read about it in **A Feast for the King** in Horizons Plus.*

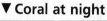
▼ Coral at night

A coral reef is home to many organisms. Some plants and animals attach to the hard surface of a reef. Other animals hide in the cracks and caves of a reef. These animals come out to feed at night. Find ten reef animals in the drawing.

The reef is also a source of much food. Some animals, such as snails and sea urchins, feed on the plants growing on the reef. These plant eaters become food for fish, crabs, and sea stars. Sharks and barracuda hunt for fish living on the reef. Other animals, such as the parrotfish in the picture, eat the coral itself. The jaws and teeth of the parrotfish are like a bird's beak. This fish uses its "beak" to bite off chunks of coral. It digests the coral animal. The droppings of the parrotfish contain ground-up lime-stone from the coral skeleton.

▲ Flamingo tongue snail on sea fan attached to reef

▼ Parrotfish eating coral

Many animals of the shallow-ocean zone have adaptations that help them move from place to place within their environment. Some animals have a shape that lets them move quickly through the water. Notice the shape of the blue shark. How does its body shape affect its movement? This stream-lined shape allows the water to pass quickly over the animal's body as it swims through the water.

▼ Blue shark

Animals of the shallow-ocean zone also have adaptations that help protect them from being eaten. Because of their coloring and body shape, some animals blend in with their environment. **Camouflage** (KAM uh flahzh) is an adaptation that helps an animal blend in with its environment. Find the flounder shown in the drawing. Flounders change color depending on the color of their sur-roundings. What part of its environment does the flounder blend with?

141

▲ Cleaner wrasse

▲ Blenny

▲ Cleaner wrasse inside mouth of coral trout

Coloring and body shape can be helpful to an ocean animal in another way. Compare the two coral-reef fish in the pictures. Look at the cleaner wrasse (ras). Scientists think that the bold stripes of the wrasse attract other fish. The wrasse cleans wounds and removes parasites from the scales of other, larger fish. The wrasse will even swim inside the mouth of a shark to feed on parasites. But the shark does not eat the wrasse. So the wrasse gets food and the shark is cleaned of parasites.

Now look at the blenny. Notice that its coloring is much like that of the cleaner wrasse. Another fish might mistake the blenny for a wrasse. As it comes near the blenny, instead of cleaning it, the blenny takes a bite out of the fish's fin! In this way the appearance of the blenny helps it obtain food.

Physical Science

CONNECTION

Find out what streamlining is. Which are the best streamlined fish in the shallow-ocean zone?

Lesson Review

1. Explain why the shallow-ocean zone has many plants and animals.
2. Describe adaptations of four animals that help them survive in the shallow-ocean zone.

Think! If you were an ocean animal, would you rather live in the intertidal zone or in the shallow-ocean zone? Give reasons for your choice.

THINKING

Skills

Constructing a classification diagram

To classify things, you start with one group. You classify the things into subgroups. You can construct a diagram to show the subgroups. The diagram can use branches to show how the subgroups are made. More branches can show still more subgroups.

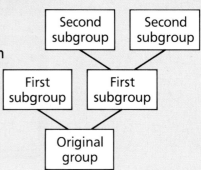

Practicing the skill

Look at the drawing of a group of shells. The shells are from animals that live in the ocean. They are called mollusks. You can classify the mollusks according to whether they have one or two shells.

1. Identify which mollusks have one shell and which have two shells.

2. Construct a two-branched classification diagram. In one branch, list the mollusks with one shell. In the other, list the mollusks with two shells.

Thinking about the skill

When might it be useful to construct a classification diagram again?

Applying the skill

You can classify one-shelled mollusks into subgroups. One group has spiral shells. The other group does not. Decide which of the one-shelled mollusks have spiral shells and which do not. Add both subgroups to your classification diagram by making another pair of branches.

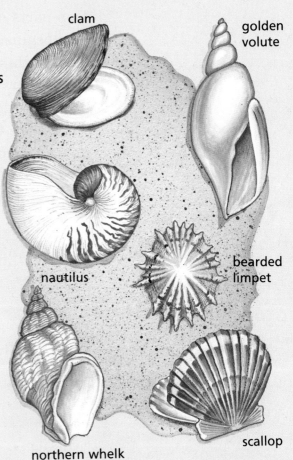

clam

golden volute

nautilus

bearded limpet

northern whelk

scallop

4. Animals of the Open-Ocean Zone

Getting Started   Imagine a place with freezing temperatures and no light. The pressure is a thousand times greater than on land. How do organisms survive in such a place?

What are the conditions of the open-ocean zone?

Some organisms actually do live under conditions like those described above. They live in the deep parts of the open-ocean zone. The open-ocean zone begins where the ocean bottom drops sharply. Point to this sharp drop in the drawing on page 129. The waters of the open ocean extend from the surface to depths of 10,000 m (32,800 feet).

Unlike the shallow-ocean zone, the open-ocean zone does not support a great number of organisms. Most of the open-ocean zone lies in the dark zone. Since light cannot reach below about 60 m (200 feet)

▼ Blue whale

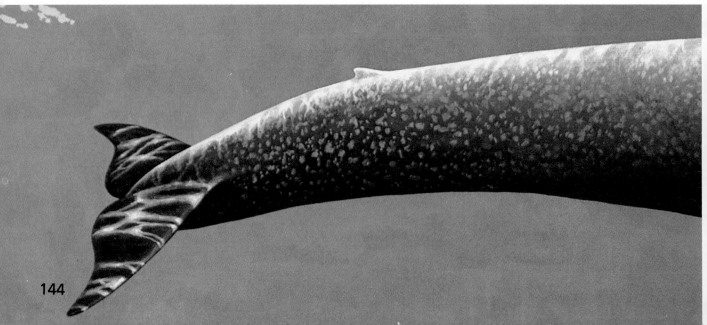

of water, producers do not survive in most of the open-ocean zone.

There is another reason that there are few producers in this zone. Most of the nutrients that producers need settle on the ocean bottom. Because the ocean bottom is so far from the light zone, there are few nutrients in the light zone. Without nutrients, the waters of the open ocean cannot support large numbers of producers.

Below the light zone of the open ocean, the waters become darker and colder. With increasing depth the pressure of the water also increases.

What animals live in the open-ocean zone?

Most plants that float in the sunlit surface waters of the open-ocean zone are microscopic. These plants are eaten by animal plankton, such as tiny shrimplike krill. Krill are eaten by the largest known animal, the blue whale. Sharks, other large fish, and whales live in the open-ocean zone.

Below the sunlit surface waters, the open ocean becomes a twilight world. Many of the animals that live in this very dim light have an unusual adaptation. They give off light. The production of light by a

145

living organism is called bioluminescence (bye oh-loo muh NES uns). On pages 122 through 124 you read about bioluminescence.

Many organisms in these dimly lighted waters use bioluminesence as they travel to the surface waters. For example, huge schools of krill are often found in the dim region during the day. At night, they move upward and feed on plant plankton. It is thought that the bioluminescence of the krill helps keep the school together.

Below 1,000 m (3,280 feet) lies the deep ocean. This is a world of total darkness. The only light here comes from the flashes of bioluminescent organisms. Most animals in the deep ocean depend on food that drifts down from the surface.

▼ Bioluminescent krill

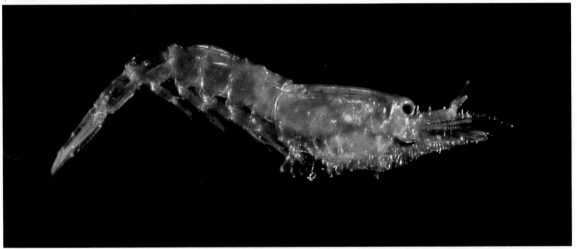

Since light cannot reach the bottom of the open-ocean zone, photosynthesis cannot occur. For this reason, scientists used to believe that producers could not live in the deep part of this zone. But they have learned that this is not so.

Scientists have discovered large vents, or openings, in some parts of the deep ocean. Heat and minerals from deep inside the earth escape from these vents. Certain bacteria use the heat and the

▼ Vent tube worms

clams

crabs

tube worms

▲ Deep-water vent community

minerals to produce food. So these bacteria are producers also. Mussels, clams, and tube worms that live near the vents use the bacteria for food.

There is much that is not known about the deep parts of the open-ocean zone. Humans cannot survive under the great pressures in this zone. Very few underwater vessels are designed to withstand such great pressures. Also, the organisms that are collected from the deep live under very great pressure. Often, the organisms cannot survive the trip up to the ocean surface. As a result, studying the bottom of the ocean is very difficult. Many people consider the ocean to be one of the last great frontiers on the earth.

Lesson Review

1. Explain why there are fewer organisms in the open-ocean zone than in the other ocean zones.
2. Describe how food is produced without light at the deep ocean vents.
3. Identify two reasons why it is difficult to study the deep ocean bottom.

Think! Suggest several ways bioluminescence may help animals survive in the darkness of the deep ocean.

147

5. Protecting the Ocean

Words to Know
ocean pollution
biodegradable
matter

Getting Started Suppose that all the producers in the shallow-ocean zone suddenly died. What would happen to life in the shallow-ocean zone?

Why is the ocean important to humans?

Humans have always turned to the ocean for food. Early humans hunted fish, clams, and other animals that lived close to shore. Today animals are harvested from every ocean zone. Fleets of ships hunt for tuna in the open-ocean zone. The fishing industry uses pictures and spotter planes to help locate schools of tuna.

Plants from the ocean are also used by people. Have you ever seen a forest of seaweed like the one in the picture? The beds of kelp shown are harvested by some people as a source of food. Substances in kelp and other seaweeds are also used to thicken ice cream, salad dressings, jellies, puddings, and toothpaste.

▼ Kelp forest

How do people harm the ocean?

Ocean pollution (puh LOO shun) is the dumping of harmful materials into the ocean. Oil in the ocean is one kind of pollution. Oil is a serious threat to ocean organisms. Oil spills and off-shore drilling accidents are the main ways that oil enters the oceans. Oil may harm ocean plants and animals by covering them or by poisoning them. For example, sea birds that are covered by oil may become unable to fly. Their feathers, which are needed for flight, become matted with oil. When they attempt to clean their oil-coated feathers, the birds may be poisoned by the oil.

▼ Oil-soaked bird

▲ Polluted waters

Oil damages living things in the intertidal zone, too. Each tide carries in more oil that can coat oysters, clams, barnacles, seaweed, and other intertidal organisms. The oil affects the ability of these organisms to feed and breathe.

Many kinds of wastes are dumped into the ocean. Some wastes dumped into the ocean are biodegradable (bye oh dih GRAY duh bul). **Biodegradable matter** is matter that can be broken down by living things. For example, most garbage from your home is biodegradable. But it takes a long time for large amounts of biodegradable materials to break down. When water is polluted with large amounts of biodegradable materials, organisms living in the water may be poisoned.

Harmful material that cannot be broken down is called nonbiodegradable. Many industrial chemicals and plastics are nonbiodegradable. Even small amounts of certain chemicals, such as mercury, can be harmful. When these materials are dumped into the ocean, they can kill organisms living in the water and along the shoreline.

Plastic products are also dangerous. Plastic bags and containers cause the death of thousands of sea turtles and other ocean animals. The animals mistake the plastic bags for food such as jellyfish.

Sea turtle caught in net ▶

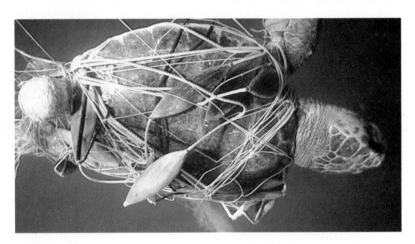

How are food chains affected by chemicals?

As you have learned, all organisms are a part of some food chain. An organism is either a producer or it is a consumer. A consumer is an organism that gets its energy from other living things. Most consumers will finally become a source of food for some other consumer in another food chain.

The balance between food chains in the ocean is very delicate. That balance is upset and can be destroyed when harmful materials enter the ocean.

Explore

Should dilution be used to solve the problem of water pollution?

Some people think that dumping small amounts of poisonous substances into the oceans does not cause pollution. They think that the substance will be harmless when mixed with a large amount of water. They believe a solution to pollution is dilution.

Materials

masking tape · marker · 6 clear plastic cups · pitcher of water · 100-mL graduate · food coloring · dropper · stirrer

Procedure

A. Use masking tape and a marker to label six cups, *1* through *6*.

B. Place 100 mL of water into cup *1*. Add one drop of food coloring to cup *1*. The food coloring represents a poison. Stir to mix well.

C. Pour 50 mL of the water in cup *1* into cup *2*. Add 50 mL of clean water to cup *2*.

D. Pour 50 mL of the water in cup *2* into cup *3*. Add 50 mL of clean water to cup *3*.

E. Pour 50 mL of the water in cup *3* into cup *4*. Add 50 mL of clean water to cup *4*.

F. Pour 50 mL of the water in cup *4* into cup *5*. Add 50 mL of clean water to cup *5*.

G. Pour 50 mL of the water in cup *5* into cup *6*. Add 50 mL of clean water to cup *6*.

H. Line the cups up in order from *1* to *6*. Compare the color of the liquid in each cup.

Writing and Sharing Results and Conclusions

1. How does the color of the water change from cup *1* to cup *6*?

2. Do you think that there is any food coloring left in cup *6*? Explain your answer.

3. Do you think that dilution is a good way to deal with pollution of water? Explain your answer.

The chemical DDT is an example of a harmful substance that affects food chains. The chemical DDT is a pesticide used in many parts of the world. DDT is sprayed on plants. DDT enters the ocean by way of rivers or from rain carrying DDT. In the ocean, DDT is absorbed by plant plankton. Follow the drawing to see how DDT ends up in the body of a bird.

▲ How DDT enters the food chain

Recently, laws have been passed that are designed to protect the oceans. Some laws prevent the dumping of harmful materials into the ocean. For example, DDT is no longer used in the United States. But many other steps must be taken if the oceans are to be protected.

Lesson Review

1. How is the ocean important to people? Give two examples.
2. Describe two causes of ocean pollution.
3. Explain how a harmful chemical dumped into the ocean can affect a food chain.

Think! Some people think we can get rid of harmful wastes by digging holes in the ocean bottom and dumping the wastes in the hole. What problems could result from this method of waste disposal?

Chapter Connections

Construct another graphic organizer. Your graphic organizer should show the main ideas of this chapter in a different way.

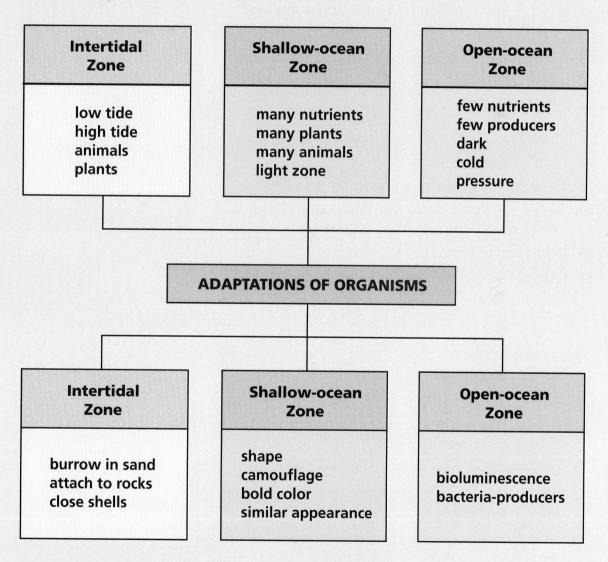

Intertidal Zone	Shallow-ocean Zone	Open-ocean Zone
low tide high tide animals plants	many nutrients many plants many animals light zone	few nutrients few producers dark cold pressure

ADAPTATIONS OF ORGANISMS

Intertidal Zone	Shallow-ocean Zone	Open-ocean Zone
burrow in sand attach to rocks close shells	shape camouflage bold color similar appearance	bioluminescence bacteria-producers

Writing About Science • Research

Scientists use special equipment to explore the oceans. Find out about some of this equipment and write a paragraph about it.

Science Terms

Write the letter of the term that best matches the definition.

1. Dumping of harmful materials into the ocean
2. A depression in rock, filled with ocean water
3. When water reaches the highest point on land
4. Ocean zone with greatest depth
5. Tiny plants and animals that float in the ocean
6. Adaptation that helps an animal blend in with its environment
7. Ocean zone that is under water during some parts of the day and above water during other parts of the day
8. Animal that produces a limestone skeleton
9. Ocean zone starting at low-tide line and ending where ocean bottom drops off sharply
10. When water reaches the lowest point on land
11. Matter that can be broken down by living things

a. biodegradable matter
b. camouflage
c. coral animal
d. high tide
e. intertidal zone
f. low tide
g. ocean pollution
h. open-ocean zone
i. plankton
j. shallow-ocean zone
k. tide pool

Science Ideas

Use complete sentences to answer the following.

1. Why is the earth often called the "water planet?"
2. How would the death of all the plant plankton in the ocean affect ocean animals?
3. Describe the three zones of the ocean.
4. Describe how conditions change in the intertidal zone during one day.
5. Give two reasons why the shallow-ocean zone has a large number of plants and animals.
6. Compare the amount of life found in the open-ocean zone with the amount of life found in the other two zones.

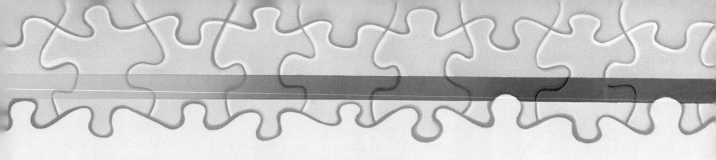

7. Suppose the deep ocean vents stopped releasing heat and minerals. What would happen to the animals living near the vents? Give reasons for your answer.

8. Describe one way ocean animals are used by humans.

9. How are seaweeds, such as kelp, used by people?

10. Discuss some of the ways oil can harm ocean organisms.

11. How can dumping plastics into the ocean harm ocean animals?

Applying Science Ideas

1. How do you think the growth in the human population will affect the ocean? Give specific examples.

2. Hurricanes can damage coral reefs. How might the animals that live on and near a reef be affected by a hurricane?

3. You have read that some ocean organisms produce substances that are useful to humans. Think about other ocean organisms and list their possible uses.

Using Science Skills

Look at the corals in the pictures. You can see that the corals have different shapes and patterns. Use the shapes and patterns to classify the corals. Construct a classification diagram for the corals shown.

Chapter 5

Change Over Time

Ancient Insects

Amber looks like brownish-yellow glass, but it is light in weight, like plastic. Amber can be polished and made into beads for jewelry. Imagine a string of amber beads. It would make an unusual present. Surprise! There is a dead insect in one of the beads!

How did the insect get into the bead? To understand how, you need to know where amber comes from. Amber formed from tree sap that hardened over a very long time. Sometimes an insect, like the one shown here, would get trapped in the sticky sap and would die. As the sap hardened, the dead insect hardened, too. Instead of rotting, the insect was preserved.

Amber formed millions of years ago. So the insects found in amber are millions of years old. Some of these insects no longer exist anywhere on the earth. Scientists study the insects in amber to learn about life in the past.

One scientist who studies amber is Dr. George Poinar, Jr. He has been interested in amber since he was a child. He used to collect pieces of amber that washed up on beaches near where he lived. Dr. Poinar likes to think about the lives of the insects he sees in amber. He is fascinated by the fact that these insects lived before there were people on the earth.

Recently Dr. Poinar got a chance to study an unusual piece of amber—one that has a frog inside. Dr. Poinar had seen many insects in amber, but this was the first time he or anyone else had seen a frog in amber. How did the frog get there?

When Dr. Poinar looked closely at the frog, he learned several things about it. The bones showed that the frog was an adult tree frog. Its back legs had been broken.

Dr. Poinar tried to figure out how the frog got into the amber. He thinks that a bird might have caught the frog. Perhaps the bird grasped the frog by its hind legs. This grasping could explain how the legs got broken. If the frog wriggled free, it might have fallen into an old tree trunk. With its legs broken, the frog could not have climbed out. Sap in the tree trunk could have trapped the frog. After millions of years, the sap hardened, forming amber.

There could be other explanations. Tree frogs climb trees. Maybe the frog just got stuck in some sap. What do you think? Can you come up with a story that solves the mystery?

Discover

How can you make a model of amber?

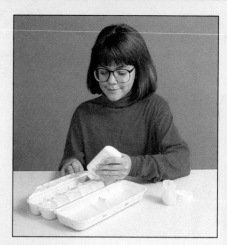

Materials   plastic foam egg carton · petroleum jelly · white glue

Procedure

Sometimes objects in amber are difficult to identify. Pieces of living things look strange in amber. Choose a small natural object or a part of an object that you think will be difficult for others to identify.

Coat the inside of one section of an egg carton with petroleum jelly. Place a thin layer of glue in this section. Add the object you have chosen. Cover the object with a thin layer of glue. When the glue is completely dry, remove the block of glue from the egg carton. Challenge others to identify the object.

In this chapter you will discover ways in which many living things have changed over time. You will learn some ideas on why these organisms have changed. You will also find out some of the ways scientists study things that lived long ago.

159

1. Evidence of Life of the Past

Getting Started Have you ever made an imprint of your hand in plaster of Paris? In a way, a hand imprint is a trace of a living thing. Scientists use imprints to study organisms that were on the earth millions of years ago.

Words to Know
fossil
petrified
radioactive
dating

Scientist studying a dinosaur bone ▼

What are fossils?

You have probably seen drawings of dinosaurs. These animals lived on the earth millions of years ago. Of course, there are no dinosaurs living on the earth today. How have scientists learned about dinosaurs if none are alive to study? Like detectives, scientists have learned about dinosaurs by studying clues that remain from these animals.

Among the most important clues are the remains of dinosaur bones. Such remains have been found in many parts of the world. Look at the dinosaur bones shown. What is one thing that can be learned about a dinosaur from its bones?

In some parts of the world, footprints of dinosaurs have been found in rock. The original footprints were not made in rock. They were made in mud or in soft soil, which later changed to rock.

Bones and footprints in rock are two kinds of fossils (FAHS ulz). A **fossil** is any kind of evidence of something that was alive a long time ago. Fossils may be remains, such as bones, of once-living things. Fossils may be traces, such as footprints in rock, of once-living things. How are an imprint in plaster of Paris and a footprint in rock alike? How are they different?

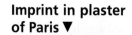
Imprint in plaster of Paris ▼

▲ Imprint of a fossil fern   ▲ Fossil dinosaur tracks

Many fossils are the remains of once-living things that are not found on the earth today. Remember that organisms that were once alive but no longer exist on the earth are extinct. Dinosaurs are among the best-known examples of extinct animals.

What are some ways fossils form?

The remains of most organisms decay before they can become fossils. Sometimes, however, things die and do not decay. Body parts such as shells, bones, and teeth sometimes do not decay. These remains can become fossils.

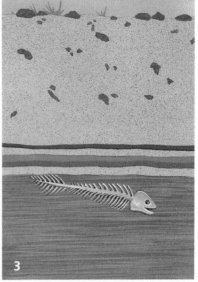

▲ How a fossil forms

Most fossils are found in rock. Refer to the drawings as you read about how fossils commonly form. Keep in mind that these events took place over millions of years. (1) Bodies of dead organisms fell to the bottom of the ocean. (2) Rivers and streams carried solid matter, such as mud and gravel, to the ocean. Some of this solid matter covered the dead organisms.

(3) After millions of years, many layers of matter built up over the first layer. The upper layers pressed down on the lower layers. Matter in the lower layers was squeezed together, forming rock. Remains of organisms trapped in the rock layers formed fossils.

Sometimes parts of the remains of dead organisms turn to stone. The remains of a living thing that has turned to stone is said to be **petrified** (PE-trih fyd). Petrified bones and shells are common types of fossils. Remains of organisms become petrified in the following way. Their remains are buried in mud under water. Minerals in the water slowly replace the hard parts of the organisms. When minerals have replaced all the hard parts, the remains have turned to stone. Look at the picture of logs in the Petrified Forest, in Arizona. Each log has turned to stone!

Logs in the Petrified Forest, Arizona ▼

Explore

How can you make a cast of a shell?

Have you ever seen human footprints in a concrete sidewalk? Have you ever seen animal tracks on a muddy trail? There is evidence of many animals and plants that lived in the ancient past. This evidence is in the form of a cast. A cast is formed when a once-living thing leaves an imprint in something. Then the imprint becomes filled in with mud that hardens. You can make a cast.

Materials
shell · petroleum jelly · modeling clay · paper cup · metric ruler · scissors · plaster of Paris · water · plastic spoon · jar

Procedure

A. Coat the outer side of a shell with a thin layer of petroleum jelly.

B. Press modeling clay into the bottom of a paper cup. Using scissors, cut off the cup about 5 cm above the level of the clay.

C. Press the outer side of the shell into the clay. Then carefully remove the shell.

D. Use a spoon to mix water and plaster of Paris in a jar. Follow the directions on the package.

E. Pour the plaster of Paris into the cup until the cup is almost full. **Caution:** *Throw the unused plaster of Paris mixture in the trash. Do not pour it down the drain of the sink.*

F. Wait at least 1 hour for the plaster of Paris to harden. Carefully remove the plaster shape by peeling away the cup, as shown in the drawing below. You now have a cast of a shell.

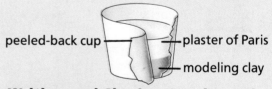

peeled-back cup — plaster of Paris — modeling clay

Writing and Sharing Results and Conclusions

1. How is the cast you just made like a fossil?

2. How is the cast different from a fossil?

3. What can a cast that was formed millions of years ago tell about life on the earth long ago?

▲ Insects preserved in amber

Sometimes scientists find the complete remains of once-living things. They found the entire body of a baby woolly mammoth frozen in ice in the Arctic. A woolly mammoth is an extinct animal that looked like an elephant.

Complete fossil insects have been found in amber. Amber is a clear, yellow material that forms from the sap of certain trees. Insects have become trapped in the sticky sap. Over time, the sap has hardened to form amber. The insects have been preserved in the amber. On page 156 and on this page at the left are insects in amber.

How do scientists find out the age of fossils?

Scientists have many ways of finding out the age of a fossil. One way is to identify the age of the rock in which the fossil is found. A fossil is about the same age as the rock layer in which it was trapped. By knowing the age of the rock layer, scientists can find the age of fossils in that layer.

To find the age of rocks, scientists use a method based on decay, or change. They know that certain

Cut-away view of rock containing fossils ▼

24 to 2 million years ago

63 million years ago

360 to 190 million years ago

164

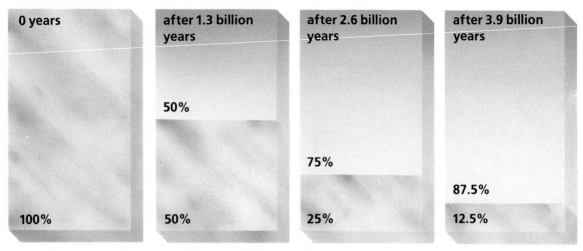

0 years	after 1.3 billion years	after 2.6 billion years	after 3.9 billion years
	50%	75%	87.5%
100%	50%	25%	12.5%

▲ **How potassium-40 decays over time**

potassium-40

argon-40

substances decay over time. One substance that is used is potassium-40. Over time, some potassium-40 decays into argon-40, as shown in the drawing.

Scientists know how long it takes for certain amounts of potassium-40 to decay into argon-40. They measure and compare the amounts of both substances in rock. By comparing the amounts, they can find the age of the rock. Then they can make a good guess about the age of the fossils in the rock.

This method of measuring the age of rocks and fossils is called **radioactive** (ray dee oh AK tiv) **dating.** By using this method, some scientists think that the earth is at least 4.5 billion years old. They think that the earliest known fossils are about 3.5 billion years old.

Lesson Review ▬▬▬▬▬

1. Define the term *fossil.*
2. Describe three kinds of fossils.
3. Describe how fossils found in rock form.
4. Identify one method scientists use to measure the age of fossils.

Think! Do you think fossils are still forming? Give a reason for your answer.

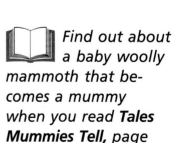

*Find out about a baby woolly mammoth that becomes a mummy when you read **Tales Mummies Tell,** page 188.*

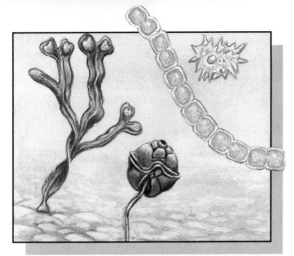

▲ Precambrian Era (3.5 billion–600 million years ago)

▼ Paleozoic Era (600 million years ago)

2. Changes in Living Things

Words to Know
era
species

Getting Started Have you ever watched a dog dig up an old bone? How long had the bone been buried? How had it changed while it was buried? Scientists ask questions like these when they study fossils.

Why do scientists study fossils?

Scientists study fossils to form ideas, or models, about life in the past. Evidence from rocks and fossils shows that the earth and the living things on it have changed a great deal over time.

The earliest living things were probably small, simple one-celled organisms. Fossils seem to show that over time, larger and more complex organisms have also formed. The earliest living things are thought to have lived in water. Land organisms probably developed much later.

The drawings on these two pages show that the history of the earth may be divided into different time periods, or eras (IHR uhz). An **era** is a main division of time in the history of the earth. What is the oldest era? In which era do you live?

166

Many extinct plants and animals are known only from their fossil remains. Some fossil remains come from extinct organisms that looked much like organisms on the earth today. Look at the drawings in this fossil record. What organism from a past era may have looked like a modern organism?

▼ Cenozoic Era (65 million years ago–present)

▲ Mesozoic Era (230–65 million years ago)

What changes are found in fossil species?

Through the study of fossils, scientists can trace how some species (SPEE sheez) change over time. A **species** is the smallest group into which living things are classified. Only members of the same species can mate and produce young that can also produce young. For example, dogs and wolves belong to two different species. They may look very much alike, but dogs and wolves usually do not mate.

All members of a species are alike in certain basic ways. For example, all dogs share certain traits. How are all dogs alike? How are they different? Although dogs differ in such traits as size and shape, they all belong to the same species.

Many scientists believe that species on the earth today are related to species that lived in the

55 million years ago

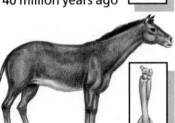
40 million years ago

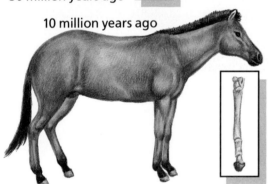
30 million years ago

10 million years ago

past. However, species alive today are different from species of the past. By studying fossils, scientists have traced the earlier forms of many species.

The drawings here show how a modern horse differs from earlier horses. Locate the earliest known horse. This animal is thought to have lived about 55 million years ago. Compare the earliest horse with the modern horse. How do they differ?

Over a very long period of time, the horse has changed in size and weight. The earliest horse was about the size of a medium-sized dog of today. It had three toes on each hind foot and four toes on each front foot. Later horses had still different feet. Over time, the toes were replaced by hoofs. A hoof is formed of one enlarged foot bone and several smaller bones covered by a hard material.

1 million years ago

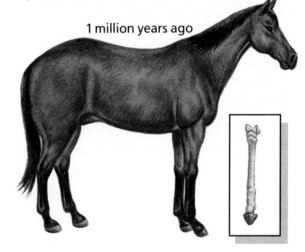

Earth Science
CONNECTION

Fossils form in types of rocks called sedimentary rocks. Use reference books to find out about how fossils form. Why are they only found in sedimentary rocks?

Lesson Review

1. Compare a modern living thing, such as a dog, with the earliest living things on the earth.
2. What is a species? Name an animal species.
3. Describe three changes in the horse over time.

Think! You are studying the fossils of a type of animal that over a million-year period moved from a cold, mountainous region to a warm, flat region. How might the species have changed?

Skills

Telling whether observations support a hypothesis

Suppose you observe that insects appear about the time flowers bloom each spring. Your observations about flowers can help you explain why insects appear. An explanation based on observations is a hypothesis. After you form a hypothesis, you can make more observations to test it.

Practicing the skill

1. Imagine that a botanist has two groups of leaves.

2. The botanist studies the color, shape, and vein pattern of a leaf from each group. Leaf A is from one group, and leaf B is from the other group. The botanist forms the hypothesis that the leaves are from the same kind of tree.

3. Observe leaves A and B. List the observations that support the botanist's hypothesis.

4. List the observations that do not support the hypothesis.

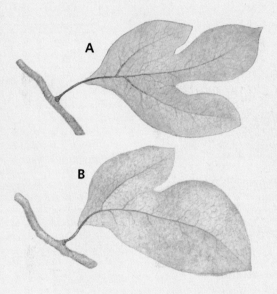

Thinking about the skill

Which observations of the leaves do you think are most important to tell whether the hypothesis is correct?

Applying the skill

Trilobites are extinct animals, but horseshoe crabs are alive today. Consider this hypothesis: Horseshoe crabs and trilobites are related. Observe the drawings of both animals. List those traits that support the hypothesis and those that do not.

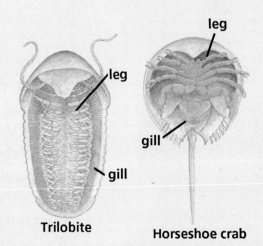

Trilobite

Horseshoe crab

3. Charles Darwin

Getting Started Imagine it is early evening. The sky is darkening. An owl is flying over a grassy field looking for a mouse for its meal. Gray mice and white mice are running through the field. The owl swoops down. Which color mouse do you think the owl will catch? Why? Which color mouse will probably survive the longest?

Words to Know
theory
evolution

Galápagos Islands

Charles Darwin as a young man

▲ Darwin's journey on *H.M.S. Beagle*

Who was Charles Darwin?

In the 1800s a scientist named Charles Darwin became interested in how species change over time. Darwin developed a theory (THEE uh ree) to explain how new species form. A **theory** is an idea that is supported by evidence. It helps to explain a set of many observations. Think again about the white mice and the gray mice in the field. Darwin might have predicted that over a long period of time only the gray mice would survive and reproduce. You will find out why Darwin's theory might have led him to make this prediction.

Charles Darwin was an English naturalist. A naturalist is a scientist who studies living things in their natural settings instead of in a zoo or in a lab. In 1831, at age 23, Darwin sailed as a ship's naturalist on a five-year voyage around the world. Trace his route on the map shown on page 170.

Wherever the ship landed, Darwin studied the living plants and animals. He also collected fossils. Darwin made notes about the many things he saw. Young Darwin spent five weeks exploring the Galápagos (guh LAHP uh gus) Islands. These are islands in the Pacific Ocean off the coast of Ecuador. Find these islands on the map. They were later to become very important to Darwin's work.

▼ Blue-footed booby

▲ Giant Galápagos tortoise

On the Galápagos Islands, Darwin found closely related species of living things. For example, he found several kinds of closely related birds. He also found many closely related reptiles and plants. Several of these organisms are shown on this page. What could account for the different, but related, species on the islands?

▲ Prickly-pear cactus

Why did Darwin study finches?

Darwin was very interested in one group of birds he found—the finches. Finches are small birds that are found throughout much of the world. Darwin might have expected that all finches on those islands would be the same species. But that is not what he found. On the 13 large islands, he found 14 species of finches. All the species seemed related, but they still differed in some ways.

When his voyage ended, Darwin began to study his collection and his notes. During the next 20 years, he formed a theory to explain how new species develop. You will read about this theory later in this chapter.

The species of finches on the different islands were alike in some ways. But the different species of finches showed differences in the shape of their beaks. The beaks were suited to the kinds of food the birds ate. The food available to the birds differed somewhat from island to island. The food also dif-

▼ **Some of the Galápagos finches and the food they eat**

fered from place to place on a single island. The different species of finches also did not mate with each other. Remember that only living things of the same species can mate and reproduce.

From his studies of the finches, Darwin formed an idea about how new species might develop. He guessed that millions of years ago some finches had arrived on the Galápagos Islands. These birds had come from South America. The finches all belonged to one species. But some of the birds had traits that suited them better for one type of diet than for another. For example, some birds had beaks that were good for cracking seeds open. Such birds tended to live where there were many seeds.

▼ Insect-eating finch

▼ Seed-eating finch

Other birds had beaks that allowed them to catch insects. These birds tended to live in regions where there were many insects. So seed-eating birds tended to live together. Insect-eating birds tended to live together.

Time passed. Several different groups of birds developed. Each group had its own diet. Each group had its own habitat. The pictures above show a seed-eating finch and an insect-eating finch. Each is shown in its own habitat. In time, such finches

Explore Together

How many ways do peanuts vary?

ACTIVITY

Materials

Organizer

20 peanuts · hand lens · metric ruler · balance · cup of water

Procedure

Investigator
Recorder

A. Predict the number of ways in which 20 peanuts vary from one another. Write down this number.

Manager,
Group

B. Carefully observe each of the 20 peanuts. Do not crack the peanuts open. You may use the hand lens, metric ruler, balance, and cup of water to gather data about the way the peanuts vary.

Recorder

C. Make a list of all the ways in which the peanuts vary. Be specific in your descriptions.

Group

D. Crack the peanuts open. Again, observe them carefully.

Recorder

E. Add to the list of the ways in which the peanuts vary.

Writing and Sharing Results and Conclusions

Group,
Recorder,

1. How did your prediction about the number of ways peanuts vary compare with your final list?

Reporter

2. What are the main ways in which peanuts vary?

3. How does your list compare with that of other members of your group?

4. Explain how some of the differences in the peanuts could be an advantage. How could some of the differences be a disadvantage?

174

became different from one another. In fact, they changed so much from one another that they could no longer mate. Over a long period of time, 14 species of finches developed. Of these 14 species, some lived on all the islands. But some could be found on only two or three of the islands.

The process of change that can produce new species from existing species over time is called **evolution** (ev uh LOO shun). This same process took place many times on the islands. Finally, 14 different species of finches had evolved.

What did Darwin conclude from his studies?

From his studies, Darwin developed a theory on how different species developed. He concluded that the environment plays a role in causing new species to form. Darwin's theory is about how evolution occurs. You will read more about Darwin's theory of evolution in the next section.

Darwin's theory of evolution was published in 1859 in a book called *The Origin of Species*. Since then scientists have gained new information on how traits are passed from parent to offspring. Much of this new information supports Darwin's theory.

▼ Kangaroo

Lesson Review

1. Who was Charles Darwin? When and where did he make his discoveries? When did he publish his theory?
2. Define the term *evolution*.
3. According to Darwin, how did the finches of the Galápagos Islands develop into different species?
4. What did Darwin conclude from his study of finches?

Think! Two Australian animals are shown here. Many Australian animals look different from animals in other parts of the world. Suggest a reason why.

▼ Duck-bill platypus

4. The Process of Change

Words to Know
inherit
variations
adaptation
natural selection

How do members of a species differ?

A trait such as fur length in the cat species is passed from parent to offspring. Fur length is said to be inherited. To **inherit** is to receive a trait from a parent.

In a family, parents and offspring are not identical. Only identical twins or triplets have the same inherited traits. Each offspring is different from its parents and from other offspring. Like members of the same family, members of the same species have differences. The cats shown all belong to the same species. But how do they differ? Slight differences

▼ Variations in cats

between members of a species are called **variations** (ver ee AY shunz).

A variation, such as eye color in cats, may not affect a living thing's survival. But another variation, such as fur length in cats, may help a cat survive under certain conditions. A cat with long hair could better survive a cold climate. What kind of variation in cats could be harmful?

How is the environment related to evolution?

Environments change over time. These changes can affect the variations that are inherited. Sometimes a certain trait helps an organism survive in a changed environment. Offspring that inherit this trait will also be better able to survive. A trait that helps an organism to survive in its environment is an **adaptation** (ad up TAY shun). For example, over time the main food in a region could change from grasses to berries. Animals adapted to eat the berries could survive. In time, animals that could eat only grass would die out.

Problem Solving

Survival of the Fittest

Imagine that you are writing a book about the evolution of animals. You are ready to write about how chipmunks will look and behave 50,000 years from now. You have predicted that the chipmunk's environment will change in this way: The climate will change from cool to very hot and dry. Forests will become deserts. The wind will blow much of the time. Dust will swirl in the air. Only low, spiny plants will grow.

How will the chipmunk change?

Draw a picture of how the chipmunk might look in 50,000 years. Describe all the ways in which it might change. Tell how each change will help the animal survive in its environment.

Darwin used the term **natural selection** for the process by which living things that are adapted to their environments survive. Well-adapted organisms then mate and have offspring with helpful adaptations. Over time, natural selection results in changes in the species.

The process of natural selection is a part of Darwin's theory. In fact, the full name of his theory is the *theory of evolution by natural selection*. Sometimes the theory is called survival of the fittest. The term *survival of the fittest* means that living things best suited to an environment survive and reproduce.

The effects of natural selection are shown in peppered moths. Peppered moths, which live in England, may be light-colored or dark-colored. The moths rest on tree trunks. They are often eaten by birds that see them on the trunks.

Before 1850, most tree trunks where peppered moths lived were light-colored. And most peppered moths were light-colored. But a few were dark-colored. As more and more factories were built in England, tree trunks became black from soot. After a while, most peppered moths were dark.

Look at the pictures of the peppered moths shown below. Which color moths would probably survive on a black tree trunk? Why? Dark-colored moths were most likely to survive on dark tree trunks. The survival of dark-colored moths was linked to the moth's environment.

▲ Moths on a light tree trunk

▲ Moths on a dark tree trunk

Lesson Review

1. What are variations?
2. Give an example of a helpful and a harmful variation in a species. Explain why the variation is either helpful or harmful.
3. Define *adaptation* and *natural selection.*
4. How is the peppered moth an example of natural selection?

Think! A species of rabbit is found in black, brown, and white. Over a long time, the climate changed from warm to very cold. Predict which color rabbits survived. Explain your answer.

150 million years ago

500 A.D.

1680 A.D.

1768 A.D.

giant lemur

dodo

Steller's sea cow

triceratops

5. Extinct Species

Words to Know
endangered
species

Getting Started You have seen pictures of dinosaurs. You may have heard of the dodo bird and the passenger pigeon, shown above. Why have you never seen any of these animals *alive?*

Why do species become extinct?

Dinosaurs, dodo birds, and passenger pigeons are all extinct. Fossil records have shown that many species have become extinct. The dinosaurs are the best-known examples of extinct animals. What happened to the dinosaurs?

About 100 million years ago, dinosaurs were plentiful on the earth. But about 65 million years ago, they all disappeared. There are many ideas about why they died off. One widely held idea is that about 65 million years ago the earth was hit by a large meteorite (MEET ee uh ryt). A meteorite is a rock that falls to the earth from space.

When the meteorite struck the earth, it might have caused huge amounts of dust to fill the air. The

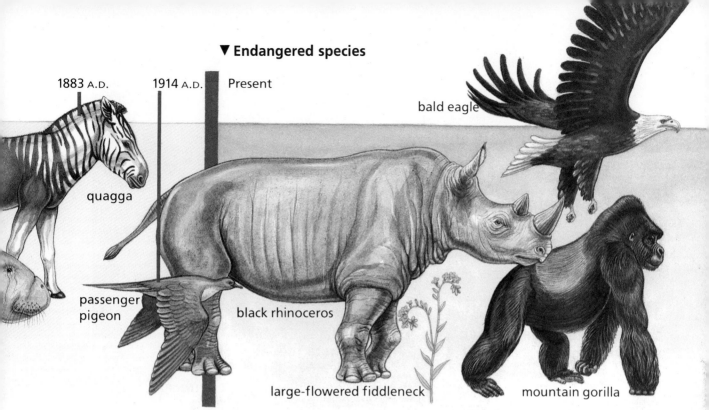

▼ Endangered species

1883 A.D.   1914 A.D.   Present

bald eagle

quagga

passenger pigeon

black rhinoceros

large-flowered fiddleneck

mountain gorilla

dust could have blocked out the sun for years, causing plants to die. The death of plants would have caused the death of plant-eating dinosaurs. Then meat-eating dinosaurs would have died because they could not eat the plant-eating dinosaurs. In time, no living dinosaurs were left on the earth.

How can modern species become extinct?

In recent times, people have caused the extinction of several species. The dodo bird and the passenger pigeon were hunted until they became extinct. A species that is in danger of becoming extinct is called an **endangered species** (en DAYN-jurd SPEE sheez).

There are many endangered animal species. Many plant species are also endangered. Which endangered organisms are shown above?

People do many things that endanger living things. They pollute the water, air, and soil with harmful chemicals. These chemicals change the natural environment. Many kinds of living things will

181

▲ Cleaning up after an oil spill   ▲ Rhinoceroses at a zoo

sicken and die if they live near the chemicals. Living things are also endangered when people cut down forests for homes and businesses. Why might the organisms become endangered?

In recent years, people have become concerned about the living things with which they share the planet. People have begun programs to protect endangered species. They have passed laws to stop or limit the hunting of some species. They are trying to control pollution of the environment. In some places, a certain amount of land may be set aside for parks, not homes. Zoos, such as the one shown, are also helping to protect endangered organisms.

Lesson Review

1. What is an endangered species? List two endangered species.
2. What is one idea about the extinction of dinosaurs?
3. What are two things that people have done to endanger species of living things?

Think! Suppose you headed a committee to protect endangered species. Describe two things your committee could do to save a species from extinction.

Chapter Connections

Use the graphic organizer to write a paragraph about an idea presented in this chapter that was new to you.

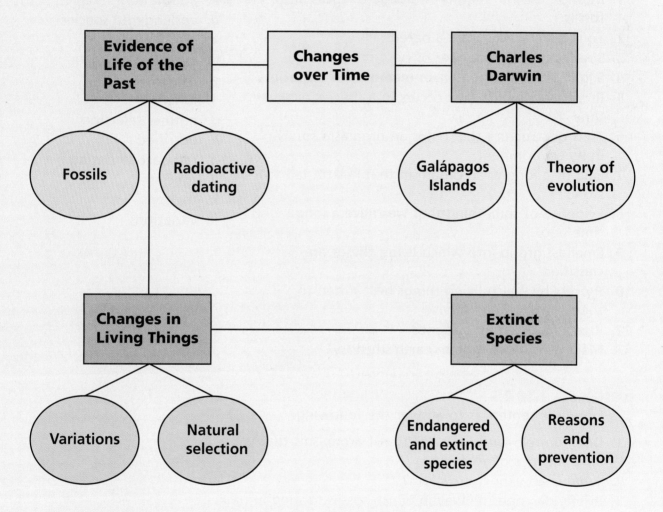

Writing About Science • Narrate

It is the year 20,001. You are a scientist digging for fossils. Tell a story about finding some bones of an animal you think lived around the year 2000. Describe the scientific techniques you would use to find out about the animal. Then write a complete description of the animal as you think it looked in the year 2000.

Science Terms

Write the letter of the term that best matches the definition.

1. Method used to measure the age of rocks and fossils
2. To receive a trait from a parent
3. Species that is in danger of becoming extinct
4. Slight differences between members of a species
5. Process of change that occurs in a species over time
6. Trait or structure that helps an organism survive in its environment
7. Said of a long-dead organism that has turned to stone
8. Evidence of something that was alive a long time ago
9. Smallest group into which living things are classified
10. Process by which living things best suited to their surroundings survive
11. Idea supported by evidence
12. Main division of time in earth's history

a. adaptation
b. endangered species
c. era
d. evolution
e. fossil
f. inherit
g. natural selection
h. petrified
i. radioactive dating
j. species
k. theory
l. variations

Science Ideas

Use complete sentences to answer the following.

1. Describe two kinds of evidence of organisms that were alive millions of years ago.
2. What is an extinct organism?
3. Briefly describe the way in which fossils formed in rock.
4. Identify and briefly describe one method scientists use to measure the age of rocks and fossils.
5. Describe how the earliest organisms probably differed from a modern mouse.
6. What is a species? Name two species you have not listed in any other answer.
7. Name a kind of hoofed animal that has changed over time. Identify three kinds of changes in the species.

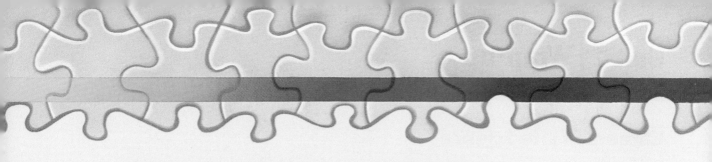

8. Who was Charles Darwin? Describe the main idea of his theory of evolution.
9. Compare the meanings of the terms *variation* and *adaptation.* Explain which adaptation helped certain peppered moths to survive.
10. What is meant by survival of the fittest?
11. How might a species become endangered? Give an example of an endangered species.

Applying Science Ideas

Scientists have studied peppered moths from 1800 to the present. They have counted the number of light and dark moths in samples of 100 moths. The table below shows the average numbers of moths counted. Figures for the years 2000 and 2025 are predictions.

Use the data in the table to prepare a bar graph. Then answer these questions. When were dark moths found in the greatest number? Do scientists predict that light moths will increase or decrease in 2025? What could account for the change in the number of dark moths in 2025?

Numbers of Moths in Samples of 100 by Year									
Kind of Moth	1800	1850	1875	1900	1925	1950	1975	2000	2025
Light	100	97	90	65	21	10	7	23	35
Dark	0	3	10	35	79	90	93	77	65

Using Science Skills

Consider this hypothesis: All species of small organisms evolve into species of larger organisms. Then observe the drawings of the evolution of the horse on page 168. Tell how your observations support or do not support the hypothesis. Find out about the extinct bird, archaeopteryx. Compare the size of this bird with that of modern birds. Tell how this information supports or does not support the hypothesis.

Careers in Life Science

Marine Biologist

Dr. Eugene Kaplan likes fish but not just for eating. Dr. Kaplan is a **marine biologist.** That means he's a scientist who studies organisms that live in the sea.

Dr. Kaplan teaches at Hofstra University in Hempstead, New York. He also runs the Hofstra Marine Biology Laboratory on the island of Jamaica. So, when he's not in his classroom, he is usually snorkeling, sailing, and teaching in the Caribbean Sea. At the Marine Biology Laboratory, students and teachers learn about the plants and animals of tropical seas.

Dr. Kaplan got the idea for the lab when he was 35 years old. He was sailing around the Caribbean with friends. "It was so beautiful," he says. "I saw coral reefs for the first time and I was hooked."

The lab is very important to Dr. Kaplan. Teachers can get training in marine biology there. Many college students study at the lab, too. They explore coral reefs in boats. They scuba dive in the warm water to study underwater habitats. They even fish with huge nets at night. They capture fish for the lab's saltwater aquarium. Then the students can study the fish from inside the lab.

"I like working with students," Dr. Kaplan says. But he also enjoys his scientific experiments. He is trying to raise new types of fish. He works with tilapia (tuh LAH pe uh). Tilapia are small fish that grow quickly and inexpensively. "One day these fish could solve some of the food problems of poor countries of the world," he says.

Marine biologists must get a bachelor's degree in biology. Then they need to go to a college or university for master's and doctoral degrees. "Curiosity and determination are also very important," Dr. Kaplan says. And, of course, they must love the sea.

Connecting Science Ideas

1. Some people break off pieces of coral reefs to take home or to sell. How might a large amount of collecting affect the food web in these coral reef ecosystems?   **Careers; Chapter 3**

2. How could a marine biologist help make people aware of the dangers of polluting the ocean with plastics?
Careers; Chapter 4

3. Explain how a flowering plant carries out four life processes.   **Chapter 1; Chapter 2**

4. You learned about the five-kingdom classification system. Protists are one of the five kingdoms. How do you think plantlike protists obtain food?   **Chapter 1; Chapter 2**

5. You read about CFCs in the atmosphere on pages 112–113. You also learned that DDT gets into ocean water. Both DDT and CFCs affect food chains. Compare how each of these pollutants might affect an Antarctic food chain.
Chapter 3; Chapter 4

6. Describe a deep ocean vent ecosystem. Include in your description the living and nonliving parts and sources of energy.   **Chapter 3; Chapter 4**

Computer Connections

Use reference books to find out about an endangered species of animal. Find out the animal's habitat, the food it eats, and why it has become endangered. Put the information you find into a class database.

Use the class database to help you design a refuge for endangered animals. Classify the animals into groups. Describe your classification system. Then describe your animal refuge.

Unit Project

Make a model of a cell. Use a sealable clear plastic bag for the cell membrane. Use a variety of materials to represent the cytoplasm and other parts of the cell. Make a key that names and describes each part of the model.

from

TALES MUMMIES TELL

Written by Patricia Lauber

Although mummies cannot talk, they can tell us many things about the past. What do you think we could learn from the mummy of a baby woolly mammoth? Join a team of scientists as they study this prehistoric animal. Find out how they uncover clues about a brief life that vanished long ago.

A Mammoth Mummy

One long-ago summer's day, a baby woolly mammoth somehow lost his mother. He was no more than seven or eight months old, so young that he had only milk teeth and still depended on his mother for food. As he wandered around his home range, near the Arctic Circle, his body fat was quickly used up. Frantic with hunger, he tried to eat dirt and plants. Then he had an accident and fell, perhaps into an icy pit, where he soon died. In the far north, summer is short. The body froze and became encased in ice. Cave-ins buried it under six feet of earth. The ground froze and stayed frozen, except for the top few inches, which thawed each summer. In this natural deep freeze, the body of the baby mammoth was preserved for thousands of years. It became a mummy, which is the term now used for any well-preserved body, whether animal or human.

A Soviet scientist measures the remains of the baby mammoth found by gold prospectors.

The mummy was found in June 1977. At that time Soviet gold prospectors were working near a stream in northeastern Siberia. One was running a bulldozer, digging out mud and frozen ground, when he struck a big block of muddy ice with something dark inside. Curious about what he had found, the prospector changed the flow of the stream and used its water to melt some of the ice. In a short time, the shape of a baby mammoth appeared.

The discovery was of great interest to Soviet scientists who study mammoths. Woolly mammoths, which were relatives of to-day's elephants, managed to survive a long period of drastic changes in the earth's climate. They lived through times when heavy snows fell, when great glaciers formed and grew so big that mile-thick sheets of ice swallowed huge areas of land for thousands of years. They lived through times when the air warmed and the glaciers shrank, releasing floods of meltwater. Yet when the glaciers last melted and drew back, about 9,000 to 12,000 years ago, the woolly mammoths died out. How and why they did remains a mystery.

We know about mammoths from the cave drawings of Stone Age peoples and from the remains of mammoths that have been found. Over the years countless bones and tusks have been found in the far north. From time to time parts of woolly mammoths have been discovered in the frozen ground, but whole mammoths are rare. The few discovered in the 1800s rotted away or were eaten by animals before scientists could study them. The ones found in this century have not been complete. The Soviet prospectors' find, which they named Dima, was the first whole mammoth mummy that modern scientists had ever had a chance to study. In addition, only once before, in Alaska, had anyone found remains of a baby mammoth.

The mummy was flown to a laboratory in the north, where it was refrigerated to keep it from rotting. Later it was flown to Leningrad for detailed study. Samples of material from the body were shared with scientists in the United States who were trying to find out, among other things, the exact relationship of mammoths and elephants.

Baby Dima and a fully reconstructed adult woolly mammoth are displayed together in a Soviet museum.

Early studies showed that Dima was about 4 feet tall and 4 feet long and weighed 198 pounds. His trunk measured 22 inches and had two "fingers" at the end, just like the ones that can be seen in cave paintings. The hide was now separated from the body, but in life Dima had had a shaggy, chestnut-colored coat. The soft, thick undercoat was 3 to 4 inches long and protected by a covering of wiry hairs up to 10 inches long. The trunk was furry and the outer ears were tiny. Like all woolly mammoths, Dima was well equipped to live in the far north, with a covering that trapped and held in body heat. By contrast, today's elephants live in warm or hot climates and are equipped to get rid of body heat. They have no fur, only bristles, on their leathery hides. Their huge outer ears provide extra surface area from which heat can escape.

A technician, at the Royal British Columbia Museum in Canada, inspects this replica of an adult woolly mammoth.

A sketch, made by one of the Soviet scientists, shows how Dima may have died by falling into an ice shaft.

It was clear that Dima had been hungry: His ribs stuck out through his skin. The stomach and other intestines provided more clues to what happened. In them was only a trace of his mother's milk. Alone, he had eaten mostly dirt. With just three milk teeth, he had not been able to chew plant food but had simply swallowed some roots, stems, grass, and grass seeds. The presence of grass seeds showed that Dima had died in summer, the time of year when these seeds form. The month was most likely August, which is late summer in the arctic.

The excellent condition of the mummy was the chief clue to the kind of place in which Dima died. It must have been a cold one, cold enough to keep the body from decaying before it froze. And because the body was buried, it must have been a place where cave-ins or landslides could occur, such as a pit or the bank of a stream.

To find the age of the mummy, scientists made use of a built-in atomic clock. This is how the clock works:

Certain kinds of atoms are radioactive—they keep breaking down by giving off tiny parts of themselves. Among these atoms are those of carbon 14, which is a radioactive variety of carbon. Carbon 14 forms when the atmosphere is bombarded by cosmic rays. When it combines with oxygen, it forms carbon dioxide. This radioactive carbon dioxide mixes with the other carbon dioxide in the air.

Plants take in carbon dioxide, which they use to make their food. And so they also take in carbon 14. Every bit of a living plant contains a tiny amount of carbon 14. Animals feed on plants or on other animals that eat plants. As a result, every animal's body also contains a tiny amount of carbon 14. The carbon 14 keeps breaking down, but new supplies are continually being added.

In this mural, a herd of woolly mammoths trudge across the tundra of northern Siberia more than 25,000 years ago.

When an animal or a plant dies, it stops taking in carbon 14. No new supplies are added, but the carbon 14 already in the tissues continues to break down. It does so at a fixed and steady rate, which is described by its half-life—the time required for half its atoms to break down.

Carbon 14 has a half-life of about 5,600 years. This means that some 5,600 years after a plant or animal dies, half the carbon 14 atoms present at the time of death are left; the rest have broken down into a different kind of atom. After another 5,600 years have passed, half of the half—a quarter—are left. After another 5,600 years, an eighth of the carbon 14 atoms are left, and so on. After some 50,000 years there is almost no carbon 14 left, although scientists can still use that tiny bit.

Because carbon 14 breaks down at this steady rate, scientists can use it to date once-living things, such as Dima, that are up to 100,000 years old. They can analyze a sample of tissue and find out how much carbon 14 is in it. They compare this result with the amount of carbon 14 in an equal amount of living tissue. They can then calculate how long ago the plant or animal died. In the same

way, if you had a clock that would run 24 hours without winding and someone told you the clock had 3 hours left to run, you would know it had been running for 21 hours.

Using one method of carbon-14 dating, Soviet scientists found that Dima's mummy was 40,000 years old. American scientists, using a different method, found the atomic clock had been running for 27,000 years. Either date makes Dima one of the oldest mummies in the world.

The studies of Dima did not solve the mystery of why woolly mammoths died out, but the mummy did tell of a brief life in a world that vanished long ago. And that is one of the chief reasons why scientists study the many kinds of mummies that have been found. Some give glimpses of single lives. Others tell much about worlds that we have never known.

Reader's Response

What did you learn about mummies that you did not know before?

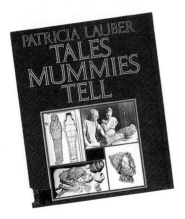

TALES MUMMIES TELL

Responding to Literature

1. How is the work of a scientist similar to that of a detective?
2. Make a list of things scientists were able to learn just by examining the contents of Dima's stomach.
3. How is carbon 14 used to learn more about mummies? Discuss your answer with classmates.
4. What do you think is the most interesting part about studying mummies?
5. Why do you think the discovery of Dima was important to the scientific world?

Books to Enjoy

Tales Mummies Tell by Patricia Lauber
If you would like to read more tales told by mummies, get a copy of this book.

Pompeii: Exploring a Roman Ghost Town by Ron and Nancy Goor
Find out about the life and times of the people who lived in Pompeii, a Roman city destroyed by a volcanic eruption that left the inhabitants mummified.

Life Begins by John Stidworthy
Learn what the fossils of prehistoric animals, from the first sea creatures to the growth of reptiles, tell about life long ago.

SCIENCE HORIZONS

PHYSICAL SCIENCE

Chapter 6

Elements and Compounds

SUPERSTUFF

A Greek myth tells the story of Daedalus (DED ul us). Daedalus made wings out of wax and feathers and used them to fly from a prison on the Greek island of Crete. No person has ever flown with such wings. But stories like this have made people dream about human-powered flight.

In 1988 a group of students and teachers from the Massachusetts Institute of Technology (MIT) went to Greece. They had invented a new aircraft and had named it the *Daedalus 88*. To honor the myth, this group decided to test their aircraft on Crete.

The *Daedalus 88* has no engine. It is powered by the pilot, who uses bicycle pedals to turn a propeller. What makes this aircraft different from others is the way it is made. The materials used were designed to be strong, flexible, and light.

The 102 ribs of the wings are made of low-weight plastic. The ribs are attached to tubes made of a thin but strong graphite material. Graphite is a form of carbon; it makes up the "lead" of a pencil. The graphite tubes are hollow, which helps to make them light. Much of the aircraft is held together by glue or yarn.

The wingspan of the *Daedalus 88* is 34 m (112 ft). These huge wings support the weight of the pilot plus the 31 kg (69 lb) of the aircraft.

The new lightweight materials used in the *Daedalus 88* made it possible for the aircraft to set a new record for human-powered flight. The aircraft stayed in the air for 3 hours, 54 minutes, 59 seconds. It flew a distance of 115 km (72 mi).

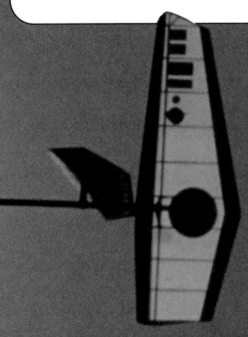

In the myth, Daedalus used feathers and wax—common things that he could find. The MIT team did not use common things. They used new materials that were designed to be both light and strong. Scientists used to look for materials with the properties that were needed. But now they invent the materials they need.

Nicknamed "superstuff," these new materials are made by putting different materials together. Each kind of superstuff has its own use. Superstuff in ceramic tiles protects the Space Shuttle from great heat as it reenters Earth's atmosphere. Another kind of superstuff is used to make artificial arms and legs.

You may have superstuff in your home. Plastic microwave cookware is made of a kind of superstuff. Superstuff that is extra bouncy is being used in sneakers. This superstuff may help you run faster or jump higher.

Discover

How would you use superstuff?

Materials   pencil · paper

Procedure

Suppose you are asked to create a new material to solve a problem. Identify a problem that might be solved with your superstuff. List the properties you would want the new material to have. Consider any drawbacks the material might have. For example, most plastics today do not break down quickly, and they can cause pollution problems. Do the advantages of your new material outweigh its drawbacks?

In this chapter you will study the building blocks from which superstuff is made. You will find out about some of the many ways building blocks can be combined to make new materials.

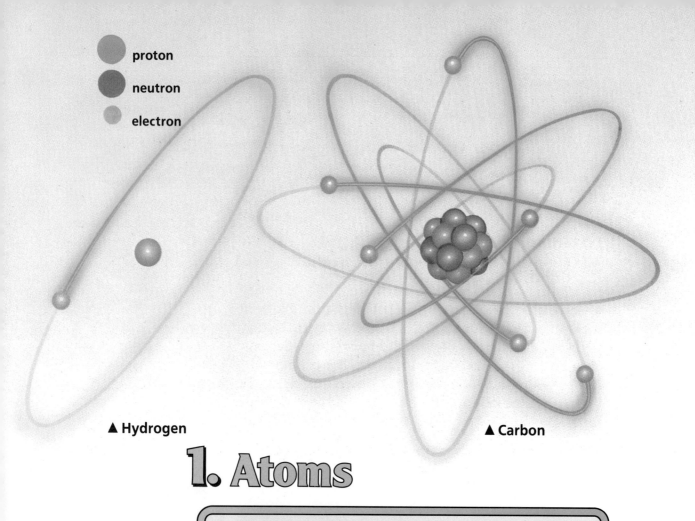

proton

neutron

electron

▲ Hydrogen

▲ Carbon

1. Atoms

Words to Know
Bohr model
electron cloud
model

Getting Started Your friend has prepared a mystery box by placing one or more objects inside a box and closing it tightly. Then your friend gives you the box. Your task is to try to tell what is in the box without opening it. How would you try to find out what the box contains?

What is the Bohr model of the atom?

You know that matter is anything that takes up space and has mass. All matter is made of tiny particles called atoms. All the things you can see around you, for example, are made of atoms.

The parts of atoms are too small to be seen, even with the most powerful microscope. How, then, do scientists know what atoms are like? You cannot see inside a mystery box. But you can shake the box and do other things to guess its contents. In the same way, no one can see inside an atom. So scientists have to form a picture of atoms in their minds. Such a mental picture of atoms is called a model.

A Danish scientist, Niels Bohr (neels bawr), developed the Bohr model of the atom. Look at the drawings below of some Bohr models. Compare them with the three-dimensional models at the left. The main parts of an atom are protons (PROH tahnz), electrons (ee LEK trahnz), and neutrons (NOO-trahnz). A proton is a particle with a positive charge. An electron is a particle with a negative charge. And a neutron is a particle with no charge.

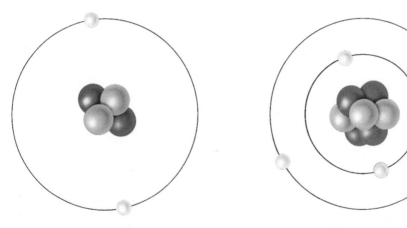

▲ Helium   ▲ Lithium

Protons and neutrons are found in the center, or nucleus (NOO klee us), of an atom. In the **Bohr model** of the atom electrons move rapidly around the nucleus in paths called orbits. Why is the Bohr model also called the planetary model?

Notice that the number of protons in each kind of atom equals the number of electrons. The carbon atom has 6 protons (6+) and 6 electrons (6−). The 6 positive charges of the protons balance the 6 negative charges of the electrons. Neutrons have no charge. So the atom as a whole is neutral.

Explore

ACTIVITY

How can you show that atoms contain charged particles?

If you rub a balloon on your hair, you may then be able to stick the balloon to a wall. If you scuff your feet on a carpet and then touch a metal lamp, you may feel a shock. What you have done is to move around some of the charged particles that are parts of atoms.

Materials
coat hanger · chair · 2 pieces of silk thread, 35 mm long · 2 capped plastic pens · paper towel

Procedure

A. Hang a coat hanger on the back of a chair. Tie the ends of two pieces of thread to the coat hanger. Tie the other ends of the threads to a pen so that the pen hangs, as shown.

B. Rub one end of the hanging pen with a paper towel. Now rub a second pen with the towel. Hold this pen near the hanging pen.
  1. Record what happens.

C. Rub the hanging pen again. Then hold the towel near the pen.
  2. Record what happens.

Writing and Sharing Results and Conclusions

1. Were the two rubbed pens in step **B** charged? What caused them to become charged?

2. Like charges repel, or push away; unlike charges attract. Did the two pens in step **B** have like or unlike charges? How do you know?

3. Did the pen and the towel in step **C** have like or unlike charges? How do you know?

4. How do your results and conclusions compare with those of your classmates?

What is the electron cloud model?

As scientists found out more about atoms, they learned that an electron does not stay on a path, like a planet stays in orbit. Instead, they found that electrons move in all directions around a nucleus. So they developed a new model. Look at the drawing. Because the electrons seem to form a cloud as they move around the nucleus, this model of the atom is called the **electron cloud model.**

▲ **Electron cloud model of helium atom**

You can compare the electron cloud model to a bicycle wheel. When the wheel is not moving, the separate spokes can be seen. But when the wheel is spinning, the spokes look fuzzy, like a cloud. Look at the pictures. How is the spinning bicycle wheel like an electron cloud, and how is it different?

▲ **An electron cloud can be compared to a spinning bicycle wheel.**

Lesson Review

1. Describe the Bohr model of a carbon atom.
2. Describe the electron cloud model of a carbon atom.

Think! Might models of the atom change in the future? Why or why not?

205

2. Elements

Words to Know
element
atomic number
Periodic Table

Getting Started Look around you. How many different kinds of matter do you see? Think how many thousands—even millions—*more* kinds of matter there are that you cannot see right now. Do you suppose that means there are millions of kinds of atoms? Why or why not?

How many kinds of atoms are there?

Matter made of just one kind of atom is called an **element.** An atom, then, can be defined as the smallest bit of an element. There are 92 natural elements. In addition, scientists have been able to make some artificial elements. So now there is a total of 109 known elements. This means that there are 109 different kinds of atoms known today.

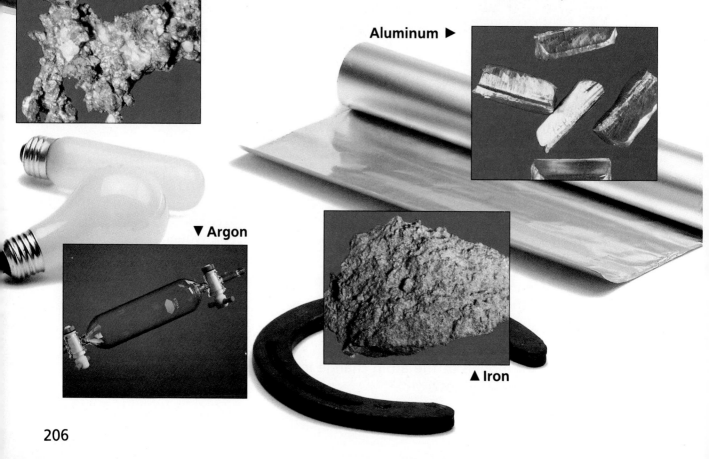

▼ Silver

Aluminum ▶

▼ Argon

▲ Iron

Look at the pictures. They show a few elements and objects made from those elements. What other objects are made from these elements?

How are atoms of the various elements different? Each kind of atom has a different number of protons in its nucleus. Look at the models of atoms on this page. How many protons does hydrogen have? How many does nitrogen have?

Every element has a different atomic number. The **atomic number** is the number of protons in an atom of an element. Look again at the models. Hydrogen has one proton, so its atomic number is 1. What is the atomic number of nitrogen?

▲ Hydrogen

What is the Periodic Table?

The **Periodic Table** is a chart that contains many facts about the elements and their atoms. The table organizes the elements according to similar properties. You can use the table to find information about any element. A simple Periodic Table is shown on the next two pages.

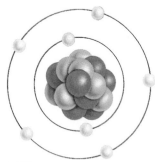

▲ Nitrogen

proton
neutron
electron

Copper ▶

▲ Carbon

The Periodic Table shown below gives the atomic number, symbol, and name of each element. Notice that the elements are arranged in rows. From left to right, the elements in the rows are in order of increasing atomic number.

The symbol of an element is usually one or two letters that stand for the name of the element. Look at the symbols for the elements in the table. The name of each element is shown below its symbol. What is the atomic number of carbon, and what is the symbol for carbon? Find the element that has atomic number 29. What is its name and symbol?

Periodic Table of Elements

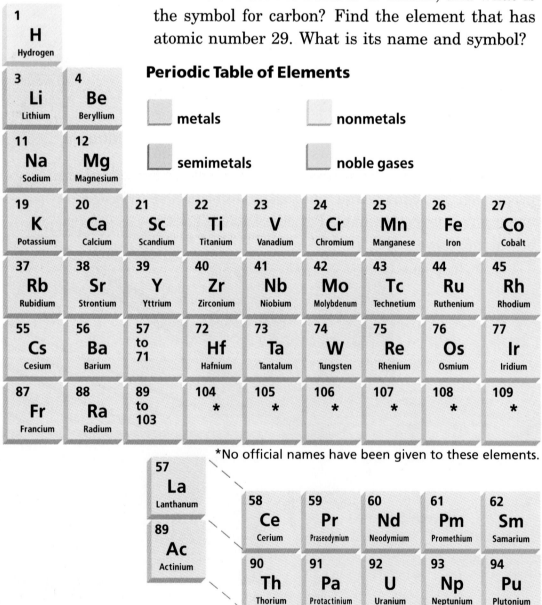

*No official names have been given to these elements.

How can the elements be grouped?

One way to group the elements is to place them in families. Notice how the elements fall into columns in the Periodic Table. All the elements in a column, from top to bottom, form a family. You can compare a family of elements to a human family. In both types of families, the members are alike in some ways. But they are not exactly alike.

Find fluorine (FLAWR een) in the Periodic Table. Fluorine and all the elements in that column are in the same family. One property of all members of that family is that they are poisonous.

					2 He Helium
Atomic Number					

5 B Boron	6 C Carbon	7 N Nitrogen	8 O Oxygen	9 F Fluorine	10 Ne Neon
13 Al Aluminum	14 Si Silicon	15 P Phosphorus	16 S Sulfur	17 Cl Chlorine	18 Ar Argon

Symbol — **6 C** Carbon — Name

28 Ni Nickel	29 Cu Copper	30 Zn Zinc	31 Ga Gallium	32 Ge Germanium	33 As Arsenic	34 Se Selenium	35 Br Bromine	36 Kr Krypton
46 Pd Palladium	47 Ag Silver	48 Cd Cadmium	49 In Indium	50 Sn Tin	51 Sb Antimony	52 Te Tellurium	53 I Iodine	54 Xe Xenon
78 Pt Platinum	79 Au Gold	80 Hg Mercury	81 Tl Thallium	82 Pb Lead	83 Bi Bismuth	84 Po Polonium	85 At Astatine	86 Rn Radon

63 Eu Europium	64 Gd Gadolinium	65 Tb Terbium	66 Dy Dysprosium	67 Ho Holmium	68 Er Erbium	69 Tm Thulium	70 Yb Ytterbium	71 Lu Lutetium
95 Am Americium	96 Cm Curium	97 Bk Berkelium	98 Cf Californium	99 Es Einsteinium	100 Fm Fermium	101 Md Mendelevium	102 No Nobelium	103 Lw Lawrencium

USES OF SOME ELEMENTS		
	Elements	**Uses**
Metals	iron mercury magnesium	making steel, magnets switches, thermometers, lamps airplane parts, flashbulbs

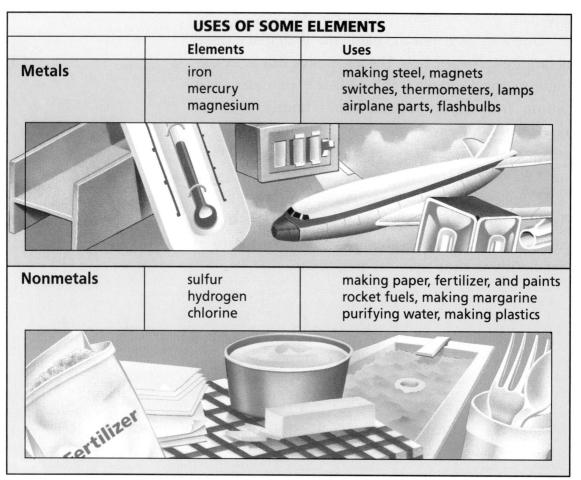

Nonmetals	sulfur hydrogen chlorine	making paper, fertilizer, and paints rocket fuels, making margarine purifying water, making plastics

Another way to classify the elements is into four groups. These are metals, nonmetals, semimetals, and noble gases. All the elements of each group have some similar properties, or traits. Find each group in the Periodic Table. Which group includes the largest number of elements?

METALS Metals are usually shiny and can be formed into shapes. They are good conductors of heat and electricity.

NONMETALS Most nonmetals have properties opposite to those of metals. Nonmetals are dull and cannot be shaped.

SEMIMETALS Semimetals have some properties of both metals and nonmetals. For example, some semimetals are shiny but cannot be shaped.

USES OF SOME ELEMENTS		
	Elements	Uses
Semimetals	silicon germanium boron	computer chips, photocells radio parts borax (a cleaner)
Noble Gases	helium neon argon	filling balloons and blimps lighted signs light bulbs, lasers

NOBLE GASES Noble gases are elements that do not combine readily with other elements.

Look at the table on these pages. Name one use of an element in each group.

Lesson Review

1. What is an element?
2. How is the atomic number of an element related to the protons in an atom of the element?
3. What is a family of elements in the Periodic Table?
4. Compare the properties of a metal, a nonmetal, a semimetal, and a noble gas.

Think! Find oxygen in the Periodic Table. What is the atomic number, name, and symbol of another member of the oxygen family?

Earth Science
CONNECTION

Minerals are natural solid substances found in the earth. Many elements, such as gold and silver are minerals. Use reference books to find out about one of these minerals.

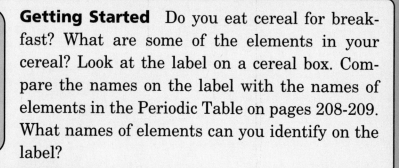
▼ Chlorine gas

3. Compounds

Words to Know
compound
chemical bonds
ions
molecule
formula

Getting Started Do you eat cereal for breakfast? What are some of the elements in your cereal? Look at the label on a cereal box. Compare the names on the label with the names of elements in the Periodic Table on pages 208-209. What names of elements can you identify on the label?

What are compounds?

How can only 109 elements make up everything on earth? The reason is that elements combine with other elements to form compounds. A **compound** is a substance formed when two or more elements combine chemically.

The properties of a compound differ from the properties of the elements that make it up. For example, the elements sodium and chlorine make up the compound called sodium chloride. Another name for this compound is table salt. Look at the chart. What properties of table salt are different from the properties of sodium and chlorine?

How are atoms joined together in a compound? When atoms combine with other atoms, chemical bonds are formed. **Chemical bonds** are forces that

▲ Sodium

▲ Table salt

PROPERTIES OF SUBSTANCES	
Substances	**Properties**
Sodium	soft silver-colored solid metal poisonous
Chlorine	greenish-yellow gas nonmetal poisonous
Table Salt (Sodium Chloride)	white crystals, solid used to season food

hold together the atoms in a compound. Atoms can form two types of chemical bonds. In both types, some of the electrons in atoms are involved.

What are ions?

One type of chemical bond forms when atoms lose or gain electrons. Atoms that have lost or gained electrons are called **ions** (EYE unz). Table salt is made of sodium ions and chloride ions. These ions form when electrons move from sodium atoms to chlorine atoms. As a result, a compound called sodium chloride is formed.

Look at the drawing below. Notice how a sodium atom loses an electron. The atom becomes a sodium ion. The sodium ion is positive because it has one more proton than electrons. Notice how a chlorine atom takes on the electron lost by the sodium atom. The chlorine atom becomes a chloride ion. The chloride ion is negative because it has one more electron than protons. The chemical bonds in sodium chloride result from the attraction between ions.

Formation of Sodium Chloride

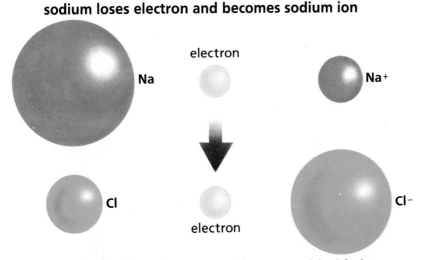

sodium loses electron and becomes sodium ion

electron

Na

Na+

Cl

electron

Cl−

chlorine gains that electron and becomes chloride ion

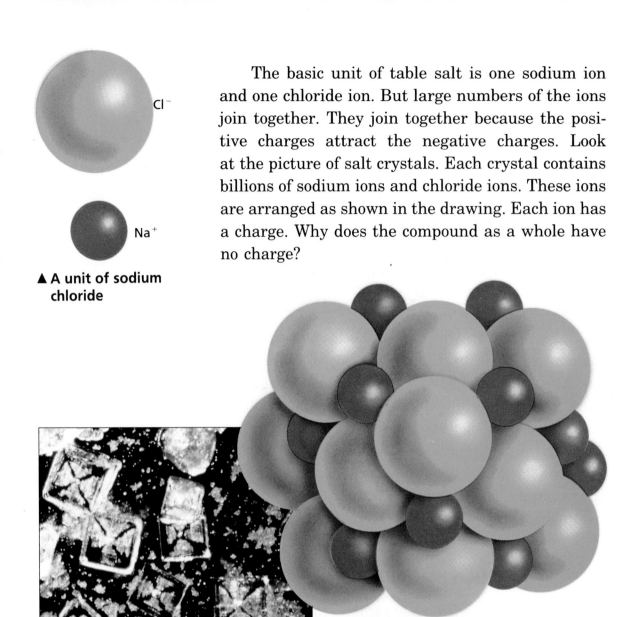

▲ A unit of sodium chloride

▲ Salt crystals magnified

▲ Sodium ions and chloride ions in a salt crystal

The basic unit of table salt is one sodium ion and one chloride ion. But large numbers of the ions join together. They join together because the positive charges attract the negative charges. Look at the picture of salt crystals. Each crystal contains billions of sodium ions and chloride ions. These ions are arranged as shown in the drawing. Each ion has a charge. Why does the compound as a whole have no charge?

What are molecules?

In a second type of chemical bond, atoms share electrons. An electron that is shared by two atoms moves around the nucleus of each atom. A particle formed by sharing electrons is called a **molecule** (MAHL ih kyool). Most compounds are made up of molecules. So the smallest unit of most compounds is a molecule. Why is the smallest unit of salt *not* a molecule?

▲ Water in liquid state

▼ Molecule of water

One example of a compound made of molecules is water. In water, atoms of hydrogen and oxygen share electrons. Look at the drawing of a molecule of water. In this molecule, two atoms of hydrogen share electrons with one atom of oxygen. All forms of water—solid, liquid, or gas—are made up of molecules like this.

Another example of a compound made of molecules is carbon dioxide. This compound is a gas used or produced by many living things. Plants use this gas in making food. Both plants and animals produce this gas during respiration. Look at the drawing of a molecule of carbon dioxide. How many atoms of each element make up a molecule of carbon dioxide?

Molecule of
carbon dioxide ▼

What is a formula?

Scientists use the symbols for the elements as a a kind of shorthand. The symbol written by itself stands for one atom of an element. For instance, H stands for one atom of hydrogen.

A **formula** is a group of symbols that shows the elements in a compound. The small numbers in a formula show how many atoms or ions of each element are in a basic unit.

For most compounds, the basic unit is the molecule. The formula for water is H_2O. This means that there are 2 atoms of hydrogen and 1 atom of oxygen in a molecule of water. The formula for carbon dioxide is CO_2. Look at the drawings here of some other molecules. What are the formulas for each of the other compounds shown?

The formula for a compound made of ions shows how many ions of each kind are in a basic unit. The formula for sodium chloride is NaCl. This means that there is 1 sodium ion and 1 chloride ion in a basic unit of sodium chloride.

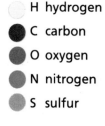

H hydrogen
C carbon
O oxygen
N nitrogen
S sulfur

▲ Carbon monoxide

▲ Sulfur dioxide

▲ Ammonia

Lesson Review

1. What is a compound?
2. What is a basic unit of sodium chloride? Explain how this unit forms.
3. What is a basic unit of carbon dioxide? Explain how this unit forms.
4. Write the formulas for sodium chloride and carbon dioxide.

Think! A molecule of a simple sugar made in plants has the formula $C_6H_{12}O_6$. Explain what the formula means.

Skills

Designing an experiment

When you set up an experiment, you try to answer a question. An experiment can be very simple. Suppose, for example, you want to know which paper towel absorbs more water, Brand X or Brand Y. You put a sheet of Brand X towel in one beaker and a sheet of Brand Y in the other. Then you pour 5 mL of water in each beaker. If both towels soak up all the water, you add another 5 mL of water to each beaker. You keep doing this until one of the towels does not absorb any more water.

Practicing the skill

1. Every chemical compound has its own characteristics. For example, some compounds dissolve more easily in water at a given temperature than others. Other compounds hardly dissolve at all. When a substance such as table salt is completely dissolved, you cannot see any crystals.

2. Your teacher will give you some table salt and sugar. Design an experiment to find out which of these will dissolve in the smaller volume of water. Use the materials in the picture. All the water you use must be at the same temperature.

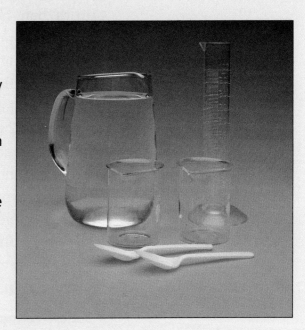

Thinking about the skill

Why would you want the temperature of the water to be the same for each compound?

Applying the skill

Will more table salt dissolve in hot water than in cold water? Design an experiment to answer that question.

4. Compounds of Carbon

Words to Know
organic
  compounds
hydrocarbon
polymer

Getting Started Think about the black substance that forms on the wick of a candle. This substance is the element carbon. There are more compounds of carbon than there are of all other elements combined! To find out why, read about the compounds of carbon.

What are organic compounds?

Organic compounds are compounds that contain carbon. Scientists once thought that most carbon compounds could be produced only by living things. Living things are called organisms, and so scientists called the compounds organic.

Carbon forms millions of compounds. How does this happen? Carbon atoms can form long chains. Other atoms can be part of such chains. For example, there are hundreds of ways compounds can be made of only carbon and hydrogen. A compound made of just the two elements hydrogen and carbon is called a **hydrocarbon** (hye droh KAHR bun).

Methane is a hydrocarbon found in natural gas. Methane is made up of one atom of carbon and four

Model of methane molecule—formula CH_4 ▼

▼ Sugar—formula $C_{12}H_{22}O_{11}$

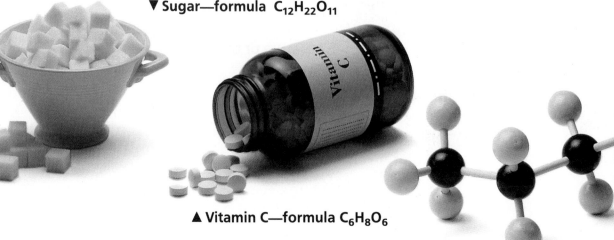

▲ Vitamin C—formula $C_6H_8O_6$

218

atoms of hydrogen. The formula for methane is CH_4. A model is one way to show how atoms are arranged in a molecule. Look at the model of methane. Each sphere in the model stands for an atom, and each stick stands for a chemical bond.

Octane is a compound found in gasoline. Look at the model of octane. Notice how the carbon atoms are all linked by chemical bonds. How can you tell that octane is a hydrocarbon? How many atoms of each kind are there in a molecule of octane?

Which of the materials shown have you seen or used? All of these materials contain organic compounds. Study the formulas for these compounds. How can you tell which ones contain oxygen as well as carbon and hydrogen?

▼ Octane—formula C_8H_{18}

▲ Rubbing alcohol—
formula C_3H_8O

Problem Solving

Go with the Flow

You may have heard of times in the past called the stone age or the iron age. You live now in a time you could call the polymer age, because you are surrounded by products made of polymers. One property of some polymers is their ability to flow. You can make a polymer like the one in the picture. Mix 30 mL of solution *A* with 10 mL of solution *B* in a paper cup. Stir until a ball forms. Different polymers may flow at different rates.

How can you invent a way to measure the rate of flow of this polymer?

Compare the appearance of solution *A* and solution *B*. What happens when you mix the solutions together? What materials might be useful for measuring the rate of flow of this polymer?

Paper-clip model of polymer ▼

What is a polymer?

A **polymer** (PAHL uh mur) is an organic compound that consists mainly of a long chain of carbon atoms. *Poly* means "many" and *mer* means "part." Polymers can be made of hundreds or thousands of parts. Each part is called a monomer (MAHN uh mur). *Mono* means "one."

To get an idea of how polymers are formed, try this. Make a chain of six paper clips. Each clip in your chain is like a monomer. Now hook other clips to the sides and ends of the first clip, as shown.

Adding side chains of different kinds forms different compounds, each with different properties. For example, side chains can make a polymer elastic, hard, tough, or resistant to heat.

Polymers are used to make a great variety of plastics and products such as fabrics, rubber goods, and toys. The model at the right shows a part of a polymer used in many products. Look at the picture of products made of polymers. Which of these objects have you used?

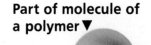

Part of molecule of a polymer ▼

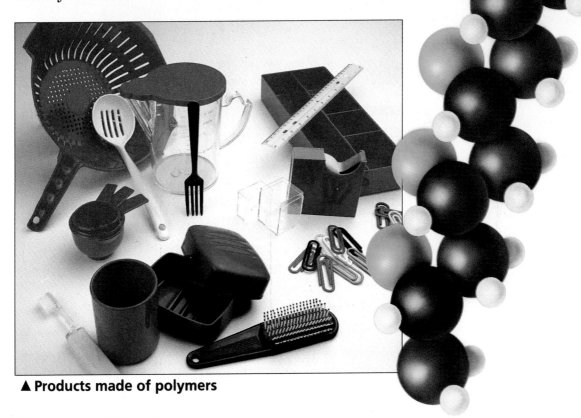

▲ **Products made of polymers**

Lesson Review

1. How can carbon form millions of compounds?
2. What is a hydrocarbon? Name two hydrocarbons.
3. What is a polymer? Name two products made from polymers.

Think! Look again at the description of the aircraft *Daedalus* at the beginning of this chapter. What parts of *Daedalus* were made of polymers?

5. Acids, Bases, and Salts

Words to Know
indicator
acid
base
salt
neutralization

What are acids and bases?

Scientists classify compounds into groups according to certain properties. Two groups of compounds are acids and bases. One property of an acid or a base is the way it changes the color of an indicator (IHN dih kayt ur). An **indicator** is a dye that changes color when mixed with an acid or a base. Litmus is an indicator that can be used to make red or blue litmus paper.

An acid turns blue litmus paper to red. A base turns red litmus paper to blue. These two color changes are shown in the picture at the left. An **acid** is a compound that turns blue litmus to red. A **base**

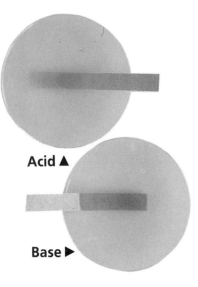

Acid ▲

Base ▶

is a compound that turns red litmus to blue. Which of the products shown on these pages are acids and which are bases?

What are some properties of acids and bases?

Acids can be weak or strong. The acids in foods are weak and have a sour taste. But strong acids, such as the muriatic (myoor ee AT ihk) acid shown, are dangerous—they can burn skin and are poisonous. Be careful never to touch or taste a material to find out if it is an acid.

Bases have a bitter taste and feel slippery. A few bases, such as baking soda, are used for cooking or for medicine. Like strong acids, strong bases can burn skin and are poisonous. Never touch or taste a material to find out if it is a base.

Many materials contain weak acids or small amounts of strong acids. Many other materials contain weak bases or small amounts of strong bases. Scientists use a scale called the pH scale to describe these materials.

ACTIVITY

Explore Together

How can you test for acids and bases?

Organizer

Materials
safety goggles · dropper bottles of vinegar (an acid), baking soda solution (a base), and 3 unknowns · red litmus paper · blue litmus paper · vial of pH paper

Procedure
Caution: *Safety goggles must be worn for this activity.*

Recorder **A.** Make a table like the one shown.

Color changes of indicators

Liquid tested	red litmus	blue litmus	pH paper

Manager **B.** Place a drop of vinegar on a strip of red litmus paper. Do not let the tip of the dropper touch the paper. Repeat with a strip of blue litmus paper.

Group, Recorder **1.** Observe the litmus paper. In your table, record the color changes of the litmus paper.

Manager **C.** Place a drop of vinegar on a strip of pH paper. Match the color on the strip with a color on a vial of pH paper.

Recorder **2.** Record the pH number of the color.

D. Repeat steps **B** and **C** for the other liquids.

Writing Results and Sharing Conclusions

Group, Recorder **1.** How does an acid affect red and blue litmus paper?

2. How does a base affect red and blue litmus paper?

3. Which of the unknowns were acids? Which were bases? How do you know?

Reporter **4.** How do your results and conclusions compare with those of your classmates?

The chart shows the pH scale. Indicator paper made with special dyes is used to test the pH of a material. An acid has a pH between 0 and 7. The lower the pH number of an acid, the stronger the acid. A base has a pH between 7 and 14. The higher the pH number of a base, the stronger the base. A pH of 7 is neutral—neither an acid nor a base. Study the chart. Which substance is more acid, milk or baking soda, and how can you tell?

▼ The pH scale

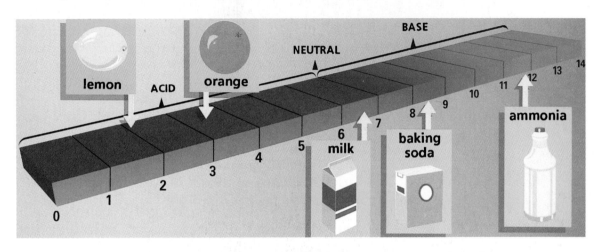

What are salts?

Salts make up another group of compounds. A **salt** can be formed when an acid is mixed with a base. The base is said to neutralize (NOO truh lyz) the acid. People sometimes take antacid tablets for an upset stomach. An antacid is a base. It neutralizes excess acid in the stomach. **Neutralization** (noo truh luh ZAY shun) is a chemical reaction, or change, between an acid and a base. The reaction forms a salt and water.

Sodium hydroxide neutralizes hydrochloric acid. When the correct amounts of these compounds are mixed, a salt and water are formed. Look at the pictures. How can you tell that the salt and water make a solution that is neutral?

Effect on litmus of an acid, a base, and a salt ▼

225

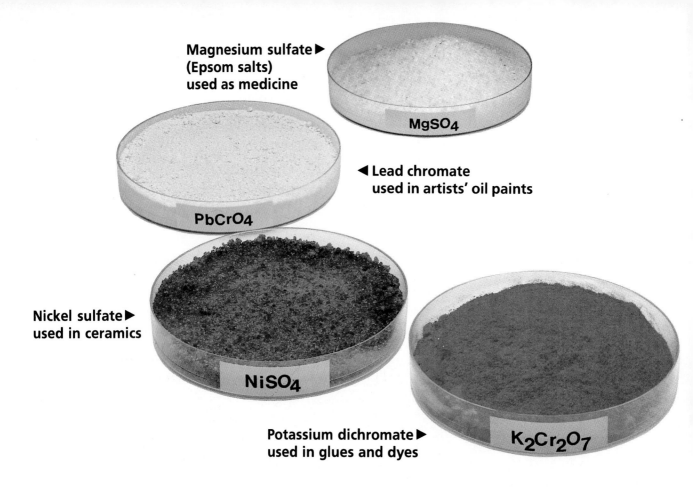

Magnesium sulfate ▶
(Epsom salts)
used as medicine

$MgSO_4$

◀ Lead chromate
used in artists' oil paints

$PbCrO_4$

Nickel sulfate ▶
used in ceramics

$NiSO_4$

Potassium dichromate ▶
used in glues and dyes

$K_2Cr_2O_7$

There are many different salts. Salts are not always white. Some salts are green, pink, or blue. Also, some salts are poisonous. Never taste a substance to find out if it is a salt.

The pictures show some salts and their uses. Notice the formulas for these salts. How can you find the names of the elements in these salts?

Lesson Review

1. What is an indicator?
2. Compare the way acids and bases affect litmus.
3. Which kind of compound, an acid or a base, has a pH number of 5? Which kind has a pH number of 12?
4. Define and give an example of neutralization.

Think! The pH of rainwater is nearly neutral—about 6.5. Do you think the pH of acid rain is higher or lower than that of rainwater? Explain your answer.

Life Science
CONNECTION

Acids can be found in the stomach. These acids break down food in the process of digestion.

Chapter Connections

Explain the connection between atoms, elements, and compounds. Use the graphic organizer to help you.

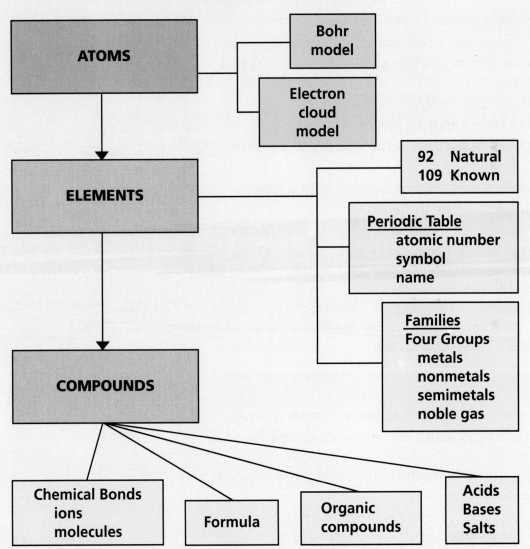

Writing About Science • Describe

You are a scientist who has discovered a new element. How might you tell if it is a metal, nonmetal, semimetal, or noble gas? Describe your element and its properties in a paragraph.

Science Terms

A. Write the letter of the term that best matches the definition.

1. Forces that hold together the atoms in a compound
2. Matter made up of just one kind of atom
3. Changes color when mixed with an acid or base
4. Group of symbols that shows the elements in a compound
5. Particle formed by sharing electrons
6. Turns blue litmus to red
7. Number of protons in the nucleus of an atom
8. Compounds of carbon
9. Formed when an acid is mixed with a base
10. Turns red litmus to blue

a. acid
b. atomic number
c. base
d. chemical bonds
e. element
f. formula
g. indicator
h. molecule
i. organic compounds
j. salt

B. Copy the sentences below. Use the terms listed to complete the sentences.

Bohr model   compound   electron cloud model
hydrocarbon   ions   neutralization
Periodic Table   polymer

1. _____ is a chemical reaction between an acid and a base.
2. In the _____ electrons seem to form a cloud.
3. Information about the elements can be found in the _____.
4. A _____ is formed when two or more elements combine chemically.
5. In the _____ electrons move in orbits like those of the planets.
6. A _____ contains only the elements hydrogen and carbon.
7. Atoms that have lost or gained electrons are called _____.
8. A _____ is an organic compound that consists mainly of a long chain of carbon atoms.

Science Ideas

Use complete sentences to answer the following.

1. Write the correct term for each number in drawing A.
2. Name the kinds of models shown in drawings A and B.
3. What is the atomic number of each atom in the drawings?
4. How do atoms of different elements differ?
5. What information is found in the Periodic Table?
6. What forms when two or more elements combine chemically?
7. Compare the basic units that make up table salt and carbon dioxide.
8. What are organic compounds?
9. Name three objects or materials made from organic compounds.
10. Compare some properties of acids and bases.

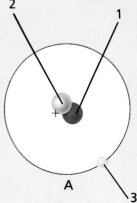

A

B

Applying Science Ideas

Astronauts may be exploring other planets in the solar system some time in the next 50 years. Do you think that the structure of atoms on Mars will be the same as the structure of atoms on Earth? Do you think the space explorers will discover new, naturally occurring elements?

Using Science Skills

An element has some properties that differ from its compounds. Steel wool contains mainly the element iron. Rusted steel wool is mostly iron oxide, a compound of iron. Design an experiment to find out whether iron and iron oxide behave the same way when they are near a magnet.

Chapter 7

Chemical and Nuclear Changes

A Problem from the Ground Up

Each night millions of Americans lock their doors, pull down their shades, and get into bed feeling safe and secure. They do not know that there is something dangerous in the basement of their homes. This invisible danger travels silently from its underground source. It enters through garage floors and through cracks in the basement walls and floors. It even winds its way up through drain pipes into sinks and showers. What kind of creature is this? It is not a creature at all but an element called radon.

Radon is one of many elements that give off energy and tiny particles of matter. The energy and tiny particles of matter are called radiation (ray dee AY shun). Radiation can harm living things. It can kill cells and cause cancer.

Elements that give off radiation have been found in surprising places. For example, some granite rocks used in buildings have been found to contain elements that give off small amounts of radiation. Most of this radiation is in such small amounts that it is not very dangerous.

What makes the radiation from radon dangerous is that radon is a gas. You do not inhale bits of granite as you walk past a granite building. But you do inhale radon if it is in the air around you. Some of the radon that is inhaled stays in the lungs. The radiation given off by the radon can harm living cells in the lungs.

Radon gas is formed in rocks below the earth's surface. The gas seeps up though rocks and soil. The amount of radon that reaches the surface depends on the kinds of rock beneath the soil. Scientists study samples of rocks to predict which places are likely to have large amounts of radon. Maps that show radon levels are based on information about where radon-producing rocks are found.

Because radon is colorless and odorless, you might not know if it is around you. People use radon detectors to measure the amount of radiation in their homes. Radiation is measured in units called picocuries (PEE koh KYOOR eez). According to the government, there should be no more than 4 picocuries in 1 L (1.1 qt) of air. Unfortunately, as many as one third of the houses in the United States may have readings above this level.

There are ways to lower the levels of radon in homes. One way is to use fans to blow air out of the basement. Another way is to seal cracks in basement floors and walls. If a house has a floor drain in the basement, a special cover can be put on it. This cover lets water flow down, while stopping radon from going up.

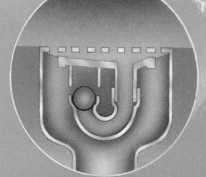

Discover

How can you find out about radon levels?

ACTIVITY

Materials   pencil · paper

Procedure

Try to find out more about radon levels near where you live. Write to local environmental groups to get information about radon. Your state's Department of Environmental Protection can also provide information about radon levels in your area. Find out where you can obtain a radon detector for your home.

If you get a radon detector, have an adult help you set it up. Follow the directions carefully. What are the results of your test?

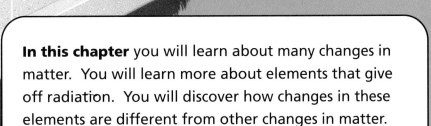

In this chapter you will learn about many changes in matter. You will learn more about elements that give off radiation. You will discover how changes in these elements are different from other changes in matter.

1. Chemical Changes

Getting Started "Three, two, one—liftoff!" Imagine you are watching a space launch. Flames and smoke rush from the rocket engine and there is a loud roar. What you see and hear are signs of change in the rocket's fuel. What kind of change takes place in the fuel?

Words to Know
chemical reaction
law of conservation of mass

What is a physical change?

Matter may change in many ways. One kind of change in matter is a physical change. Changes in the size, shape, or state of a substance are physical changes. A substance is an element or a compound. Remember that substances are made of particles called atoms, ions, and molecules.

During a physical change the particles of substances do not change. So no new substances form. For example, water changes physically when it changes state. You know that water is made of molecules of H_2O. Water remains H_2O regardless of whether it exists as ice, as liquid water, or as water vapor. What physical change in water is shown here?

▼ Melting ice

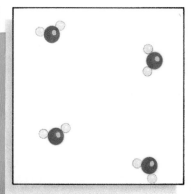

▲ H_2O—solid   ▲ H_2O—liquid   ▲ H_2O—gas

Remember that atoms in molecules are held together by chemical bonds. Notice that these bonds in water do not change when water changes state. This is true for all physical changes—there are no changes in chemical bonds.

What is a chemical reaction?

Another kind of change in matter is a chemical reaction, or change. In a **chemical reaction,** one or more substances change to form new substances. Each new substance has some properties that are different from those of the original. During a chemical change, molecules and ions *do* change.

The burning of a rocket fuel is a chemical reaction. One rocket fuel is hydrogen. It is mixed with oxygen when the rocket is fired. The hydrogen and oxygen react and water vapor is formed. Look at the picture and drawing of this reaction.

▼ Burning rocket fuel

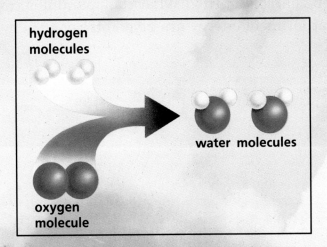

hydrogen molecules

oxygen molecule

water molecules

Burning hydrogen ▶

$$2H_2 \quad + \quad O_2 \quad \rightarrow \quad 2H_2O$$
hydrogen   oxygen   water

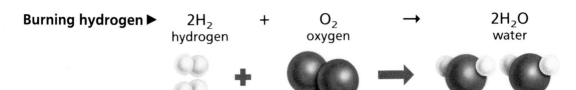

*Read about a planet where substances react in unexpected ways in **The Green Book,** page 354.*

Hydrogen plus oxygen forms water. In this change, chemical bonds in molecules of hydrogen and oxygen are broken. New chemical bonds form between atoms of hydrogen and oxygen. Look at the chemical equation and models above.

The + in the equation means "reacts with," and the arrow means "forms." The equation says that two molecules of hydrogen react with one molecule of oxygen, forming two molecules of water. How is this change different from a physical change?

Energy changes always take place in chemical reactions. Chemical energy is stored in chemical bonds. When bonds change during a reaction, chemical energy may change to other forms of energy. Heat is given off when hydrogen and oxygen react. Think back to the sight and sound of a space launch. When rocket fuel burns, not only heat but also sound and light are given off.

*Tracy learned that her family's new house was haunted — haunted with radon! But where did it come from? What could she do? Find out when you read **The Radon-Haunted House** in Horizons Plus.*

Have you seen charcoal burning? Study the models and equation below. What elements combine when charcoal burns? What compound is formed? What forms of energy are given off?

$$C \quad + \quad O_2 \quad \rightarrow \quad CO_2$$
carbon   oxygen   carbon dioxide
(charcoal)

▼ Burning charcoal

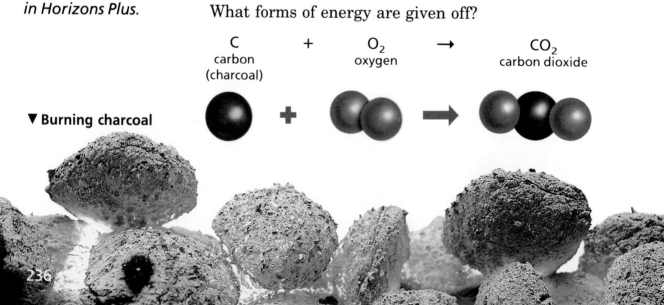

Explore

What are some signs of a chemical change?

ACTIVITY

You can often observe signs of chemical changes when cooking. Baking soda may be added to foods, such as pancakes, to make them "light," or fluffy. Bubbles of gas form in the batter as the pancake cooks. The bubbles of gas are one sign of chemical change.

Materials
safety goggles · spoon · baking soda · small and large sealable plastic bags · calcium chloride · graduate · bromothymol blue (BTB)

Procedure
Caution: *Wear safety goggles for this activity.*
A. Place one spoonful of baking soda and two spoonfuls of calcium chloride in a large sealable plastic bag. Mix the solids.
B. Pour 10 mL of BTB and 10 mL of water into a small sealable plastic bag.
C. Place the small bag into the large bag. Do not seal the small bag. Do not let the liquids spill out of the small bag.
D. Press most of the air out of the large bag, and then seal it.
E. Invert the large bag so that the liquids spill and mix with the solids.

1. What changes do you observe inside the bag?
2. What do you observe about the temperature of the bag?

Writing and Sharing Results and Conclusions
1. What kind of change, chemical or physical, occurs when the liquids mix with the solids?
2. What observations helped you answer question 1?
3. How do your results and conclusions compare with those of your classmates?

In one type of chemical reaction, two elements combine to form a compound. An example is the combining of hydrogen and oxygen to form water. In another type of chemical reaction, a compound breaks down into elements. For instance, water may break down into hydrogen and oxygen. This change occurs when an electric current is passed through the water. Look at the drawing of the setup and equation for this change. In which molecules are chemical bonds broken? What new chemical bonds are formed?

Breaking down water ▶

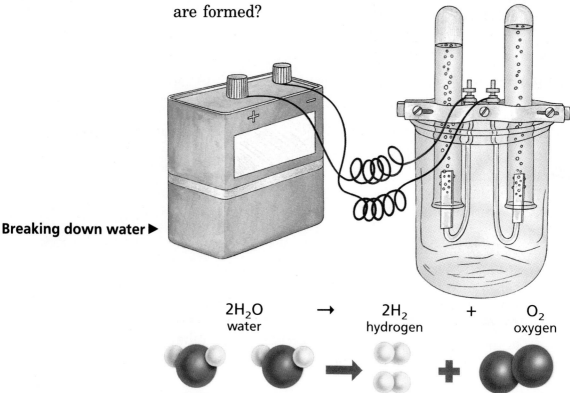

$$2H_2O \rightarrow 2H_2 + O_2$$

water   hydrogen   oxygen

What is the law of conservation of mass?

In all kinds of chemical changes, chemical bonds are formed and broken. But in these changes, atoms are neither created nor destroyed. They are only re-arranged. The fact that matter cannot be created or destroyed by any chemical reaction is called the **law of conservation of mass.**

238

Mass is a measure of the amount of matter in an object. A balance is used to measure mass. Did you ever see a flashbulb used to take a picture? What is the mass of the flashbulb shown here?

Suppose the flashbulb is used to take a picture. There is a flash when magnesium combines with oxygen inside the bulb. As you can see in the equation, magnesium oxide forms.

Now look at the same flashbulb "burned out." What is its mass? How does this reaction show the law of conservation of mass?

Remember that chemical energy is often changed into another form of energy in chemical changes. In a flashbulb, chemical energy is stored in magnesium and oxygen. When the bulb is used, chemical energy changes to light.

▼ **Reaction in a flashbulb**

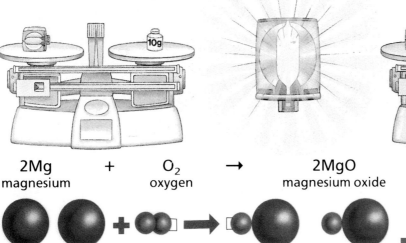

$2Mg$	+	O_2	→	$2MgO$
magnesium		oxygen		magnesium oxide

Lesson Review

1. Name and describe a physical change.
2. Name and describe a chemical change.
3. What is the source of energy that is released during a chemical change?
4. State the law of conservation of mass.

Think! What energy change occurs when electric current is used to break down water?

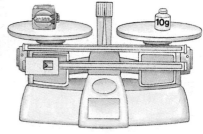

Life Science
CONNECTION

Respiration is the process by which living things obtain energy from food. Use reference books to find out the chemical equation for respiration.

2. Using Chemical Reactions

Words to Know
oxidation
corrosion
synfuel

What is slow oxidation?

A chemical change in which oxygen reacts with other substances is called **oxidation** (ahks ih DAY shun). When a substance oxidizes (AHKS ih dyz ez), it reacts with oxygen.

Oxidation may be slow or rapid. Rusting is one kind of slow oxidation. Iron rusts when it combines with oxygen from the air. Steel contains iron, and some kinds of steel can also rust. Water must be present for rusting to take place. Rust is a reddish-brown powder. How can you tell that each object shown has rusted?

Rusting is one type of corrosion (kuh ROH zhun). The **corrosion** of a metal is a chemical change in which the metal combines with elements such as oxygen. This corrosion can slowly destroy objects made of iron or steel.

Salt speeds up the corrosion of iron. The rusty truck in the picture may have been driven on roads spread with salt used to melt ice and snow. Or it may have been kept near a seashore, where there is salt spray in the air.

Today the metal in most new car bodies is coated with a thick tarlike material. How does this coating help prevent corrosion?

What is rapid oxidation?

Some oxidation reactions are rapid. Burning a fuel such as oil, coal, or wood is rapid oxidation. Think back to the chemical reaction in which rocket fuel is burned. Why is this change an example of rapid oxidation? The picture shows another use of fuel. What energy changes take place when the fuel burns?

▼ Burning fuel in a torch

Problem Solving

Spoilsport

Suppose you take a bite of an apple or a banana. You then leave the fruit on a table for several hours. What happens? You may have noticed that the fruit darkens. Chemical changes cause this darkening. How might oxidation be one of these changes?

How can you prevent darkening of sliced fruit?

Since the fruit will not be eaten, you may experiment with it. Check with your teacher before you try out your ideas. What material or condition that you tried works best at keeping the fruit from turning dark? What is the worst method you tried?

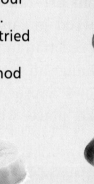
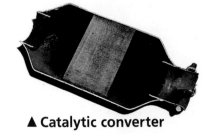

Gasoline is also a kind of fuel. When gasoline burns, heat is released. The heat is changed into energy of motion in a car engine. The burning of gasoline in a car engine also produces poisonous, or toxic, gases. These gases are given off in the exhaust of the car. These gases pollute the air.

A way to reduce air pollution from car exhausts is now being used. The picture shows a catalytic (kat-uh LIHT ihk) converter that is built into cars. This device causes gasoline to burn more completely. In this way, smaller amounts of toxic gases are formed and added to the air.

▲ **Catalytic converter**

◀ Household products that contain flammable or toxic chemicals

Sometimes rapid oxidation can be dangerous. If a substance is burned very fast, there may be an explosion. A flammable (FLAM uh bul) chemical is one that can burn rapidly and may explode. Many flammable chemicals are also toxic. Look at the picture. In what ways should people be careful in using the materials in these containers?

*If you know enough about chemical reactions, you can be the most successful treasure hunter in history! See how as you try **Investigating Chemical Reactions.***

What is a synfuel?

Most of the energy used today comes from oil, natural gas, and coal. Supplies of natural gas and oil are being used up rapidly. So scientists are developing synfuels (SIHN fyoo ulz). A **synfuel,** or synthetic fuel, is a fuel put together from other materials.

Coal is one fossil fuel that is plentiful. Methane, a gas that occurs naturally, can also be made as a synfuel from coal. Methane can be used directly as a fuel for cooking and heating. Or the methane can be changed into gasoline for use in cars, buses, and trucks.

The picture shows a chemical plant in which coal is made into methane gas. The chemical changes that take place can be shown simply in two steps. Look at the equations below. (1) Carbon in the coal reacts with steam. The gases carbon monoxide and hydrogen are produced. (2) These two gases then react. Methane and water are produced.

(1) C + H_2O $\rightarrow$ CO + H_2
carbon   water   carbon monoxide   hydrogen

(coal)   (steam)

Plant where a synfuel ▶ is made

(2) CO + $3H_2$ $\rightarrow$ CH_4 + H_2O
carbon monoxide   hydrogen   methane   water

Lesson Review

1. Define *oxidation.* Give an example of slow oxidation.
2. How can the corrosion of iron be prevented?
3. Give an example of rapid oxidation.
4. Define *synfuel.* What synfuel is made from coal?

Think! Gasohol is a synfuel made by mixing gasoline with alcohol. Alcohol can be made from corn. How might gasohol help conserve fossil fuels?

Skills

Using symbols to communicate ideas

Chlorine bleach is a chemical that can damage some fabrics but not others. A shirt might have a symbol on the label that says bleaching is allowed. The symbol would have Cl, for chlorine. Symbols show some ideas more quickly than words can.

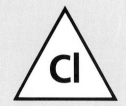

Practicing the skill

1. You are going to design symbols that will warn students about chemical dangers. A circle with a diagonal bar is a symbol that is used by many people. This symbol means *do not.* When this symbol appears with a small picture, it means that you should not do or use what is pictured.

2. Look at the examples. Tell what each one means.

3. What symbol could you make that would tell someone to keep fire away from a chemical? Draw the symbol.

4. Draw other symbols that will tell about other dangers. Draw a symbol to tell that a chemical should not be inhaled. Draw another symbol to show that a chemical should not be stored in a glass bottle.

Thinking about the skill

Why do you think a symbol might be better than using words alone?

Applying the skill

You drew some symbols to say what not to do with some chemicals. Now draw a symbol to say *Handle this with gloves.* Draw another to say *Keep this cool.*

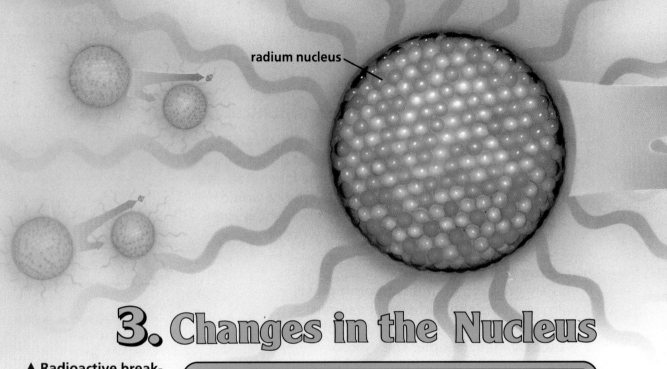

radium nucleus

3. Changes in the Nucleus

▲ Radioactive break-
down of radium

Getting Started Have you ever heard of the domino effect? Dominoes can be set up so that when one domino falls down, it causes two others to fall. These two dominoes cause four more to fall, and so on. This is a model of a chain reaction. Why does this kind of reaction have this name?

Words to Know
nuclear reaction
radioactive
  elements
nuclear fission
nuclear reactor

Tracy learned that her family's new house was haunted — haunted with radon! But where did it come from? What could she do? Find out when you read **The Radon-Haunted House** *in Horizons Plus.*

What is a nuclear reaction?

You know that atoms are rearranged forming different substances in chemical changes. The nuclei of atoms do not change in a chemical reaction. (*Nuclei* is the plural of *nucleus*.) But sometimes the nuclei of atoms *do* change. A reaction in which nuclei change is called a **nuclear** (NOO klee ur) **reaction**. In a nuclear reaction, nuclei of elements change into nuclei of other elements.

Some nuclear changes take place in radioactive (ray dee oh AK tihv) elements. **Radioactive elements** are elements whose nuclei naturally break down into other nuclei. As these elements break down, they give off particles and energy.

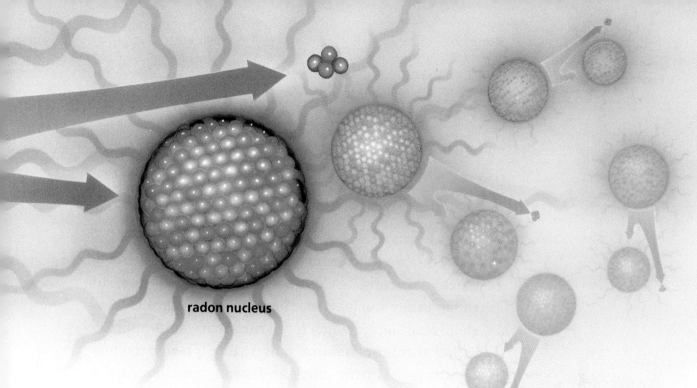

radon nucleus

The radon gas you read about at the beginning of the chapter is radioactive. Radon is formed in the earth from radium, which is also radioactive. Look at the drawing. It shows how a radium nucleus breaks into a radon nucleus and a helium nucleus.

The wavy lines in the drawing stand for energy. As the nuclei of radioactive atoms break down, energy is released. Some of this energy is heat, and some is gamma (GAM uh) rays. Gamma rays are a form of energy that you cannot see or feel. But this energy is powerful enough to pass through many materials.

Another word for the particles and gamma rays given off by radioactive elements is radiation (ray-dee AY shun). Radiation is both useful and dangerous. A symbol that means "radioactive" is printed on containers of radioactive materials. Find this symbol in the pictures.

▲ Uses of symbol for radioactive materials

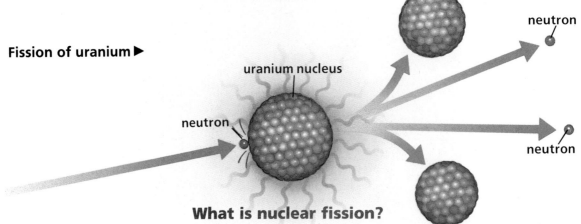

uranium nucleus

neutron

neutron

neutron

What is nuclear fission?

The breakdown of radioactive elements takes place naturally. Scientists have learned how to cause other nuclear reactions to take place. A nuclear reaction in which large nuclei are split apart is called **nuclear fission** (FIHSH un). *Fission* means "splitting." During nuclear fission, smaller nuclei are produced and energy is released.

Nuclei of uranium atoms can be made to split by bombarding them with neutrons. Then a nuclear chain reaction can take place. Look at the numbers in the drawing as you read about the steps in this reaction.

(1) A neutron strikes a uranium nucleus. The nucleus splits and more neutrons are set free. Energy as heat and gamma rays is also released. (2) Two of the free neutrons strike two more uranium nuclei. The nuclei split in the same way as before. (3) Four of the neutrons formed strike four more nuclei. The nuclei split. How many nuclei will be split by neutrons released from these four nuclei?

Nuclear chain reaction ▼

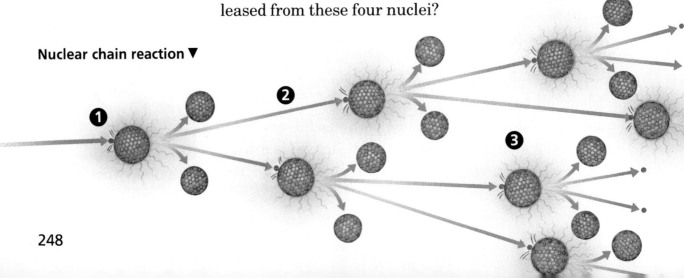

What is a nuclear reactor?

A nuclear chain reaction that is not controlled can release energy so fast that an explosion takes place. But when the chain reaction is controlled, energy is released slowly. A **nuclear reactor** is a device in which a nuclear chain reaction is controlled. There the energy is released slowly.

Look at the numbers in the drawing as you read about how a reactor works. (1) The core of the reactor contains rods of a fuel such as uranium. When neutrons strike the rods, fission starts. (2) Control rods go through the core. By raising or lowering these rods, workers can control the speed of the chain reaction. (3) A liquid absorbs heat that is released by the reaction and carries the heat away. (4) The core is covered by thick shielding. The radiation produced in the reactor is dangerous, but it cannot pass through the shielding.

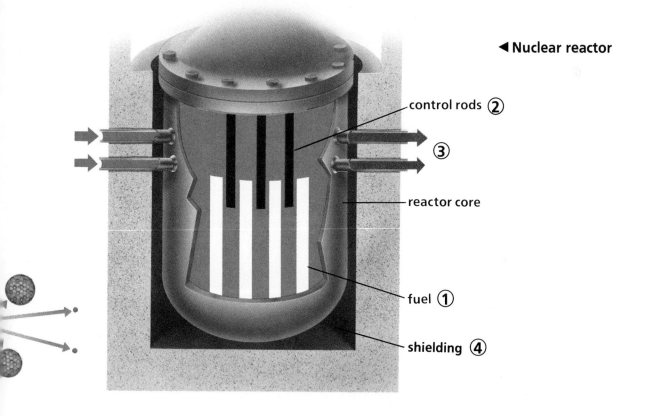

◀ Nuclear reactor

control rods ②

③

reactor core

fuel ①

shielding ④

What is a nuclear power plant?

A nuclear power plant uses heat released in a nuclear reactor to produce electrical energy. Look at the numbers in the drawing as you read about the steps of this process.

(1) A controlled fission reaction takes place inside a sealed reactor. Energy from the fission is released as heat. (2) This heat is used to change water into steam in a boiler. (3) The steam turns the blades of a machine called a turbine (TUR bihn). (4) The moving blades turn a generator (JEN ur ayt ur) that produces electric energy. (5) Used steam goes through pipes that are cooled by lake water. Steam changes to water that is returned to the boiler. Here, the water becomes steam again. But the lake water never comes in contact with the water heated by the nuclear reactor.

▼ Nuclear power plant

Nuclear power plants have many advantages that other kinds of power plants do not have. Nuclear power plants do not give off smoke and gases that pollute the environment. They do not use scarce fossil fuels. Once built, nuclear power plants are not costly to run.

But there are some problems with nuclear power plants. You know that nuclear fission gives off radiation. Even after the fuel for fission is used, some radioactive wastes are left. They continue to give off dangerous radiation for hundreds of years.

How are other products of reactors used?

Nuclear reactors provide energy for power plants. Reactors are also used to make radioactive forms of many elements. The pictures show a few of the many ways these elements are used.

Picture *A* shows a photograph made by radiation from a radioactive element that was fed to a patient. Doctors use pictures like this to diagnose certain disorders. The patient in picture *B* is being treated for cancer with a radioactive element. The research worker in picture *C* is using a radioactive element to study how the body fights disease.

Medical uses of radioactive elements in
(A) Diagnosis
(B) Treatment
(C) Research ▼

A

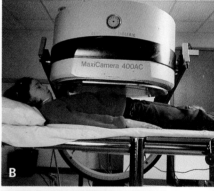

B

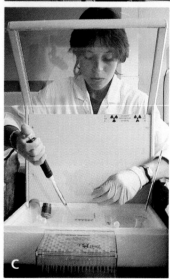

C

Lesson Review

1. Describe the radioactive breakdown of radium.
2. Describe the fission of uranium.
3. Trace the steps in the production of electrical energy from a nuclear reactor.
4. What is one use of a radioactive element?

Think! Water used to remove extra heat from a nuclear power plant is returned to its source—a lake or river. The lake or river then becomes warmer. What problems might be caused by this warming?

How safe is nuclear power?

On April 26, 1986, a fire started at the Chernobyl nuclear power plant in the former Soviet Union. It quickly got out of control. A cloud full of radioactive material poured into the air. Then that material started to fall from the cloud. People could not drink the water after the material fell in it. Thousands of people had to leave their homes. Many people became sick. Some of them died.

As the days passed, winds blew the radioactive cloud across much of Europe. Radioactive material continued to fall from the cloud. In some places, fresh vegetables could not be eaten because of the radioactive material that had fallen on them. They had to be thrown away. If cows ate grass in those places, the milk had to be thrown away too.

As people read about the Chernobyl accident, they wondered if such a thing could happen in the United States. Some experts say that it could not happen here. American nuclear power plants have many safety systems to prevent such accidents.

STS

Radiation Fallout from Chernobyl Disaster, 1986

Other experts are not as sure. There are about 100 nuclear power plants in the United States. Small accidents have happened in some of them. One accident happened at Three Mile Island in Pennsylvania. Only a small amount of radioactive material leaked out. But there is no way to be sure that a larger leak would never happen.

The Chernobyl accident made it clear that nuclear power has risks. But it has some advantages over other energy sources. Fuels such as oil and coal are being used up. Nuclear fuel is plentiful in the United States. The burning of fossil fuels pollutes the air. Nuclear power plants do not cause this kind of pollution.

Are the advantages of nuclear power worth the risks? No one yet has a definite answer. But it is a question everyone should think about.

Critical thinking

Suppose you must decide whether or not a nuclear power plant should be built in your town. What information would you need to make your decision? Where would you find this information?

Using what you learned

Would the people in your community allow a nuclear power plant to be built nearby? If there is one already, how do people feel about it? Make up a questionnaire to find out what people think about nuclear power. Ask five people to answer your questions.

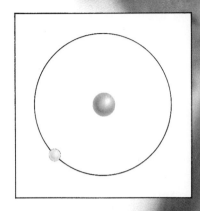

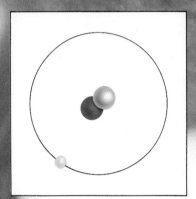

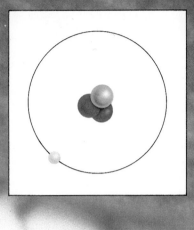

▲ Three forms of hydrogen

4. Nuclear Fusion

Getting Started Think about helium, the gas used to fill balloons. It may seem odd, but scientists discovered this element on the sun before they discovered it on the earth! You will learn how reactions that form helium produce the sun's energy.

Words to Know
nuclear fusion

How is energy produced on the sun?

You know that nuclear fission is a type of change in which large nuclei split. In another type of change, nuclei join together. A change in which small nuclei join to form a larger nucleus is called **nuclear fusion** (FYOO zhun). *Fusion* means "putting together." Fusion begins with the smallest of all atoms—those of hydrogen.

Look at the three forms of hydrogen atoms in the drawing above. Notice that their nuclei differ. How many neutrons does each of the other two forms have? The form of hydrogen that has one neutron is needed for fusion.

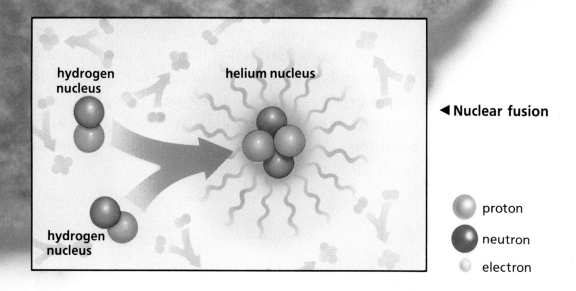

hydrogen nucleus

helium nucleus

hydrogen nucleus

◄ Nuclear fusion

proton
neutron
electron

Nuclear fusion is the process by which the sun produces energy, including the sunlight you see. The drawing above shows a simple fusion reaction. Fusion on the sun is complex and involves the fusion of hydrogen nuclei to form helium nuclei.

How may fusion produce useful energy on the earth?

Can the fusion of hydrogen be used to produce useful energy on the earth? Many scientists are doing experiments to produce fusion in a reactor. A fusion reactor would produce energy that could be changed into electrical energy. Many people believe that nuclear fusion will be the solution to many future energy problems.

There are several reasons for this belief. The form of hydrogen needed for fusion is easily obtained from water. The supply of water is almost without limit. Uranium is needed for fission. But the supplies of uranium are limited. Fission can produce large amounts of energy, but fusion can produce even more. Unlike fission, the fusion reaction does not give off radioactive wastes.

Why have power plants using fusion not been built? You know that fission is used in power plants. No energy has to be added to the fuel to start the fission process. But this is not true of fusion. Such reactions take place only at extremely high temperatures. Great amounts of energy are needed to reach these temperatures.

Fusion reactor ▶

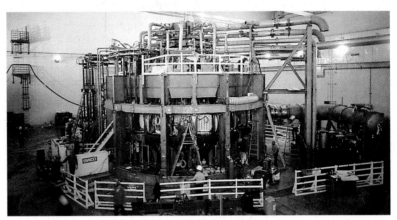

Workers inside fusion reactor ▼

Look at the picture of the fusion reactor in Princeton, New Jersey. A temperature of 50 million degrees C (122 million degrees F) has been produced in this reactor. This is hot enough for fusion to take place. But the amount of energy it takes to reach this temperature is greater than the amount of energy produced. To be useful, a fusion reactor must do the opposite. The fusion must produce more energy than it uses.

Lesson Review

1. Define *nuclear fusion.*
2. Describe a fusion reaction that takes place on the sun.
3. What are four reasons fusion may help solve the world's energy problems in the future?

Think! A form of hydrogen made up of atoms that have one proton and one neutron is sometimes called "heavy hydrogen." Why is this a good name?

Chapter Connections

Write a paragraph explaining the differences between physical, chemical, and nuclear changes. Use the graphic organizer to help you.

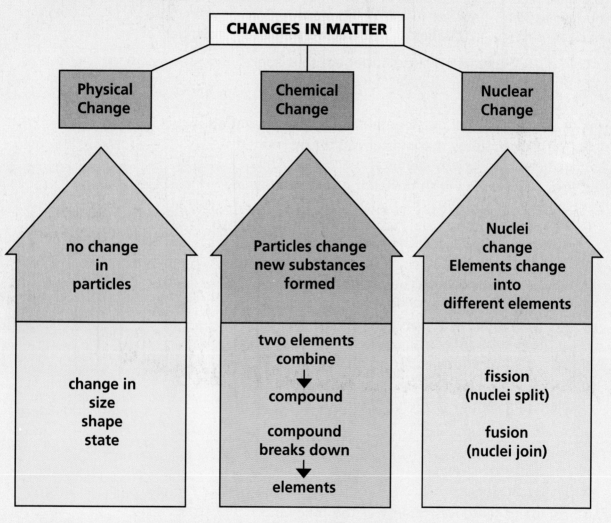

CHANGES IN MATTER

Physical Change

Chemical Change

Nuclear Change

no change in particles

change in size shape state

Particles change new substances formed

two elements combine
↓
compound

compound breaks down
↓
elements

Nuclei change Elements change into different elements

fission (nuclei split)

fusion (nuclei join)

Writing About Science • Persuade

Suppose a large power plant is going to be built near your home. How would you react? Consider the pros and cons of nuclear power. Then write a letter to a local newspaper explaining your opinion. Be sure to support your ideas with facts.

Science Terms

Copy the sentences below. Use the terms listed to complete the sentences.

chemical reaction   corrosion   law of conservation of mass
nuclear fission   nuclear fusion   nuclear reaction
nuclear reactor   oxidation   radioactive elements   synfuel

1. In a _____ reaction large nuclei are split apart.
2. A device in which a nuclear chain reaction is controlled is a _____.
3. A _____ is a fuel put together from other materials.
4. The _____ states that matter cannot be created or destroyed by any chemical reaction.
5. Any reaction in which nuclei of atoms change is called a _____.
6. Elements whose nuclei naturally break down into other nuclei and give off radiation are called _____.
7. Any reaction in which chemical bonds are formed or broken is called a _____.
8. Any change in which oxygen reacts with another substance is called _____.
9. In _____ small nuclei join to form a larger nucleus.
10. A chemical change in which metals react with elements such as oxygen is called _____.

Science Ideas

Use complete sentences to answer the following.

1. Classify each of the following as a physical change or a chemical change: melting ice, burning rocket fuel.
2. Why is boiling water a physical change rather than a chemical change?
3. Why is breaking down water into hydrogen and oxygen a chemical change rather than a physical change?

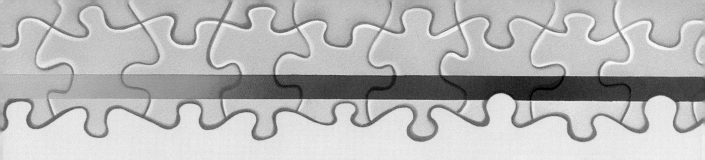

4. What change in energy takes place when hydrogen and oxygen combine?

5. Describe an experiment that illustrates the law of conservation of mass.

6. What substances combine when iron rusts?

7. Classify each of the following as slow oxidation or rapid oxidation: burning of fuel, corrosion of iron.

8. Look at drawings *A, B, C,* and *D*. Each shows a molecule that is part of the process of making a synfuel. Write the letter of the drawing that shows each of the following: water, methane, carbon monoxide, hydrogen.

9. Which drawing shows a molecule of a synfuel? Write its name and formula.

10. Look at drawings *E* and *F*. What is one way in which the two reactions shown are similar?

11. What device produces both energy and radioactive elements from controlled nuclear chain reactions?

12. What kind of nuclear change is shown in drawing *G*?

A

B

C

D

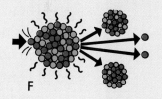

E

Applying Science Ideas

1. A chemical heating pad warms up when the substances in it are mixed together and start a chemical reaction. Where does the heat come from?

2. Scientists are not sure what to do with radioactive wastes from nuclear reactors. Some are stored underground. But many people think this is not the best way to dispose of these wastes. What are some reasons that such storage might be unsafe?

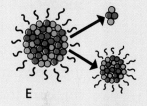

F

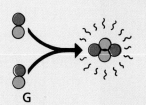

G

Using Science Skills

Suppose you visit a country where you do not know the language. At a gas station, you notice a warning sign telling you to avoid breathing the gasoline fumes. Draw the symbol that could warn you about this danger.

Light

Making a Glow of It

Shhh! The show at the Living Light Center in Philadelphia, Pennsylvania, is about to start. The house lights are dimmed, but the children do not notice. They talk excitedly as they wait for the show to start. Soon the room is completely dark. Suddenly the audience gasps! On the stage they can see the bright lights of a puppet theater.

As the children look in wonder they can see the glowing hair of their friends. For most of these children, these lights are the first they have ever seen. These children are visually impaired.

This is not a medical miracle. The children's eyes have not changed. What is different is the kind of light being used on stage.

Ultraviolet (ul trah VYE uh lit) waves, also called black light, caused the strange effects that the children saw. Black light is an invisible form of energy. When some objects absorb this energy, they give off visible light. Such objects are described as fluorescent (floo uh RES unt). When seen in black light, these objects glow. They look about 20 times brighter than they do in ordinary light. This increase in brightness can help some people who are almost blind see objects they never saw before.

Black light and fluorescent materials have many uses. More than 600 minerals are fluorescent. Because so many minerals are fluorescent, black light can be used to identify them. Calcite is a mineral that glows hot pink under black light.

Have you ever had your hand stamped with a special ink as you entered a fair or an amusement park? When the ink dries, the mark is invisible and waterproof. It will not wear off for many hours. If you leave the park and then wish to return later, you must pass your hand under a black light to make the stamp visible.

Doctors who prescribe contact lenses use black light. The doctor puts harmless fluorescent dye in the person's eyes. Under the black light, the dye makes the contact lenses glow. The size and shape of the lenses against the eyes show how well the lenses fit.

Discover

How can black light be used in new ways?

Materials   pencil · paper

Procedure

You have learned that there are special inks that can be seen only with black light. These inks may be used to stamp your hand at an amusement park. How else could inks and black lights be used?

Identify a problem that could be solved by using fluorescent ink and black light. Then explain how you solved the problem.

In this chapter you will learn about other kinds of radiant energy that people cannot see. You will learn more about how light behaves.

1. Energy You Can See

Words to Know
wavelength
frequency
intensity
electromagnetic
spectrum

Getting Started Think about the last time you made waves in water. Perhaps you sat at the edge of a pool and stirred the water with your foot. Or you may have dropped a pebble into a pond. You could see waves. Light also travels in waves. Are light waves anything like water waves? As you read about light, you will find out.

How can you describe a light wave?

Light is energy that you can see. Light is one kind of radiant (RAY dee unt) energy. All radiant energy travels in waves. Radiant energy is always moving. As you will learn, there are kinds of radiant energy that you cannot see.

Light travels in waves that are in some ways like water waves. Imagine you are in a sailboat on a lake, as shown in the picture. A powerboat moves by,

◀ Sailboat riding on wave

making waves in the water. The sailboat floats on these waves.

As shown in the drawing, each high point of both a water wave and a light wave is called a crest. Each low point is called a trough (trauf). The sailboat rises on a crest, drops into a trough, and rises again on the next crest.

The distance between two crests is the same as the distance between two troughs. The distance between the crest of one wave and the crest of the next is called the **wavelength.** Find the wavelength in the drawing. How can you describe wavelength in terms of troughs? Different waves, either water waves or light waves, have different wavelengths.

Another characteristic of both water waves and light waves is the rate at which they move. The rate at which the water waves pass by the sailboat is their frequency (FREE kwun see). If two waves pass by each second, the frequency is 2 waves per second. What is the frequency if three troughs pass by each second?

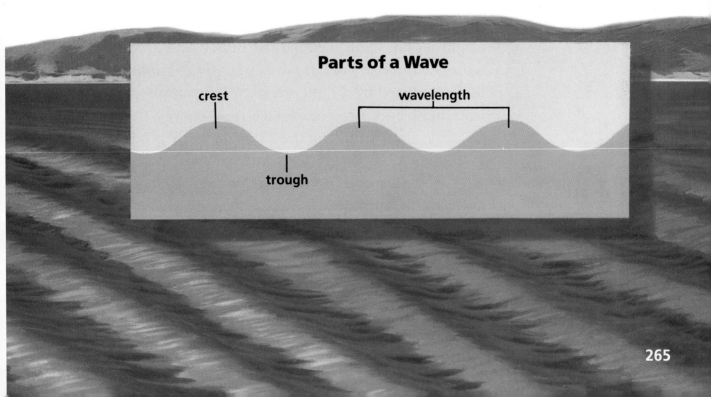

Parts of a Wave

crest

wavelength

trough

The **frequency** of a light wave is the number of waves that pass by a point each second. You read that different light waves have different wavelengths. Different light waves also have different frequencies. But there is a relationship between wavelength and frequency. The shorter the wavelength of a wave, the greater its frequency. Which light wave in the drawing below has the shorter wavelength and the greater frequency?

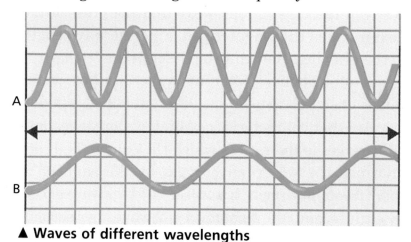

▲ **Waves of different wavelengths**

How does brightness vary?

You know that light can vary in brightness. The brightness of light is called **intensity** (ihn TEN suh tee). The intensity of light depends on the amount of light produced by a light source. For example, a 60-watt light bulb uses more electrical energy than a 25-watt light bulb. So the 60-watt bulb produces more light than the 25-watt bulb.

The intensity of light also changes with distance from the light source. Look at the drawing. Near the source of the light, the intensity is the greatest. As light travels away from the source, it spreads out over a larger area. As a result, the

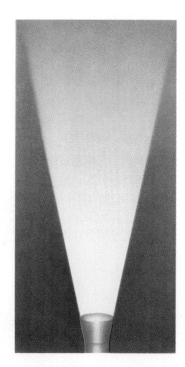

◀ **Relation of intensity to distance**

intensity of light decreases as the distance from its source increases. When would more light strike a page of this book, when the page is near a lamp or when it is farther away?

How do various kinds of radiant energy differ?

Radiant energy includes waves of different wavelengths and frequencies. The drawing shows some types of radiant energy arranged in order of wavelengths and frequencies. This arrangement is called the **electromagnetic spectrum** (ee lek-troh mag NET ihk   SPEK trum).

Radio and television waves have the longest wavelengths and the lowest frequencies. Gamma rays have the shortest wavelengths and the highest frequencies. Notice that visible light is near the middle of the electromagnetic spectrum. As you will learn, the color of light depends on its frequency.

The electromagnetic spectrum ▼

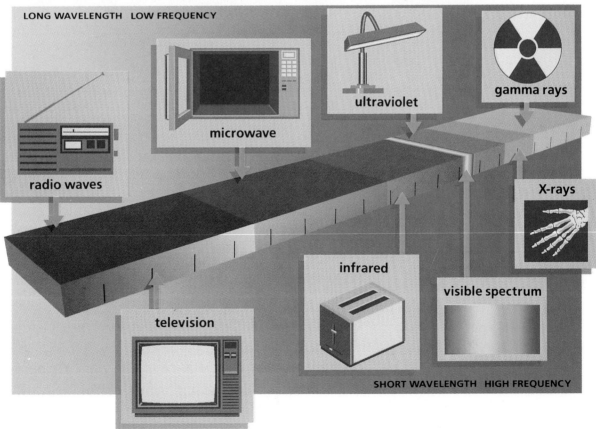

LONG WAVELENGTH   LOW FREQUENCY

gamma rays

ultraviolet

microwave

radio waves

X-rays

infrared

visible spectrum

television

SHORT WAVELENGTH   HIGH FREQUENCY

Radiant energy in different parts of the electromagnetic spectrum has different effects and uses. Radio and television waves are used in communications. Microwaves are used in microwave ovens to heat or cook foods quickly.

Most of the radiant energy produced by a heat lamp, a toaster, or a gas flame is made up of infrared (ihn fruh RED) waves. All warm objects give off some infrared waves. With special film, infrared waves can be used to take pictures in the dark. The warmer areas are red and white. The cooler areas are blue and purple. Which are the warmest areas in the picture of the houses?

▲ Picture taken with infrared waves

Have you ever had a suntan or a sunburn? Ultraviolet (ul truh VYE uh lit) waves coming from the sun can tan or burn your skin. Ultraviolet waves can cause skin cancer.

As you read at the beginning of this chapter, ultraviolet waves are sometimes called black light because they cause some objects to give off visible light.

Radiant energy called X-rays can pass through many materials, including your skin. So X-rays can be used to take pictures of structures inside the body. X-rays may also damage living cells. Notice that this person is wearing a protective shield. Dentists and doctors are careful not to expose people to X-rays any more than necessary.

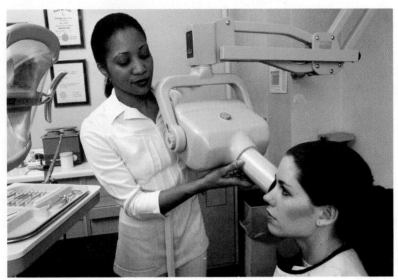

▲ X-ray machine in use

As described in Chapter 7, radioactive elements give off radiant energy called gamma rays. These rays can destroy living cells. In the proper use of nuclear energy, living things must be shielded from gamma rays.

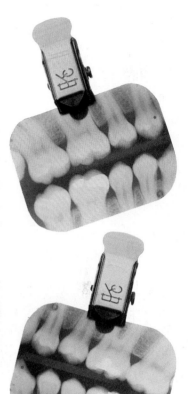

▲ Dental X-ray pictures

Lesson Review

1. Define *wavelength* and *frequency.* How is wavelength related to frequency?
2. How is the intensity of light related to the distance from a light source?
3. Name seven kinds of radiant energy in the electromagnetic spectrum.

Think! Suppose you are reading a book by a lamp but you are not getting enough light. What are two changes you could make that would increase the brightness of light on the book? Explain why each change would help.

Life Science
CONNECTION

Bees use certain wavelengths of light to find their way between sources of food and their hives. Use reference books to find out more about this.

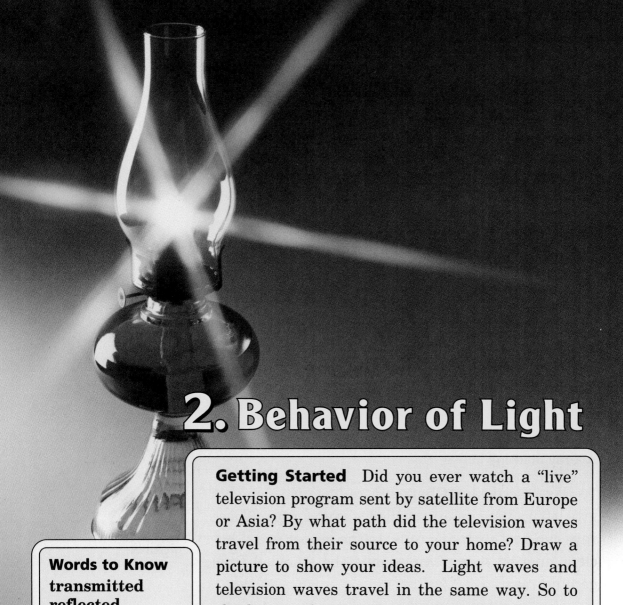

2. Behavior of Light

Getting Started Did you ever watch a "live" television program sent by satellite from Europe or Asia? By what path did the television waves travel from their source to your home? Draw a picture to show your ideas. Light waves and television waves travel in the same way. So to check your ideas, read about how light travels.

Words to Know
transmitted
reflected
absorbed
transparent
translucent
opaque
refraction

How does light travel?

Scientists have learned much about light by studying how it behaves. They have found that light waves travel in straight lines. Light waves can change direction. When light waves strike an object, some of the waves bounce off. But the paths of the waves to and from the object are straight lines.

Scientists have also found that light travels in all directions from a source. Suppose you place a lighted lamp in the center of a room. Light will travel out from the lamp in all directions. No matter where in the room you are, some light waves will reach you.

An object casts a shadow because light travels in straight lines and does not curve around the object. Suppose you use a small lamp as a light source to cast the shadow of a comb. As shown, the straight lines of light form the shadow. Now suppose you move the comb closer to the light source. Use drawings A and B to describe what then happens to the shadow.

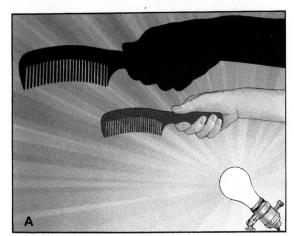

▲ Using a comb to make shadows

What happens when light strikes matter?

Light from the sun that reaches the earth first travels through outer space. Outer space is nearly a perfect vacuum (VAK yoo um). Any space that contains little or no matter is a vacuum. In a vacuum, light travels at about 300,000 kilometers per second (186,000 miles per second). This speed is so great that it is hard to imagine. If light could travel in a circular path, it could go around the earth more than seven times in just 1 second!

When light waves from the sun reach the earth, the first matter they strike is air. Most light passes

Problem Solving
Say Cheese

Long before the invention of modern cameras, people used pinhole cameras both for fun and to investigate the behavior of light. The pinhole camera shown in the drawing is a closed box with a tiny hole at one end. A waxed paper screen covers the other end.

How does the action of a pinhole camera show that light travels in straight lines?

Design and build your own pinhole camera. Make sure that light enters the camera only through a tiny hole. Aim the camera at a brightly lit object in a dark room. Look through the camera as shown. What kind of image do you see? How do you explain how it looks?

through air. Light that passes through matter is said to be **transmitted** (trans MIHT ted) by the material. Light is transmitted by air as well as by other gases, most liquids, and some solids.

Suppose that light strikes an object but is not transmitted. What happens to the light? Some of the light is **reflected** (rih FLEK ted), or bounced off, from the surface of the object. You see most objects because light is reflected from their surfaces to your eyes. For example, you can see the moon because the part of its surface facing the sun reflects sunlight that strikes it.

Light that is not reflected or transmitted by a material is **absorbed** (ab SORBD), or trapped. What happens to light that is absorbed? Most of it is changed to heat and warms the matter that absorbs it. Whenever you are warmed by standing in direct sunlight, you feel this effect.

Materials can transmit light in two different ways. Look at the picture. The clear glass door is transparent (trans PER unt). A **transparent** material lets light pass through it without scattering the light. So you can see objects clearly through a transparent material. Besides clear glass, what are some other examples of transparent materials?

The glass brick window is translucent (trans LOO-sunt). A **translucent** material lets some light pass through it, but it scatters the light. So you cannot see objects clearly through a translucent material.

An **opaque** (oh PAYK) material does not transmit light. Most solids are opaque. In the picture, which structures are opaque? Liquids usually do transmit light, but they can become opaque if small particles of opaque material are scattered through them. Tempera paint and milk are examples of opaque liquids.

▼ **Building made of various materials**

When does the direction of light change?

Light travels in a straight line. But the direction in which light travels can change if the matter through which it is traveling changes. Compare the pictures of light passing from air into water. In picture *A*, the light strikes the water at a right angle. The light continues to travel through the water in a straight line. In picture *B*, the light strikes the water at an angle other than a right angle. Notice how the light changes direction as it enters the water.

▲ A   No refraction

▲ B   Refraction

Refraction of light from a pencil ▼

The change in direction of light when it passes from one kind of matter to another is called **refraction** (rih FRAK shun). Light that is refracted appears to be bent. Refraction, or bending, is caused by the change in the speed of light as it passes from one material to another. In the example given, the two materials are air and water.

Refraction can produce many surprising effects. Look at the picture of a pencil in a glass of water. Refraction of light reflected from the pencil causes the pencil to look broken. Light from the pencil is refracted as it moves from the water into the air. The light is again refracted as it passes from the air through the glass.

Light also changes direction when it is reflected from a surface. Look at the picture of light moving through a thin plastic thread called an optical fiber. As light moves through the fiber, it seems to curve around corners. But the light really travels in straight lines. The drawing shows how the light is reflected from the inner walls of the fiber. In the next section, you will learn how mirrors and lenses reflect and refract light.

Path of light in optical fiber ▶

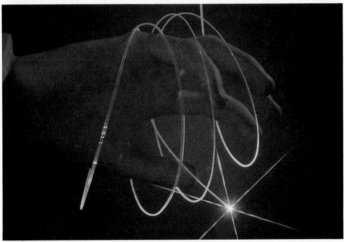

▲ Optical fibers

Lesson Review

1. Why does an object in front of a light source produce a shadow behind the object?

2. What are three things that may happen to light that strikes matter?

3. How do the following compare in the ways in which they transmit light: a transparent material, a translucent material, and an opaque material?

4. What happens to a beam of light that enters a glass window at an angle other than a right angle?

Think! Many light bulbs used in reading lamps are made with frosted glass. So are the glass doors in shower stalls and some inside walls in office buildings. How does frosted glass affect the intensity of light passing through it?

3. Mirrors and Lenses

Getting Started Suppose you are in a dark room. There is a mirror in front of you and a picture behind you. Why is it not possible for you to see the picture? Then someone turns on a ceiling light in the room. The path the light travels makes it possible to see the picture. Describe that path.

Words to Know
plane mirror
concave mirror
convex mirror
convex lens
concave lens

What are two kinds of reflection?

When light strikes a surface it is reflected. The reflection of light can be irregular or regular. Light that strikes a rough or uneven surface, such as a wall, is reflected in all directions, or scattered. This kind of reflection is irregular.

Light that strikes a smooth and shiny surface produces a regular reflection. Any such smooth and shiny surface acts as a mirror. What you see in the mirror is called an image. Look at the picture of a lake. Is the reflection of the landscape on its surface irregular or regular?

Wherever a beam of light strikes a reflecting surface, the light is reflected at the same angle as it strikes the surface. As you know, mirrors reflect light. A mirror in which the reflecting surface is flat is a **plane mirror.**

Look at the drawing of a flashlight and a plane mirror. Find the incoming beam of light striking the mirror and the reflected beam of light. Notice the angles drawn between the red line and each of the light beams are the same.

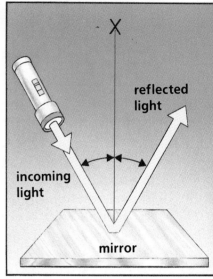

▲ Plane mirror

What are two kinds of curved mirrors?

Some mirrors are not plane, but curved. A **concave** (kahn KAYV) **mirror** is a mirror in which the reflecting surface curves inward. Look at picture *A*. When you look into a concave mirror, you see a larger image of yourself. A **convex** (kahn VEKS) **mirror** is a mirror in which the reflecting surface curves outward. Look at picture *B*. When you look into a convex mirror, you see a smaller image of yourself. A convex mirror also makes things seem farther away than they really are.

▼ Concave mirror

▼ Convex mirror

Explore

ACTIVITY

How does a periscope work?

To see your face, you use a mirror. To see the back of your head, you use two mirrors. In a somewhat similar way, you can use a periscope (PER ih skohp) to see above heads at a parade. A periscope contains two mirrors arranged so it is possible to see over or around objects.

Materials
chalk · 2 mirrors, each 5 cm square · pencil · metric ruler · food-wrap carton · tape · scissors

Procedure

A. Use chalk to print a letter *F* on the chalkboard. Hold a mirror so you can see an image of the *F* in the mirror.
   1. Draw what you observe.

B. Use a pencil and a metric ruler to draw a 5-cm square at each end of one side of a food-wrap carton. Draw a line across each square, as shown in drawing *B*.

C. Tape two mirrors along the lines inside the carton, as shown in drawing *C*.

B   C   D

D. Use scissors to cut two holes in the carton, as shown in drawing *D*.
   2. Predict how the *F* will look through the periscope.

E. Look at the *F* through the periscope.
   3. Draw what you observe.

Writing and Sharing Results and Conclusions

1. Copy drawing *D*. Add lines to the drawing that trace the path of the light from the *F* to your eye. Why is the image of the *F* in the periscope not reversed?

2. How do your results and conclusions compare with those of your classmates?

How do lenses affect light?

A lens is a transparent object that refracts, or bends light. Like a curved mirror, a lens may be convex or concave. A **convex lens** is a lens that is thicker in the middle than it is at the edge. A **concave lens** is a lens that is thinner in the middle than it is at the edge.

Compare the picture of light passing through a convex lens with the picture of light passing through a concave lens. Notice that light passing through the convex lens comes together to form a small, bright spot and then spreads apart. But light passing through the concave lens spreads apart and does not come together.

Why do the two kinds of lenses have different effects on light that passes through them? Remember that light changes direction, or bends, when it passes from air to glass. Look again at the pictures. How does the light bend when it strikes the convex lens? How does the light bend when it strikes the concave lens?

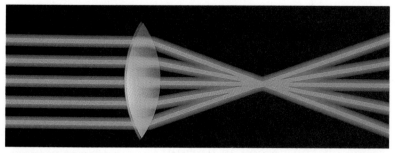

▲ Convex lens   ▼ Concave lens

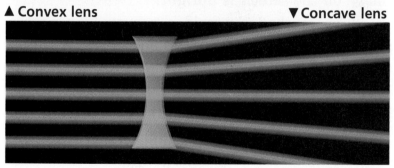

What kinds of images do convex lenses form?

Look at the drawing of a simple camera. The lens in this camera is a convex lens. When light enters the opening in a camera, an image appears on the film inside the camera. If the lens is moved back and forth until the image is clear, then the image is in focus. This image is a picture of the object that is opposite the opening in the camera.

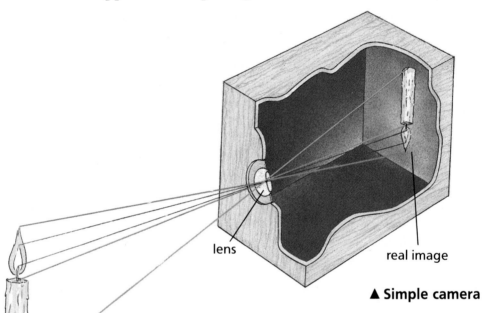

lens

real image

▲ **Simple camera**

The image formed on the film of a camera is called a real image. It is real because you can see it on the film when it is developed. Notice that the image on the film is upside down. The image formed on a screen by a slide projector is also a real image. How are slides placed in a projector so that the image on the screen is upright?

Suppose that you held a convex lens near a printed page, as shown. You would see a larger image of the page. In this case, the convex lens is being used as a magnifier. This image is upright, but it is not called a real image, because it cannot be formed on a surface like a film or a screen. The image can be seen only through the lens.

object

**Lens used
as magnifier** ▼

How do eyeglasses work?

Like a camera, the human eye has a convex lens. This lens forms a real image on the retina, or back wall of your eye. Look at drawing A. Notice that an upside-down image of the tree forms on the retina. Your brain interprets the image right side up.

The lenses in the eyes of some people form clear images of close objects but not of distant ones. These people are nearsighted because the image of a distant object is focused in front of the retina. Look at drawing B. Eyeglasses made with concave lenses help a nearsighted person see distant objects clearly. Look at drawing C. How does the concave lens change the focus of the light?

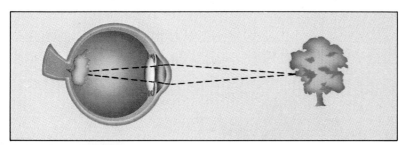

▲ A   Normal eye

▲ Tree in focus

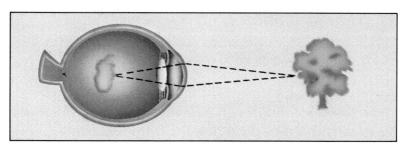

▲ B   Nearsighted eye

▲ Tree out of focus

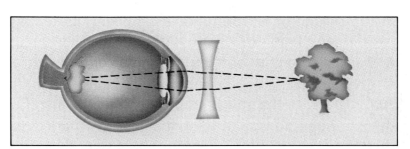

▲ C   Nearsighted eye with concave lens

▲ Tree in focus

The lenses in the eyes of some other people form clear images of distant objects but not of close ones. These people are farsighted because the image of a close object is focused behind the retina. Look at drawing *A*. It shows the eye of a farsighted person. Farsighted people have difficulty reading or sewing. But they can be helped by eyeglasses with convex lenses. Look at drawing *B*. How does the convex lens change the focus of the light?

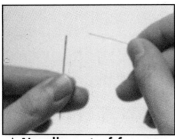

▲ Needle out of focus

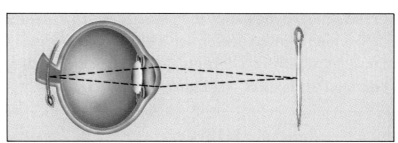

▲ A   Farsighted eye

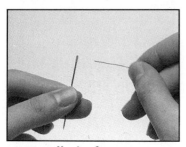

▲ Needle in focus

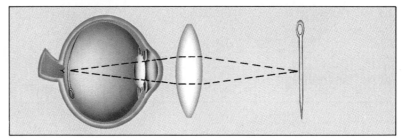

▲ B   Farsighted eye with convex lens

Lesson Review

1. How is the reflection of light from this page different from reflection of light from a mirror?

2. Describe how a plane mirror produces an image.

3. Which kind of mirror, concave or convex, produces a larger image? Which produces a smaller image?

4. Describe the path of light through a convex lens.

5. Compare the image produced by the lens in a camera with the image produced by a magnifier.

Think! Suggest a way of using a mirror to send a message from one ship to another on a clear day.

Skills

THINKING

Testing how one variable affects another

In an experiment, you can observe how things change. Anything that can change in an experiment is called a *variable.* When one variable changes, it may cause another variable to change. In the experiment below, distance from the viewer and the height of an object are variables.

Practicing the skill

1. Stand a mirror in a piece of clay. Place it on a table, near one end.

2. Measure and record the height of an object that is a little taller than the mirror. Stand the object directly in front of the mirror.

3. Rest your chin on the end of the table and look at the mirror.

4. Have a partner move the object until you see all of it in the mirror.

5. Measure and record the distance between the mirror and the object.

6. Repeat steps **2–5** with objects of different heights.

7. Describe how an object's height affects how far from the mirror the object must be before you can see all of it in the mirror. Write your description.

Thinking about the skill
When did you discover how the variables affected each other?

Applying the skill
Construct a test to find out how tall a mirror has to be for you to be able to see your entire reflection. This length may be different for your teacher. Why might the length be different?

How have lasers become a part of daily life?

Have you ever seen a laser light show? Thin beams of colored light shoot back and forth to the beat of rock music. In movies and videos, lasers light up the screen. But lasers are not just for entertainment. Since their first use in 1960, lasers have changed the way many things are done.

Lasers are useful because they produce a powerful beam of pure light. Ordinary light contains several different wavelengths of light that spread out in all directions. In contrast, lasers produce light of just one wavelength. The light waves move in one direction, forming a narrow concentrated beam.

Because lasers can send and interpret signals, they are used in communications. Lasers carry telephone calls and television signals through optical fibers. At supermarket checkouts, lasers scan the bar codes on packages you buy.

Lasers also play compact disks (CDs) in CD players. A CD has a spiral track. The track is as thin as a hair. If the track were stretched out, it would be several kilometers long. On the track, sound is recorded in a code. A pattern of billions of microscopic pits forms the code.

and Society

STS

When a CD player is turned on, the disk spins hundreds of times in a minute. A laser sends out a beam. The beam moves along the spiral track, from the center to the edge of the disk. When the beam strikes the track, it reads the code. It changes the code into electrical signals. Inside the speakers, the electrical signals are changed into sound.

In medical science, lasers have broken new ground. Doctors use lasers for delicate eye surgery. Laser light beams cut more cleanly than knives do. They seal blood vessels instantly, so there is less bleeding with laser surgery. Some medical lasers can be tuned to different wavelengths, just as a radio can be tuned to different stations. With these lasers, doctors can remove birthmarks from skin. Lasers can also be used to destroy some growths caused by cancer.

Lasers are used in industry and science. Some lasers cut and weld airplane parts. Others measure small movements in the earth's crust. Laser research done today may help find new sources of energy in the future.

Critical thinking

Suppose you were writing a story about how lasers could help to save human lives. Which uses of lasers would be most helpful for this purpose?

Using what you learned

Find out if there is a laser scanner used at the checkout of a nearby department store, video store, supermarket, or library. Find out what information the laser can read from scanning a bar code. Discuss your findings with your class.

4. Seeing Colors

Getting Started If you shine a white light on a red rose, the rose looks red. If you shine a white light on a green leaf, the leaf looks green. If you shine a red light on a red rose, the rose still looks red. But if you shine a red light on a green leaf, the leaf looks black. How do you think this observation can be explained?

What causes different colors of light?

Light that does not appear to have any color is called white light. But when white light is passed through a glass prism (PRIHZ um), the light breaks up into bands of color. A prism is a clear, wedge-shaped block. Together all the bands of visible light make up the **visible spectrum.**

The visible spectrum contains all the colors of the rainbow. Together these colors form white light.

▼ Visible light spectrum

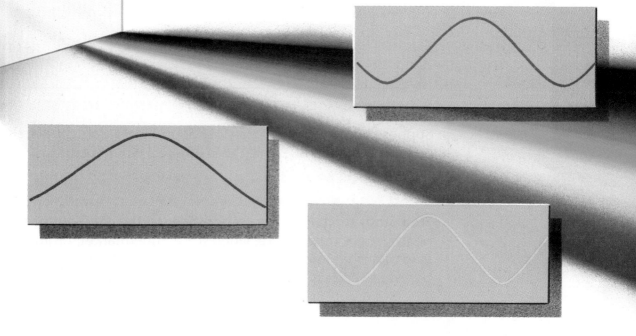

Look at the drawing. What is the order of the colors in the visible spectrum?

How does one color of light differ from another? Waves of different colors of light have different frequencies. Red light has the lowest frequency. Violet light has the highest frequency. Orange, yellow, green, and blue light have waves with frequencies between those of red and violet.

When white light passes through a prism, waves of different frequencies refract at different angles. As a result, the waves are spread apart into the color bands of the visible spectrum.

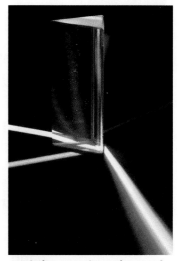

▲ Light passing through prism

What objects produce or transmit colors?

An object has color because it is either producing light, transmitting light, or reflecting light. An object that produces light is said to be **luminous** (LOO muh nus). The color of a luminous object is the color of the light that it gives off. The gas flame in the picture produces blue light. If a luminous object gives off all colors of light at once, what color will you see?

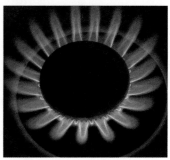

▲ Luminous flame

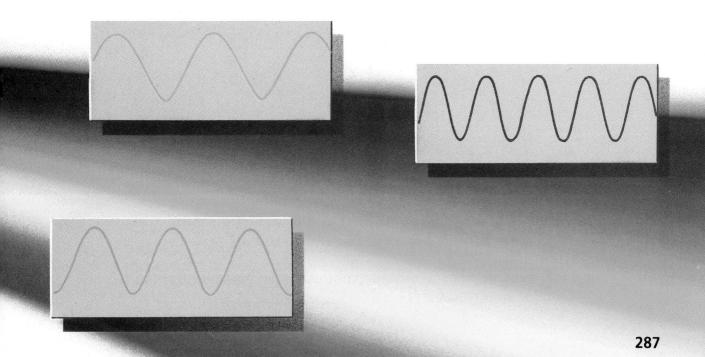

Explore Together

How can you make white light from colored light?

Organizer

Materials

3 flashlights · red, blue, and green cellophane · 3 rubber bands

Procedure

Manager

A. Cover the end of a flashlight with a piece of red cellophane. Fasten tightly with a rubber band, as shown in drawing A. In the same way, cover a second flashlight with blue cellophane and cover a third flashlight with green cellophane.

Investigator

B. Darken the room. Direct the light from one flashlight onto a white wall or screen. Repeat with each of the other two flashlights.

Recorder

1. What do you observe with each flashlight?

Group Investigator

C. Direct red light and blue light from the flashlights onto the screen so that the circles of light overlap, as shown in drawing B. Repeat using all the possible combinations of two or three colors.

Group, Recorder

2. What do you observe? Make a table to record your observations.

A

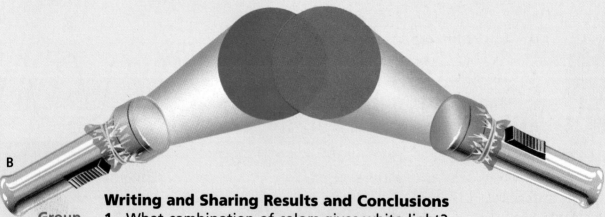

B

Writing and Sharing Results and Conclusions

Group, Reporter

1. What combination of colors gives white light?

2. How do your results and conclusions compare with those of your classmates?

288

The color of a transparent or translucent material or object depends on the color of the light it transmits. A red film over a flashlight bulb transmits most of the red light waves. But the film absorbs nearly all of the other colors. So the light transmitted by the film appears red. Why does the traffic light in the picture appear yellow?

▲ **Yellow traffic light**

What objects reflect colors?

The color of an opaque material or object depends on the frequencies of light it reflects. The drawing shows what happens when white light strikes a red car. The car reflects the red frequencies of light. All the other frequencies of light are absorbed by the car. The color of most opaque materials or objects can be explained in the same way. When white light strikes a green leaf, why does the leaf look green?

What causes an opaque material or object, such as the white part of this page, to look white? When white light strikes the page, nearly all the light is reflected and little of the light is absorbed. So the page looks white.

▼ **Red car in white light**

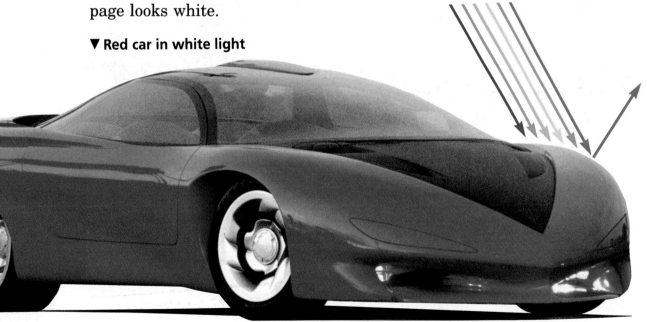

What causes an opaque material or object, such as the print on this page, to look black? When white light strikes the print, nearly all the light is absorbed and little of the light is reflected. So the print looks black.

Sometimes an object has a color when you look at it in white light, but the same object looks black in colored light. Look at the drawing. A green leaf absorbs red light that strikes it. But there is no other color in the red light shining on the leaf. The leaf reflects no light, so it looks black.

*Could Elena use what she had learned in science class to help her family sell flowers? Find out in **The Gold at the End of the Rainbow** in Horizons Plus.*

▲ Green leaf in white light   ▲ Green leaf in red light

Lesson Review

1. What happens to white light that passes through a glass prism?
2. Name, in order of their frequencies, the colors of the visible light spectrum.
3. What determines the color of a luminous object, a transparent object, and an opaque object?

Think! What is the difference between the red of a stoplight and the red of a printed DANGER sign?

Life Science
CONNECTION

What parts of the visible light spectrum are used by plants to make food?

290

Chapter Connections

Write a paragraph based on information in one of the boxes of the graphic organizer. Use details from the chapter.

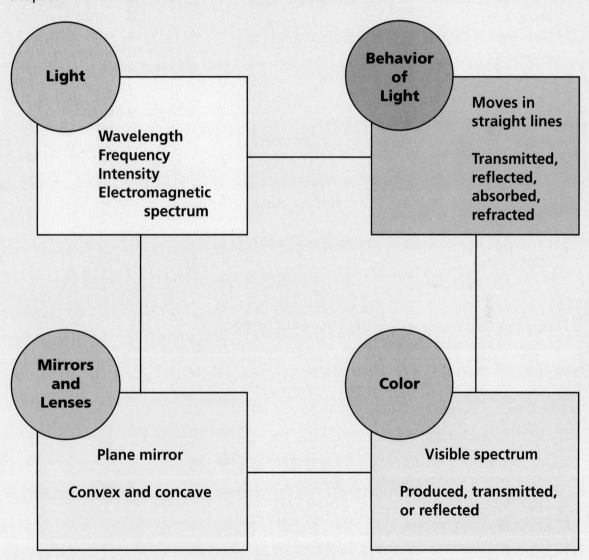

Light

Wavelength
Frequency
Intensity
Electromagnetic
 spectrum

Behavior
of
Light

Moves in
straight lines

Transmitted,
reflected,
absorbed,
refracted

Mirrors
and
Lenses

Plane mirror

Convex and concave

Color

Visible spectrum

Produced, transmitted,
or reflected

Writing About Science • Research

Find out what holograms are and how they are used. Write a report to share with the class.

Chapter 8 Review

Science Terms

A. Write the letter of the term that best matches the definition.

1. Number of waves that pass by a point each second
2. Lens that is thinner in the middle than at the edge
3. Mirror with flat reflecting surface
4. Change of direction of light
5. Distance between crests in a wave
6. Mirror in which the reflecting surface curves inward
7. Brightness of light
8. Mirror in which the reflecting surface curves outward
9. Lens that is thicker in the middle than at the edge

a. concave lens
b. concave mirror
c. convex lens
d. convex mirror
e. frequency
f. intensity
g. plane mirror
h. refraction
i. wavelength

B. Copy the sentences below. Use the terms listed to complete the sentences.

absorbed   electromagnetic spectrum
luminous   opaque   reflected   translucent
transmitted   transparent   visible spectrum

1. Light is not transmitted by an _____ object.
2. All forms of radiant energy are arranged in order of wavelength and frequency in the _____.
3. Light passes through a _____ object without being scattered.
4. Light that is trapped by matter is _____ .
5. Light passes through and is scattered by a _____ object.
6. All the bands of light you can see make up the _____.
7. Light that bounces off a surface is _____ .
8. Light is produced and given off by a _____ object.
9. Light that passes through matter is _____ .

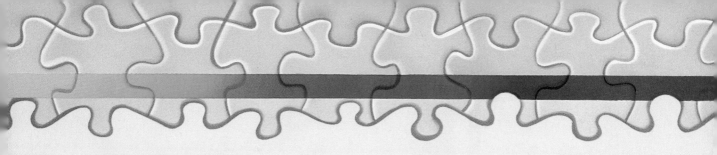

Science Ideas

Use complete sentences to answer the following.

1. Which waves, those in drawing *A* or drawing *B*, have a higher frequency? Which waves have a longer wavelength?

2. In what path does light travel from a source?

3. What happens to light that strikes a transparent material, a translucent material, and an opaque material?

4. What causes light to be refracted?

5. How is the reflection of light by a mirror different from its reflection by other surfaces?

6. Compare the sizes of the images produced by a convex mirror and a concave mirror.

7. Which drawing, *C* or *D*, shows a concave lens? Which shows a convex lens? Which type of lens can cause a beam of light to come together in a small bright spot?

8. What colors of light make up white light? How can white light be separated into these colors?

9. Why does a blue flame look blue? Why does a blue scarf look blue in white light? Why does white light passed through a blue filter look blue?

Applying Science Ideas

1. What is the advantage of a convex mirror used as a side-view mirror on a truck? What must the driver keep in mind for safety when using such a mirror?

2. What are two devices found in many homes that use lasers to communicate through sound?

Using Science Skills

How could you find out what color a yellow object appears to be when different colored lights are shined on it? What are the variables?

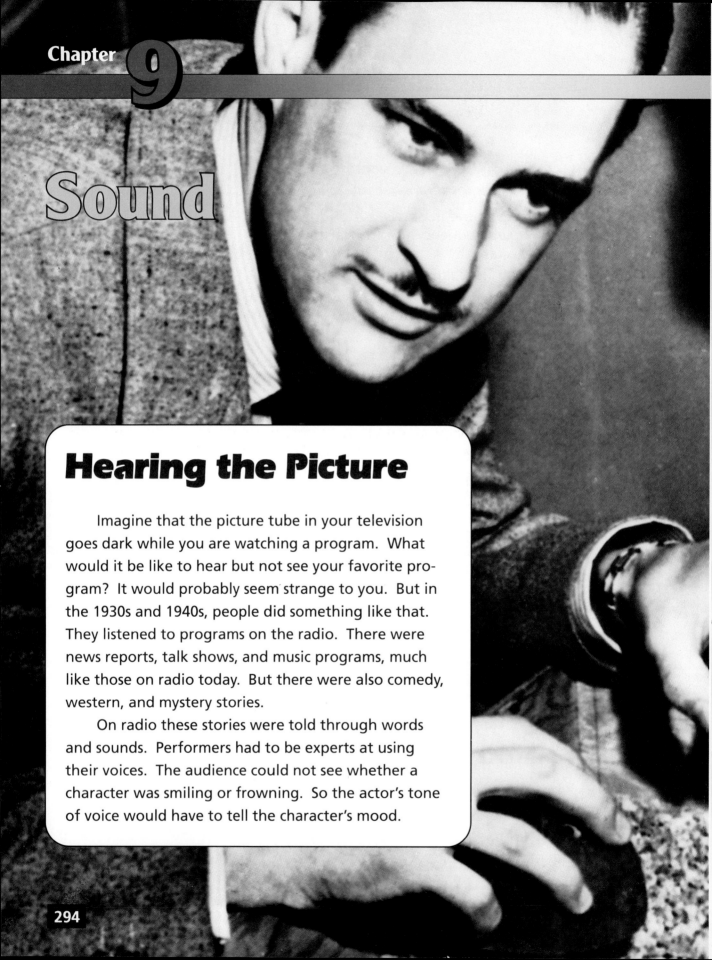

Sound

Hearing the Picture

Imagine that the picture tube in your television goes dark while you are watching a program. What would it be like to hear but not see your favorite program? It would probably seem strange to you. But in the 1930s and 1940s, people did something like that. They listened to programs on the radio. There were news reports, talk shows, and music programs, much like those on radio today. But there were also comedy, western, and mystery stories.

On radio these stories were told through words and sounds. Performers had to be experts at using their voices. The audience could not see whether a character was smiling or frowning. So the actor's tone of voice would have to tell the character's mood.

Listeners could not see the weather around a character. But they could hear the roar of wind and the crash of thunder. They could also hear the crunch of footsteps in snow. Listeners used these sounds as a guide. Then they used their imagination to fill in the details of what was happening in the story.

Sounds also suggested the time of day. Chirping birds or a crowing rooster made the audience think of morning. The sound of crickets suggested nighttime. The hoot of an owl made the night a bit mysterious.

The old radio shows used different kinds of sounds. There were sounds made with human voices. Some radio performers specialized in only one kind of sound. For example, one woman could make the sound of a crying baby.

Sounds not made by voices were also used. Suppose a cowboy was galloping away on a horse. A horse could not run around in the radio studio. So the sound-effects person hit two halves of a coconut together. The audience heard hoof beats. Suppose firefighters were rescuing people from a burning building. The sound-effects person would crumple cellophane near the microphone. The audience heard the sound of crackling flames.

Radio shows also used sound-effects records. There were about 500 different records. A record might have the sound of a car crash on one side and the sound of a plane taking off on the other. The records helped to tell the story. But the sound-effects person had to be careful. If there was a mistake, the audience might have expected a car crash but instead heard a plane take off!

Today a few radio stations still have stories that use sound effects. And sound effects are used in television and movies, too. But most of these sounds are made with electronic devices. A synthesizer is a machine that can make the sound of almost anything—from the loud roar of a jet engine to the happy cluck of a farmyard chicken. Sound is still important for telling a story. But using sound is a lot easier now than it used to be. The only thing people have to do now is push a button!

Discover

How can you create sound effects?

Materials tape recorder with microphone · various objects for making sound effects

Procedure

Put on a radio play. Choose a short story that you know or make up a story. It should be a story in which you can use lots of sounds. Decide which sounds you need. Then use your imagination to think of ways to make these sounds. Test your ideas.

Work in groups of five or six. Record your play on a tape recorder. Then play your story back to the class. See if other students can figure out what your sounds are and how you made them.

In this chapter you will learn more about different kinds of sounds. You will find out how sounds are made and how they travel. You will also discover some uses for sounds.

Cymbals ▶

◀ Mandolin

Clarinet ▶

1. Energy You Can Hear

Getting Started Place a plastic ruler flat on your desk so that half of the ruler extends over the edge. Hold the ruler down tightly against the desk as you strike the free end. How is the motion you observe related to the sound you hear? What happens if you stop the motion?

Glass vase shattered by sound ▼

What is sound?

Sound, like light, is a form of energy. Do you remember how energy is defined? Energy is the ability to do work or move objects. Think about whether sound fits this definition. Have you heard that the noise of an explosion can rattle windows and cause dishes to fall off shelves? A high note from a human voice can shatter glass, as shown in the picture. What are some other examples of how sound can move things?

The rapid back-and-forth movement of matter that may produce sound is called **vibration** (vye-BRAY shun). The ruler produced a sound because it vibrated. When you speak, air passing over your vocal cords causes them to vibrate. Look at the instruments on the opposite page. When each instrument produces sound, what vibrates? How could you cause the vibration?

How does sound travel?

Like light, sound travels outward in all directions from its source. For example, suppose you ring a bell in the center of your classroom. Students sitting anywhere in the room can hear the sound of the ringing bell.

Sound is similar to light in another way. Both of these forms of energy travel in waves. You can use a spring toy to make a model of a sound wave. Suppose you squeeze together a group of coils at one end of the spring, as shown in picture *A*. When you let go, a wave moves through the spring. Each of the pictures labeled *B* and *C* shows the spring shortly after the picture above it.

▼ **Wave traveling through a spring**

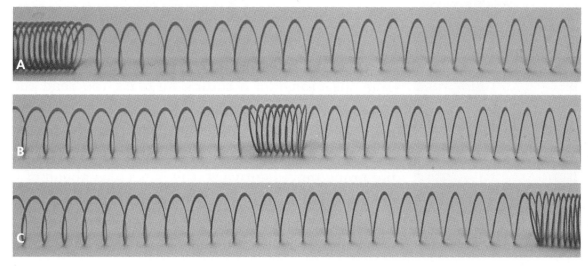

Problem Solving

Off the Record

Before 1877, sound had not been recorded. Then Thomas Edison discovered how to use his voice to start a needle vibrating in the same patterns as sounds from his voice. The needle scratched wavy grooves in tinfoil wrapped around a rotating drum. When the drum was again rotated, the needle moved through the wavy grooves and vibrated in almost the same pattern as before. Thus, the sound of Edison's voice was played back.

How can you get sound from a record without using a record player?

Get a record that no one wants. Use a pencil to spin the record, as shown. What other materials will be useful? Ask a friend to help you carry out your plan.

Vibrating tuning fork ▼

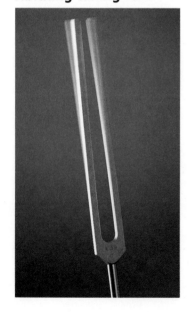

A sound wave moves through matter, such as air, much like a wave moves through a spring. Notice what happens when a tuning fork is struck to make it vibrate. The picture at the left shows how the prongs move back and forth.

The steps describe how a sound wave moves from the prongs of a tuning fork. As you read the steps, look at the numbered drawings on the next page. (1) When the tuning fork is at rest, the fork is surrounded by molecules in the air. (2) As a vibrating prong moves outward, the molecules ahead of it are crowded together. (3) When the prong moves back toward the center, it leaves a region that has fewer molecules than usual.

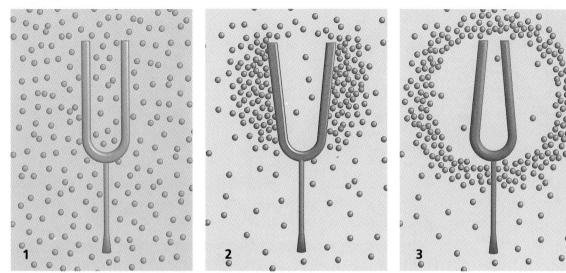

▲ Sound wave moving from tuning fork

The region of a sound wave in which the molecules are crowded together is a **compression** (kum-PRESH un). The region of a sound wave in which particles are spread apart is a **rarefaction** (rer uh-FAK shun). Find these two regions in the drawings.

As the tuning fork vibrates, it causes molecules in the air to move. The molecules bump into other molecules nearby, causing them to move. This process continues from molecule to molecule. The result is a series of compressions and rarefactions that make up sound waves.

Unlike light waves, sound waves do not travel through a vacuum. Recall that a vacuum is a space in which there is no matter. And without matter, there can be no sound waves.

Lesson Review

1. Give an example that shows that sound is a form of energy.
2. How is sound produced?
3. How does sound travel through the air?

Think! How might hearing-impaired people keep perfect time to music from a piano they cannot hear?

Life Science
CONNECTION
Contact an audiologist to find out how a hearing aid works.

compression

rarefaction

2. Sound Waves

Getting Started Cut off one-third of a drinking straw so that you have two straws of different lengths. Squeeze your lips together and blow through each straw. Which straw makes a higher sound and which makes a lower sound? How can you cut another straw to make a sound that is in between these two sounds?

Words to Know
amplitude
pitch

How can you describe a sound wave?

You can see a picture of a sound wave on the screen of a device called an oscilloscope (uh SIHL uh-skohp). Look at the picture and the drawing. Compare the particles with the wavy line in the drawing. The compressions, in which particles are crowded together, appear as upward curves in the line. The rarefactions, in which particles are spread apart, appear as downward curves in the line.

Three characteristics are used to describe a sound wave. These are wavelength, frequency, and amplitude (AM pluh tood). Look at the drawing. As with a light wave, the wavelength of a sound wave is the distance from the crest of one wave to the crest of the next. The frequency is the number of waves that pass a point in each second.

▼ Oscilloscope

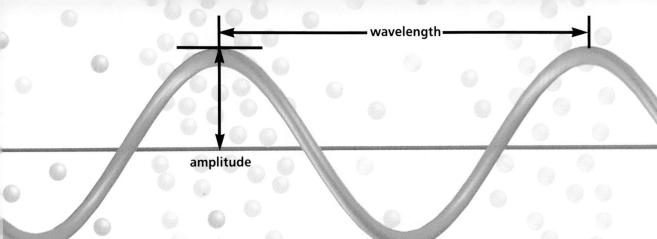

wavelength

amplitude

A third characteristic of a sound wave is its amplitude, indicated by the height of the wave. Look at the drawing. As you will learn, **amplitude** is a measure of the amount of energy in a sound wave.

How are frequency and pitch related?

Pitch is how high or low a sound seems. You can make sounds that differ in pitch by blowing through straws of different lengths. Or you can sing a high note and then a low note. Which of the animals shown produces a high-pitched sound? Which produces a low-pitched sound?

Pitch depends on the frequency of sound waves. Long waves have low frequencies, which produce sounds with a low pitch. Short waves have high frequencies, which produce sounds with a high pitch. Which sound wave shown in the drawings has the higher frequency?

▲ High-frequency sound waves

▼ Low-frequency sound waves

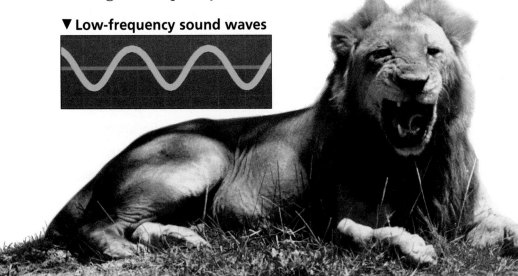

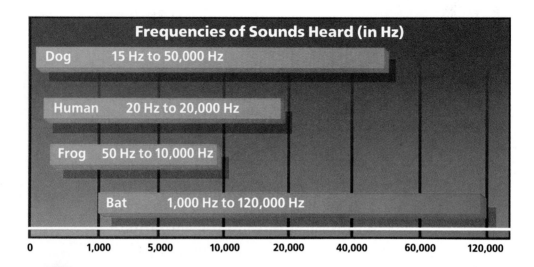

Frequencies of Sounds Heard (in Hz)

Dog	15 Hz to 50,000 Hz
Human	20 Hz to 20,000 Hz
Frog	50 Hz to 10,000 Hz
Bat	1,000 Hz to 120,000 Hz

0	1,000	5,000	10,000	20,000	40,000	60,000	120,000

The frequency of sound is measured in units called hertz (herts). The symbol for hertz is Hz. Sounds have a wide range of frequencies. Most people can hear sounds that have frequencies between about 20 Hz and 20,000 Hz. Which animals listed in the table can hear sounds too high-pitched for most people to hear?

How are amplitude and intensity related?

Sounds differ not only in pitch, but also in loudness. Imagine you are the girl playing the flute in the picture. Why does blowing hard into the flute make a louder sound than blowing lightly? Blowing into the flute harder takes more energy, so the sound waves produced have more energy.

The more energy the sound wave has, the louder the sound seems. The intensity of a sound is the amount of energy it has. You hear intensity as loudness. Recall that the amplitude, or height, of a sound wave is a measure of the amount of energy in the wave. So the greater the intensity of a sound, the greater its amplitude. How can you tell which of the two sound waves shown represents a more intense sound?

▼ Loud

▼ Soft

Explore Together

How can you change the pitch of sound?

ACTIVITY

Organizer

Materials
wide rubber band · scissors · ice-cream stick
rectangular or square plastic container

A

Procedure

Manager
A. Use scissors to cut a wide rubber band into two bands, one wider than the other, as shown in picture *A.*

B. Stretch each band around a rectangular plastic container, as shown in picture *B.*
Pluck the wider band. Using the same amount of force, pluck the other band.

Group, Recorder
1. Describe what you hear when each band is plucked.

Investigator
C. Now place an ice-cream stick between the two bands and the container, as shown in picture *C.*

Group, Recorder
2. Predict what will happen if you pluck each band now. Test your prediction.

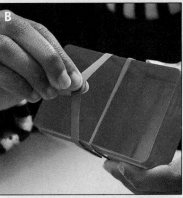
B

Writing and Sharing Results and Conclusions

Group, Recorder
1. What do you hear each time a band is plucked?

2. How are the width and length of a vibrating band related to the pitch of the sound it produces?

Reporter
3. How do your results and conclusions compare with those of your classmates?

C

Loudness (dB)	
140	Low-flying jet plane
120	Riveting machine
110	Loud rock band
80	Vacuum cleaner
60	Talking
10	Breathing

The intensity, or loudness, of sounds is measured in units called decibels (DES uh bulz). The symbol for decibels is dB. The intensity of your voice when you speak is about 60 dB. Sound levels above 140 dB may be painful. Over a period of time, sound levels above 90 dB can damage your hearing. Which sounds listed in the table at the left may be harmful?

How do sounds vary in quality?

Pitch and loudness are two ways that sounds differ. Another way sounds differ is in quality. For example, you hear distinct sounds made by different musical instruments. Imagine the sound of a saxophone and a guitar playing the same note at the same loudness. You can tell which note comes from which instrument by the quality of its sound.

Why do sounds differ in quality? The sound made by each kind of instrument has a different mixture of frequencies. Compare the wave patterns produced by a saxophone and a guitar. Each wave pattern was a different mixture of frequencies. But they have the same pitch because they have the same basic frequency.

▼ Guitar

▼ Saxophone

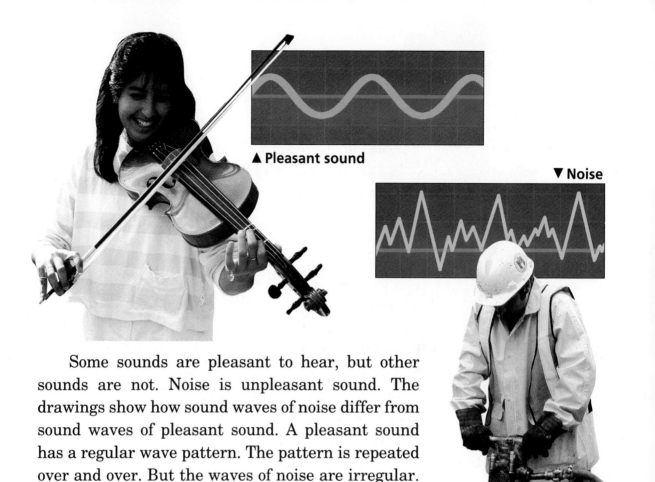

▲ Pleasant sound

▼ Noise

Some sounds are pleasant to hear, but other sounds are not. Noise is unpleasant sound. The drawings show how sound waves of noise differ from sound waves of pleasant sound. A pleasant sound has a regular wave pattern. The pattern is repeated over and over. But the waves of noise are irregular. They do not have a repeated pattern.

Noise pollution is any very loud or unwanted sound and its effects. You have read how loud sounds can damage hearing. Very loud or unwanted sound can also cause illness. Think of some loud sounds or some annoying sounds. What are some ways that noise pollution can be reduced?

Lesson Review

1. Describe three characteristics of a sound wave.
2. How is pitch related to frequency?
3. What is the intensity of a sound? How is intensity related to amplitude?
4. Why does a sound with the same pitch sound different when played by different instruments?

Think! Why do some people who work at airports or on construction sites wear ear protectors?

 *Make music while you learn about pitch and frequency. Try **MUSICSHAPES**!*

◀ String telephone

3. The Behavior of Sound

Getting Started Gently tap the eraser end of a pencil on your desk and listen to the sound it produces. Press your ear to the desk and tap the pencil again with the same amount of force. What have you shown about the behavior of sound?

What happens when sound strikes matter?

Three things may happen when sound strikes matter, depending on the kind of matter. Some of the sound may be transmitted, or passed through the matter. Some of the sound may be absorbed, or trapped, and some of the sound may be reflected, or bounced off. In these ways the behavior of sound is similar to the behavior of light.

What did you notice when you tapped your pencil on your desk? You probably observed that sound travels easily through your desk. It travels through other solids as well. Have your ever used a string telephone like the one in the picture? The cups and the string are also solids that transmit sound better than air does.

308

Use the numbers in the pictures to trace how sound is transmitted. (1) The sound is transmitted from the girl's voice through the air to the first cup. (2) Next, the sound is transmitted through three solids—the first cup, the string, and the second cup. (3) Then the sound is transmitted through the air to the boy's ear. Why might you hear sounds through the string telephone that are too soft to hear through the air alone?

Liquids, such as water, can also transmit sound. Suppose a swimmer standing in shallow water strikes two stones together under the water. Imagine you are another swimmer standing in the water some distance away. If you listen with one ear under the water you can easily hear the sound made by the stones when they are struck.

When sound waves strike solid matter, such as a wall, some of the sound is transmitted. Some of the sound is absorbed. You may hear music from a radio playing in the next room because some of the sound passes through the wall. But the wall absorbs some of the sound. So the sound seems softer than it would if you were in the same room as the radio.

▲ Reflection of sound in Zion National Park, Utah

Not all of the sound that strikes solid matter is transmitted or absorbed—some is reflected. That is, the sound bounces off the solid matter the way a tennis ball bounces off a wall. Sound reflected back to its source is an echo. Have you been in a place where you could hear echoes? Such places often have a large wall or cliff that reflects sound. How could you hear an echo of your voice in the echo valley of Zion National Park, Utah, shown here?

How do different materials affect sound?

Look at the picture of a living room. When sound strikes soft materials, much of the sound is absorbed. A sound insulator (IHN suh layt ur) is a material that absorbs most of the energy of sound waves. Drapes and carpets are good sound insulators. What sound insulators do you see in the picture of the living room on the next page?

Look at the picture of the gymnasium. When sound strikes hard materials, like bare floors, much of the energy is reflected. Hard materials are poor sound insulators because they reflect sound.

Rooms in which much sound is absorbed are usually quieter than rooms where much sound is reflected. Suppose you turn on a radio and place it in the middle of the gymnasium. Then without changing the loudness control, you place the same radio in the middle of the living room. In which room is the radio likely to seem louder, and why?

▼ **Living room**

▼ **Gymnasium**

What is the speed of sound?

The speed of sound depends on the kind of matter through which it travels. The speed of sound is expressed in meters per second. Sound travels through air at about 344 meters per second, which is about 0.2 miles per second. Put another way, sound travels through air about 1 kilometer (0.6 mile) every 3 seconds.

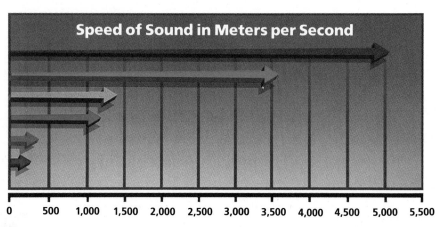

Kind of matter	Speed of Sound in Meters per Second										
iron (solid)											
copper (solid)											
water (liquid)											
alcohol (liquid)											
air (gas)											
carbon dioxide (gas)											
	0	500	1,000	1,500	2,000	2,500	3,000	3,500	4,000	4,500	5,000	5,500

▲ Lightning

Suppose there was an explosion 1 km away from where you are sitting. It would take 3 seconds for the noise to reach your ears. Look at the table above. It gives the speed of sound through different materials. Compare the speed of sound in solids, liquids, and gases. Through which state of matter does sound travel the fastest?

Look at the picture. You may know that lightning causes thunder. Lightning and thunder occur at almost the same time. So why do you usually see a lightning flash before you hear thunder? Light travels so fast that it reaches you almost instantly. Sound travels much more slowly than light. So the light from a lightning bolt can reach you several seconds before the sound of the thunder.

Lesson Review

1. What happens to sounds that are transmitted, absorbed, and reflected?

2. Which makes a better sound insulator, a hard material or a soft material? Explain your answer.

3. In which state of matter does sound travel the fastest? In which state of matter does sound travel the slowest?

Think! Suppose you see a flash of lightning and hear thunder 6 seconds later. About how far away did the lightning strike? Explain your answer.

Earth Science

CONNECTION

Sound pollution can be harmful to your health. Find out what sound pollution is. What can be done to reduce this form of pollution?

Skills

Using what you know and observe to make predictions

Suppose you observe a friend moving a pin close to a balloon. You cover your ears because you know that a pin can cause a balloon to burst with a loud sound. You use what you observe and what you know to predict what will happen.

Practicing the skill

1. Blow across the mouth of an empty test tube. Listen to the sound it makes.

2. Put water in another tube until it is one-fourth full. Then blow across it and listen. Which test tube makes a higher sound?

3. Put water in the empty test tube until it is half full. Predict how it will sound when you blow across it. Write your prediction.

4. Now blow across the half-full test tube.

5. Describe what you heard. Was your prediction correct?

Thinking about the skill

What musical instruments do you know of that use air and tubes to make sounds?

Applying the skill

Set up two test tubes, one empty and one half full of water. Predict which test tube will make the higher sound when tapped gently on top with a spoon. Tap each test tube and listen to the sound. Describe what you heard. Decide if your prediction is correct.

4. Using Sound

▲ Dolphin using echolocation

Words to Know
infrasonic sound
ultrasonic sound
sonar

What is echolocation?

Suppose you shout in a valley with your eyes closed. What would an echo tell you about the land around you? What would the time it takes to hear the echo tell you? This example is somewhat like the way many animals use reflected sound to "see without their eyes." This method is called echolocation (EK oh loh kay shun).

Look at the drawing of a dolphin using echolocation to find food. The dolphin sends out a clicking sound that travels through the water and strikes a school of fish. The sound is reflected off the fish and travels back to the dolphin. If it takes a long time for the sound to return, the dolphin senses that the fish are far away. If it takes a short time, the dolphin senses that the fish are nearby.

What is "silent sound"?

Have you ever heard of "silent sound"? The term refers to frequencies of sound that most people cannot hear. Recall that frequency determines pitch, or how high or low a sound seems. Recall also that people can hear sounds between 20 Hz and 20,000 Hz. Thus, the frequencies of silent sounds are below 20 Hz and above 20,000 Hz.

There are two types of silent sounds. Some have low frequencies and some have high frequencies. Sound with a frequency below 20 Hz is called **infrasonic** (in fruh SAHN ihk) **sound**. Sound with a frequency above 20,000 Hz is called **ultrasonic** (ul-truh SAHN ihk) **sound**. As the table on page 304 shows, some animals hear certain sounds in these regions. Many animals make use of those sounds.

Elephants, for example, communicate with different sounds. These animals make a trumpeting call when angry or faced with danger. This call is sound that people can hear. Elephants also call with infrasonic sounds. Scientists think male elephants use infrasonic sounds to warn other males to stay away. The animals may also use silent sounds to find lost elephant calves.

▲ Sonogram of
unborn baby

How is ultrasonic sound used?

Doctors use ultrasonic sound in many ways. When ultrasonic sound is directed at a person's body, it can make a picture called a sonogram (SAHN-uh gram). The sonogram is made when sound waves are reflected off of the parts of the person's body. This sonogram shows a baby growing inside the mother's body. From a picture like this a doctor can tell if the baby is growing normally.

Doctors also use ultrasonic sound to diagnose and treat illnesses. The waves can help doctors detect heart disorders, tumors, gallstones, and kidney stones. Look at the picture below. When kidney stones are found, a probe may be inserted in the body. Ultrasonic sound given off by the probe breaks up the stones into small pieces, which then pass from the body.

Ultrasonic sound is used in many ways in industry. In the picture at the left, a worker is using ultrasonic sound to find cracks in metal. Ultrasonic sound is also used to weld metal together. The safety of a car or an airplane that you ride in may depend upon such uses of ultrasonic sound.

Finding cracks
in metal ▼

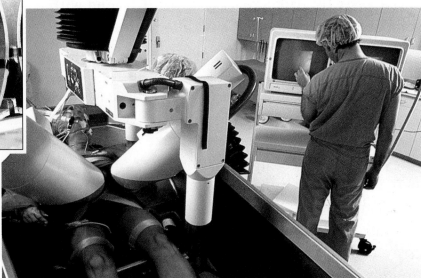

Treating
kidney stones ►

Explore

ACTIVITY

How does a megaphone work?

If you have watched a cheerleader in action, you know what a megaphone can do. A megaphone directs the sound of a voice and makes it louder. So people at a ballgame can hear the cheers from a greater distance than they could otherwise.

Materials
heavy paper · tape · ticking clock · meterstick

Procedure

A. Roll up and tape together a sheet of heavy paper to make a cone, as shown in the picture. Make the opening at the small end large enough to speak into. This cone is a megaphone.

B. Have a friend stand across the room. Point the megaphone toward your friend and whisper into it. Ask your friend to walk toward you until your voice is heard.

C. Put down the megaphone and whisper as before.

1. Predict how close your friend must come before hearing your voice. Test your prediction.

D. Place a ticking clock on a table and stand where you cannot hear it. Hold the megaphone to your ear.

2. How close to the clock must you be to hear it with the megaphone? Use a meterstick to find out.

3. How close must you be to the clock to hear it without the megaphone? Find out.

Writing and Sharing Results and Conclusions

1. What are two ways a megaphone can be used?

2. What behavior of sound allows a megaphone to work?

3. How do your results and conclusions compare with those of your classmates?

Sonar is a method of using ultrasonic sound to locate objects under water. Sonar is used to find schools of fish and to explore shipwrecks. Another use of sonar is to map the ocean floor. A sonar map of the ocean floor is shown.

To see how sonar works, look at the drawing below. Short bursts of ultrasonic sound waves are sent out from a ship. The sound strikes an object under the water. The waves then bounce back to the ship. Scientists can measure the time it takes for the waves to reach the object and be reflected. They can then figure out how far away the object is. Compare sonar with the dolphin's use of echolocation as shown on page 314. How are sonar and echolocation alike, and how are they different?

▼ **Sonar map**

▼ **How sonar works**

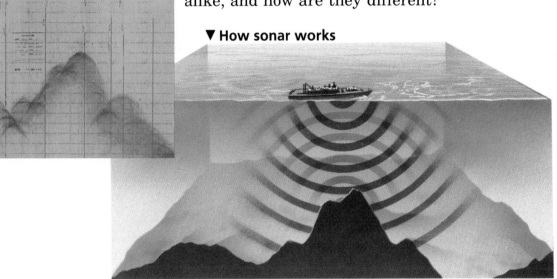

Lesson Review

1. Explain how a dolphin uses sound to find food.
2. What is the difference between infrasonic sound and ultrasonic sound?
3. Name two ways that people use ultrasonic sound.
4. How does sonar locate an underwater object?

Think! Could a synthesizer similar to the one you read about at the beginning of this chapter be used to make silent sounds? Explain your answer.

Chapter 9 Putting It All Together

Chapter Connections

Choose a partner. Explain the information in two of the boxes of the graphic organizer to your partner. Have your partner explain the other two boxes to you.

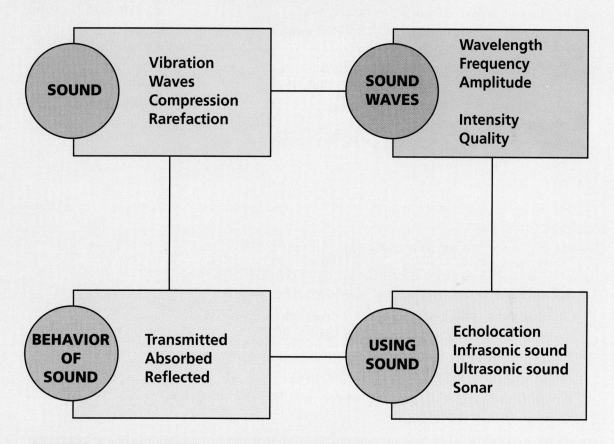

Writing About Science • Classify

Make a chart like the one shown below. Sit quietly at home for 5 minutes. Concentrate on the sounds you hear during that period of time. Fill in the chart as you listen.

SOUND	SOURCE OF SOUND	FREQUENCY (HIGH,LOW)	INTENSITY (LOUD,SOFT)
backfire	car	low	loud

Science Terms

Write the letter of the term that best matches the definition.

1. Rapid back-and-forth movement that may produce sound
2. Region of crowded particles in a wave
3. Region of spread-apart particles in a wave
4. How high or low a sound seems
5. Sound with a frequency below 20 Hz
6. Sound with a frequency above 20,000 Hz
7. The amount of energy carried by a sound wave
8. Method of using ultrasonic sound to locate objects under water

a. amplitude
b. compression
c. infrasonic sound
d. pitch
e. rarefaction
f. sonar
g. ultrasonic sound
h. vibration

Science Ideas

Use complete sentences to answer the following.

1. How does the rattling of windows by the noise of a low-flying plane show that sound is a form of energy?
2. Compare the way a sound wave moves through air with the way a wave moves through a spring toy.
3. Which number in the drawing represents a compression? Which number represents a rarefaction?
4. Which number in the drawing shows amplitude? Which number shows wavelength?

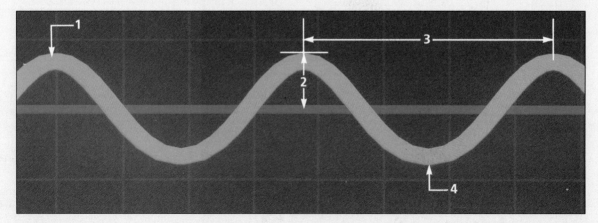

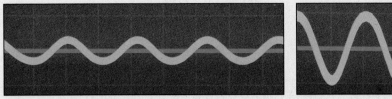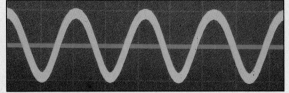

5. In what way are these two sound waves alike? In what way are they unlike?

6. Compare the sound waves of noise with the sound waves of pleasant sound.

7. Why does a note produced by a saxophone differ in quality from the same note produced by a guitar?

8. What is an echo?

9. Compare the speed of sound in water, air, and iron.

10. Which sounds are too high-pitched for people to hear, and which sounds are too low-pitched?

11. Name one medical use and one industrial use of ultrasonic sound.

12. Describe the path of sound waves in sonar. How do scientists use sonar to determine distance?

Applying Science Ideas

1. An office manager wants to reduce noise pollution in the office. What kinds of floor and window coverings would be best to use? Explain your answer.

2. Imagine you are one of two astronauts on the moon. You try to communicate with the other astronaut by tapping on your helmet with a rock. The helmet vibrates, but no sound is made. Why is there no sound outside?

Using Science Skills

Look at the musical instrument shown. Predict which tubes will make the higher sound when hit with the hammer.

Chapter 10

Electrical Energy

AT YOUR SERVICE

Computers for people with all kinds of disabilities are now an actual fact. Some people are unable to use their eyes, hands, or fingers. These people can get information into and out of a computer in other ways. They can do this by moving their head, by speaking words, or even by twitching a muscle.

Special computers for the blind speak the words that are on the screen. Therefore, seeing the screen is not necessary. Some computers for the blind even produce printouts in Braille. People who cannot use their hands are helped by robot arms that lead disks into a computer. Other new computers also help disabled people.

322

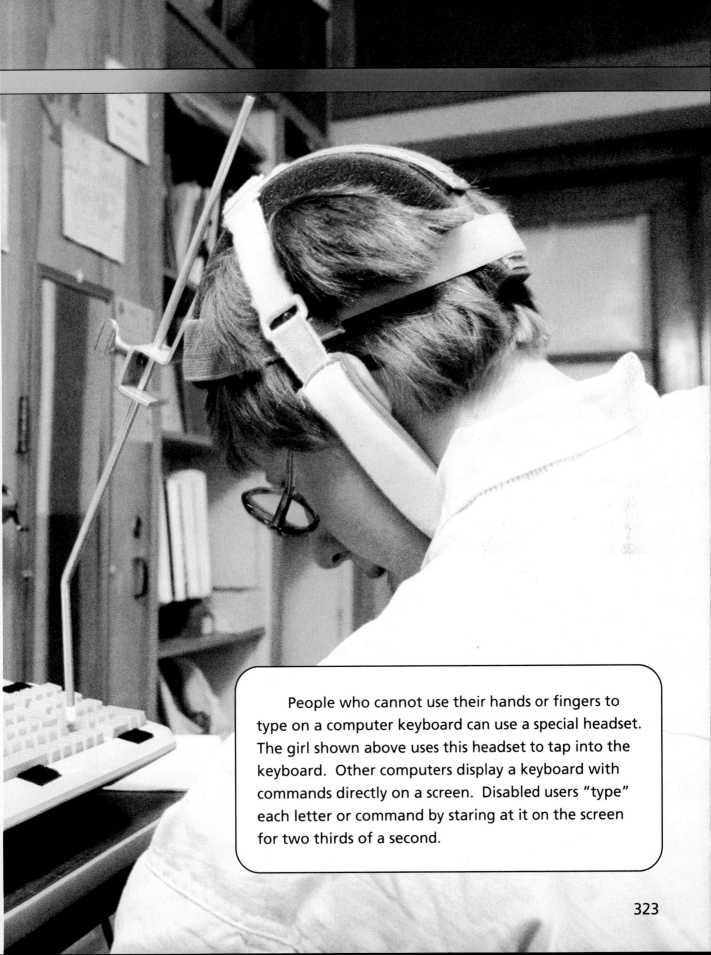

People who cannot use their hands or fingers to type on a computer keyboard can use a special headset. The girl shown above uses this headset to tap into the keyboard. Other computers display a keyboard with commands directly on a screen. Disabled users "type" each letter or command by staring at it on the screen for two thirds of a second.

323

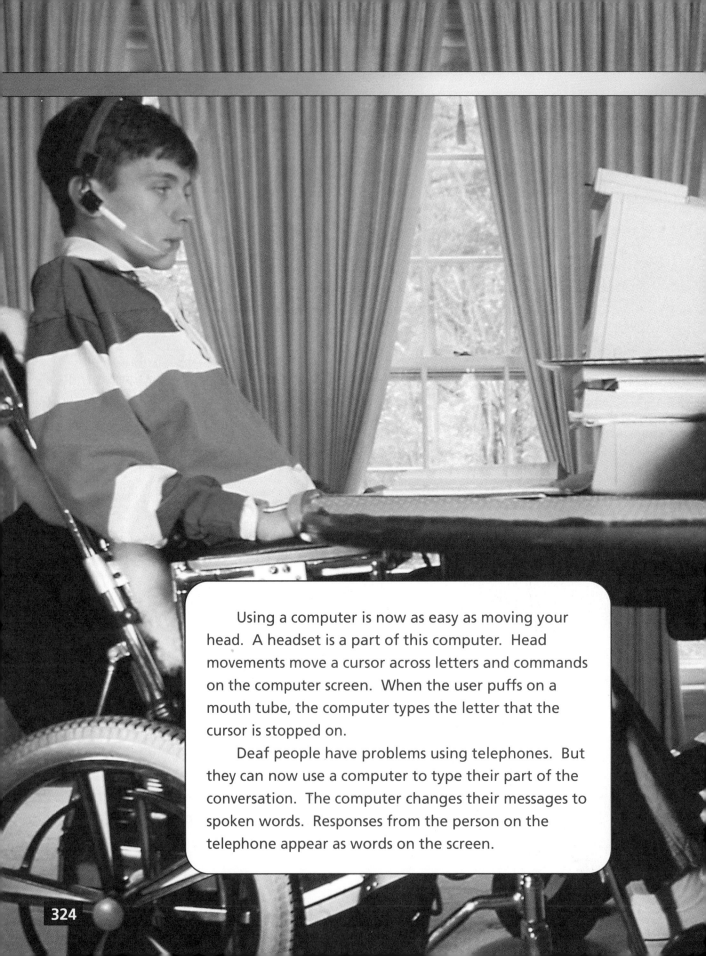

Using a computer is now as easy as moving your head. A headset is a part of this computer. Head movements move a cursor across letters and commands on the computer screen. When the user puffs on a mouth tube, the computer types the letter that the cursor is stopped on.

Deaf people have problems using telephones. But they can now use a computer to type their part of the conversation. The computer changes their messages to spoken words. Responses from the person on the telephone appear as words on the screen.

Discover

How can you change a video game to help a disabled friend?

Materials white construction paper · pencil · markers

Procedure

Make a list of electronic video games that you play. Suppose you have a disabled friend who cannot play your favorite video game. Design an extra feature or change the game so that your friend can play.

In this chapter you will learn more about electricity and electronics. You will learn about amazingly tiny chips that contain the "brains" of computers.

1. Charges and Circuits

Getting Started   Tear off two strips from a roll of clear plastic tape. Make each strip about 8 cm (3 inches) long. Hold one end of each strip. Bring the smooth sides of the two strips toward each other. What happens? How do you explain what happens?

What is static electricity?

People often use the word "electricity" to refer to electrical energy. This form of energy involves the movement of electrons. You know that an atom has a nucleus made of protons and neutrons. A proton has a positive charge, and a neutron has no charge. Electrons move around the nucleus. An electron has a negative charge. How can you tell that the atom shown is neutral?

Electrons often move away from one object and collect on another object. Both objects then have electric charges. A neutral object that loses electrons becomes positive. And a neutral object that gains

▼ **Atom of beryllium**
neutron
electron
proton

extra electrons becomes negative. An electric charge that collects on the surface of an object is called **static electricity.**

The picture at the left shows a plasma sculpture. The surface of the globe has a positive electric charge. The touch of a hand on the sculpture increases the positive charge. As a result, a kind of "red lightning" can be seen in the globe. This is one effect of static electricity.

Look at the picture of tape that has been pulled from a roll. When you tear a strip of tape from a roll, electrons move from the strip to the roll. Since the strip lost electrons, it now has a positive charge. Since the roll gained electrons, it now has a negative charge. Unlike charges attract. Like charges repel, or push away from each other. The two strips of the tape repel because they have like charges. Why would the roll attract a strip of tape pulled from it?

Static electricity is often a nuisance. Clothes rubbing against one another in a dryer may become charged. Why do the clothes shown stick together?

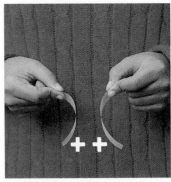

▲ Charged tape

▼ Charged clothes

Static electricity can also be helpful. Machines that produce static electric charges have many uses. One of these uses is in a room air cleaner. Look at the numbered drawings as you read about the air cleaner. (1) Dirty air passes through a filter that removes large dust and dirt particles from the air. (2) The filtered air strikes a wire mesh that gives a positive charge to small particles such as those of smoke and pollen. (3) A grid that has a negative charge attracts the positively charged particles. The particles stick to the grid. (4) The air passes through a carbon filter that absorbs odors from the air. (5) A fan pulls clean air into the room.

▼ **Air cleaner**

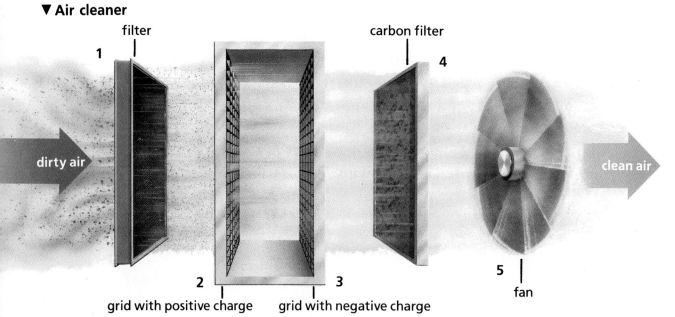

What is an electric current?

Electricity is most useful in an electric current. An **electric current** is a continuous movement of electrons through a conductor. A conductor is a material through which electrons move easily. Metals are good conductors.

As with anything that moves, electrons must be set in motion by some source of energy. You must pedal a bicycle to keep it moving on a rough road. You are the energy source that keeps it moving. Electrons also need a source of energy to keep moving as a current. Sometimes this energy comes from a battery.

Look at the picture of a simple electric circuit (sur kiht). An electric circuit is a complete pathway on which electrons can move. This circuit is made up of a battery, two wires, and a light bulb.

Electrons move continuously throughout the circuit. The electrons move from the negative terminal, or end, of the battery, through the bulb, and back to the positive terminal. Inside the bulb, some of the electrical energy is changed to heat and light.

An electric circuit may be closed or open. When a circuit is closed, it provides a complete, unbroken path for electrons. If the circuit is open, the path is incomplete, or broken. Most circuits in the electric devices you use have switches. Find the switch in the drawing of a circuit in a flashlight. The purpose of a switch is to close or open a circuit. Why do the electrons move through the switch when it is "on," but not when the switch is "off"?

▲ Simple electric circuit

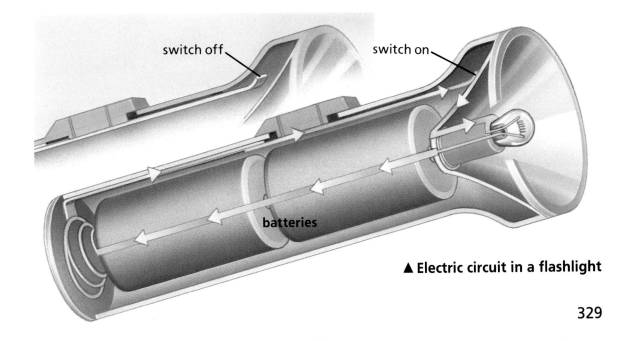

switch off

switch on

batteries

▲ Electric circuit in a flashlight

Explore Together

How does a series circuit compare with a parallel circuit?

Organizer

Materials
safety goggles · 2 size-D batteries in holders, connected as shown · 2 flashlight bulbs in holders · 4 test leads

Procedure
Caution: *Wear safety goggles for this activity.*

Investigator

A. Make a circuit like the one in picture *A*.

Group, Recorder

  1. What do you observe?

  2. Predict what will happen if you unscrew one of the bulbs.

Manager Recorder

B. Unscrew one of the bulbs.

  3. Record what you observe.

Investigator

C. Make a circuit like the one in picture *C*.

Group, Recorder

  4. What do you observe?

  5. Predict what will happen if you unscrew one of the bulbs.

Manager Group, Recorder

D. Unscrew one bulb.

  6. Record what you observe.

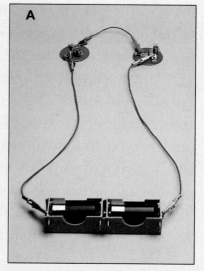

A

Writing and Sharing Results and Conclusions

Group, Recorder

1. Which of the two circuits you made is a series circuit and which is a parallel circuit?

2. How are a series circuit and a parallel circuit alike? How are they different?

Reporter

3. How do your results and conclusions compare with those of your classmates?

C

What are series and parallel circuits?

There are two types of electric circuits. One type is called a series circuit. A **series circuit** is a circuit in which the electrons have only one path on which to move. Picture A shows a series circuit. Suppose one bulb is removed from its socket. Would the other bulb light? Why or why not?

Another type of electric circuit is a parallel circuit. A **parallel circuit** is a circuit in which electrons have more than one path that they can follow. Look at picture B. Trace a path along which electrons can move through the red bulb without going through the green bulb. Now trace a path on which electrons can move through the green bulb without going through the red bulb. Suppose one bulb is removed from its socket. Would the other bulb light? Why or why not?

▲ A   Series circuit

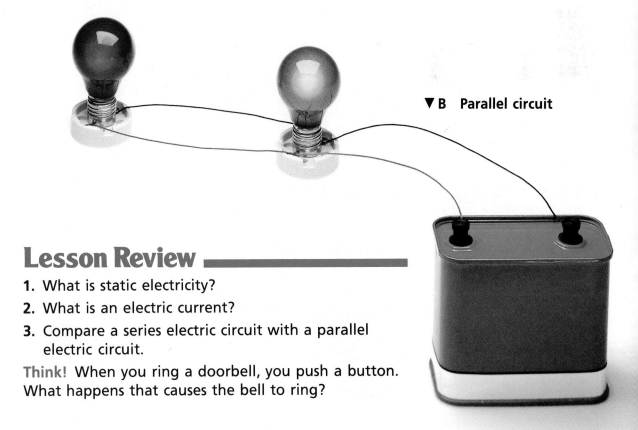

▼ B   Parallel circuit

Lesson Review

1. What is static electricity?
2. What is an electric current?
3. Compare a series electric circuit with a parallel electric circuit.

Think! When you ring a doorbell, you push a button. What happens that causes the bell to ring?

2. Producing Electricity

Words to Know
generator

Getting Started Have you ever heard the saying, "You cannot get something for nothing?" Think about how this saying applies to the electrical energy you use every day. Where does that energy come from?

What is a hydroelectric power plant?

Most of the electrical energy you use comes from power plants. There are several different kinds of power plants. Look at the picture of a hydroelectric (hye droh ee LEK trihk) power plant. *Hydro* means "water." Towers carry wires off into the distance. These wires may supply electrical energy to homes that are far from the power plant. Where does the

▼ Hydroelectric power plant

dam

falling water

energy in these wires come from? It comes from the energy stored in water behind a dam like the one in the picture.

The water behind the dam has stored energy because of its position. As falling water flows through the dam, the potential energy of the water changes into kinetic energy.

Now look at the drawing. In a hydroelectric power plant, water moves through turbines (TUR-bihnz). A turbine is a kind of wheel with blades, as shown. The moving water strikes the blades, causing the turbines to spin. As the turbines spin, they turn coils of wire in a generator (JEN ur ayt-ur). A **generator** is a machine that changes mechanical energy into electrical energy.

How does a generator work? Look at the drawing of a model generator. Find the coil of wire and the magnet. Lines of force make up the magnetic field that surrounds the magnet. When the wire coil turns, it cuts across the lines of force, causing electrons to move through the wire. In a real generator, many coils of wire turn in a magnetic field. The mechanical energy of spinning turbines is thus changed into electrical energy.

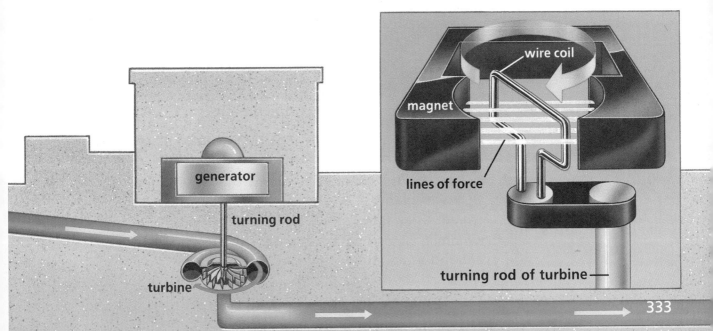

generator

turning rod

turbine

wire coil

magnet

lines of force

turning rod of turbine

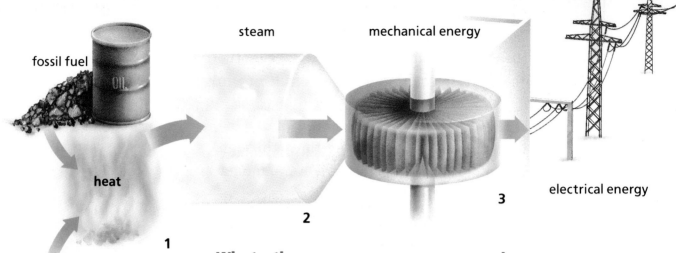

steam   mechanical energy

fossil fuel

heat

electrical energy

3

2

1

nuclear fuel

▲ **Energy changes in nuclear and fossil fuel power plants**

What other energy sources are used in power plants?

In some power plants, the energy in a fossil fuel or a nuclear fuel is changed into electrical energy. Coal, oil, and natural gas are fossil fuels. As the fossil fuel burns, its chemical energy changes into heat. When atoms of a nuclear fuel such as uranium are split, nuclear energy is released as heat.

Look at the numbers in the drawing as you read about the energy changes in fossil fuel and nuclear power plants. (1) Either chemical or nuclear energy is changed into heat. This heat is used to change water to steam. (2) The energy of moving steam is used to turn the turbines connected to a generator. (3) As in a hydroelectric plant, the energy of the spinning turbines is changed into electrical energy. But steam, not falling water, turns the turbines.

Lesson Review

1. What is an electric generator?
2. Describe the changes in energy that take place in a hydroelectric power plant.
3. Describe the changes in energy that take place in power plants that have steam turbines.

Think! Some homes have generators that use a windmill. Name one advantage and one disadvantage of wind as an energy source.

Earth Science
CONNECTION

Find out why coal, oil, and natural gas are called fossil fuels.

Skills

Defining terms based on observations

By observing a process or a thing, you can write an operational definition for it. An operational definition is a definition that is based on your observations of what something is or does. On page 327, *static electricity* is defined as "an electric charge that collects on the surface of an object." One operational definition of *static electricity* might be "the force that makes two strips of tape repel each other after they have been torn from a roll."

Practicing the skill

1. Observe the pictures of the flashlight, the fan, and the hair dryer. Each of these three devices has a switch.

2. Think about what happens to each of these devices when you move the switch to the "on" and "off" positions. For each device, write a different operational definition for the term *switch.*

  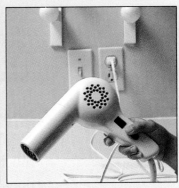

Thinking about the skill

Suppose you are told to turn on a switch. You do not know what the word *switch* means. Look up *switch* in the dictionary. Compare the definition you find with the operational definition. Which definition would be more useful to you?

Applying the skill

You know that many electrical devices have a plug. Think about what a plug does. Write an operational definition for *plug* that tells what it does.

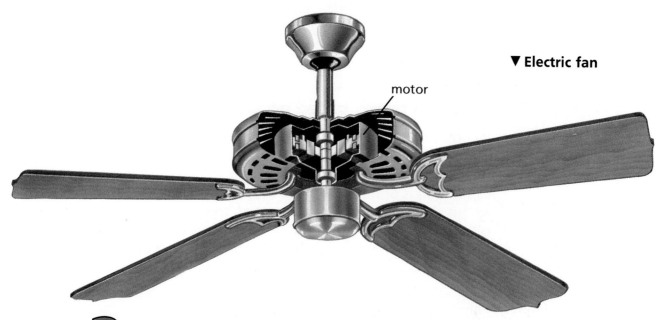

motor

3. Using Electrical Energy

Getting Started When you use electrical energy, it is nearly always changed to some other form of energy. Make a list of some electric devices you use. What energy changes take place in each device on your list?

How is energy changed in motors?

▼ Electromagnet

In a motor, electrical energy is changed to mechanical energy. Find the motor in this fan. How does a motor work? You know that in a generator a magnet produces an electric current. But the opposite can also happen—an electric current produces a magnetic field. Whenever electrons move through a coil of wire, the wire itself becomes a magnet. This kind of magnet is called an electromagnet (ee LEK troh mag niht). Perhaps you have made an electromagnet from wire coiled around an iron nail, like the one shown.

Remember that every magnet has a north pole and a south pole. The north poles of magnets repel one another. So do the south poles. But the north pole of one magnet attracts the south pole of another. This behavior of magnets is used in a motor.

Look at the numbered drawings as you read about a model motor. The model shows just one loop of the wire coil of an electromagnet. (1) A permanent, or fixed, magnet is placed around the coil. The north pole of the fixed magnet attracts the south pole of the coil, causing the coil to turn. (2) The north pole of the coil becomes lined up with the south pole of the fixed magnet. (3) At this moment, a device attached to the coil changes the direction of the current in the coil. This change reverses the poles of the coil. Now the two like poles of each magnet are near each other. They repel, so the coil turns again. The direction of the current changes after each half turn. So the coil keeps turning. In this way, electrical energy is changed to mechanical energy.

In a real motor, there are several spinning electromagnets. These can be attached to a rod that is made to spin. This rod may turn a gear or a wheel. Look again at the fan. What part of the fan turns when the rod spins?

▼ **Simple electric motor**

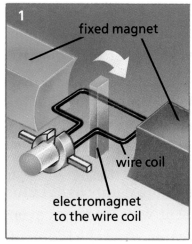

fixed magnet

wire coil

electromagnet to the wire coil

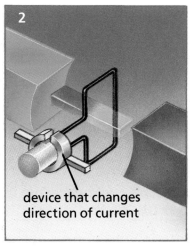

device that changes direction of current

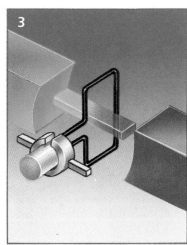

How is energy changed in heaters and light bulbs?

Electrons move through some conductors more easily than through others. Materials that slow down or stop the movement of electrons are said to have resistance (rih ZIHS tuns). Whenever electrons move through a conductor, some of the electrical energy is changed to heat. The amount of heat produced depends on the resistance of the conductor. The greater the resistance of the conductor, the greater the amount of heat produced.

▼ Heater

▼ Copper wire

▼ Nichrome wire

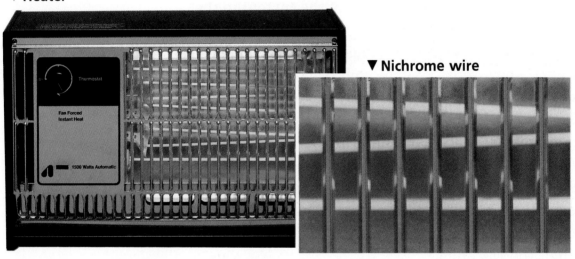

Look at the picture of an electric heater. The wires of this heater are made of a metal called nichrome (NYE krohm). Nichrome is a conductor that has high resistance. Because nichrome has high resistance, the coils get very hot when electric current passes through them. But notice that the wires of the cord are made of copper. The metal copper is a conductor that has low resistance. Why is the wire in the cord made of copper instead of nichrome?

In an incandescent (ihn kun DES unt) light bulb, the filament, (FIHL uh munt) or wire, becomes even hotter than the coils of the heater. Find the filament in the drawing. The filament is a long, thin piece of wire made of tungsten (TUNG stun). The metal tungsten is a conductor that has high resistance. Long, thin conductors also have high resistance.

The filament is twisted so that the long wire will fit in a small space inside the bulb. The resistance of the wire is very high. When electrons move through the wire, this high resistance causes much of the electrical energy to change to heat. The wire gets so hot, some radiant energy is produced as light. The wire glows white-hot.

The hot bulb of an incandescent lamp can give you a bad burn if you touch it. But you can touch a fluorescent (floo uh RES unt) bulb without being burned. Why does a fluorescent bulb stay cool? A fluorescent bulb produces very little heat. Most of the electrical energy in the bulb is changed to light. Look at the drawing. The bulb is a glass tube filled with mercury gas. As electric current passes through the tube, electrons bump into the mercury atoms. The mercury atoms gain energy. They lose this energy by giving off radiant energy in the form of ultraviolet waves. The waves strike the inside coating of the tube and cause it to glow.

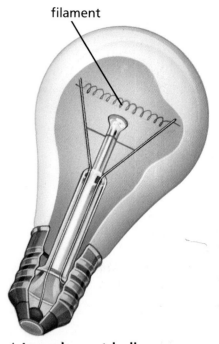

filament

▲ **Incandescent bulb**

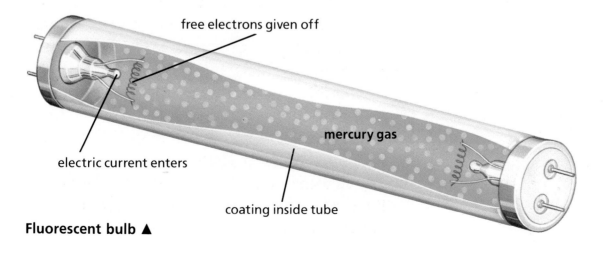

free electrons given off

mercury gas

electric current enters

coating inside tube

Fluorescent bulb ▲

What are fuses and circuit breakers?

Why is it dangerous to use a lamp cord in which the insulation, or covering, is worn off? A person might touch the bare wires and get an electric shock. Another danger is that the two wires in the cord might touch each other. If the wires do touch each other, the current can go directly from one wire to the other, without passing through the lamp. This path for the current is called a short circuit.

A short circuit has very low resistance. Because of the low resistance, a large amount of current can move through a short circuit. Another cause of too much current in a circuit is connecting too many electric devices to one outlet. A short circuit can cause great amounts of heat, which may start a fire.

Circuit breakers and fuses protect buildings against fire. A circuit breaker, as shown, has a switch. The switch opens if there is too much current in a circuit. A fuse has a metal strip that melts and breaks, or "blows," if a circuit becomes too hot. Find the metal strip in the pictures of the fuses. Why does the current stop when a circuit breaks?

▼ Good fuse

▼ "Blown" fuse

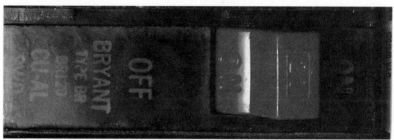

▲ Circuit breaker closed   ▼ Circuit breaker open

How can you make a model of a fuse?

The electric circuits in some homes are not the only ones that have fuses. Electric circuits in televisions and other appliances also have fuses. So do electric circuits in cars, buses, and trains. All fuses help make electricity safe. Think of how many ways you depend on fuses for your safety!

Materials

safety goggles · steel wool · petri dish · 2 lumps of modeling clay · 2 test leads · 6-volt battery

Procedure

Caution: *Wear safety goggles for this activity.*

A. Pull three 4-cm strands of wire from the steel wool. Twist the strands together. The twisted strands of steel wool will be the fuse in the circuit you will make.

B. Make a circuit like the one in the picture. Stick two test leads into two lumps of clay set in a petri dish. Attach the steel wool to the clips of the test leads. Do not connect the clip to the negative terminal of the battery.

C. Close the circuit by attaching the test lead to the negative terminal. Wait 3 or 4 seconds.

1. What happens?

2. After 3 or 4 seconds, is the circuit open or closed? Explain your answer.

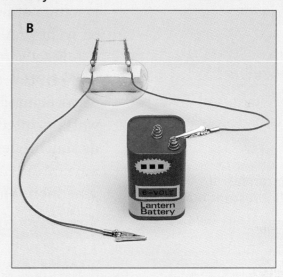

B

Writing and Sharing Results and Conclusions

1. How are your model and a fuse in an electric device alike? How are they different?

2. How do your results and conclusions compare with those of your classmates?

How is electrical energy measured?

Each day great amounts of electrical energy are used in homes, schools, offices, and factories. You use a certain amount of electrical energy when you watch television for an hour. You use a different amount of electrical energy when you read for an hour by the light of a lamp.

Did anyone ever tell you to turn off a light? Someone must pay for all the energy you use. But before you can pay for it, the amount you use has to be measured. This person is reading a meter that measures the amount of electrical energy used.

You know that electrical energy is used to do work. The amount of work that is done in a certain period of time is called power. Small amounts of electric power are measured in watts. Large amounts of power are measured in kilowatts (KIHL-oh wahts). A kilowatt is 1,000 watts.

Electric devices have the number of watts they use printed on them. A light bulb may have 100 watts printed on it, and a small motor may have 200 watts printed on it. The 200-watt motor uses twice as much energy as the 100-watt bulb in the same amount of time. Which of the bulbs in the picture uses more energy in the same amount of time?

▲ Reading an electric meter

Incandescent and fluorescent bulbs ▼

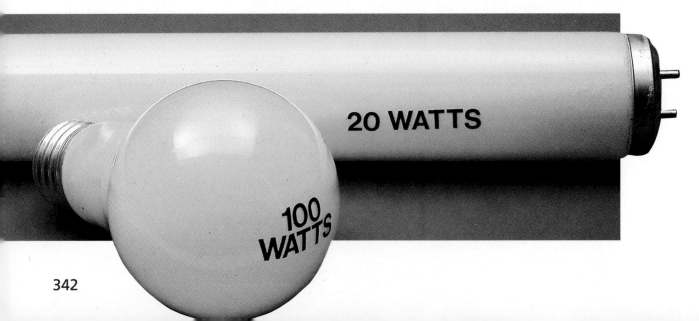

20 WATTS

100 WATTS

Electric companies measure how much electrical energy a customer uses in kilowatt-hours. A **kilowatt-hour** is a unit equal to 1,000 watts of electrical energy used for 1 hour. So a 200-watt motor runs for 5 hours before it uses a kilowatt-hour of energy. Look again at the bulbs in the picture. Use a calculator to find how long each one can operate before it uses a kilowatt-hour of energy.

In a building an instrument called a meter measures the amount of electrical energy used. Do you know where the meter is at your home? The meter shows how many kilowatt-hours of energy have been used in your home. Each kilowatt-hour costs a certain amount of money. Look at the picture of an electric bill. How many kilowatt-hours of energy were used during the month?

```
THIS IS YOUR CURRENT BILL CALCULATION

CUSTOMER CHARGE                      $        4.57
ENERGY CHARGE      937 KWH @ $.09750         91.36
ENERGY ADJ CHG     937 KWH @ $.008542-        8.00CR
CURRENT PERIOD CHARGES               $       87.93
09/28/89 TO 10/27/89
   FOR  29 DAYS


           METER                 METER READING
           NUMBER                CURRENT
```

◀ Electric bill

Lesson Review

1. What energy change takes place in a motor?
2. What energy changes take place in electric heaters and light bulbs?
3. How do fuses and circuit breakers work?
4. What is a kilowatt-hour?

Think! Is the part of a toaster that produces heat made of a material with high resistance or low resistance? Explain your answer.

Life Science
CONNECTION

Some doctors use electricity to heal bones. Use reference books to find out about this use of electricity.

▲ Electronic devices

4. Circuits on Chips

Getting Started What is 3,579 × 467? Time yourself as you solve this problem two ways. Solve it first with pencil and paper. Then solve it with an electronic (ee lek TROHN ihk) calculator. Compare the times. What makes the calculator so fast? Its "brain" is a kind of computer chip, as you will learn.

Words to Know
integrated
  circuit
microprocessor

What kind of circuits are found on chips?

You know that electrical energy can be changed to mechanical energy, heat, and light. Electrical energy can also be used to carry data, or information. Numbers, words, sounds, and pictures are all data. Devices that use electrical energy to carry data are commonly called electronic devices.

A computer and a calculator are two kinds of electronic devices. All the things in the picture are also electronic. Which of these things have you used?

344

You have learned about series and parallel circuits. In both these kinds of circuits, the parts are connected by wires. A different kind of circuit, called an integrated (IHN tuh grayt ihd) circuit, is found in electronic devices. An **integrated circuit** is a circuit in which all the parts and connections are on a tiny chip. A chip is a thin slice of silicon.

An integrated circuit on a chip is smaller than a fingernail. Yet the circuit contains thousands of electronic parts and their connections. How can so many parts be made so small? First, a drawing of the integrated circuit is made, as shown. Then the drawing is reduced, or made smaller, by photography. This chip is shown at its actual size.

Did you solve the math problem at the start of this section? Why does the calculator work so fast? The integrated circuit on the chip has a huge number of parts. Also, electrons travel very short distances through the tiny chip. So the chip can carry out thousands of math operations in a second.

▼ **Chip on a paper clip**

▼ **Drawing of integrated circuit**

How does a computer work?

Like calculators, computers have chips that work with numbers. Computer chips can also work with words and other data. Such chips are called microprocessors (mye kroh PRAHS es urz). A **microprocessor** is a computer on a chip.

Computers have parts called hardware and software. The physical parts of a computer system are hardware. A microprocessor, sometimes called the central processing unit (CPU), is hardware. Chips that store information, called memory chips, are hardware. So are input units, such as disk drives, keyboards, and joysticks. Output units, such as monitors and printers, are also hardware.

Programs, or instructions that tell a computer what to do, are software. Many different programs can be run on most computers. You may run some software to play games and other software to do schoolwork. The usefulness of all computers depends on software designed to do certain jobs.

▼ 1 Input units

joystick

disk drive

program on disk

mouse

keyboard

What happens when you run a program on a computer? Refer to the numbered pictures on these pages as you read on.

1. You load, or enter, a program in an input unit called a disk drive. The program is stored in the memory chips of the computer. You then use one or more input units to tell the computer what to do. You may use the keyboard to give commands or to write. You may use a mouse to give commands. You may use a joystick to play a game.

2. The program is a set of instructions for the CPU. As you use the imput units to tell the computer what to do, the CPU follows the instructions of the computer program stored in the memory chips.

3. The result of the work, or output, appears as words or pictures. You can see the output on the monitor, or screen. A printer may print the output on paper. Output may also be stored on memory disks inside or outside the computer.

▼ 2   Processing

CPU

▼ 3   Output units

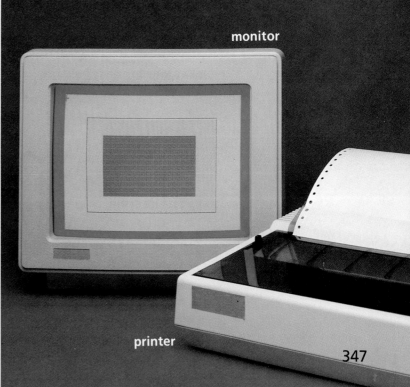

monitor

printer

Problem Solving
The Right Connection

A light-emitting diode (DYE ohd), called an LED, is a part found in electronic circuits. You have probably seen a colored light on a computer disk drive. This light is given off by an LED in a circuit in the computer.

How is an LED in a circuit different from a flashlight bulb?

First make a circuit with a flashlight bulb in it. What materials will you need? Then make circuits that include the diode. How many ways can the diode be connected as part of a circuit? How are different circuits that have the diode in them different? What do you think the use of the diode is in a circuit?

New uses for computers are being invented all the time. You may soon be able to speak into a computer and it will instantly type out what you have said. You may use a computer to translate Japanese into English, quickly. What are some other new ways home computers may be used?

Lesson Review

1. What is an integrated circuit?
2. What is a microprocessor?
3. Describe three steps of running a computer program.

Think! At the beginning of this chapter you read about computers that help disabled people. What special kinds of input units and output units do each of these computers have?

Chapter Connections

Draw the shapes of the graphic organizer on a sheet of paper. Then try to fill them in without looking at your textbook.

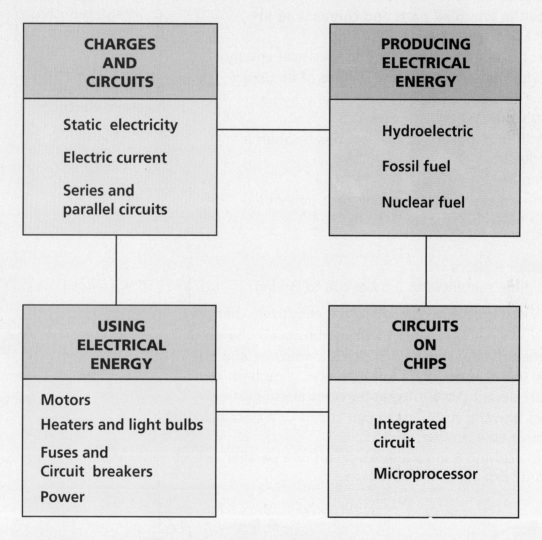

CHARGES AND CIRCUITS

Static electricity

Electric current

Series and parallel circuits

PRODUCING ELECTRICAL ENERGY

Hydroelectric

Fossil fuel

Nuclear fuel

USING ELECTRICAL ENERGY

Motors

Heaters and light bulbs

Fuses and Circuit breakers

Power

CIRCUITS ON CHIPS

Integrated circuit

Microprocessor

Writing About Science • Inform

Think about how you got ready for school this morning. Write a paragraph about getting ready for school a morning when the power was out. How would your morning routine be different without electrical energy?

Science Terms
Write the letter of the term that best matches the definition.

1. Circuit in which the electrons have more than one path on which to move
2. Circuit in which all parts and connections are contained on a chip
3. Changes energy of motion into electrical energy
4. Charge that collects on the surface of an object
5. Equal to 1,000 watts of electrical energy used for 1 hour
6. Continuous movement of electrons through a conductor
7. Computer on a chip
8. Circuit in which the electrons have only one path on which to move

a. electric current
b. generator
c. integrated circuit
d. kilowatt-hour
e. microprocessor
f. parallel circuit
g. series circuit
h. static electricity

Science Ideas
Use complete sentences to answer the following.

1. How can a neutral object become negatively charged?
2. How can a neutral object become positively charged?
3. Name one way static electricity is a nuisance and one way that it is useful.
4. In an electric current, what particles are in motion?
5. Does drawing *A* show an open circuit or a closed circuit? Explain your answer.
6. Does drawing *B* show a series circuit or a parallel circuit? Explain your answer.

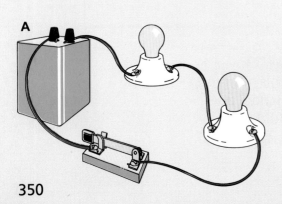

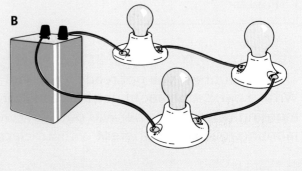

7. What energy change takes place in an electric generator?

8. What turns the turbine in a hydroelectric power plant, and what turns the turbine in a fossil-fuel or nuclear power plant?

9. How does energy change in an electric hot plate that glows red when it is hot?

10. What are two reasons that a fuse may "blow" or the switch of a circuit breaker may open?

11. In what units do electric companies measure how much electrical energy a person uses?

12. What name is given to devices that use electrical energy to carry data?

13. What kind of circuit contains thousands of electronic parts and connnections on a chip?

14. Chips found in calculators and home computers can calculate, solve problems, and do other jobs. What are these chips called?

Applying Science Ideas

1. Suppose the charge for 1 kilowatt-hour of electrical energy is $0.58. Use a calculator to find how much it would cost a homeowner to operate a 200-watt bulb for 50 hours. Explain your answer.

2. In what way is a computer like a human brain? How is it different?

Using Science Skills

Suppose a casserole is placed in a microwave oven, which is then turned on. When a toaster plugged into the same outlet as the oven is turned on, both the oven and the toaster stop working. An adult helps you find that the circuit breaker has opened. Use this information to write an operational definition of *circuit breaker*.

Careers in Physical Science

Radiological Technician

Sarah King was in a car accident at the age of 14. That is when she had her first X-ray. Now she X-rays other people.

Sarah is a **radiological technician** (ray de uh LAHJ ih kul   tek NIHSH un). She works at a medical center in Bethlehem, Pennsylvania. Her job begins when a doctor requests an X-ray for a patient. Perhaps a child has flipped over on a bicycle or has fallen from a tree. Sarah takes X-ray images to find out if there are broken bones.

Sometimes she X-rays babies who have trouble breathing. The X-ray is used by doctors to find blocked air passages. X-rays can also detect foreign objects in the body. Little children sometimes do something very dangerous. They swallow tiny objects. "Once a child had swallowed a safety pin," says Sarah. "I took an X-ray that showed doctors just where it was."

When Sarah gets ready to X-ray a patient, she must first make sure the patient is in the right position. That is so the X-ray will come out clear. Sarah must cover the parts of the patient's body that are not being X-rayed with a lead apron. X-rays cannot pass through lead. The lead apron prevents unnecessary exposure to radiation.

Sarah must protect her own body, too. She stands behind a lead shield as she operates the X-ray machine. She also wears a badge that monitors her monthly exposure to radiation.

X-ray images are an important tool for doctors who diagnose illnesses. But, since radiation is used, the machines must be handled with care. Sarah had to be 18 to get her job. She also needed a high school diploma. Then she took a special training course to get a radiographic technician's license.

"It's an interesting job," Sarah says. "I like working with people and knowing that I'm doing something important."

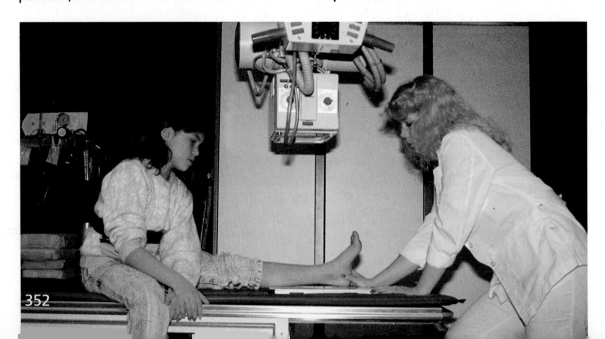

Connecting Science Ideas

1. The radiological technician you read about follows important safety precautions to prevent overexposure to X-rays. Name some other dangerous forms of energy waves and the workers who should be protected from them.
   Careers; Chapter 7; Chapter 8

2. Is the formation of table salt from its elements a physical change or a chemical change? Explain your answer.
   Chapter 6; Chapter 7

3. Is carbon monoxide a hydrocarbon? Is carbon monoxide formed by a chemical change or a nuclear change? Explain your answers. **Chapter 6; Chapter 7**

4. How are the color of light and the pitch of sound similar? **Chapter 8; Chapter 9**

5. On pages 260–263 you read about a kind of light that can be seen by visually impaired people. On pages 294–297 you learned about the use of sound effects. Imagine that you are planning a puppet show for visually impaired children. How could you use light and sound to help your audience enjoy the show more? **Chapter 8; Chapter 9**

6. The term *electron* has been used several times in this unit. How are electrons part of the discussion of atoms, the formation of ions, and electrical energy? **Chapter 6; Chapter 10**

Unit Project

Construct an electric quiz board for other students to try. On a large sheet of paper, make a list of questions next to a list of answers which are out of order. Mount this paper onto pegboard. Push a brass fastener through the pegboard next to each question and answer. Turn over your board and plan parallel circuits that will light a bulb when someone touches wires that connect a question and its answer. Use a D-cell battery to provide power for your circuits.

from

THE
GREEN
BOOK

Written by Jill Paton Walsh

Illustrated by Lloyd Bloom

Properties of matter on Earth are known. But would they be the same on another planet? In this science fiction story, a young girl tells about a group of people who survive a disaster that leaves Earth dying. They travel to another planet where rain falls from a cloudless sky, grass breaks like glass, and trees are as tough as metal. Join these pioneers as they try to survive in their new home.

The Guide said they must set a guard over the camp all night. "Any kind of living thing, harmless or savage, may be here," he said. The wilderness seemed so beautiful and so still it was hard to believe that, but they chose five of the men to take turns on watch.

And only just in time, for soon after the watch was chosen, the night came upon us. A curtain of deep lilac light swept across the lake, obscuring the sight of the mountain, and sinking almost at once to a deepening purple, then inky darkness. It got dark much quicker than it would have done on Earth—in less than half an hour. The darkness was complete for a moment or two; and then as our eyes got used to it, it was pierced by hundreds of bright and unknown stars— nameless constellations shining overhead. People began to

spread their bedding in the tents, and to settle to sleep, and as they did so, a gust of air shook the tent walls, and there was a sighing sound of wind in the woods, and a lapping of water on the shore close by, unseen in the dark. And then the air was quite still again, and it began to rain, heavily and steadily, though the stars were still bright and clear above. When Pattie fell asleep, she could hear Father and Malcolm talking together in low voices at the other end of the tent.

"There must be no dust at all in this atmosphere," said Malcolm. "That would scatter light and delay the dark. No wonder it feels so invigorating to breathe."

Father took his turn on watch, but nothing stirred all night, he said. The rain stopped in an hour or so, and not so

356   Science in Literature

much as a gust of air moved anywhere around. At the sudden return of daylight, all was well.

The next day the land hopper was fitted out. It "was a small craft that could carry four men and a scanning viewer to make tapes for the computer in the spaceship. It could hover about forty feet up and glide over water and dry land. It was going to explore the whole planet, looking above all for any sign of life, any possible enemy creature. It had a navigation program built in, sensitive to the planet's own gravity. A lot of people wanted to go on the trip, and the Guide had to choose the crew like a raffle, pulling names out of a bag. Father stayed. The people who stayed would have to look for materials to build houses. Tents would not do forever.

Of course, we went first to the woods, to cut down trees. A party of grownups went, carrying saws and axes, and the children went with them to watch. The light in the wood was all ruby-red and crimson where the sun struck down through the red leaves overhead. The trees wouldn't be cut down. The saw blades were blunted as soon as they cut through the soft gray bark. The trees were far harder than wood on Earth. Arthur suggested trying a hacksaw, and that did better, bringing out of the cut in the tree trunk a fine silver dust like metal filings. The work went very slowly and was very boring to watch; after they had been working an hour, the cut was only an inch or so deep.

Father began walking around the wood, looking for twigs on the ground. When he found some, he broke them and held the broken ends to the light. He showed Arthur and Joe what he saw.

"Look, this stuff has a different structure from wood. It's made of lots of little rods joined together. It's very hard to saw, but I guess it will be easy to split."

"I hope you're right," said Arthur. "It will take ten years to build a single house if we have to saw planks and it takes as long as this!"

"And how long would it take to plane and shape wood for window frames and furniture?" asked Jason's father.

"Children, go and gather up as many of these twigs as you can carry, and take them down to the beach," Father said. "We don't even know if this wood will burn yet, and if it doesn't burn, we will have to find something else for fuel." So the men took turns at the hacksaw, and the children gathered twigs all morning.

Father was right about the splitting. The tree trunk that had taken so long to cut through across the grain split easily and straight along its length when wedges were banged in at one end with a hammer.

"We could use them just like this," said Arthur. "Round sections outward, flat edges in, like log cabins."

"As for windows," said Father, "I doubt if we'll need them"—for the sunlight was striking through the pale stuff of the split log as though it were frosted glass. A little more trial and error showed that nails were useless. Even the best ones turned their points at once on the tree trunk, but it was very easy to drill, and screws would hold well in it.

Meanwhile, on the beach, Joe set light to the pile of twigs the children had carried from the wood, and discovered at once that the trees would burn. The twigs caught fire easily and blazed brilliantly with a bright blue flame, so hot and fast-burning that the fire had to be dampened with sand before the meal could be cooked on it. "We shall need to be careful making huts out of this, " said Malcolm. "We shall need stone chimneys and hearths, I think."

When we had eaten, and brewed a can of coffee on the fierce little bonfire, we quenched it with water, and then the children found in the ashes curious shiny lumps of molten stuff, too hot to hold, and streaked in green and blue and orange, which had formed on the sand where the fire had blazed. A conference was going on among the grownups.

Cutting trees was going to be a terrible labor, and would soon blunt all the blades we had. They had tried axes instead of saws, but though the axes would split the tree easily, they just bounced off the side of the trunks.

Father looked thoughtfully at the fused lumps in the dead fire. "What if we tried fire?" he asked. "Perhaps heat would soften the stuff."

"We'd have to be very careful," said Malcolm. "It does burn very easily, and we don't want to start a forest fire."

So when they had eaten, the work party returned to the forest edge, and looked for a tree standing apart from its neighbors. A can of fuel was fetched from the supplies, and poured slowly and carefully in a ring around the foot of the tree. The grownups brought buckets of sand from the lake shore, to muffle the fire if it got out of hand. Then they lit the ring of kindling around the base of the tree. The flames roared up the tree, burning the bark off very fast, to the very top, and running along the branches to their tips. At the bottom, where the trunk was ringed with fire, a soft red glow began to show on the bare translucent trunk. Then, using the longest saw blade they had, so that they could stand back clear of the fire, the men began to saw through the red-hot band of the tree trunk—and the wood cut like butter, smoothly and easily. The tree toppled and fell, crashing through the outermost branches of neighboring trees, and thudding on the ground in a shower of torn twigs and leaves. Everyone cheered and shouted.

Reader's Response
Would you like to be a member of this group of space pioneers? Explain why or why not.

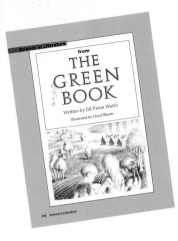

Selection Follow-up

THE
GREEN
BOOK

 Responding to Literature

1. How is the new planet similar to Earth? How is it different?

2. Explain the differences between trees on Earth and trees on the new planet.

3. Do you think the group could have survived if its members had not worked together? Discuss your answer with classmates.

4. If you were going to leave Earth to live on a new planet, what would you take with you to help you survive?

5. Pretend that you are a member of the group. Write a journal entry that tells how you feel about living on the new planet.

 Books to Enjoy

The Green Book by Jill Paton Walsh
Trees that melt are only the beginning. Read the book, and discover gray flowers, green jellyfish, and giant dancing moths.

A Wrinkle in Time by Madeleine L'Engle
If you like science fiction, try this book about a girl who enters the fifth dimension to help stop the destruction of Earth.

Silent Killers: Radon and Other Hazards by Kathlyn Gay
In **The Green Book**, people cannot live on Earth. Read about present-day hazards to health and efforts to clean our planet.

SCIENCE
HORIZONS

EARTH SCIENCE

Movements of the Earth's Plates

Darkness at Dawn

In A.D. 62 an earthquake shook the Roman city of Pompeii. Marble statues and columns fell as the ground shook. In the reservoir, which held the city's water, waves crashed back and forth. Then the walls of the reservoir broke, flooding the city. Damage from the earthquake and flood was great.

As the years passed, the city recovered. People rebuilt their homes and stores. Public buildings again were decorated with tiled walls and marble statues. The city once more took its place as a center of trade. What the people of Pompeii did not know was that the earthquake had shaken nearby Mount Vesuvius. Seventeen years later Pompeii faced a new disaster—Mount Vesuvius erupted.

Early in the afternoon of August 24, A.D. 79, a huge cloud rose from the mountain. The cloud was shaped like an oak tree, with the bottom of the cloud resembling the tree trunk. Later in the day an even greater explosion shattered the air. Ashes began to fall, gently at first, and then with greater force.

The mountain had exploded. By evening the sky rained hot ashes. Cracked blackened stones fell on the people of Pompeii. The roar coming from the mountain blocked out all other sounds. Most people stayed indoors, waiting for the ash storm to end. A few ran into the streets, in spite of poisonous smoke that filled the air.

During the night, rivers of melted rock flowed down the mountain. By dawn this burning river was close to the walls of the city. Clouds of ash blocked the light from the sun. During this dark morning the mountain exploded again. The force of the explosion pushed tons of ash and melted rock over the walls of the city. They city and the people in it were quickly buried. The melted rock hardened as it cooled.

More than 1,600 years passed before the sun shone again on Pompeii. Scientists first began to dig out the city in 1748. As they worked, they marveled at each new discovery. They found theaters, gardens, shops, and well-paved streets.

In some places, workers found strange hollows in the hardened rock. These hollows were a mystery until a scientist used plaster to fill in one of the spaces. When the surrounding rock was removed, the mystery was solved. The plaster cast had the shape of a human being. The hollows were places where people had been when they were buried. All that was left was the imprint each person had left in the rock.

Today, visitors go to Pompeii to see what life was like in A.D. 79. The visitors wonder about the people who were buried under rock so long ago.

Discover

ACTIVITY

Can you identify an object from its imprint?

Materials clay · mystery objects

Procedure

The impressions seen at Pompeii did not always show shapes in great detail. Scientists must often draw conclusions based on such incomplete information. Find out how much you can learn from imprints.

Select an object such as a small plastic animal or toy or any other object that will leave an imprint in clay. Form two slabs of clay. Make an imprint by placing the object between the slabs and pushing them together. Carefully separate the slabs of clay. Challenge a classmate to identify the object you used to make the imprint.

In this chapter you will explore the forces that destroyed the city of Pompeii. You will discover how movements of the earth's crust create both earthquakes and volcanoes.

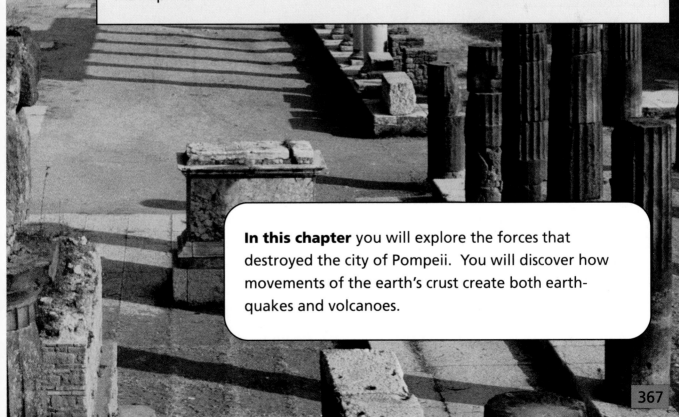

1. Origin of the Earth

Getting Started Make a drawing of what you think the earth was like shortly after it was formed. Write a brief description that explains your drawing.

Words to Know
atmosphere
hydrosphere

How did the earth begin?

The earth may have formed about 4.6 billion years ago. Most scientists believe it formed from particles in a dust cloud around the newly formed sun, as shown above. It is thought that the particles came together due to gravitational attraction. As they rushed together, much heat was produced.

Early in its history, scientists think that the earth was partly melted, or molten (mohl tun). It is believed that even now part of the inside of the earth is molten.

Heat in the newly formed earth caused volcanoes to erupt. The volcanoes released gases. These gases—carbon dioxide, methane, sulfur dioxide, and others—probably formed the earth's original atmosphere (AT mus feer). The **atmosphere** is the mixture of gases that surround the earth. Later, plants that grew on the earth changed the atmosphere. They used carbon dioxide and released oxygen. Today about one fifth of the atmosphere is oxygen. Most of the atmosphere is nitrogen.

Water vapor from the early volcanoes probably helped form the hydrosphere (HYE droh sfihr). The **hydrosphere** is all the parts of the earth that are water. It includes oceans and lakes, rivers, underground water, glaciers, clouds, and even water vapor in the air. You can see much of the hydrosphere in these pictures.

▲ The earth seen from space

◀ A river

Within the partly melted earth, molten elements began to move. Heavy elements, such as iron, sank toward the center of the earth. Lighter elements, such as silicon (sihl ih kahn), rose to the surface. As a result of this separation, three different layers formed within the earth.

What are the layers of the earth like?

The layers of the earth are the crust, the mantle, and the core. Look at the drawing on the next page. Locate each layer as it is described.

CORE The densest layer is the core, which has two parts. The outer core is liquid. The inner core is thought to be solid. Heavy metals, such as iron and nickel, probably make up most of the core.

MANTLE The mantle is less dense than the core and is made of heavy rock material. The part of the mantle closest to the core is solid. Above that part there is a plasticlike region. The outer part of the mantle is a hard, rigid solid.

CRUST The crust is the least dense layer. It is made of light rock material. The continents and the ocean floor are made of rocks of the crust. Like the part of the mantle just beneath it, the crust is mainly a hard, rigid solid.

Lesson Review

1. Describe how some scientists believe the earth may have formed.
2. Compare the formation of the atmosphere with that of the hydrosphere.
3. Describe the layers of the earth.

Think! The whole earth has an average density almost twice that of the crust. What does that tell you about the earth's interior?

Skills

Constructing a scale model

In a scale model the sizes of all the parts have the same relationship to each other as they do in the real object. Imagine that you want to construct a scale model of a table. The table itself is 150 cm long, 75 cm wide, and 73 cm high. You want the model to be one-tenth the size of the real thing. The scale-model table would have a length of 15 cm, a width of 7.5 cm, and a height of 7.3 cm.

Practicing the skill

1. The earth has three sections: the crust, the mantle, and the core. The crust is about 20 km thick, the mantle is about 2,900 km thick, and the core is about 3,500 km thick to its center. You will construct a scale model of the earth. The model will be a section of the earth. It should look like the picture of a wedge cut from the earth.

2. To construct your model, use three colors of modeling clay, one for each layer. Use 1 mm of clay for each 200 km of the earth's thickness. The core will be 17.5 mm. How thick will the mantle be?

Thinking about the skill

Suppose you have very little clay with which to construct your model. How could you construct the model with less clay?

Applying the skill

Observe the picture of Mount Mayon, an active volcano in the Phillipines. It is shaped like an almost perfect cone. It reaches 2,514 m above the sea. Construct a model of the mountain. Use 1 cm of clay for every 200 m of mountain.

371

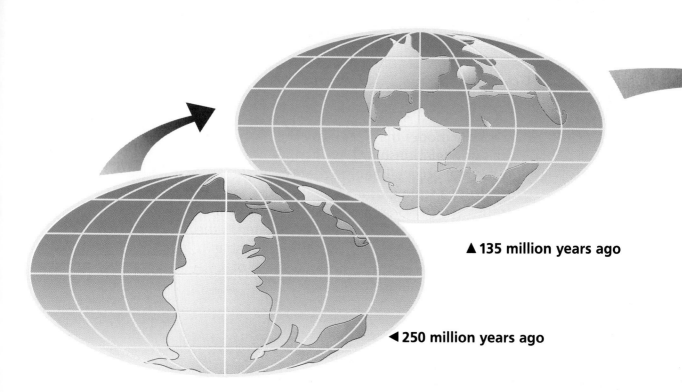

▲ 135 million years ago

◄ 250 million years ago

2. Moving Continents

Getting Started Look at a globe of the earth. It shows the continents and the oceans. Do you think the continents were always in their present locations? Explain why or why not.

Words to Know
lithosphere
plate tectonics

What is the idea of continental drift?

Is it possible that Africa and South America once fit together like pieces of a jigsaw puzzle? The German scientist Alfred Wegener (VAY guh nur) thought so. He proposed the hypothesis of continental drift. According to this idea, all the continents were once a single supercontinent. This supercontinent then broke into smaller continents, which slowly drifted apart.

That the continents seem to fit together is just one piece of evidence Wegener used to support his

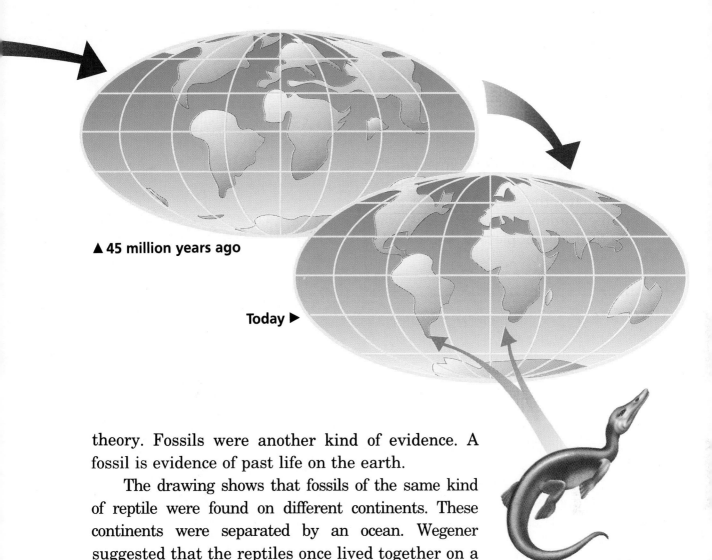

▲ 45 million years ago

Today ▶

▲ Mesosaurus—an early reptile

theory. Fossils were another kind of evidence. A fossil is evidence of past life on the earth.

The drawing shows that fossils of the same kind of reptile were found on different continents. These continents were separated by an ocean. Wegener suggested that the reptiles once lived together on a single supercontinent. Later, the reptiles were separated when the supercontinent broke up and the pieces drifted apart.

Wegener's third piece of evidence in support of continental drift is related to climate. India is a country near the equator. Why would you not expect to find glaciers there? But materials left by glaciers have been found in India. The presence of these materials suggests that India was once at a different latitude. Latitude is the distance north or south of the equator. Look at the map. Between what latitudes does most of India lie?

30°N

20°N

10°N

▲ Map of India today

Explore

Were the continents once one large supercontinent?

When putting together a jigsaw puzzle, you probably look first for the pieces with straight edges. That is the easy part. Those pieces form the border of the puzzle. But when you try to fit the other pieces together, what must you look for?

Materials tracing paper · scissors · world map or globe

Procedure

A. Carefully trace the outline of the continents shown below.

B. Cut out the continents you traced. Write the letter of the continent on each piece.

C. Try to fit the continents together to form one supercontinent.

Writing and Sharing Results and Conclusions

1. Which continents seem to fit together?

2. How well does this show that the continents were once one supercontinent?

3. How do your results differ from those of your classmates?

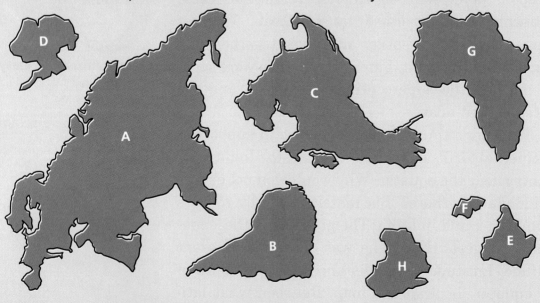

Although the evidence seemed to support the idea of continental drift, there was one problem. Wegener could not explain how the continents moved apart. He suggested that the earth's continental crust—the crust that makes up the continents—slid over the ocean-floor crust. Most scientists did not accept this idea. Years later, however, new evidence was found that helps explain how the continents move.

What is the idea of sea-floor spreading?

Many features of ocean floors are like those on land. For example, deep underwater canyons, called trenches, have been found. Ocean trenches are usually deeper than canyons on the land.

Another feature of some ocean floors is a mid-ocean ridge. A mid-ocean ridge is a long chain of mountains. Mid-ocean ridges run through the Atlantic, Pacific, and Indian Oceans. In the center of each ridge is a valley with huge cracks, called fissures (fihsh urz).

▼ **Mid-ocean ridges**

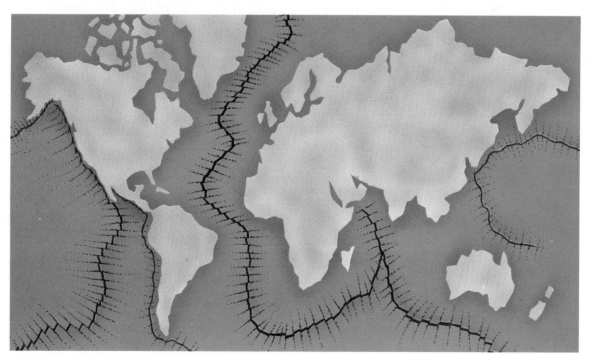

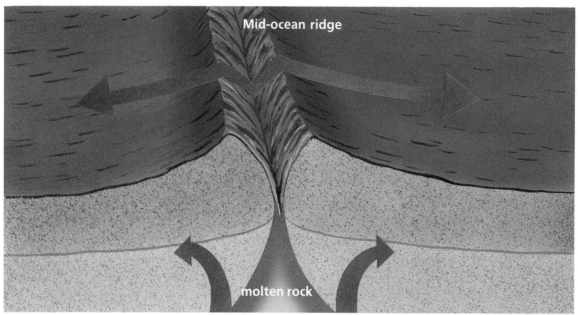

▲ **Sea-floor spreading**

The fissures puzzled scientists for a long time. They wondered how and why the fissures formed. Studies of what may have caused the fissures finally led to the theory of sea-floor spreading. This theory suggests that the sea floor spreads apart at the Mid-Ocean Ridge. Look at the drawing. It shows how molten rock from the mantle is squeezed up through the fissures in the valley. The molten rock spreads to either side. New ocean-floor crust and ridges form as the molten rock hardens. You can see in the drawing how the sea floor spreads. Where would you expect to find the oldest sea floor?

What is the theory of plate tectonics?

The theory of plate tectonics (tek TAHN ihks) explains Wegener's hypothesis, or idea, of continental drift. A plate is a huge slab of solid, rigid rock in the lithosphere (LIHTH oh sfihr). The **lithosphere** is the earth's crust plus the rigid upper part of the mantle. The term *tectonics* means large movements of the crust. The theory of **plate tectonics** states that the

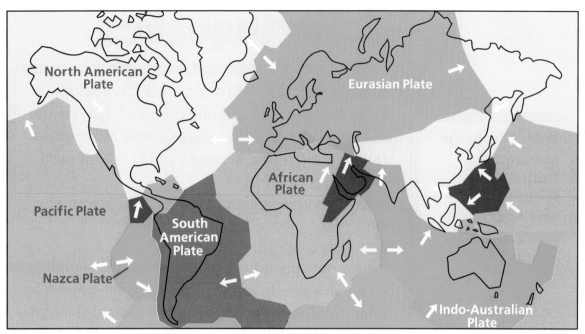

▲ Major plates of the lithosphere

lithosphere is made of plates that move very slowly.

The lithosphere is made of more than 25 plates. Seven of these are major plates. A plate is usually made of both ocean-floor crust and continental crust. Look at the drawing above. The arrows show the general direction of plate movements. From where do most of the major plates get their names?

The plates of the lithosphere "float" on the plastic part of the mantle. Scientists think that movement in the plastic region causes the plates to move. As the plates move, the continents are carried along. Study the drawing. What happens when plates collide?

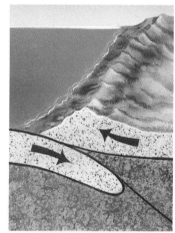

▲ Colliding plates

Lesson Review

1. What evidence supports continental drift?
2. What may take place at a mid-ocean ridge?
3. Explain the theory of plate tectonics.

Think! If the plates move as they are thought to move, what do you think may happen in the future?

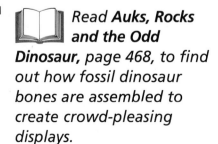

*Read **Auks, Rocks and the Odd Dinosaur**, page 468, to find out how fossil dinosaur bones are assembled to create crowd-pleasing displays.*

3. Earthquakes

Getting Started Have you ever felt your house shake from a loud clap of thunder? Maybe the windows even rattled. Imagine those effects multiplied many times. What do you think an earthquake might feel like?

What is an earthquake?

An **earthquake** is a shaking and trembling of the earth's crust. Earthquakes can be caused by a sudden shifting of rocks along a break in the earth's crust. The break in the earth's crust is called a **fault.** The fault shown here is the San Andreas fault, in California.

Most earthquakes occur at the boundaries of plates. A plate boundary is an edge of a plate. Moving plates have great amounts of energy. When plates "grind" against each other, large forces build. In time, enough force develops to cause a sudden movement of the plates.

Sliding plate boundary ▶

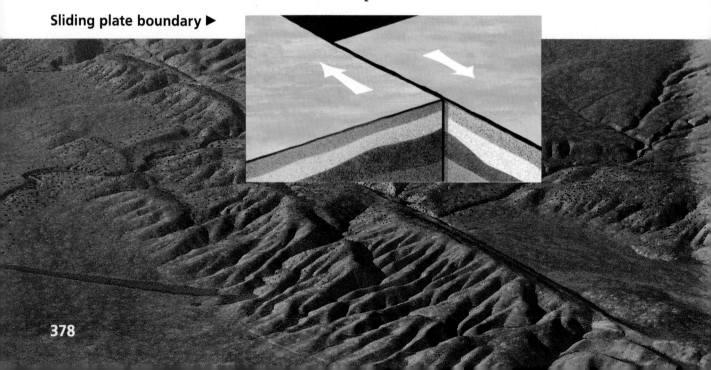

378

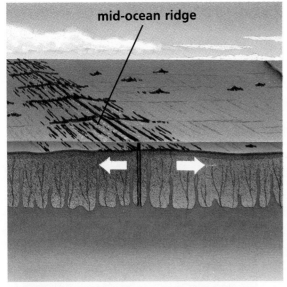

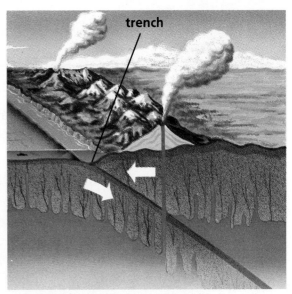

▲ Plates moving apart at boundary   ▲ Colliding plate boundary

In one type of plate boundary, plates slide past one another, as in the drawing on page 378. The San Andreas fault is a sliding-plate boundary. Cities near this fault have experienced several strong earthquakes.

Two other types of plate boundaries are shown here. The drawing on the left shows a boundary along which plates move apart. A mid-ocean ridge is this type of boundary. In another type of boundary, plates collide. Usually at such boundaries, one plate slides beneath another plate to form a trench. But sometimes the plates collide and buckle up to form mountains.

How are earthquakes measured?

The strength of an earthquake can be measured. One way to do this is to measure the amount of shaking, or vibration. When an earthquake occurs, the vibrations begin at a point underground, called the **focus.**

Earthquake vibrations move as waves through the earth. These waves can be detected on the earth's surface with a seismograph (SYZ muh graf).

Problem Solving

When Push Comes to Shove

Buildings may crumble during an earthquake. The force on the buildings is similar to a sudden strong gust of wind hitting the buildings from the side.

How can a building be made to withstand an earthquake?

Use an empty cereal box to represent a tall building. Place the box on a piece of sandpaper, 23 cm x 28 cm. What happens when you jerk the sandpaper? Think of ways to keep the box from falling over when the sandpaper is jerked about 8 cm. (You may not use glue or tape!) Test the method you predict will work best. Describe your method and tell how well it worked.

▲ Seismograph and recording

A **seismograph** is an instrument that measures and records earthquake waves. A recording of some earthquake waves can be seen in the picture.

The height of the strokes on the recording are related to the numbers 1 to 10 on the Richter (RIHK tur) scale. The Richter scale is used to measure the strength of an earthquake. The higher the number, the stronger the earthquake.

What are some effects of earthquakes?

Another way to describe the strength of an earthquake is by how it affects structures and people. Some earthquakes can hardly be felt; others cause much damage.

Often many people may be injured or killed when buildings collapse because of an earthquake. Underground water and gas pipes may break, and landslides can occur.

Look at the map. It shows where earthquakes occur in the United States. Where do the strongest earthquakes occur?

Scientists try to predict where and when earthquakes will occur. They look for clues that show which rocks in the lithosphere are under stress. Rocks that are under stress are most likely to move. Another clue is changes in the properties of the rocks. Sometimes a gas locked in the rocks may be released when the rocks are under stress. Even with such clues, exact predictions of where or when earthquakes will occur cannot be made.

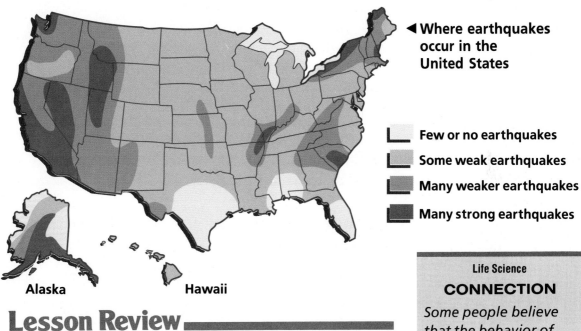

◄ **Where earthquakes occur in the United States**

Alaska　　　　**Hawaii**

- Few or no earthquakes
- Some weak earthquakes
- Many weaker earthquakes
- Many strong earthquakes

Lesson Review

1. Where on the earth do most earthquakes occur?
2. What are two ways by which the strength of an earthquake is measured?
3. What are some effects of a strong earthquake?

Think! Study the map on this page. Predict if an earthquake is likely to occur where you live.

Life Science
CONNECTION

Some people believe that the behavior of some animals changes before an earthquake. Use reference books to find out more about using animal behavior to predict earthquakes.

How can people prepare for earthquakes?

Earthquakes occur in many places around the world. Usually there is a fault in the rock below the earthquake area. If scientists know there is a fault somewhere, they know that an earthquake is likely to occur in that place. But is there any way to know that an earthquake is coming?

Scientists have developed tools to help them predict when earthquakes may occur. One tool is the tiltmeter. It shows tiny changes in the slope of the ground. A creepmeter is a tool that measures how far the ground has moved. Seismographs sense the vibrations deep in the earth. These tools help scientists observe changes near a fault. Yet scientists cannot predict the time and place of an earthquake.

In December of 1988 there was an earthquake in Armenia. The earthquake measured 6.9 on the Richter scale. In October of 1989, a major earthquake shook San Francisco, California. The San Francisco earthquake measured 7.1.

Although it was a stronger earthquake, the loss of life and damage in California was far less than in Armenia. Over 25,000 people lost their lives in the Armenian tragedy. Fewer than 100 people died in California because many newer buildings were constructed to withstand earthquakes.

STS

The buildings that did collapse in San Francisco were older ones. Since 1971 California has enforced strict building codes. Foundations must be built to move with the ground. Buildings must be constructed on layered steel and rubber that act like shock absorbers. Homes must be built of either reinforced cement or flexible wood frames.

Although newer buildings in California have been built to withstand earthquakes, many of the roads and bridges have not been. Nor have they been reinforced according to the newest building codes. The technology to make bridges and highways earthquake proof is available, but costly.

In many places people must decide if money should be spent to make older structures safe from earthquakes. Although San Francisco experiences many small earthquakes each year, earthquakes occur infrequently in many other cities. People in each city must answer the question, "Should millions of dollars be spent to prepare for something that rarely occurs?"

Critical thinking

1. Compare learning to predict earthquakes with learning to build earthquake-resistant buildings. Which could save more lives? Give reasons for your conclusions.

2. How do you think governments can protect people from earthquakes that occur in cities?

Using what you learned

Use your imagination to design an earthquake-resistant house. Describe some new way the house might be built. Think up new materials from which to make it. Draw your design and explain it to the class.

4. Volcanoes

Getting Started Do you know what a "soda-pop eruption" is? You do know if you have ever opened a bottle of warm soda pop that had been shaken. How is a soda-pop eruption similar to a volcanic eruption?

What is a volcano?

A **volcano** is an opening in the earth through which molten rock material reaches the earth's surface. The structure that forms when the molten material cools and hardens is also called a volcano. Many such structures are a type of mountain. Mount Vesuvius, which you read about in the beginning of this chapter, is such a mountain.

▼ **Kilauea erupting on the island of Hawaii**

Follow the drawing as you read how a volcano forms. (1) Molten rock mixed with gases within the earth is called **magma.** Magma forms in the mantle and moves up through fissures until it reaches the crust. (2) Magma collects in underground openings called magma pools. (3) As the gas in the magma comes near the earth's surface, the pressure on it is reduced. This can cause an eruption.

In an eruption the magma is forced up from the magma pool to the earth's surface. Magma that reaches the earth's surface is called **lava.** The cones of volcanic mountains are made of lava and lava fragments.

Where are volcanoes found?

Look at the map showing the location of many of the earth's volcanoes. Notice that, like earthquakes, most volcanoes occur along plate boundaries.

How a volcano forms ▶

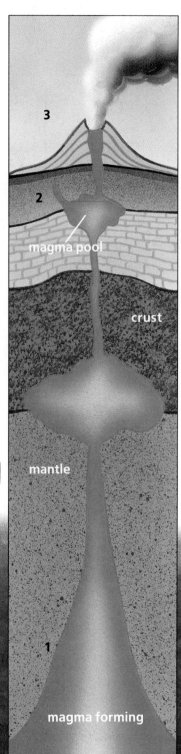

▼ **Locations of many volcanoes and earthquakes**

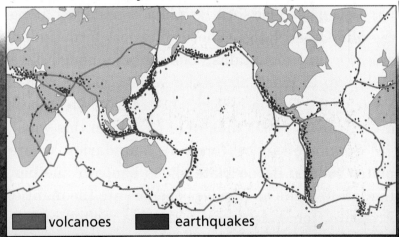

volcanoes   earthquakes

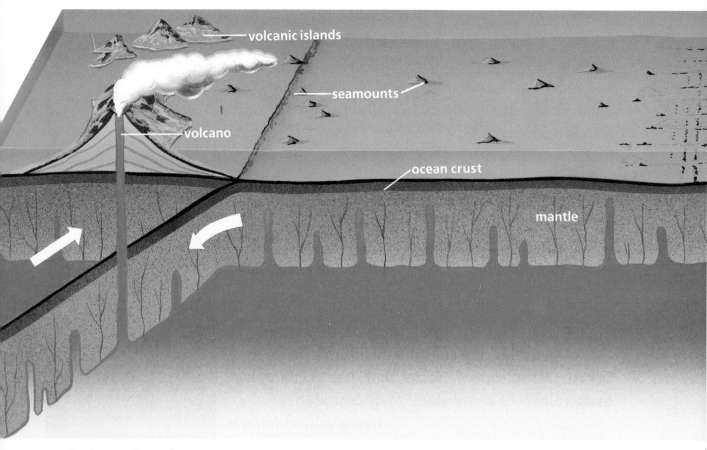

labels on image: volcanic islands, seamounts, volcano, ocean crust, mantle

▲ The formation of volcanoes on the ocean floor

Who was the goddess Pele? Would she cause the volcano to erupt? Read about her in *Goddess of Fire* in Horizons Plus.

Volcanoes also form at plate boundaries along the Mid-Ocean Ridge. These volcanoes form undersea volcanic mountains. Sometimes enough lava builds up to reach above the surface of the water. Then a volcanic island forms. Iceland and the Azores are volcanic islands that were formed in this way.

Some volcanoes form at boundaries where plates collide. If one plate slides beneath another, that plate melts as it moves deeper into the mantle. Pressure from below may cause this melted rock to rise to the surface, forming volcanoes and volcanic islands.

Some volcanoes are not found at plate boundaries. These volcanoes are located in the middle of an ocean plate. Such volcanoes are called seamounts. There are thousands of seamounts on the

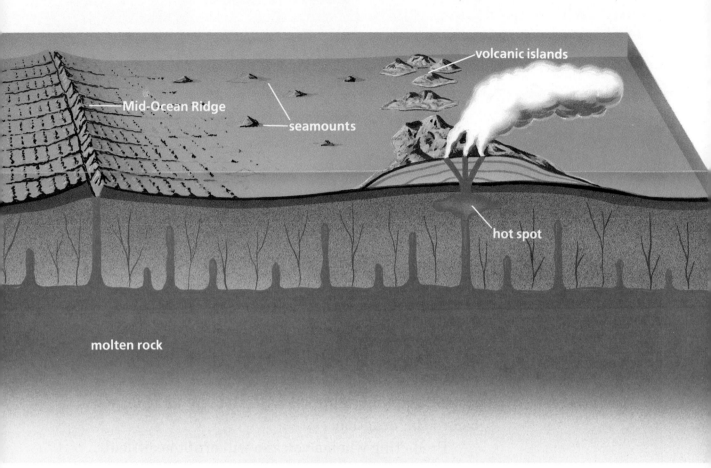

volcanic islands

Mid-Ocean Ridge

seamounts

hot spot

molten rock

ocean floor. Many of these seamounts formed long ago at mid-ocean ridges. They were moved away from the ridge as the seafloor spread.

Other seamounts form when a plate moves over a hot spot. A hot spot is a region of molten rock in the earth's mantle. A seamount forms on the part of the plate over the hot spot. The Hawaiian Islands are believed to have formed from a hot spot. Look at the seamounts in the drawing. A new seamount forms each time another part of the plate passes over the hot spot. In which direction does this show the plate is moving?

How may a volcanic eruption be predicted?

Mount St. Helens, a volcano in the state of Washington, erupted violently on May 18, 1980. The

▲ Mount St. Helens after the eruption

hot lava and gases killed people, plants, and animals. Compare the picture of Mount St. Helens as it looked after the eruption with the one as it looked before the eruption.

Predicting when a volcano will erupt is difficult, and the predictions are often unreliable. Records of a volcano's past eruptions are often used to predict when the volcano may erupt again. Suppose a volcano erupted every 25 to 30 years for the last 100 years. When do you predict it might erupt again?

Scientists cannot go inside a volcano to study it. Instead they look for clues that indicate gases are building up in the volcano. The buildup of gases occurs before an eruption. One clue to the buildup of gases is a change in the shape of the volcano. Before Mount St. Helens erupted, a bulge formed on one side of the volcano.

Changes in the shape of a volcano can be measured with an instrument called a tiltmeter. The tiltmeter is placed in a level position on the volcano. If the position changes, it may indicate that the shape of the volcano has changed.

▼ Mount St. Helens before the eruption

Laser beams are also used to detect small changes in the shape of the land. The laser beam is aimed at a certain point on the volcano. The time it takes for the beam to travel from the sending station to that point is known. If the travel time changes, the distance between the two points has changed. This means that the land has moved and an eruption may soon occur.

Sometimes earthquakes occur before a volcano erupts. The number and strength of these earthquakes are also clues to the possible time of an eruption.

▲ Scientist measuring the change in a volcano's shape

Lesson Review

1. Describe the movement of magma as it relates to a volcanic eruption.
2. Why do volcanoes form at plate boundaries and hot spots?
3. Describe three methods used to try to predict when a volcano will erupt.

Think! Many people think only of the destruction that is caused when a volcano erupts. What good, do you think, can result from a volcanic eruption?

389

5. Mountain Building

Words to Know
fault-block
 mountain
folded mountain
volcanic
 mountain
dome mountain

Getting Started From pictures, you know that some mountains are high and pointed. Other mountains are more rounded at the top. What do you think causes different mountains to have different shapes?

What are the different kinds of mountains?

Mountain ranges are found on nearly all the earth's continents and on the ocean floor. Mountains can be classified into four groups—fault-block, folded, volcanic, and dome. Each kind of mountain has its own characteristics.

The mountains in the picture are fault-block mountains. A **fault-block mountain** is formed when a block of rock is raised along a fault. The

Formation of a fault-block mountain in the Teton Range ▼

Teton Range, in Wyoming, formed this way. These mountains are among the most beautiful in the world. They seem to rise up along a straight line from a flat desert plain.

Compare the picture of these mountains with the drawing of how they formed. How does the movement of these rock layers differ from the movement of rock layers that form the folded mountains in the picture on this page?

A **folded mountain** is formed when rock layers are squeezed together, as shown in the drawing. Some of the highest mountains in the world are folded mountains. Mount Everest, in the Himalayas, is a folded mountain that is 8,848 m (29,021 feet) high.

Scientists think that most folded mountains form at boundaries where plates collide. The drawing shows how the Himalayas may have formed. The folded rock layers probably formed when the plates

▼ **Formation of a folded mountain in the Himalayas**

Explore Together

How are folds formed in folded mountains?

Organizer

Materials
wax paper · red, blue, and green modeling clay · metric ruler · plastic knife · 2 blocks of wood

Procedure

Manager

A. Place a long sheet of wax paper on your desk. Do all of this activity on the wax paper.

Investigator, Manager

B. Form two strips of red clay, each 1 cm x 3 cm x 10 cm. Join the strips at one end to make a strip 20 cm long.

Investigator, Manager

C. Repeat step **B** with the blue clay and with the green clay.

Investigator

D. Stack the long strips of colored clay. Place a block of wood at each end of the stack. Push the blocks toward each other.

Group, Recorder

    1. What do the different colors of clay represent?

    2. Describe what happens to the clay.

Investigator, Recorder

E. Cut off the top one fourth of the stack of clay.

    3. Draw a picture of how the stack of clay looks.

Writing and Sharing Results and Conclusions

Group, Recorder

1. What evidence of folding can be seen in the clay?

2. When do rock layers become folded?

Reporter

3. How do the folds in your clay compare with the folds in your classmates' clay?

carrying India and Asia collided. As the plates collided, pressure caused folding of rocks that made up the plates. Pressure also caused the sediments on the ocean floor to crumple and fold.

A volcanic mountain differs from other mountains in its shape and in the way it is formed. **Volcanic mountains** are formed from molten rock material that reaches the earth's surface from deep inside the earth. Most volcanic mountains, such as the one in the picture, are cone shaped. The cones are made up of layers of lava and ash.

During "quiet" eruptions, lava pours out of the volcano, cools, and hardens. During "explosive" eruptions, ash and cinders are thrown high into the air. In both kinds of eruptions, materials fall back onto the sides of the mountain, increasing its size.

Some volcanic mountains are made only of hardened lava. These mountains are not as high as the cone-shaped volcanic mountains and their sides are not as steep.

▼ **Formation of Mount Fuji—a volcanic mountain**

Not all mountains form by faulting, folding, or volcanic activity. A **dome mountain** is formed when a large area of the earth's surface is slowly bent upward. Look at the picture. You can see why this kind of mountain is called a dome mountain.

Some dome mountains form when the crust is pushed upward by huge collections of magma below the surface. This process of mountain building is shown in the drawing of a dome mountain.

▼ **Formation of a dome mountain in the Appalachians**

Lesson Review

1. How do volcanic mountains differ from other kinds of mountains?
2. Describe how folded mountains, fault-block mountains, and dome mountains are formed.

Think! Why are many mountain ranges found on the coasts of continents?

Chapter Connections

Copy the graphic organizer. Add more information to it so that it could be used to study for a chapter test.

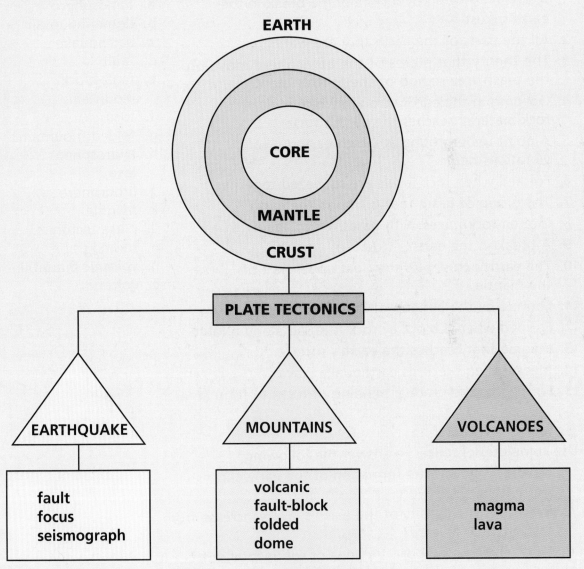

EARTH

CORE

MANTLE

CRUST

PLATE TECTONICS

EARTHQUAKE

MOUNTAINS

VOLCANOES

fault
focus
seismograph

volcanic
fault-block
folded
dome

magma
lava

Writing About Science • Imagine

Imagine you are a mountain being formed by forces discussed in this chapter. Write a paragraph about the experience of becoming a mountain.

Chapter 11 Review

Science Terms

Write the letter of the term that best matches the definition.

1. A sudden shifting of rocks along a break in the earth's crust
2. All the parts of the earth that are water
3. The theory that plates of the lithosphere move on the plasticlike region of the Earth's mantle.
4. Opening in the earth through which molten rock material reaches the earth's surface
5. A point underground at which earthquake vibrations begin
6. Formed when rock layers are squeezed together
7. The group of gases that surround the earth
8. Molten rock mixed with gases within the earth
9. A break in the earth's crust
10. The earth's crust plus the rigid upper part of the mantle
11. Formed by the buildup of "new" rock
12. Formed when a block of rock is raised along a fault
13. Magma that reaches the earth's surface
14. Measures and records earthquake waves
15. Formed by the gradual bending of rocks to form an arch

a. atmosphere
b. dome mountain
c. earthquake
d. fault
e. fault-block mountain
f. focus
g. folded mountain
h. hydrosphere
i. lava
j. lithosphere
k. magma
l. plate tectonics
m. seismograph
n. volcanic mountain
o. volcano

Science Ideas

Use complete sentences to answer the following.

1. In what way was the formation of the early earth's atmosphere and hydrosphere similar?
2. Why does the density of the earth's layers increase from the crust to the core?
3. What evidence supports the idea of continental drift?
4. What is a mid-ocean ridge?
5. What causes an earthquake, and where do the earthquake vibrations begin?
6. How do magma and lava differ?

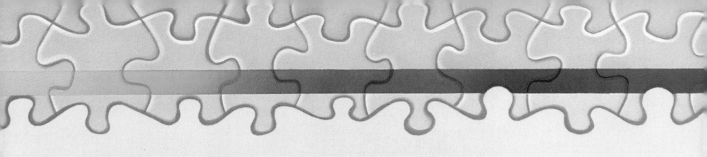

7. What are seamounts, and where do they form?
8. What clues do scientists look for when trying to predict when a volcano will erupt?
9. Name the four types of mountains.
10. Which type of mountain forms mainly at the boundaries where plates collide?

Applying Science Ideas

1. Suppose there was an earthquake where you live. Would you be safer in a building or in an open field away from buildings and other structures?
2. You have read how destructive an earthquake and a volcanic eruption can be. Which would be easier to prepare for—an earthquake or a volcanic eruption? Explain your answer.

Using Science Skills

The dome-shaped mountain in the picture is called Half Dome. It rises 2,700 m (8,858 feet) above the sea. What other information would you need to make a scale model of Half Dome?

Chapter 12

Weather and Climate

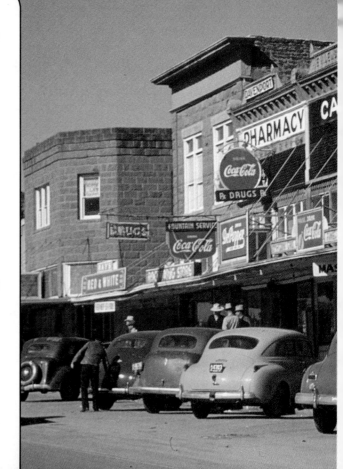

The Great Indoors

In the past, where did people go to shop, to meet, or to celebrate? Most towns and cities had a street called Main Street, where people would gather. Main Street was the center of a town's activities.

Today, the local shopping mall has replaced Main Street as a place to gather. Americans spend more time in malls than anyplace except their home, school, or workplace. Some malls look very much like Main Street. There are tree-lined walkways, bubbling fountains, and park benches. And of course, there are stores.

How did the mall replace Main Street? The first part of the change was made when people moved from cities to suburbs. These people wanted to shop in stores near their homes.

The second part of the change came in the 1950s. In 1953, architect Victor Gruen was asked to design a shopping center in Minnesota. In that part of the country, the summers are hot and the winters can be bitterly cold. Gruen had noticed that the amount of business in local stores was related to the weather. On mild days, sales were up. On bad-weather days, sales were down.

Gruen wondered how he could produce perfect weather all year. The answer was obvious to him. He would enclose the whole shopping center and heat or cool the entire space as needed. This would be the first of many enclosed, climate-controlled malls.

Since the first enclosed mall, malls have changed to include much more. They are places for walking or jogging. Inside a mall, people can exercise without the stress of extreme heat or cold. Most malls include several restaurants. Some malls house police stations, hotels, and offices. Others may include hospitals, health clubs, and even chapels. It would be possible for a person to be born, live, work, and exercise—all within a mall!

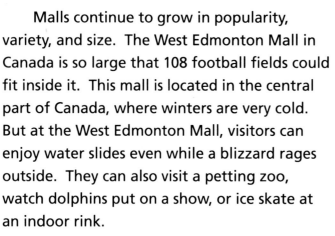

Malls continue to grow in popularity, variety, and size. The West Edmonton Mall in Canada is so large that 108 football fields could fit inside it. This mall is located in the central part of Canada, where winters are very cold. But at the West Edmonton Mall, visitors can enjoy water slides even while a blizzard rages outside. They can also visit a petting zoo, watch dolphins put on a show, or ice skate at an indoor rink.

Shopping malls create an endless spring—perfect weather for shopping. But heating and cooling these large spaces uses great amounts of energy. Some people wonder whether heating and cooling shopping malls is a good use of limited energy resources.

Discover

ACTIVITY

How can you keep climate-controlled air inside a mall?

Materials   pencil · paper

Procedure

In a climate-controlled mall, it is important to keep the warmed or cooled air inside. Each time an outer door is opened, air from inside the mall is mixed with the air from outside the mall. Malls are often designed with one or more ways of limiting the mixing of air in doorways.

Find out about an enclosed mall near your home. How is the mall designed to help control the climate inside? What other ways can you think of to keep the air inside from mixing with the air from outside? Design an improved entryway for a mall. Show your design to the class. Explain the advantages and disadvantages of your design.

In this chapter you will learn what causes changes in the weather and how weather is forecast. You will also learn how climate has changed over time.

1. Weather

Getting Started Many schools close when there is too much snow for students to get to school. School officials must decide early in the morning whether or not to close for the day. What data do they need to make the decision?

What determines weather?

Weather is the condition of the atmosphere at a given time and place. Weather is the result of many factors. Some weather factors are air temperature, air pressure, humidity, and the amount of cloud cover. Other weather factors are wind speed and direction, and the type and amount of precipitation. Describe the weather shown in the two pictures. In what ways do the weather conditions differ?

You are probably familiar with weather factors such as temperature, wind, and precipitation. Most likely you know that humidity is the water vapor in the air. You may also know that air pressure is the pressing force of air. What you may not know is how a change in any of these factors causes a change in the weather.

▼ A spring day

402

How do air masses and fronts affect weather?

Weather at the earth's surface is closely related to moving bodies of air called air masses. An **air mass** is a large body of air that has about the same temperature and humidity throughout.

An air mass forms when a body of air stays over the same region for several days. During this time, the air takes on the temperature and humidity conditions of the surface beneath it. An air mass is described by its temperature and its humidity. An air mass may be either cold or warm, and it may be either moist or dry.

Look at the map. It shows the regions where most air masses that affect weather in the United States form. Find the polar regions on the map. Air masses that form over the polar regions tend to be cold. Those that form over tropical regions tend to be warm. Air masses that form over water tend to be moist. Those that form over land tend to be dry. How would you describe an air mass that forms over water in a polar region?

Air masses that affect the United States ▼

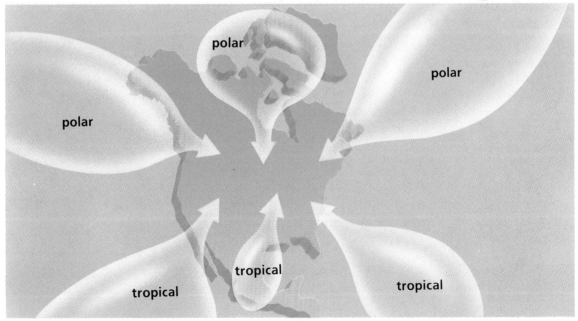

403

After an air mass forms, it moves across the earth's surface. As an air mass moves, it causes changes in weather conditions. According to the maps, in what direction do air masses tend to move across the United States?

An air mass and its weather conditions are called a weather system. Most air masses are high-pressure systems, or highs. Highs result from cool, dense air pressing on the earth's surface near the center of an air mass. This usually results in clear, dry weather. The arrows on the map show the direction of winds within a high-pressure system. You can see that in a high, air moves from the center of the air mass outward in a clockwise direction.

As a high moves into a region, the air pressure and wind direction in the region change. As the center of the high comes closer, the air pressure in the region rises. After the center has passed, the air pressure in the region falls. When will the air pressure be highest? On the two days shown on the maps, how does the wind direction in Billings change?

Knowing about weather can help you find where travelers from a distant planet might be hidden. Try **Climatrolls: A Weather Simulation.**

Movement of an air mass ▼

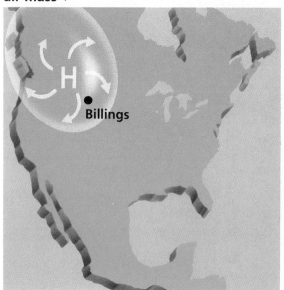

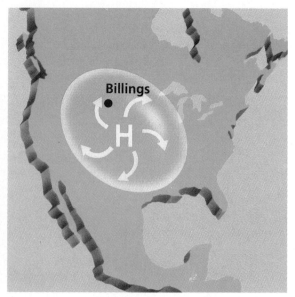

Explore

ACTIVITY

How can weather maps show how fronts and weather patterns move and change?

Until about a hundred years ago, people predicted the weather using only their senses. A change in the weather was as important to people then as it is today. But today, weather predictions are made with the aid of weather maps.

Materials
5 weather maps, same size and shape · paper · glue · sheet of clear acetate or clear plastic · red and blue wax pencils

Procedure
A. For 5 days in a row, collect the weather maps and forecasts found in the newspaper. Be sure both are dated.

B. Arrange the maps and forecasts by date on a large sheet of paper. Glue them in place.

C. Lay a sheet of acetate over the first map. Line up the top left corner of the acetate with the top left corner of the map.

D. Trace any cold fronts on the map with the blue pencil. Trace any warm fronts with the red pencil. Label these lines *1*, to stand for the first day.

E. On the same sheet of acetate, repeat steps **C** and **D** with each of the other maps. Each time, label the lines to show the correct day.

D

Writing and Sharing Results and Conclusions

1. In what general direction do fronts seem to move?

2. For the 5 days studied, did warm fronts or cold fronts seem to move faster?

3. What kind of weather does a warm front bring? What kind does a cold front bring?

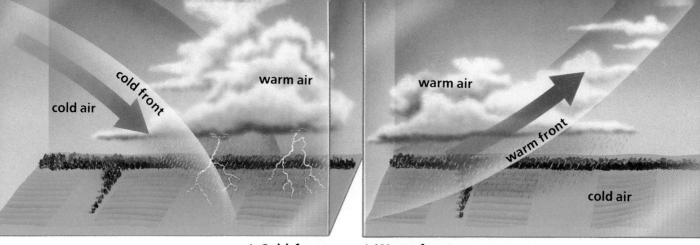

▲ **Cold front**   ▲ **Warm front**

As air masses move, they come in contact with other air masses. The boundary between two air masses is called a **front.** When a cold air mass overtakes a warm air mass, a cold front forms. When a warm air mass overtakes a cold air mass, a warm front forms.

Low-pressure systems, or lows, form along fronts. The low pressure is produced when warm air rises over denser cold air. In a low-pressure system, air moves in a counter-clockwise direction.

As warm air rises along a front, the air cools. Water vapor in the cooling air condenses, causing clouds and precipitation to form. Cold fronts often produce heavy rain or snow that lasts for a short time. After the front passes, the weather is usually clear, cool, and dry. Warm fronts produce rain or snow that may fall for several days. After a warm front passes, the weather is often hazy and warm.

Lesson Review ━━━━━━━━

1. What are four factors that make up the weather?
2. What two weather factors are used to describe an air mass?
3. What type of weather occurs with a high-pressure system and with a low-pressure system?

Think! A cold front is 400 km west of your town. What data do you need to predict if or when this front will pass through your town?

Skills

Estimating temperatures

Meteorologists collect temperature readings from many places in a region. When they make weather maps, they sometimes use lines to connect all the places that have the same temperature. These lines are called isotherms.

Practicing the skill

Look at the map that shows a part of Arizona on a hot July day. Notice the isotherms. The numbers on each isotherm tell the temperature.

1. What is the temperature in Tucson? What is the temperature in Clifton?

2. The temperature of a place that is not on an isotherm must be estimated. Phoenix is about halfway between the isotherms for 42°C and 38°C. You might therefore estimate that Phoenix's temperature is 40°C. Estimate the temperature in Globe and Silver Bell.

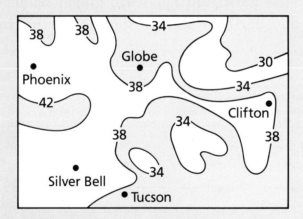

Thinking about the skill

Suppose you lived in Silver Bell and saw the map shown in a newspaper. You used the map to estimate the temperature that day in Silver Bell. How could you check that your temperature estimate was accurate?

Applying the skill

Measure the temperature at several places around your school. Then choose an area located between two of those places. Estimate the temperature in that area.

2. Moving Air

Words to Know
global winds
prevailing winds
jet stream

Getting Started Has your family ever planned a trip? It would be helpful to know what kind of weather to expect. How might the weather affect your plans for the trip?

How does air move around the earth?

The air covering the earth is always in motion. In general the air moves in large bands that circle the earth. The bands of moving air that circle the earth are called **global winds.** Global winds flow between a series of high and low pressure belts that also circle the earth. The global winds and pressure belts are shown in the drawing.

If the earth did not turn, global winds would blow due north or south. But the earth's rotation

Global winds and pressure belts ▼

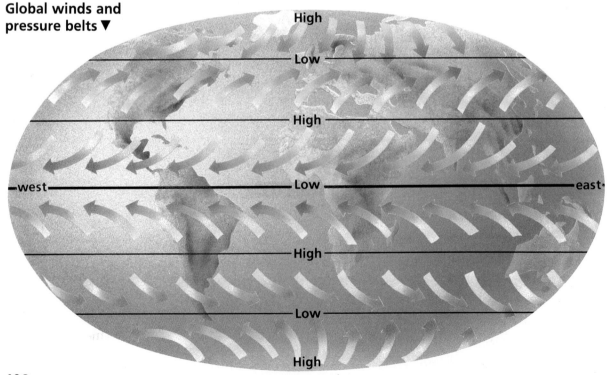

High
Low
High
west — Low — east
High
Low
High

408

helps to cause global winds to curve. In the Northern Hemisphere the winds curve to the right. So winds blowing from the north become northeasterly winds. Winds blowing from the south become southwesterly winds. In the Southern Hemisphere, the earth's rotation causes winds to curve to the left. Winds blowing from the south become southeasterly winds. What happens to winds blowing from the north?

Winds that blow from the same direction over long distances are called **prevailing** (pree VAYL-ihng) **winds.** The global winds map shows the general direction of the prevailing winds. However, the direction of these winds in a given region can be affected by the surface over which they travel.

Look at the prevailing winds map of Africa. Notice that some of the prevailing winds blow for long distances across land. Other winds blow from across the oceans. How do the prevailing winds seem to affect the region into which they move?

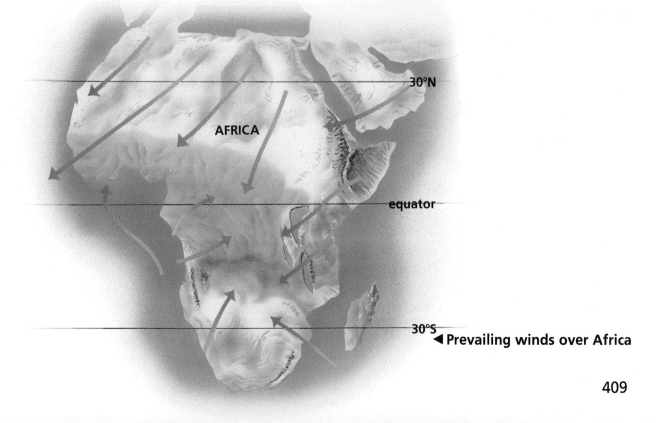

◄ **Prevailing winds over Africa**

▲ The jet stream over the United States

You may have noticed that in your area winds are always changing direction. These are local winds caused by weather conditions over small regions. Local winds occur within only about 1 km (0.6 mile) above the earth's surface.

How do jet streams affect the weather?

The troposphere (TROH poh sfihr) is the layer of the atmosphere nearest the earth's surface. Air masses and fronts move in the general direction of prevailing winds near the bottom of the troposphere. But strong winds very high in the troposphere also help steer the movement of weather systems. These strong winds are called jet streams. **Jet streams** are narrow bands of very fast-moving air high in the troposphere. They reach speeds of up to 370 km (230 mi) per hour. The clouds in the picture trace the path of a jet stream.

A jet stream moving eastward is shown in the drawings. It is located where cold air moving away from the North Pole meets warmer air moving toward the pole. The drawing on the left shows the path of the jet stream in winter. The drawing on

▼ Jet stream in the winter

▼ Jet stream in the summer

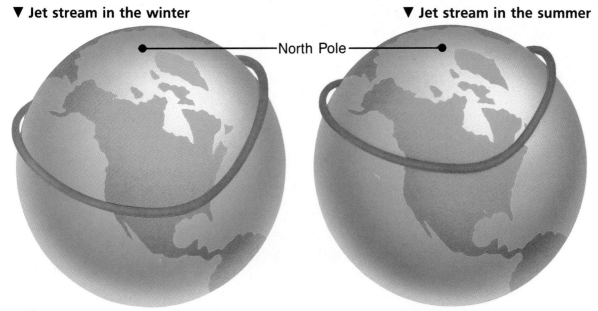

North Pole

the right shows the path of the same jet stream in summer. The winter path is much farther south than the summer path. This path steers cold air into regions that normally have warm temperatures.

Jet streams wander north and south as they travel. Sometimes they move far off their normal path. Such changes in the paths of jet streams may result in milder than normal winters or cooler than normal summers. Changes in the jet streams may also cause droughts (drouts). A drought is a long period of time during which there is below normal amounts of rainfall. The conditions shown in the picture occurred during a drought in 1983.

Farmer in his field during a drought ▼

Lesson Review

1. What are global winds?
2. How would the direction of a prevailing wind affect the movement of an air mass?
3. What are jet streams? How do they affect weather?

Think! How would the global winds be affected if the earth rotated in the opposite direction?

3. Technology and Weather

Words to Know
artificial satellite
cloud seeding

Getting Started This picture of clouds was taken from high above the earth's surface. Computers were used to add the colors. How can such views of the earth's surface help people predict the weather?

How is technology used to predict weather?

An **artificial satellite** (ahrt uh FIHSH ul SAT uh lyt) is an object made by people that orbits another object in space. Satellites made by people are a product of technology (tek NAHL uh jee) used to predict weather. Data gathered by satellites make weather forecasts more accurate.

Some satellites, such as the GOES satellites, orbit above the same part of the earth's surface all the time. The picture below was taken by a GOES satellite. GOES satellites can send back pictures of

Picture taken by a GOES satellite ▼

▲ Satellite pictures used to track a hurricane

one fourth of the earth's surface every 30 minutes. This means that the movement of a group of clouds or a storm can be watched constantly. Using satellite pictures such as these, a hurricane can be tracked from day to day. In this way, warning can be given to people in its path.

GOES satellites also collect data from instruments at weather stations around the world. Because satellites collect the data, some weather stations can be run without people working there. This means that weather stations can be set up in places where humans cannot live or work.

How is radar used to collect weather data?

Radar is used to collect some weather data. Radar devices send out radio waves. When the waves strike rain or snow, they are reflected, or bounced back, to a radar receiver. These reflected waves show up on a radar screen.

Radar can locate rain or snow within a range of about 100 km (60 mi). An advanced kind of radar, called Doppler (DAHP lur) radar, can detect how much rain or snow is falling. It also can detect how fast a storm is moving toward or away from the radar device.

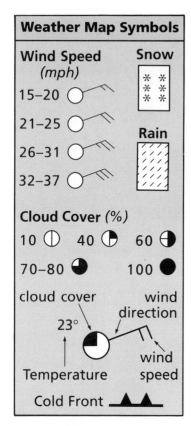

Weather Map Symbols

Wind Speed *(mph)*

15–20

21–25

26–31

32–37

Snow

Rain

Cloud Cover *(%)*

10   40   60

70–80   100

cloud cover

23°

Temperature

wind direction

wind speed

Cold Front

How are computers used to forecast weather?

Satellites do not send actual photographs back to the earth. Instead they send radio signals. These signals are then changed into pictures by computers on the earth.

Computers also are used to process other weather data from satellites and from weather stations throughout the world. There are hundreds of such stations in North America alone. In the United States, weather data from these stations are sent to the National Weather Service (NWS). At the NWS, computers use the data to make weather maps. The satellite picture on the left can be used to make the weather map on the right. Maps such as this are sent to meteorologists across the country. A meteorologist is a scientist who studies the weather. Meteorologists use the maps along with data from their own instruments to make local forecasts.

▼ **Satellite picture**

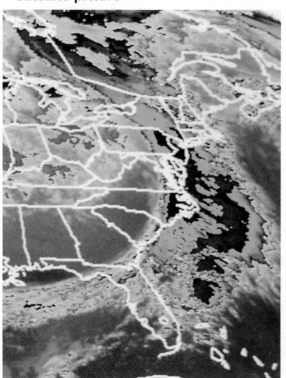

▼ **Weather map**

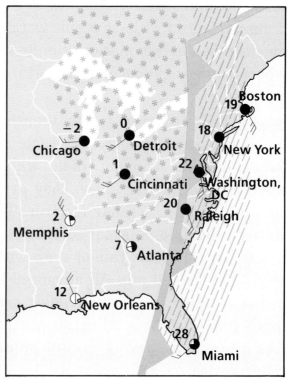

414

How can technology change the weather?

There are a number of ways to change the weather using technology. For example, cloud seeding is a method used to cause clouds to release precipitation. In **cloud seeding,** small solid particles of carbon dioxide or silver iodide are scattered in clouds to cause rain. The plane in the picture is seeding clouds.

▼ **A plane scattering cloud seeding crystals**

The clouds that are seeded have low temperatures and much moisture. The solid particles serve as surfaces around which moisture can condense and droplets can form. If the droplets grow large enough, they fall as rain or snow. Some people do not think that cloud seeding is a good idea. They believe that by causing clouds to release moisture in one region, other regions may not get enough.

Lesson Review

1. What kinds of weather data do satellites and radar provide?
2. How are computers used in weather forecasting?
3. What is the purpose of cloud seeding?

Think! What are some advantages of being able to view weather conditions from space?

Physical Science
CONNECTION

Use reference books to find out other uses of computers in forecasting weather.

How can lightning be detected before it strikes?

You see a flash of lightning. Then you hear a rumble of thunder. The light, followed by the sound, is the familiar pattern of a thunderstorm. Lightning is produced when opposite electrical charges build up in clouds and on the ground. The charges grow stronger and stronger. Then an electric spark leaps between the cloud and the ground or between clouds. That spark is lightning.

When lightning strikes the earth's surface, it can start fires. And it can kill. Each year, lightning kills about 100 people in the United States.

Nothing can prevent lightning. But now something can be done to let people know it is on the way. There is an early warning system to detect lightning. It is a system of over a hundred sensors. These sensors are located across the country. Each sensor rests on top of an antenna. The antenna picks up radio signals from charges in the lightning. The sensor records the strength and direction of each lightning bolt. A computer collects the information.

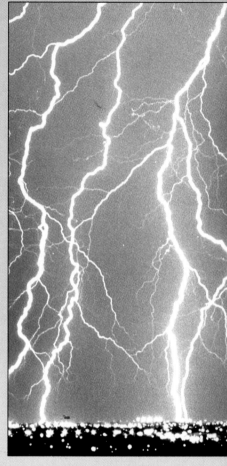

and Society

STS

▲ Lightning sensor

The collected data are used to track electrical storms. The warning system is hooked up to telephones. People that are part of the early warning system are called automatically when an electrical storm is due in their area.

Since the sensors were first used, millions of flashes have been detected. The sensors alert power companies of storms. Company crews can be ready to fix power failures that may be caused by lightning strikes. The warning sensors send lightning information to weather services as well. Airline pilots also get warning of lightning before they take off.

NASA has use for lightning detection, too. If lightning were to strike a spacecraft, the results could be a disaster. NASA is working on lightning sensors that will be put into satellites. As the satellites orbit, these sensors will detect lightning around the world.

Detecting lightning before it reaches a place can save lives. But for lightning detection to be effective, people must be prepared for lightning coming to their area. Being prepared means following safety rules during an electrical storm.

Critical thinking

Suppose an airline pilot is ready to take off for a city located due east. The lightning early warning system sends a message. Lightning is located 200 kilometers due east of the airport. The pilot takes off anyway. What might be some of the pilot's reasons?

Using what you learned

Does your local power company receive early warnings about lightning that is moving in your direction? Perhaps your local television station uses a weather service that gets thunderstorm information from an early warning system. Write letters to find out.

A parade on New Year's Day ▼

4. Climate

Getting Started The parade in the picture took place on New Year's Day. You know that it is winter on New Year's Day. Why do you think the weather in this place is like this in the winter?

Words to Know
climate
latitude
altitude
tropical climate
polar climate
temperate
  climate

What is climate?

From the picture, you can see that places around the world have different climates. **Climate** (KLYE mut) is the average of weather conditions for a region over a long period of time. It is usually described by the yearly range of temperatures and the amount of precipitation in the region. The climate of a region results from several factors. These factors include latitude (LAT uh tood), nearness to mountains and large bodies of water, prevailing winds, and altitude (AL tuh tood).

How does latitude affect climate?

Latitude is the factor that most affects the temperature of a climate. **Latitude** is the distance north or south of the equator. Regions near the

418

equator have the lowest latitudes. These regions have the highest average yearly temperatures. Regions near the poles have the highest latitudes. Regions near the North and South Poles have the lowest average yearly temperatures.

▼ **Least slanted rays**

The differences in temperature among regions at different latitudes are due mainly to the angle at which the sun's rays strike the earth. The drawing shows why this is true. Notice that the sun's rays strike the earth at different angles. Which part of the earth's surface receives the least slanted rays? Which part receives the most slanted rays?

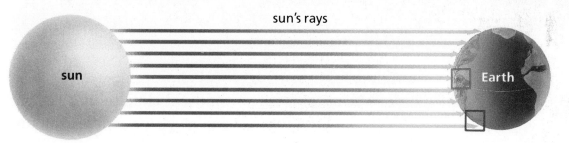

sun's rays

sun

Earth

The earth's surface is heated least by slanted rays of the sun. The more slanted the rays are, the less they heat the earth's surface. Look again at the drawing. Which part of the earth's surface will be heated most by the sun? Which part will be heated least?

▲ **Most slanted rays**

Latitude also affects the amount of rain or snow in a region. Earlier you learned about pressure belts and the pattern of air movement around the earth. There are low-pressure belts near the equator (0° latitude) and near latitudes 60° North and 60° South. Regions near these latitudes tend to have high amounts of rain or snow.

The high-pressure regions of the earth are near the poles (90° latitude) and near latitudes 30° North and 30° South. High-pressure regions tend to have low amounts of rain or snow.

▲ Air moving over a mountain

What factors affect local climate?

Mountains affect the local climate in a region. They change the movement of air masses. Mountains also change patterns of precipitation. The drawing shows air being forced up over a mountain. As the rising air cools, water vapor in the air condenses and forms clouds. Rain or snow falls on the side of the mountain where the air is rising. By the time the air reaches the top of the mountain, it has lost most of its moisture. So the air that moves down the other side of the mountain is dry.

Large bodies of water affect the climate of nearby land. Places near water often have more rain or snow than places far from water. Places near large bodies of water also have smaller differences between their summer and winter temperatures than do places far from water. Water heats and cools more slowly than does land. When the water is cooler than nearby land, the air over the land is cooled. When the water is warmer than nearby land, the air over the land is warmed.

El Niño *means "boy child." But there is nothing childish about the damage El Niño can cause, as Kwame would find out. Find out in* **El Niño** *in Horizons Plus.*

The prevailing winds over an area affect climate. Regions where the prevailing winds blow from over land receive little precipitation. Regions where the prevailing winds blow from over the oceans receive a lot of precipitation.

Altitude affects climate. **Altitude** is the distance above sea level. At high altitudes the air temperature tends to be lower than at low altitudes. The palm tree and the mountain shown are both near the equator. Yet the top of the mountain, which is almost 6 km (about 3.5 mi) above sea level, is covered with snow. What does that tell you about the temperature at the top of the mountain?

▲ The affect of altitude on local climate

What are the major climate zones?

The earth's surface can be divided into three major climate zones. These zones are based mainly on temperature. The map shows the location of each climate zone. Find the tropical, temperate (TEM pur-iht), and polar climate zones.

The three major climate zones ▼

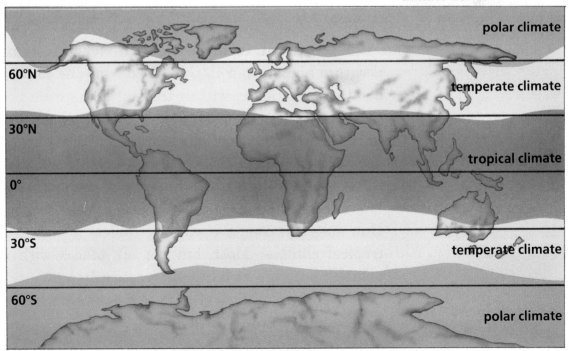

polar climate

60°N — temperate climate

30°N

tropical climate

0°

30°S — temperate climate

60°S

polar climate

Problem Solving

For the Record!

An ad agency was filming a commercial in November. They needed a setting with a lot of snow. To find such a place, they called the National Climatic Data Center in Asheville, North Carolina. The man in the picture works at the Center. According to the Center's computer records, Stampede Pass, Washington, was a good location. Each year Stampede Pass had an average of 163 cm (64.2 in) of snow in November.

What is the best time to have a class picnic where you live?

Think about the climate where you live. Are some times of the year too cold or too warm? Are these times different from the most rainy times of the year? Use resources and records in your public library to find the best time for your picnic. What did you decide would be the best time? Explain why you chose that time.

A **tropical climate** has an average temperature higher than 18°C (64°F) during the coldest month. Most places with a tropical climate lie between latitudes 30° North and 30° South. According to the map, about how much of the earth's surface does this include?

A **polar climate** has an average temperature lower than 10°C (50°F) during the warmest month. How does this compare with the coldest month in a tropical climate? Most, but not all, places with a polar climate are at latitudes greater than 60°.

The average summer temperature in a **temperate climate** is above 18°C (64°F) and the average winter temperature is below 10°C (50°F).

Most regions with a temperate climate lie between latitudes 30° and 60° north and south of the equator. In such regions, weather changes with the seasons.

Most of the United States is in the temperate climate zone. According to the climate map you just saw, what parts of the United States are not in this zone? One area that is not in the temperate climate zone is Alaska. Alaska is north of 60° latitude and is in the polar climate zone. Hawaii and most of Florida are parts of the United States in the tropical climate zone. Look at the pictures showing all three climate zones. What can you tell about each climate zone from these pictures?

▼ **Temperate climate**

▼ **Polar climate**

▼ **Tropical climate**

Lesson Review

1. What is climate?
2. What two conditions are used to describe climate?
3. Name four factors that affect the climate of a region. List the most important factor first.
4. Describe the three climate zones.

Think! Boston, Massachusetts and Sioux Falls, South Dakota, are at the same latitude. Why are winter temperatures in Boston milder than those in Sioux Falls?

Life Science
CONNECTION

Find out what a biome is. How are biomes and climates related?

A glacier ▼

5. Changing Climates

Words to Know
ice ages
glacier
greenhouse
 effect
ozone

Getting Started   In 1987 a huge iceberg broke off the ice cap at the South Pole. The iceberg was larger than the state of Delaware. What climate changes might cause an increase in the number of such icebergs?

How has the earth's climate changed?

Evidence shows that throughout its history, the earth has had periods of warming and periods of cooling. The periods when the world climate became cooler are called **ice ages.** The most recent series of ice ages began about 1 million years ago. At one time, much of Canada and the northern United States were covered by glaciers (GLAY shurz). A **glacier** is a large body of moving ice. The drawing shows how much of North America was covered by ice as recently as 10,000 years ago.

Scientists think that during the ice ages, average temperatures were only a few degrees cooler than they are now. Between the ice ages average temperatures became warmer and much of the glaciers melted. Since the last ice age, temperatures have slowly been rising.

There are several theories about what may cause natural changes in climate. Most scientists think that one factor in climatic changes is a change in the shape of the earth's orbit. Scientists believe that another factor may be a change in the angle at which the earth's axis is tilted.

What activities can change the climate?

Many scientists think that human activities are changing the earth's climate today. If that is true, people may have to change the ways they live. They will have to change some of their activities to stop or slow the climate changes.

Look at the pictures. These human activities may seem harmless. But using hair spray in an aerosol can can affect climate. Paving a parking lot or building a shopping center can also cause climatic changes. Cities are built, fossil fuels are burned, chemicals are released into the air, and forests are cut down. These and similar activities take place all over the world. All these activities help to warm the atmosphere.

▲ Using hairspray

◀ Paving a road

How can burning fossil fuels change climate?

Carbon dioxide, together with water vapor and other gases, act like the glass of a greenhouse. Energy from the sun passes through the greenhouse glass and is absorbed inside. Much of the absorbed energy is changed to heat. This heat warms the air in the greenhouse. The warmed air is trapped. It cannot escape through the glass.

Carbon dioxide in the atmosphere also traps heat. Some of the sun's energy that enters the atmosphere is absorbed by the earth's surface. The absorbed energy is changed to heat. Carbon dioxide traps some of the heat, keeping it close to the earth's surface. The trapping of heat by gases in the atmosphere is called the **greenhouse effect.**

Some of the greenhouse effect happens naturally. But the activities of humans are adding more carbon dioxide than normal to the atmosphere. Humans burn fossil fuels such as coal, natural gas, fuel oil, and gasoline for energy. When these fuels are burned, carbon dioxide is produced and released into the air. The added carbon dioxide causes increased warming of the atmosphere.

The greenhouse effect ▼

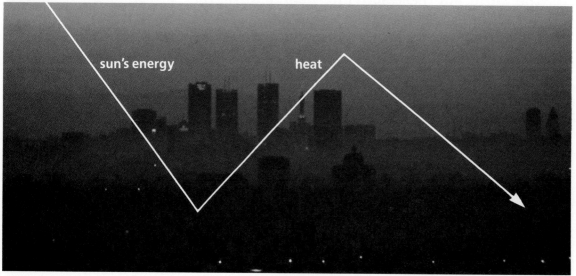

sun's energy

heat

426

ACTIVITY

Explore Together

How can you demonstrate the greenhouse effect?

Organizer

Materials

felt-tip pen · 3 shoeboxes · 3 thermometers · tape · plastic wrap · sheet of clear acetate

Procedure

Manager A. Use a felt-tip pen to label three shoeboxes A, B, and C.

Investigator B. Place a thermometer in each box. Tape the thermometers to the bottoms of the boxes near the center.

Investigator C. Cover box A with plastic wrap and tape it in place.

Investigator D. Cover box B with a sheet of acetate and tape it in place. Leave box C uncovered.

Group, Recorder   1. Which of the three boxes is your control?

Recorder E. Read the temperature on each thermometer. Record the temperatures in a chart such as the one shown.

Manager F. Place the three boxes next to each other in direct sunlight.

Group, Recorder   2. Predict what will happen to the temperature reading on each thermometer.

Recorder G. Read and record the temperature shown on each thermometer every 5 minutes for 30 minutes.

Group, Recorder   3. Draw a line graph of your recorded data for each box.

Time (minutes)	Temperature (°C) in Box		
	A	B	C
start			
5			
10			
15			
20			
25			
30			

Writing and Sharing Results and Conclusions

Group, Recorder 1. What happened to the temperature in each box?

2. Using your results, explain how the greenhouse effect warms the earth.

Reporter 3. How do your results and conclusions compare with those of your classmates?

What other factors can change climate?

Cities are usually warmer than rural regions. There is less evaporation of water in cities than there is elsewhere. Evaporation is a cooling process. In rural regions, water is absorbed into the ground or it runs off into rivers and lakes. Water can evaporate from these places. In cities, water runs off into storm drains and sewers. So there is little water on the surface to evaporate.

There is another reason why cities are warm. The buildings and paved streets absorb much energy from the sun and change it to heat. The heat from these surfaces raises the temperature of the air around them.

Chemicals called chlorofluorocarbons (klor oh-floor oh KAHR bunz) are harmful to the atmosphere. These chemicals are also known as CFCs. CFCs trap the earth's heat even more than carbon dioxide does. CFCs account for about 15 percent of the greenhouse effect.

The items in the picture contain CFCs. If the coolant in an air conditioner leaks, CFCs get into the air.

▼ Items containing CFCs

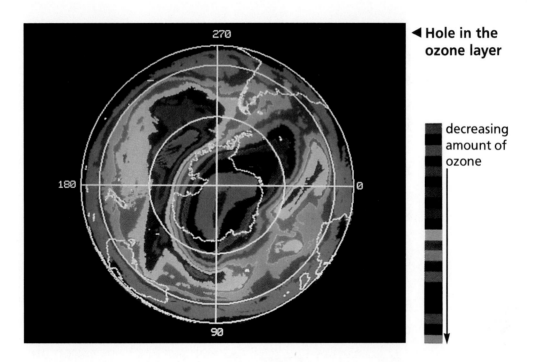

◄ Hole in the ozone layer

decreasing amount of ozone

Ozone (OH zohn) is a gas in the upper atmosphere. Ozone absorbs most of the ultraviolet (UV) radiation from the sun. Besides trapping heat, CFCs may also be destroying the ozone layer of the atmosphere. The map shows a hole that has already formed in the ozone layer. Destruction of the ozone layer would allow more UV radiation to reach the earth. UV radiation causes sunburn and skin cancer.

Cutting down and burning trees of the rain forests also leads to an increase in the greenhouse effect. Rain forests are found in the tropical climate zone. Many of the forests are being cleared to provide land for other purposes.

As you know, green plants take in carbon dioxide as part of their food-making process. They also release large amounts of water vapor into the air. Cutting the rain forests increases the amount of carbon dioxide in the air. It also decreases the water vapor added to the air. The decrease in water vapor may affect rainfall patterns around the world.

Burned trees of a rain forest ▼

429

With more CFCs and carbon dioxide in the air, the atmosphere will become warmer. The maps show how much the world's temperatures may increase by 2015 if the current warming continues. Ice in the polar regions could melt. This could raise sea level and flood shore regions. The rate of evaporation may increase. So the levels of lakes would go down.

An increase in temperature could also cause rainfall and snowfall to increase in some places and decrease in others. Regions that now have polar climates might become major crop producers. Today's farmlands might become tomorrow's deserts. So you can see, people all over the world must be concerned about future climate changes.

▼ 1990

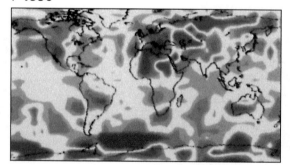

▼ 2015

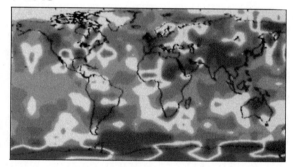

Change in temperature (°C)

Lesson Review

1. What is an ice age?
2. Name four activities of humans that can change climate.
3. What is the greenhouse effect? How does it occur?
4. What might happen if the earth's temperature rises?

Think! Suppose in the future that instead of warming, the earth's temperatures cooled and another ice age occurred. What changes might such an ice age bring?

Chapter Connections

Copy the graphic organizer. Watch a weather forecast on television. Put a check mark by each term in the graphic organizer that is used during the forecaster's presentation.

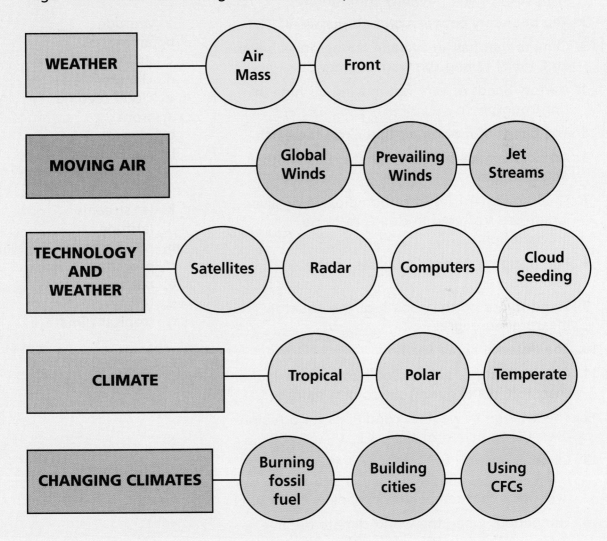

WEATHER — Air Mass — Front

MOVING AIR — Global Winds — Prevailing Winds — Jet Streams

TECHNOLOGY AND WEATHER — Satellites — Radar — Computers — Cloud Seeding

CLIMATE — Tropical — Polar — Temperate

CHANGING CLIMATES — Burning fossil fuel — Building cities — Using CFCs

Writing About Science • Classify

The climate people live in affects the way they live. Make a chart to show how food, clothing, shelter, and human activity may be different in each climate zone. Then use the chart to help you write a paragraph about your ideas.

Science Terms

Write the letter of the term that best matches the definition.

1. A large body of air that has about the same temperature and humidity throughout

2. The boundary between two air masses

3. Climate that has an average temperature below 10°C (50°F) during the warmest month

4. Narrow bands of very fast-moving air high in the troposphere

5. The bands of moving air that circle the earth

6. An object made by people that orbits another object in space

7. Small solid particles of carbon dioxide or silver iodide are scattered in clouds to cause precipitation

8. The trapping of heat by gases in the atmosphere

9. The distance north or south of the equator measured in degrees

10. The distance above sea level

11. Climate that has an average temperature higher than 18°C (64°F) during the coldest month

12. The average of weather conditions for a region over a long period of time

13. Climate in which the average summer temperature is above 18°C (64°F) and the average winter temperature is below 10°C (50°F)

14. The periods when the world climate became cooler

15. A large body of moving ice

16. A gas in the upper atmosphere

17. Winds that blow from the same direction over long distances

a. altitude
b. air mass
c. artificial satellite
d. climate
e. cloud seeding
f. front
g. glacier
h. global winds
i. greenhouse effect
j. ice ages
k. jet streams
l. latitude
m. polar climate
n. prevailing winds
o. ozone
p. temperate climate
q. tropical climate

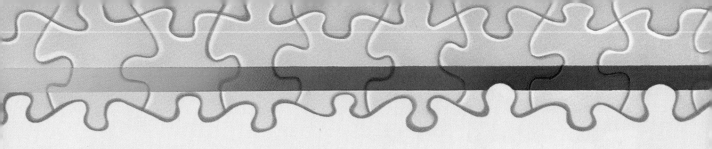

Science Ideas
Use complete sentences to answer the following.
1. Describe the weather on any day using at least five weather factors.
2. What would the weather be like on a day when a warm front is passing through your area? What would the weather be like after the front passes?
3. Suppose the jet stream has just moved south of your town. Why might the weather there change?
4. How is radar used to locate rain?
5. What are the two major conditions you would need to know to describe a region's climate.
6. Describe the conditions of a tropical climate, a polar climate, and a temperate climate.
7. What happened to much of the United States during the last ice age?
8. How does the use of CFCs affect the earth's atmosphere?

Applying Science Ideas
1. Describe some of your daily activities that may be helping to change the earth's climate.
2. What would be the danger of living in a low-lying shore region if the earth's temperatures continue to increase?
3. What are some benefits of having an early warning system to detect lightning?

Using Science Skills
The map shows a part of Kansas. You can see that in Topeka and in Lyndon the temperature is 20°C. In Lawrence and in Ottawa the temperature is 24°C. About what temperature would you estimate it is in Overbrook?

Chapter 13

Beyond the Solar System

Calling All Extraterrestrials

Picture an alien from space. Does it have three eyes? Is it green? Maybe it looks like the movie character E.T. Interest in aliens is not new. For years, people have been fascinated by the idea of creatures from space. But are there really aliens in space? There may be. Scientists are looking for them right now.

Scientists looked for aliens earlier in this century, too, when many people thought that there might be life on Mars or Venus. In 1905 the astronomer Percival Lowell claimed that he had found life on Mars. He said he saw dim lines crisscrossing the surface of Mars. Lowell thought the lines were canals built by Martians. He believed the canals carried water to modern cities. A newspaper at that time even ran a front-page headline that read "There Is Life On Planet Mars." Imagine picking up the morning paper and reading about Martian neighbors!

Many people get excited and even frightened when they hear about creatures from space. In 1938 the radio star Orson Welles broadcast a famous story called *War of the Worlds.* The story is about a Martian attack on Earth. In his broadcast, Welles described Martians landing in New Jersey. His description was so vivid that over 1 million radio listeners believed the story and panicked.

Scientists today still want to learn if there is life in space. The scientists at SETI are searching for intelligent life in space. SETI stands for Search for Extraterrestrial Intelligence. Harvard University scientist Paul Horowitz heads one of the SETI projects. Finding other life in the universe would be "the most important discovery in the history of the world," Horowitz says. Then he adds, "I hope it happens soon, and I hope I am the one who finds it."

AT THIS VERY MOMENT SPACE SHIPS FROM THE BEYOND MAY BE ON THEIR WAY TO DESTROY OUR PLANET!

H. G. WELLS'
The War of the Worlds

Just deciding how to find other life in the universe is a real challenge. Paul Horowitz is waiting for a "call" from outer space. He hopes the call will be "heard" by a 25-m (84-ft) radio antenna located in the city of Cambridge, Massachusetts. It is the largest system of any kind that is searching for life in space.

The dish antenna picks up radio signals from space. But answering a call from space is not as easy as answering a telephone. Scientists pick up many radio signals from space. Some of these signals come from the sun and other stars.

The puzzle for scientists is how to identify a radio signal that is being sent by a living thing in space. Maybe it would be a series of repeated notes. Maybe it would be a loud crash to get the attention of someone listening. A computer analyzes all the signals that the dish receives to see if any of them might have been sent by beings in space.

How long will it be before we find out if there are other beings in space? So far we have been searching for over 80 years. Some scientists think that Earth is 5 billion years old. The universe may be 15 billion years old. It is the opinion of some scientists that it may take 5,000 years to find a signal sent by a being in space. But it could happen much sooner.

Discover

What might life be like somewhere other than on Earth?

Materials   pencil · paper

Procedure

Harvard scientist Paul Horowitz has said that finding life somewhere else in the universe would be "the most important discovery in the history of the world." Pretend that you are a scientist and have heard from an alien in space. Prepare a radio interview with this alien.

Discuss the alien's home, likes, dislikes, needs, and so on. Decide what form of communication you need to use for the alien to understand you. Explain your form of communication to the class. Then present your radio interview to your class.

In this chapter you will learn how distances to objects in space are measured. You will learn about the life and death of stars. Finally you will find out how people are exploring space.

1. Distances in Space

Words to Know
astronomical
unit
light-year

Getting Started   Use a metric ruler to measure the length of this book. Give your answer in centimeters and in meters. Measure the distance from your seat to the chalkboard. Give your answer in centimeters and in meters. Which unit was easier to use for each measurement?

sun

1 AU =
149,600,000 km

Which units are used for distances in space?

You can see that different units can be used to measure distance. Some units are more useful for measuring short distances. Others are more useful for measuring long distances. In the drawing, which unit is used to express distances between cities?

Distances in space are so great that units such as kilometers are not convenient to use. The **astronomical unit** (as truh NAHM ih kul YOON iht), or AU, is a unit used to measure distances in the solar system. An astronomical unit is equal to 149.6 million km (93 million miles). This length is the average distance between the earth and the sun.

◀ The distance between
the earth and the
sun is 1 AU.

4,669 km

New York

San Francisco

Earth

The table below shows the distances from the sun to the planets in kilometers and AUs. What is the distance between Neptune and the sun in AUs? What is the distance in kilometers? Notice how using AUs makes these distances easier to write.

Planet	Distance from Sun (km)	Distance from Sun (AU)
Mercury	57,900,000	0.387
Venus	108,200,000	0.723
Earth	149,600,000	1.000
Mars	227,900,000	1.524
Jupiter	778,400,000	5.203
Saturn	1,427,000,000	9.539
Uranus	2,896,600,000	19.182
Neptune	4,520,000,000	30.214
Pluto	5,899,900,000	39.439

Distances between objects outside the solar system and the earth are greater than distances within the solar system. To express distances between objects beyond the solar system, a unit called a light-year is used. A **light-year** is the distance light travels in 1 year. Light travels about 300,000 kilometers (186,000 miles) in 1 second. In 1 year, light travels a distance of about 9.5 trillion kilometers (about 6 trillion miles). It takes about 8 minutes for light from the sun to travel to the earth.

▼ Expanding cloud of gas

Outside the solar system, Proxima Centauri (PRAHK suh muh sen TOR eye) is the nearest star. It is 4.3 light-years from the earth. How long does it take light to reach the earth from this star?

In A.D. 1054 astronomers saw a star explode. The star actually exploded in about 3000 B.C. It took the light more than 4,000 years to reach the earth. Look at the picture of an expanding cloud of gas. This cloud shows where that star once was.

How are distance and travel time related?

Distances can also be expressed by the time it takes to travel from one place to another. For example, you might say that your cousin's house is 1 hour away by car. Suppose you traveled at 88 kilometers per hour (55 miles per hour). At that speed, it would take you 1 hour to reach your cousin. But it would take you 6 months to reach the moon.

A spacecraft can travel at a speed of about 48,000 kilometers per hour (29,760 miles per hour). Moving at this speed, such a craft would reach the moon in about 8 hours. The same craft would reach Proxima Centauri in about 96,500 years.

Distance can be expressed in time traveled ▼

Lesson Review

1. Why is it inconvenient to use meters when describing the distance from the earth to the sun?

2. Define *astronomical unit* and *light-year*.

3. Suppose you are measuring three distances: (a) from Austin, Texas, to Fresno, California; (b) from the sun to Jupiter; and (c) from the earth to the star Sirius. For each distance, which unit of measurement would be easiest to use?

Think! Astronomers sometimes say, "When you look out into space, you are looking back in time." What do they mean?

THINKING

Skills

Relating two-dimensional and three-dimensional shapes

The pictures in this book are shown on flat pages. A picture on a page has only height and width. A shape that has only height and width is two-dimensional. The pictures show real objects. Real objects have height, width, and depth. Real objects are three-dimensional. You can match two-dimensional shapes with three-dimensional objects.

Practicing the skill

1. Study the picture of the earth. It is a two-dimensional view.

2. From what you can see in the picture, Earth has a round shape. What other information does this picture provide about the earth?

3. You cannot be sure of the overall shape of the earth from the picture. What other information is not provided in the picture?

4. Now examine a globe. A globe is three-dimensional. What does a globe show you that the picture cannot show?

Thinking about the skill

When might a three-dimensional model be more useful than a two-dimensional picture?

Applying the skill

Look at the drawings. Each drawing is a two-dimensional shape. Make a three-dimensional shape out of clay. The object should have sides that look like the drawings.

 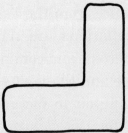 

Orion

Big Bear

2. Observing Stars

Getting Started When people of long ago looked into the night sky, they saw pictures. The Big Bear, shown above, is one of the pictures they saw. In the Big Bear there are three stars in the tail and four stars across the bear's back. These seven stars form the Big Dipper. Do you see a dipper in these stars? If not, what do you see?

When and where can constellations be seen?

A group of stars that seem to form a picture is called a **constellation** (kahn stuh LAY shun). Many of the constellations were named by the ancient Greeks. The stars in a constellation are not all the same distance from the earth.

Constellations are named for such things as animals, heroes, and common objects. Across the top of this page and the next are several constellations. It may help you to picture the shapes if you play "Connect the Dots" with the stars. For example,

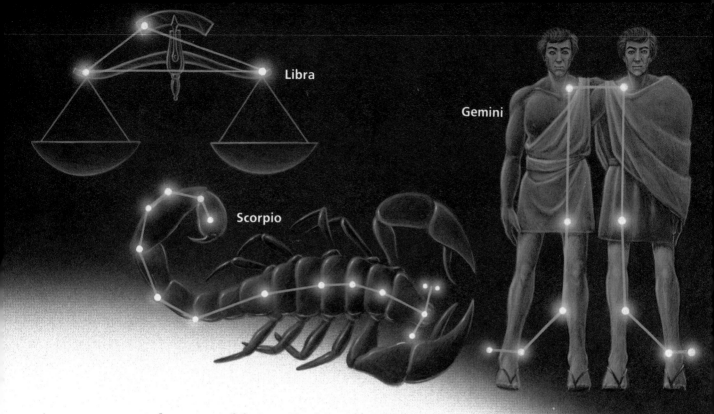

Libra

Gemini

Scorpio

connect the stars of Orion. Perhaps you can picture a hunter. Connect the stars of Gemini (JEM uh nye), and you may be able to see a pair of twins.

Just as the sun appears to move across the daytime sky, stars appear to move across the night sky. They appear to move from east to west. You probably know that the earth spins on its axis. Because the earth is spinning, the sun and nearly all stars *appear* to be moving across the sky.

One star seen from the northern half of the earth seems to stay in the same place. This star is Polaris (poh LAR ihs), also called the North Star. It is found almost directly above the North Pole.

Those constellations that are close to Polaris can be seen all year from the northern half of the earth. This is because the paths followed by such constellations do not dip below the horizon. Due to the earth's spinning, a group of constellations appears to circle Polaris. Look at the picture at the right. It was taken over several hours. It is known as a time-lapse photograph. What do you observe?

Constellations close to Polaris ▼

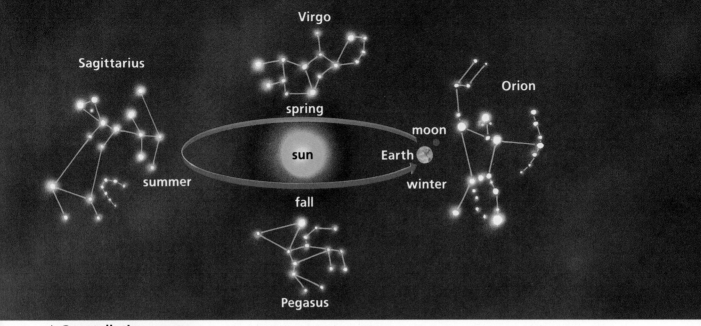

Constellations that are not near Polaris seem to "rise" and "set," just as the sun does. These constellations can be seen only at certain times of the year. As the earth moves along its orbit, it faces different parts of the sky. So different groups of stars can be seen at different times of the year. From the drawing on this page, which constellation can be seen in spring?

A light telescope in an observatory ▼

What modern devices are used to study stars?

Today people still enjoy locating the constellations. But the study of constellations does not help scientists learn about the nature of stars. Scientists now use many instruments to study the stars.

A common way to study the stars is with a telescope (TEL uh skohp). A telescope makes distant objects appear brighter, clearer, and larger. It shows details that cannot be seen with the eyes alone. A **light telescope** is a device that gathers light from stars and other objects in space. The telescope shown here gathers light with a mirror and lenses. Light telescopes let you see many stars that are too dim to be seen with the unaided eye.

Not all telescopes gather light waves. A **radio telescope** is a device that gathers radio waves from objects in space. Some objects in space, such as stars and planets, give off radio waves. Radio waves pass through space and then are collected by large dish-shaped antennas on the earth. The larger the dish, the more radio waves the telescope can collect. The picture shows a radio telescope with its large dish for collecting radio waves. Data collected by radio telescopes were used to produce the radio maps shown on this page. Computers interpret the data and produce the maps. These maps show regions in space where radio waves are given off.

▼ Sky maps produced by radio telescopes

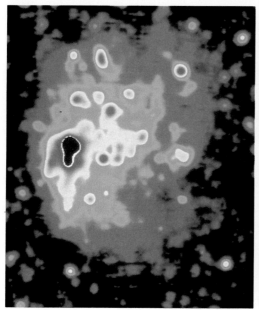

A radio telescope in New Mexico ▶

In some ways, radio telescopes are more useful than light telescopes. A light telescope can be used only when the sky is clear and only at night. A radio telescope can "see" through dense cloud cover and pollution. A radio telescope can be used during the day as well as at night.

Explore

How can you construct a spectroscope?

In 1666 the English scientist Isaac Newton made a tiny hole in a window shutter. With the shutter closed, he held a special kind of glass in front of the hole. A beam of light passed through the glass. On his white wall, Newton saw a rainbow of colors. He had built the first spectroscope!

Materials

scissors · piece of cardboard · cardboard tube from paper toweling
sharpened pencil · metric ruler · masking tape · diffraction grating

Procedure

A. Cut two identical circles from a piece of cardboard. The circles should just seal the two ends of a cardboard tube.

B. With a pencil, punch a hole 0.5 cm in diameter in the center of one of the cardboard circles.

C. Tape a piece of diffraction grating over the 0.5 cm hole.

D. Tape the circle with the diffraction grating to one end of the cardboard tube. Make sure the grating faces inward.

E. Cut the other cardboard circle in half. Tape the two halves to the other end of the tube. Leave a narrow slit between them.

F. Seal the ends of the tubes very carefully with tape.

G. Aim the slit end at a light bulb. Look at the light through the end with the diffraction grating.

H. Aim the slit end of the tube at another light source in your room. **Caution:** *Do not aim the tube at the sun. The bright light could injure your eyes.*

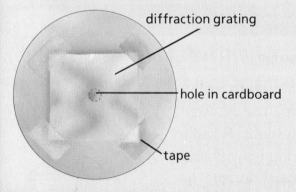

diffraction grating

hole in cardboard

tape

Writing and Sharing Results and Conclusions

1. How did the two light sources seen through the tube compare?

2. What does the diffraction grating do to the light that passes through it?

3. How could this device be used to study stars?

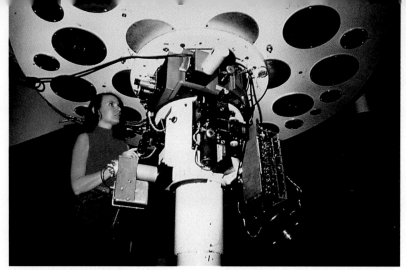

▲ A spectroscope

The spectrum of helium gas ▼

What does starlight tell us about stars?

Fingerprints can be used to identify people. The light given off by a star can be used as a "star fingerprint." Scientists can use the light of a star to "fingerprint," or identify, the gases in a star. They use a spectroscope (SPEK troh skohp), shown above, to study the starlight. A **spectroscope** is a device that separates light into a band of colors. Such a pattern is called a spectrum.

Each kind of glowing gas in a star produces a spectrum. This spectrum is different from that produced by any other gas. Such a spectrum is like a "fingerprint" of that gas. A spectrum of helium gas, found in most stars, is shown. The spectrum of a star shows the kinds of matter in that star.

Lesson Review

1. What is a constellation?
2. Name and describe a well-known constellation.
3. Give examples of two different types of telescopes. Explain when each can be used.
4. What information does a spectroscope provide about a star?

Think! The spectrum produced by a star does not match any spectrum ever seen before. What might be concluded?

3. Characteristics of Stars

Words To Know

magnitude
nebula
red giant
white dwarf
black dwarf
supernova
neutron star
black hole

Getting Started Imagine that you are at one end of a football field at night. At the other end are two lights. One is a huge stadium light at the top of a pole. The other is a flashlight. Which light is brighter? Suppose the stadium light is moved 10 km away. The flashlight is moved 1 m away. Which light looks brighter?

▲ Comparing the magnitude of two stars

What affects a star's brightness?

Stars differ in brightness. Scientists call the brightness of a star its **magnitude** (MAG nuh tood). The magnitude of a star depends on three things. First, it depends on the distance the star is from the earth. The closer the star, the brighter it will appear. Look at the two stars shown. They are the same in every way except one. They have the same size and the same temperature. But they vary in their distance from the earth. Star A is closer to the earth. Which star—A or B—will appear brighter?

448

Problem Solving

Star Light, Star Bright

Imagine that tonight you will be viewing the stars from an open field. You notice that the stars vary in magnitude. A bright star will look bigger than a dim star. You have brought a 3" x 5" card. Holes of different sizes are punched in the card.

How can you use a 3" x 5" card to compare the magnitude of some stars?

Show other members of your class how you can use the card to compare magnitude. How could you improve upon this simple device? How could you compare the magnitude of the stars forming your favorite constellation?

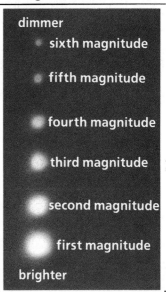

Second, magnitude depends on the size of the star. Suppose two stars are the same distance from the earth and have the same temperature. Imagine that one star is much larger than the other. The larger star will be brighter than the smaller star.

Third, how bright a star appears depends on the temperature of the star. Suppose two stars are the same in every way except for temperature. The star with the higher temperature will be brighter.

Early astronomers ranked stars according to how bright they looked. The brightest stars were called stars of the first magnitude. The dimmest stars were called stars of the sixth magnitude. At the right is a magnitude scale. It shows that stars with the greatest magnitude have the lowest numbers on the scale. For example, a very bright, nearby star, such as the sun, will have a very low number. Stars with the least magnitude have the highest numbers on the scale. A very dim, distant star has a very high number on the scale.

▼ Magnitude scale

dimmer
- sixth magnitude
- fifth magnitude
- fourth magnitude
- third magnitude
- second magnitude
- first magnitude
brighter

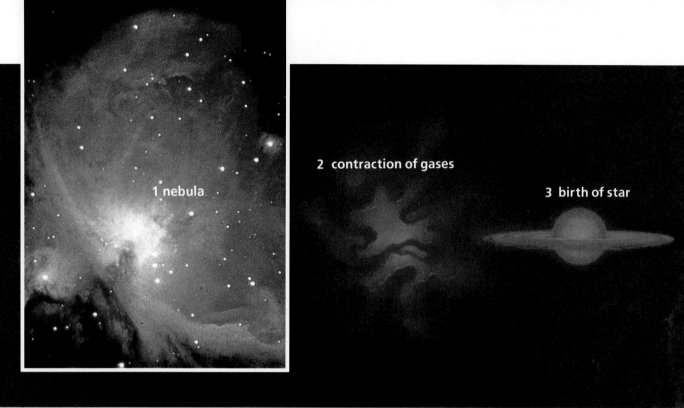

1 nebula

2 contraction of gases

3 birth of star

▲ Life cycle of a star like the sun

What is the life cycle of a star?

Scientists believe that stars go through a "life cycle." Stars are "born," they exist for a while, and then they "die." During their life cycles, stars change in temperature and brightness. The life cycle of a star may take billions of years.

Refer to the pictures above to see the life cycle of a star with an average mass, such as our sun. (1) Scientists think that stars are born in nebulas (NEB-yuh luz). A **nebula** is a huge cloud of dust and gases. A famous nebula, called the Great Nebula in Orion, is shown. (2) Gases contract, or come together, inside a nebula. The contracting gases form a small core of gases. Inside this core, the temperature becomes very high. (3) Finally, the temperature is high enough to cause nuclear reactions. These reactions produce energy. The star begins to glow. A star is then "born."

Many scientists believe that the mass of a new star affects the star's lifespan. In general, stars that

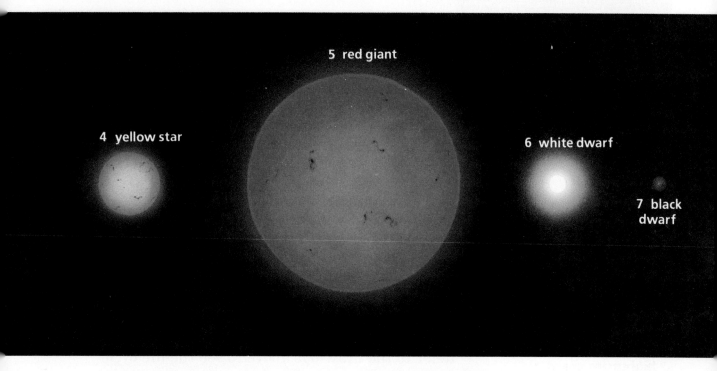

4 yellow star

5 red giant

6 white dwarf

7 black dwarf

begin with a very low mass have the longest life. Such stars take a very long time to use up their supply of fuel. Stars that are born with a very large mass often have the shortest life. They use up their supply of fuel very quickly.

The mass of a star affects the stages of a star's life cycle. (4) Stars with about the same mass as the sun begin life as yellow stars. Such stars remain as yellow stars for about 10 billion years. (5) As they age, these stars slowly change into red giants. A **red giant** is an old star that has greatly enlarged and is cool compared with a yellow star.

(6) After its fuel is used up, a red giant will collapse and become a white dwarf. A **white dwarf** is an old, very dense star. A white dwarf may be only as large as the earth but have a mass as great as the sun. (7) As it cools, a white dwarf becomes a black dwarf. A **black dwarf** is the remains of a white dwarf star that has used up all its fuel. It does not give off any light.

1 nebula

3 red giant

2 blue star

▲ **Life cycle of a high-mass star**

📖 *Myla was not an ordinary traveler. Her voyage was not an ordinary trip. Learn why she had to leave Elan in **Final Call For the Stars** in Horizons Plus.*

Refer to the drawings above to see the life cycle of a star that starts out with a high mass. (1) As with all stars, the star first forms in a nebula. (2) It develops into a blue star, a very hot star with a high mass. This star uses up its fuel quickly. (3) After only a few million years, the blue star enters old age. In old age, a blue star can change into a red giant. A red giant can expand and contract a number of times. Then it explodes.

(4) The violent explosion of a star that has a high mass is called a **supernova** (soo puhr NOH-vuh). Much of the star's mass is lost during this explosion. The supernova may shine more brightly than millions of stars combined. The shining cloud of matter may be visible for thousands of years. Locate the supernova in the drawing of the life cycle of a high-mass star.

(5) After the supernova stage, the star that remains may become a neutron star. A **neutron star** is a very small, very dense star. Scientists found a spinning neutron star, called a pulsar, at the

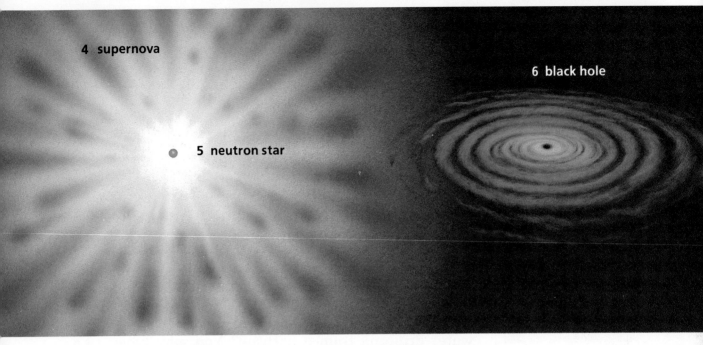

4 supernova

6 black hole

5 neutron star

center of the Crab Nebula. A pulsar gives off regular bursts of energy.

(6) A star that began with a very high mass may end up as a black hole. A **black hole** is a small region in space resulting from the collapse of a massive star. The gravitational attraction of the matter in a black hole is so great that no light can escape.

The explosion that occurs when stars die provides dust and gas for new stars. New stars come from old stars. At this very moment, somewhere out in space, a new star is about to be born.

Lesson Review

1. What three things affect the magnitude of a star?
2. Trace seven main stages in the life cycle of a star that has a mass about the same as that of the sun.
3. Beginning with the blue-star stage, describe five stages in the life of a high-mass star.

Think! A supernova can occur near the end of a star's life cycle. Yet, a supernova is also related to a star's birth. How are the birth and death of stars related?

453

4. Stars in Motion

Words to Know
galaxy
spiral galaxy
elliptical galaxy
irregular galaxy
universe

Getting Started Have you ever watched the water draining from a bathtub? You may have noticed that the draining water formed a spiral shape. This spiral is somewhat like the shape formed by the huge group of stars to which our sun belongs.

What is a galaxy?

The stars you can see at night and the sun belong to a group of stars called a galaxy (GAL uhk-see). A **galaxy** is a huge rotating group of stars. You can see a galaxy in the picture above. Some astronomers believe there are trillions of galaxies. Each galaxy is like a giant island made of billions of stars moving through space. Stars in a single galaxy are light-years apart. Galaxies are separated in space by distances of hundreds of thousands or by millions of light-years.

In 1987 scientists discovered the most distant galaxy ever seen. At the left is a computer-made picture of this galaxy. The galaxy may be 15 billion light-years away from the earth.

Computer picture of a distant galaxy ▼

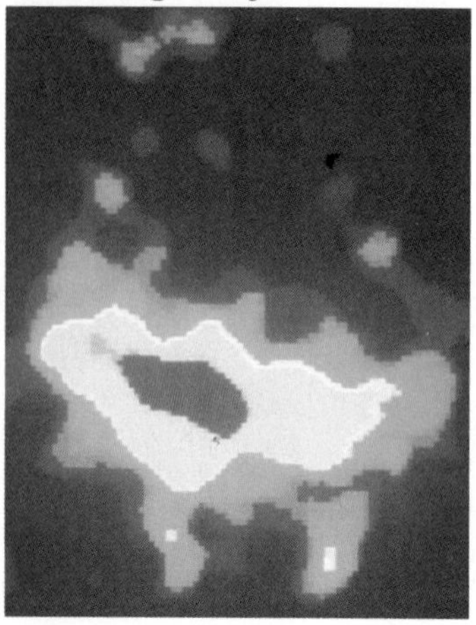

454

What are the shapes of galaxies?

On a clear, moonless night, far from the city lights, you can see part of the Milky Way galaxy. The Milky Way galaxy is a huge collection of stars that includes the sun and hundreds of billions of other stars. This galaxy is thought to have a central part and arms that spiral out from it. The drawing below shows two views of the Milky Way. One is a top view of the galaxy. The other is a side view. From the side, it looks a bit like a slim watch with a watchband. The central part of the galaxy—the "watch"—is about 5000 light-years thick. It is bright because of the great number of stars.

Scientists think that our solar system is about three fifths of the way from the center of the Milky Way galaxy. Our solar system is thought to be in one of the galaxy's spiral arms. Notice that our solar system is marked with Xs in the drawing.

▼ **Top view and side view of the Milky Way galaxy**

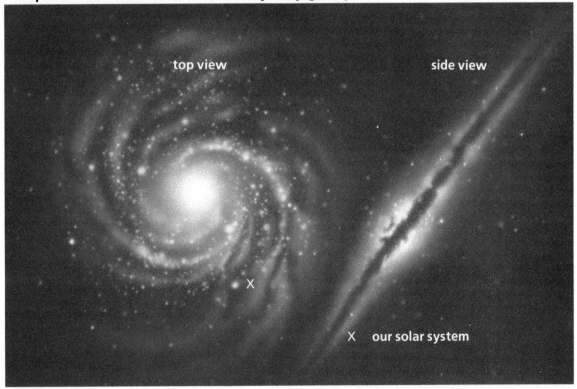

top view   side view

X

X   our solar system

▼ An ellipitical galaxy

▼ An irregular galaxy

Not all galaxies are like the Milky Way. Galaxies have different shapes. Scientists classify galaxies into three types based on their shapes. A **spiral galaxy** is a galaxy that has arms coming out from a central region. An **elliptical** (ee LIHP tih kul) **galaxy** is a galaxy that is shaped like a football. This type of galaxy does not have arms, as you can see in the picture. Most of the known galaxies are elliptical. An **irregular** (ihr REHG yoo lur) **galaxy** is one that has no specific shape. Locate the irregular galaxy in the picture above.

What is one theory on how the universe began?

The **universe** (YOON uh vurs) is everything that exists, including space and all objects in it. Many scientists believe that the universe is expanding like a balloon that is being blown up. Scientists call this idea about the expansion of the universe the expanding-universe theory. This theory suggests that the Milky Way, and other galaxies, are moving through space. Further, it suggests that galaxies are moving away from each other.

456

Some scientists believe that the universe began as a concentrated mass of matter, as shown in drawing *A*. A huge explosion, shown in drawing *B*, scattered matter and energy throughout space. The stars and galaxies formed later, when parts of this matter began to collect, as shown in drawing *C*. Scientists refer to this idea about how the universe formed as the big-bang theory.

Galaxies may still be moving outward from the center of that first huge explosion. Some scientists think the universe will continue to expand. Others think that one day it will collapse in upon itself.

▼ **The big-bang theory of how the universe began**

  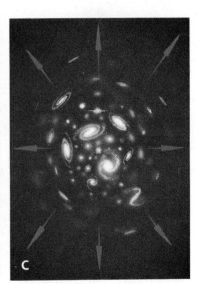

Lesson Review

1. What is a galaxy?
2. Name and describe the galaxy in which our solar system is found.
3. What is the difference between a spiral galaxy, an elliptical galaxy, and an irregular galaxy? Draw each of these galaxies on a sheet of paper.
4. What is the big-bang theory?

Think! If the universe is expanding, what effect is this having on the density of the universe?

5. Exploring Space

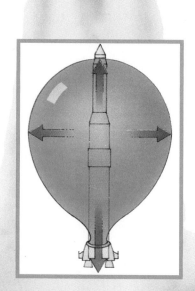

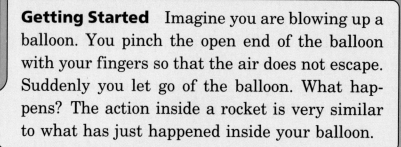

Words to Know
rocket
space shuttle
space station

Getting Started Imagine you are blowing up a balloon. You pinch the open end of the balloon with your fingers so that the air does not escape. Suddenly you let go of the balloon. What happens? The action inside a rocket is very similar to what has just happened inside your balloon.

How do rockets work?

A **rocket** is a spacecraft that contains a powerful engine. It can launch people and equipment into space. Such a spacecraft can overcome the earth's gravity. Gravity is the force that attracts objects toward the center of the earth. For example, the force of gravity causes a ball thrown up into the air to fall back to the earth.

Recall the imaginary balloon you just let go of. Air was pushing against all inside surfaces. The force was equal in all directions. When you let go of the open end, air escaped. But it still pushed on the closed end. So, the balloon shot away. Similar forces occur inside a rocket.

Look at the drawing that compares a balloon and a rocket. The force of the gases pushing against the top of the rocket is not balanced by a force against the bottom. Instead, gases escape from the bottom opening in the same way that gases escape from the neck of a balloon. The unbalanced force causes the rocket to move upward.

◀ **A rocket liftoff compared to a rising balloon**

458

▼ Parts of the space shuttle

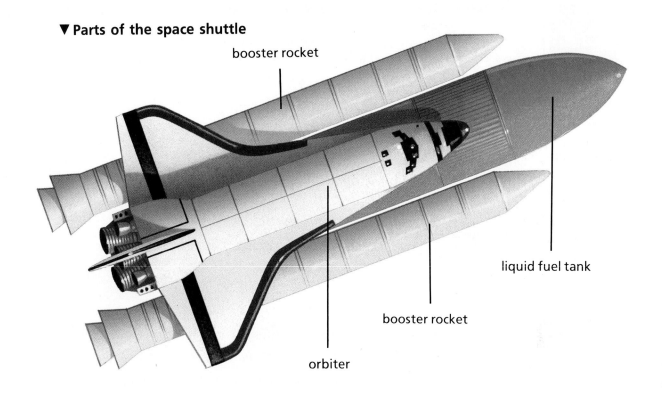

booster rocket

liquid fuel tank

booster rocket

orbiter

What are the parts of the space shuttle?

The **space shuttle** is a spacecraft that carries passengers and equipment into space. Like most other spacecraft, the space shuttle is launched into space by rockets. But the space shuttle is different because it can be reused. It consists of three main parts. One part is the orbiter, which carries passengers and equipment. The orbiter has three engines. Find the orbiter in the picture.

A second main part of the space shuttle is a large outside tank that holds liquid fuel. Two booster rockets that hold solid fuel make up a third main part of the shuttle. After the booster rockets have used up their fuel, they fall to the earth. These rockets can be reused in later flights. The large fuel tank uses up its fuel and falls back to the earth.

Only the orbiter reaches space and circles the earth. When the orbiter returns to the earth, it lands on a runway, much as an airplane does.

Explore Together

How does a rocket move?

Materials

Organizer

scissors · fishing line · balloon · twist tie · drinking straw
masking tape

Procedure

Investigator

A. Work with a partner. Cut a 9-m length of fishing line. Attach one end of the fishing line to a doorknob.

Manager

B. Blow up a balloon. Attach a twist tie to the open end of the balloon so that air will not escape.

Investigator

C. Tape a drinking straw to the balloon as shown. The balloon and straw make up your rocket.

Investigator

D. Slide the loose end of the fishing line through the drinking straw.

E. Hold the string tight and in a straight line. Remove the twist tie. Observe how your rocket moves.

F. Draw a picture of the balloon on the string. With an arrow, show the direction in which the balloon moves.

Recorder

1. How far did your rocket travel?
2. How can you make your rocket travel farther?

G. Repeat steps **A–F**. This time, find a way to make your rocket travel farther.

Group and Reporter

Writing and Sharing Results and Conclusions

1. What makes your rocket move?

2. How do your results and conclusions compare with those of your classmates?

▲ Voyager space probe

How are space probes and satellites used?

A device called a space probe can study objects in space. Unlike the space shuttle, a space probe does not have humans aboard. It carries only computers and instruments. The instruments collect and send back data to the earth for study by scientists. Many facts about the solar system have come from space probes that flew by the planets.

The Voyager space probes have sent back data about the giant outer planets. In 1989 the space probe Galileo was sent on a journey to Jupiter. It should reach that planet in 1995.

A satellite is a body that orbits another body in space. For example, the moon is the earth's natural satellite. A satellite that is made by people is called an artificial satellite. Artificial satellites are of many different shapes and sizes. The Hubble telescope, also called the Space Telescope, is one type of artificial satellite. Shown at the right, it is a light telescope designed to orbit above the earth's atmosphere. It can see the universe more clearly than any telescope on the earth's surface.

▼ Construction of the Space Telescope

▲ How a space colony
on Mars might look

Life Science
CONNECTION

*Use reference books
to find out how
astronauts exercise
while in space.*

How will space be explored in the future?

On pages 434–436 you read about space aliens. In the future, humans will study space from space stations. A **space station** is a spacecraft that stays in orbit for long periods. People live on and do experiments in a space station. The United States Skylab was the first space station, orbiting the earth in 1973. A larger Soviet space station, Mir, was sent out in orbit in 1986.

Someday, spacecraft may return to the earth with medicines and other goods made at a space station. Spacecraft may stop at the space station to get fuel and other supplies. Scientists are planning space stations for the moon and Mars. There may be working space colonies on Mars by the middle of the twenty-first century.

Lesson Review

1. Briefly describe how a rocket works.
2. What is the space shuttle? What are its three main parts?
3. Describe one kind of artificial satellite.
4. List three uses of space stations.

Think! What conditions will be needed in a space station to house people for long periods of time?

Chapter Connections

Look at the graphic organizer and explain each term that appears in the boxes. In your own words compare your explanations with those in your textbook.

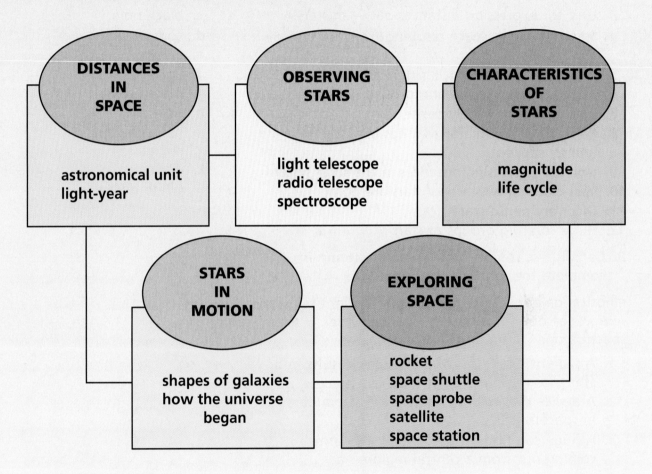

DISTANCES IN SPACE

astronomical unit
light-year

OBSERVING STARS

light telescope
radio telescope
spectroscope

CHARACTERISTICS OF STARS

magnitude
life cycle

STARS IN MOTION

shapes of galaxies
how the universe began

EXPLORING SPACE

rocket
space shuttle
space probe
satellite
space station

Writing About Science • Create

Suppose that a spacecraft without people aboard will soon be launched to look for intelligent life in outer space. Make a series of drawings to be placed in the spacecraft. The purpose of the drawings is to inform the other intelligent life about life on Earth. Include directions to Earth. Write a paragraph explaining what you drew and why you drew it.

Science Terms

A. Write the letter of the term that best matches the definition.

1. Old star that is greatly enlarged but cool
2. Brightness of a star
3. Unit for expressing distances between stars
4. Small region in space resulting from collapse of a massive star
5. Everything that exists, including all of space
6. Group of stars that seem to form a pattern
7. Very small, extremely dense star
8. Remains of dwarf star that has used up its energy supply
9. Unit for expressing distances in the solar system
10. Vast cloud in which new stars are born
11. Old, very dense star
12. Huge rotating groups of stars

a. astronomical unit
b. black dwarf
c. black hole
d. constellation
e. galaxy
f. light-year
g. magnitude
h. nebula
i. neutron star
j. red giant
k. universe
l. white dwarf

B. Copy the sentences below. Use the terms listed to complete the sentences.

elliptical galaxy   irregular galaxy   light telescope
radio telescope   rocket   space shuttle   space station
spectroscope   spiral galaxy   supernova

1. A violent explosion of a star that results in a star's losing much of its mass is a _____.
2. A device that gathers radio waves from objects in space is a _____.
3. A huge rotating group of stars with arms coming out from a central region is a _____.
4. A _____ is a spacecraft that contains a powerful engine and can launch equipment and people into space.
5. A huge rotating group of stars that is shaped like a football is an _____.
6. A spacecraft that stays in orbit for long periods of time is a _____.
7. A device that breaks light into different colors and is used for studying the stars is a _____.

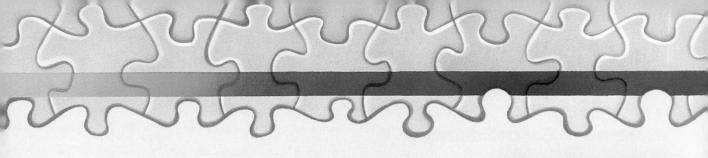

8. Astronomers use a _____ to gather light so that space objects can be seen more clearly.

9. A spacecraft that carries passengers and equipment into space is a _____.

10. A huge rotating group of stars with no special shape is an _____.

A

Science Ideas
Use complete sentences to answer the following.

1. Distinguish between a light-year and an astronomical unit. When would each be used?
2. Define *constellation*. Name and describe a constellation you could see tonight.
3. Describe how the following could be used by an astronomer: spectroscope, radio telescope, and telescope.
4. What are some of the characteristics used to tell one star from another?
5. What is magnitude? On what does it depend?
6. Place the stages in the life cycle of a high-mass star, shown at right, in the correct order.
7. Name and describe the group of stars to which our solar system belongs.
8. Name and describe three main types of galaxies.
9. Briefly describe the big-bang theory.
10. How does a rocket work?
11. Name and describe a device used to explore space.

B

C

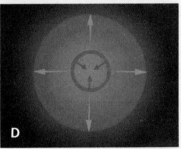

D

Applying Science Ideas
Explain why some stars in a constellation may appear to be much brighter than other stars in that constellation.

Using Science Skills
The picture on page 459 shows the parts of the space shuttle and its shape. What other information would a three-dimensional model show?

Careers in Earth Science

Seismologist

"As a child I was always asking questions," says Waverly Person. Waverly still asks a lot of questions, mostly about earthquakes. Waverly Person is a **seismologist.** He is a scientist who studies how and why earthquakes happen.

Waverly Person is the chief of the National Earthquake Information Service. Its headquarters is in Denver, Colorado.

The Service has monitors all over the world that keep track of movements in the earth's crust. When the crust moves, the monitors beam the information to satellites. The satellites beam it to the National Earthquake Information Service.

Waverly and his staff also study data that they collect from each earthquake. The data include the strength of each quake, how long it lasts, and where it is located.

Waverly makes sure that relief agencies know where a quake has happened. Then they can send food, supplies, and equipment to help people. "There is no sure way to warn people before a quake," says Waverly. "But one day our research might help us to say exactly when an earthquake will happen."

Do you think you might like to be a seismologist? You'll need a college degree. It helps to like math, geology, and other sciences. Waverly says it is also important to learn about computers. Waverly Person has been a seismologist for 30 years. But he still likes his job a lot. "It's very exciting," he says. "No two earthquakes are alike. I am always learning something new."

Connecting Science Ideas

1. Imagine that you are designing a very tall office building. What kind of helpful information could the National Earthquake Information Service provide?   **Careers; Chapter 11**

2. How has the movement of continents affected the kinds of air masses that move over North America?
   Chapter 11; Chapter 12

3. In what ways do different parts of the hydrosphere contribute to the weather?   **Chapter 11; Chapter 12**

4. You read about the presence of rock layers left by glaciers in India. Use what you know about climate zones to explain how the presence of these rock layers supports the theory of continental drift.   **Chapter 11; Chapter 12**

5. How is the way the earth may have formed different from the way a star with a low mass forms?   **Chapter 11; Chapter 13**

Computer Connections

Choose a star. Use reference books to find out about the star, including its distance from Earth, its magnitude, the constellation in which it is located, and the season in which it can be seen. Enter the information you find into a class database. Use the class database to help you make four star charts — one for each season.

Unit Project

With a partner, make a model of a seismograph. Fill a shoebox with sand and put the lid on. The shoebox will represent the crust of the earth. Place the box on a table. Wrap a rubber band around the box and slip a felt-tip pen under the rubber band. The pen should be parallel to the top of the table and stick out beyond the end of the box. Your partner should move a pad of paper slowly past the pen as you shake the table. Try this several times and compare the recordings on the sheets of paper.

from

Auks, Rocks and

by Peggy Thomson

the Odd Dinosaur

Antrodemus is one of the many treasures housed at our National Museum of Natural History in Washington, D.C. Find out how Arnold Lewis was able to piece together the 268 fossil bones of this meat-eating dinosaur and make it stand upright again for the first time in millions of years.

Meet *Antrodemus* 145 million years after his life. A skeleton of dark fossil bones, he has been caught in action, moving fast toward a meal, which for him is not leafy vegetation but a leaf-eating *Stegosaurus* almost as big as himself.

In 1979 when the hall of dinosaurs was remade, planners thought it needed something fierce. It needed gaping jaws and saw-teeth, a predator in action. The plant-eating dinosaurs are huge and strange looking, with spikes and great plates and horns, but they are not *doing* much of anything. A meat eater on the move would impress people.

Meat eaters are in short supply. Fewer of them lived, and because they lived in exciting and dangerous ways they tended to be damaged. By good fortune the museum had a fine specimen. And Arnold Lewis was the person to prepare it for exhibit.

He had two years, till the new hall opened, to clean up the bones and stand *Antrodemus* on his feet in a hunting position. As such work goes, two years is not much time. But Lewis was an old hand, and it helped to have a specimen in such good condition.

Most dinosaurs in museums are composites, put together from scraps, like cars from spare parts. This skeleton, though, had been a great find. It was practically complete. If the fossil hunters who quarried it in the 1880s in Colorado hadn't thrown the tail over the cliff (they thought it belonged to another animal), it would have been just about perfect.

The bones were amazingly hard, too unlike most dinosaur bones, which are rotten, punky, crumbly. And they were easy to see because they were black, and the rock they were imbedded in was a pale sand color. Most often the colors blend, and it is difficult to tell where the rock ends and the bone begins. Lewis knew he was lucky.

Part of the work had already been done. The skull and some bones had been freed from the rock back when the animal was first written up for scientific papers. Still, it took Lewis six months just to grind away rock from the remaining bones to see what he had. He used chisels and picks and power drills, and he proceeded with caution. If a tool slipped, he'd nick a bone or dent it or scratch it. If he dropped a pelvic bone, it would shatter like glass.

All along he was reading up on *Antrodemus* and looking at photographs and at an old drawing with the bones numbered 1 through 238 (not counting some 30 bones in the head). When an artist made him a new drawing to work from, it showed *Antrodemus* running, one leg lifted high. The pose was dramatic, just what the new hall needed, but too dramatic, Lewis thought. So did the dinosaur expert, Nicholas Hotton.

The men agreed. Lifted that high, the leg would have pulled out of its socket. They made cardboard cutouts based on the drawing. They moved the leg around with pins and lowered it a lot.

Antrodemus, said Hotton, was no runner, no jumper, but a strider. He'd read the information in the bones, as paleontologists do. *Antrodemus* was a powerful strider, moving out at a tilt like a chicken's. He kept his front legs at the ready for grabbing prey and holding it. As he strode, his hind legs swung back and forth like pendulums, like the legs of elephants. Fossil tracks found on the ground show footprints that are even and narrowly spaced—left, right, left, right. The prints also show that the tail was not dragged but held up as a mighty counterweight.

Lewis, with a rhinoceros-size chicken in mind, sawed a shape to size out of wood, matching it to the position of the cardboard cutout. Then he built a giant sandbox and piled up sand to support the bones while he laid them out. "Without it," he said, "I'd have needed five hands." When the

bones of the neck were joined, they formed a kind of half circle. Once all such curves and angles were established, Lewis could bend his steel for the framework and start attaching bones to it, lifting and lowering the largest of them with chain hoists hung from a ceiling beam.

In life the animal balanced, seesaw fashion, across the hips. Much of the front part was hollow with lungs and such. And the back was weighted with muscle. But without the meat, the skeleton is front-heavy, so the frame has to make up for it. The frame carries the weight. Yet it has to be almost out of sight so that people seeing the dinosaur will marvel at it and not at museum handiwork.

There was of course the matter of the missing tail. Lewis had to copy one. He made a rubber mold from a tail in a Utah museum and then cast a new tail by pouring plastic into the mold. He replaced ribs, all but five or six of which were splintered, some in hundreds of pieces. He hung the all right ribs, then tied on wires for the missing ones and built them up with fiberglass tape and with papier-mâché. Trickiest to reconstruct was the belly armor, the ribby bit that floats free without a backbone connection. Lewis kept it light, attached to the nearest rib.

The one piece of guesswork was the sternum, or breast bone. The real bone existed, but it was shattered, and there was none to copy that was reasonably intact. "In such a quandary," Lewis says, "you go to other dinosaurs that walked on two feet. You check them out and their closest living relatives, too, which happen to be crocodiles." In the end he took his design from the sternum of a crocodile. As a friend in the lab says, "Sometimes Arnie has to hum a few bars and hope he gets it right."

Once done, the patching looked spotty. Lewis then painted the pipes and all his homemade pieces. He did not try for the closest match but purposely kept his paint lighter than the black of the bones. He was going by the museum's six-foot-six inch rule. At a distance of six feet, the difference between real bones and fakes ought not to hit people in the eye. Close up, at six inches, if it can't be seen at all, then people are being tricked.

Lewis met his deadline. He'd put in two full years of brain work and muscle work, of heaving and hauling and delicate, close work, too. He'd used all his expertise in bones and stones and his skills at sculpting, painting, welding. And he was done on time.

Now at least once a week, sometimes still in his blue denim apron, splotched from fossil work in progress, he comes from his lab to look at *Antrodemus*. He thinks about the lunging tilt and the leg lift that puzzled him so long and about all the nicks and bumps on bones, which came, he thinks, from fights, and the big deformity on the collar bone, from a serious injury.

When someone in the crowd says, "*Antrodemus* was a tough customer," Lewis is the first to agree.

Reader's Response
What do you think was the most difficult step in putting together the skeleton of *Antrodemus?*

A Case of Mistaken Identity

If you visit the Hall of Dinosaurs at the National Natural History Museum in Washington, D.C., you may look for *Antrodemus,* but you will not find him. Instead, you will see the huge skeleton of the meat-eating predator, *Allosaurus.* Why will you see *Allosaurus* and not *Antrodemus?* The answer lies in a case of mistaken identity that took place about seventy years ago.

In 1920, Charles W. Gilmore, the curator of the division of vertebrate paleontology at the Smithsonian Institution was responsible for the mistake. Using information that had come to him from the work of other paleontologists, Mr. Gilmore identified the fossil remains of a huge meat-eating dinosaur as *Antrodemus.* However, later discoveries and more up-to-date information proved him wrong. The dinosaur he mistakenly identified as *Antrodemus* is today recognized by most paleontologists as *Allosaurus.* It is *Allosaurus* whose huge, fierce skeleton is the central attraction at the Smithsonian's Hall of Dinosaurs.

This case of mistaken identity demonstrates an important lesson. The horizons of science are constantly growing and changing as new information is uncovered. Perhaps, one day you will make a discovery that will contribute to the expansion of those horizons.

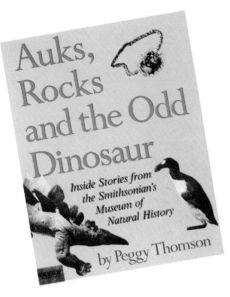

Auks, Rocks and the Odd Dinosaur

 ## Responding to Literature

1. Why have so few fossils of meat-eating dinosaurs been found?

2. Arnold Lewis decides not to rebuild the fossil with its front legs raised high. Explain why.

3. What surprised you most about the process of piecing together the skeleton of *Antrodemus*?

4. Write a story telling how *Antrodemus* might have injured his collar bone. Share it with your classmates.

5. Today most scientists believe that *Antrodemus* is *Allosaurus*. What made them change their minds?

 ## Books to Enjoy

Auks, Rocks and the Odd Dinosaur by Peggy Thomson
Each article in this book tells about one object on display at the National Natural History Museum. And each is told from an insider's point of view.

Dinosaurs: A Journey Through Time by Dennis Schatz
Putting the bones of a dinosaur back together is a real challenge. Learn more about what it takes to do it right.

Mighty Mammals of the Past by John Stidworthy
Take a closer look at fossils of dinosaurs and other creatures that lived both before and after dinosaurs.

SCIENCE
HORIZONS

HUMAN BODY

Growth and Development

CLASP

Many children live far from where their grandparents live. These children may not have a patient
older person with whom to share games, stories, hugs,
and friendship. They may not have a chance to know
any older people. But a group of lucky children and
grandparents in Great Neck, New York, have very close
ties with each other. Yet they are not even related!

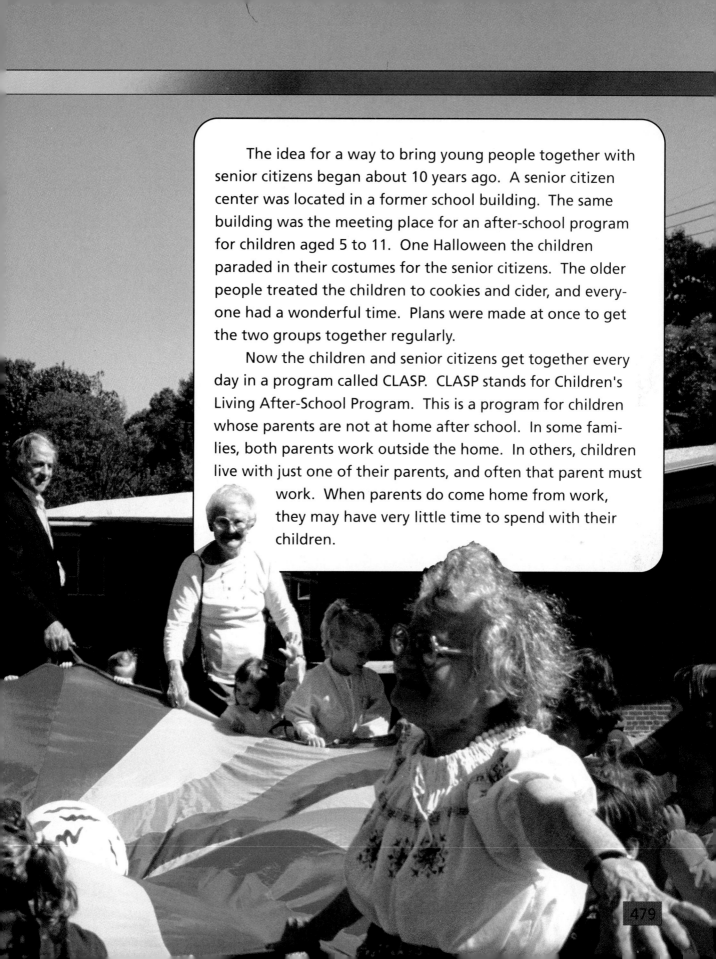

The idea for a way to bring young people together with senior citizens began about 10 years ago. A senior citizen center was located in a former school building. The same building was the meeting place for an after-school program for children aged 5 to 11. One Halloween the children paraded in their costumes for the senior citizens. The older people treated the children to cookies and cider, and everyone had a wonderful time. Plans were made at once to get the two groups together regularly.

Now the children and senior citizens get together every day in a program called CLASP. CLASP stands for Children's Living After-School Program. This is a program for children whose parents are not at home after school. In some families, both parents work outside the home. In others, children live with just one of their parents, and often that parent must work. When parents do come home from work, they may have very little time to spend with their children.

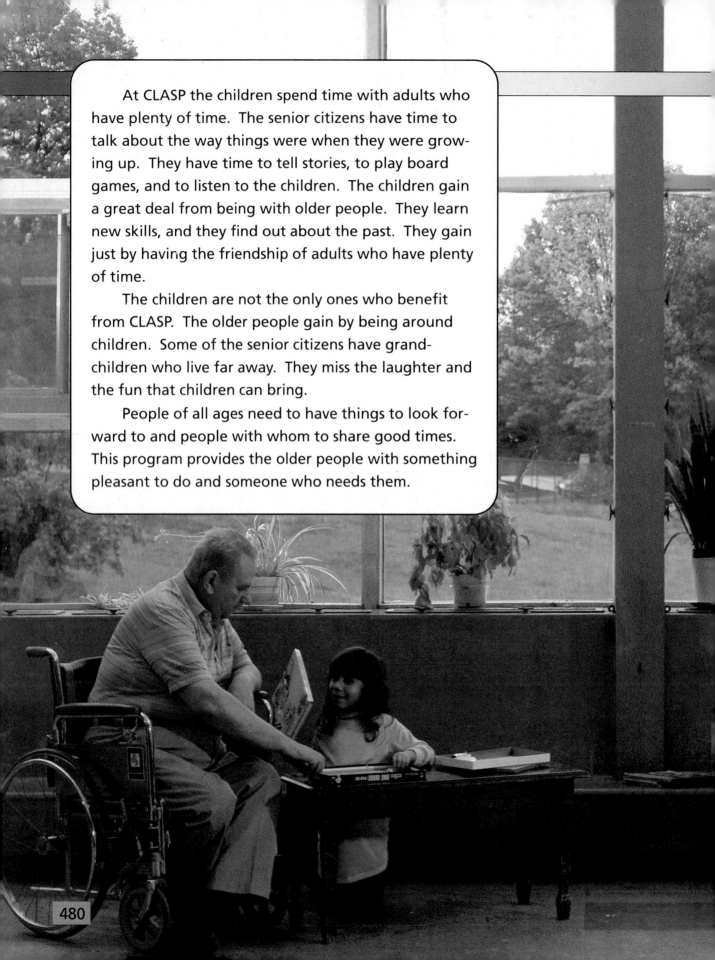

At CLASP the children spend time with adults who have plenty of time. The senior citizens have time to talk about the way things were when they were growing up. They have time to tell stories, to play board games, and to listen to the children. The children gain a great deal from being with older people. They learn new skills, and they find out about the past. They gain just by having the friendship of adults who have plenty of time.

The children are not the only ones who benefit from CLASP. The older people gain by being around children. Some of the senior citizens have grandchildren who live far away. They miss the laughter and the fun that children can bring.

People of all ages need to have things to look forward to and people with whom to share good times. This program provides the older people with something pleasant to do and someone who needs them.

Discover

How can people help one another?

Materials   pencil · paper

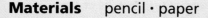

Procedure

　　Contact some senior citizens and think of ways that you can help each other. You might want to send birthday cards and holiday cards. You might want to visit once a week or once a month. List the different things you might do. Show this list to your teacher. If possible, put your plan into action.

In this chapter you will learn about how people grow—from before they are born to adulthood. You will also learn how certain qualities are passed from parent to child.

Words to Know
reproduction
sperm
egg
chromosomes
meiosis

1. Reproduction

Getting Started Tear a piece of paper in half. Now you have two pieces of paper. Did the piece of paper reproduce? Will the small pieces of paper ever grow larger?

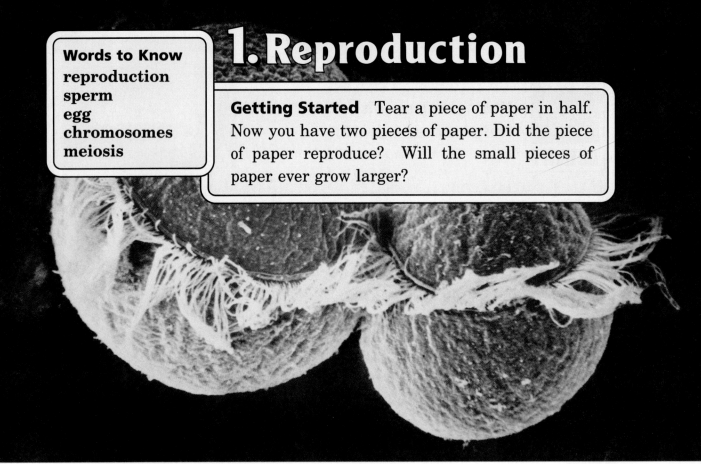

▲ A protist dividing

What is reproduction?

You know that paper is not living. A piece of paper can be torn in half, but the small pieces of paper cannot grow. One main difference between living and nonliving things is that living things grow by producing more cells. Nonliving things do not. Also, living things can make more of their own kind. The process by which living things produce other living things of the same kind is **reproduction** (ree pruh DUK shun). Nonliving things do not reproduce.

Some living things reproduce by just splitting in half. This process is called cell division. One-celled organisms, such as the protist shown, reproduce this way. This protist can reproduce every few hours.

Some simple living things reproduce by budding. The animal shown in the picture, a hydra, is budding. In budding, as in cell division, there is only one parent. When only one parent reproduces, the process is called asexual reproduction.

In many-celled organisms, reproduction usually involves two parents. When two parents produce a living thing, the process is called sexual reproduction. One parent is male, and the other is female.

Cells produced by each parent join to form a new living thing. The cells that join are called sex cells. The **sperm** is the sex cell produced by the male parent. The **egg** is the sex cell produced by the female parent. As you can see in the drawing, the egg cell is much larger than the sperm cell. Notice that the sperm has a tail. The tail helps the sperm move toward the egg.

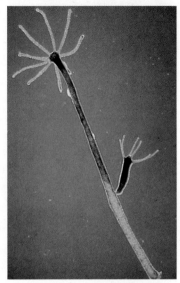

▲ **Hydra budding**

How are eggs and sperm formed?

In Chapter 1 you learned how body cells reproduce by mitosis (mye TOH sihs). Each new cell contains the same number and kind of chromosomes (KROH muh sohmz) as the parent cell. **Chromosomes** are structures in the nucleus of a cell that carry information about the characteristics of the living thing.

▼ **Human egg cell**

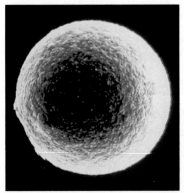

▼ **Human sperm cell**

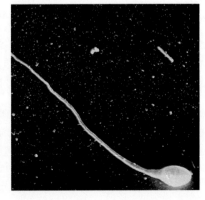

▼ **Egg and sperm**

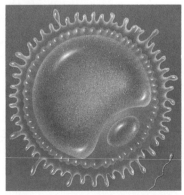

ACTIVITY

Explore

What happens to chromosomes during meiosis?

Each individual has a different combination of characteristics. Half the characteristics are from the mother's side of the family, and half are from the father's side. This activity will help you understand how chromosomes carry these characteristics on to the new individual.

Materials
large sheet of paper · pencil · yarn of two different colors
metric ruler · scissors

Procedure
A. Draw and label the circles and arrows as shown.
B. Cut six pieces of yarn of one color. Two pieces should be about 2 cm long. Two should be about 4 cm long, and two should be about 6 cm long. These will represent chromosomes in the female. Place the yarn pieces in the female cell.
C. Repeat step **B** with the other color of yarn, representing chromosomes in the male.
   1. How many chromosomes are there in each cell?
   2. How many pairs of chromosomes are there in each cell?
D. Take the two long pieces of yarn from the female cell and place one in each circle below that cell. Repeat with the other pieces of yarn.

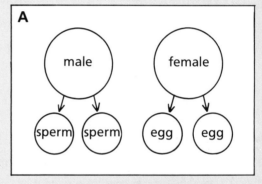

E. Repeat step **D** with the yarn from the male cell.
   3. How many chromosomes are there in each new cell?
   4. Are there pairs of chromosomes in any of the new cells?

Writing and Sharing Results and Conclusions
1. When you separated the pairs of yarn pieces in steps **D** and **E**, what cell process were you showing?
2. How does a baby get characteristics from both parents?

Chromosomes are made of a substance called DNA. Human body cells have 23 pairs of chromosomes, or 46 chromosomes. Body cells are not like sex cells. An egg and a sperm each have only 23 chromosomes, one from each pair.

You know that body cells reproduce by mitosis. Sperm and eggs are produced by a different kind of cell division. **Meiosis** (mye OH sihs) is the kind of cell division that produces sex cells. Another name for meiosis is *reduction division*. The drawing shows that the number of chromosomes is reduced to one-half when eggs and sperm are formed.

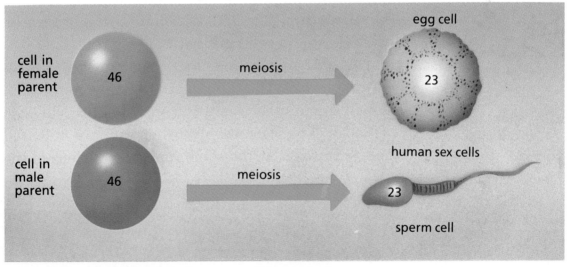

▲ **Formation of egg cell and sperm cell by meiosis**

Lesson Review

1. What is reproduction? How does asexual reproduction compare with sexual reproduction?
2. What are male sex cells called and what are female sex cells called?
3. By what process are sex cells formed?

Think! Does meiosis take place in an organism that reproduces by asexual reproduction? Why or why not?

Physical Science
CONNECTION

Use reference books to find out what elements are found in DNA.

2. The Developing Individual

Getting Started Often the larger and more complex an organism is, the longer it takes for its young to develop. A kitten is born after 2 months of development. A human baby is born after 9 months of development. Many changes take place in the baby during that time.

Words to Know
fertilization
zygote
embryo
fetus

What happens when a sperm joins an egg?

In humans, as in all mammals, the sperm joins with the egg inside the body of the female. **Fertilization** (fur tul ih ZAY shun) is the process by which a sperm cell joins with an egg cell.

During fertilization, the head of the sperm enters the egg. The tail remains outside. As you can see in the drawing, only one sperm enters the egg. The 23 chromosomes of the sperm are released inside the egg. At the same time, the nucleus of the

▼ Fertilized egg dividing

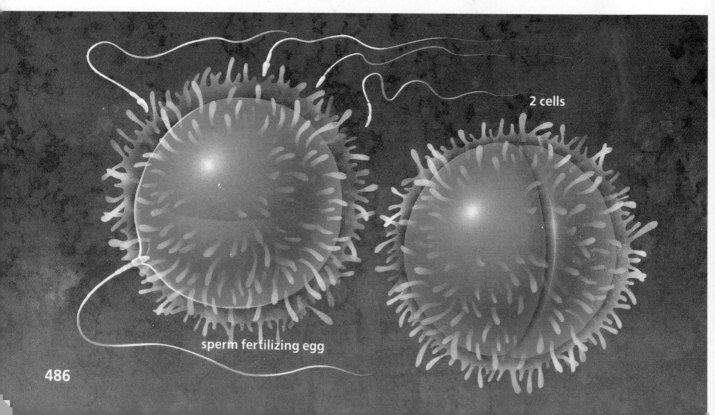

2 cells

sperm fertilizing egg

486

egg opens, and its 23 chromosomes are released into the cell. A fertilized egg is called a **zygote** (ZYE goht). In the zygote, these 23 pairs of chromosomes make up the normal number of 46 chromosomes.

What happens after fertilization?

Look at the drawing. After fertilization the single-celled zygote divides into two cells. The two cells become four, and so on. In about 3 days the zygote has developed into a ball of 16 cells. This kind of cell division is mitosis.

For the first 2 months after fertilization, the developing organism is called an **embryo** (EM bree oh). Organs and systems begin to form in the embryo. Soon the heart will start to beat.

Many changes take place in the embryo as it develops. But after 2 months it is only about as long as your thumb. The embryo can be harmed by viruses or poisons in its mother's system. What does this tell you about the importance of the health of a woman who is going to have a baby?

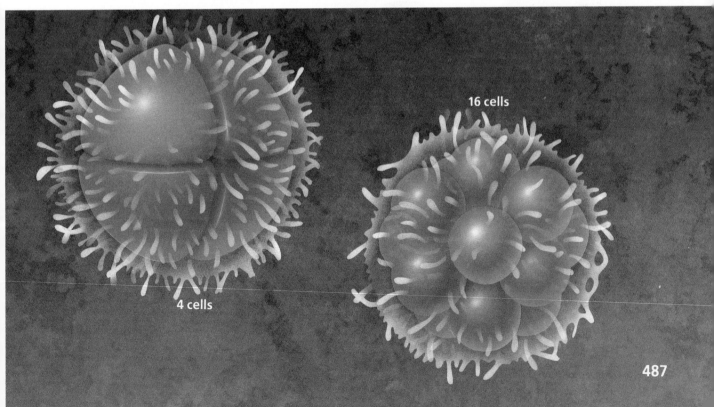

4 cells

16 cells

At the beginning of the third month of development, the organism is called a **fetus** (FEET us). At this stage the organs have formed. The kidneys already function. The fetus also has many reflexes. One is the sucking reflex. How does such a reflex help prepare the baby for life after birth?

From the third to the sixth month of development, a fetus grows rapidly. It moves and has periods when it sleeps and when it is awake. It can swallow, hiccup, make a fist, and kick. After 6 months of development, its eyes are open and it is about 32 cm (12 inches) long.

In the last 3 months of development, a fetus continues to grow. Scientists believe it can hear sounds. By the end of 9 months of development, the fetus is about 50 cm (20 inches) long.

What happens at birth?

About 270 days after fertilization, the baby is ready to be born. At birth, strong muscle contractions push the baby out of the mother's body. The

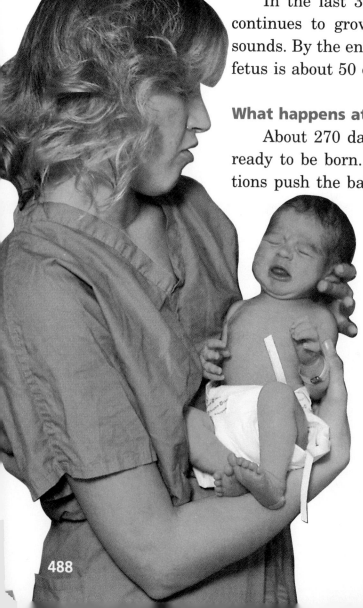

◄ Newborn baby

newborn baby begins to breathe on its own. Reproduction of a new human being is complete.

Sometimes a baby is born before the 9 months of development are complete. Such a baby is said to be premature (pree muh TOOR). Premature babies may need special care. For example, they tend to get cold easily. This is because they do not have the extra layers of fat that babies born at 9 months have. Without these layers, a premature baby needs to be in a special warming unit called an incubator. The temperature in an incubator is kept only a few degrees below body temperature.

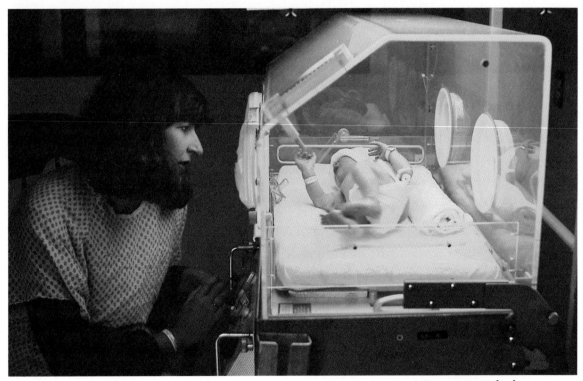

▲ Premature baby in incubator

Lesson Review

1. Describe what takes place during fertilization.
2. What are the main differences between a zygote, an embryo, and a fetus?

Think! In what ways might a 7-month premature baby be different from a 9-month baby?

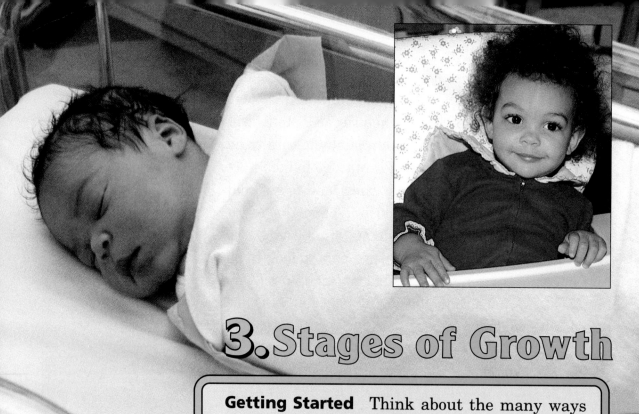

3. Stages of Growth

Getting Started Think about the many ways in which you have changed since you were born. What are some of the things you learned to do in the first 3 years of life? How will you be different 10 years from now?

Words to Know
infancy
childhood
adolescence
adulthood

What are infants like?

A newborn baby is called an infant. This time in life is called infancy (IHN fun see). **Infancy** is the stage between birth and 1 year of age.

As soon as it is born, a baby must be able to get the things it needs to survive. The baby needs to breathe in oxygen. It needs food. The baby also needs to rid its body of wastes.

From the moment of birth, some living things can get the things they need to survive. A newborn baby can breathe, so it gets the oxygen it needs. But it cannot search for food on its own. It cannot find shelter. Human babies depend on adults for care. Look at the picture of the newborn baby. How is this baby like an adult? How is it different?

When does a baby become a child?

The two pictures on page 490 show the same child. One picture was taken the day the child was born. The second one was taken on the child's first birthday. How has the child changed?

Think how much infants learn in their first year of life. They learn to sit up. Then they learn to crawl. Many infants begin to walk during this time. They learn to recognize the people who care for them. They may begin to feed themselves. But they still need much care.

The stage from 1 year to about 12 years is called **childhood.** Children can do many more things than infants can. Think about all you have learned during childhood. You have learned to walk, talk, read, solve problems, and do much to take care of yourself. But most children still depend on adults for food, clothing, shelter, and many kinds of care.

▼ Stages of growth

Problem Solving

Lend Me a Hand

Suppose that you are in charge of making children's gloves. You want to make gloves for children who are 10 to 12 years old. You need to find out what size or sizes to make for children of these ages. Think about what measurements you need. Make a list of each kind of measurement.

How would you determine what size or sizes of gloves are needed to fit your classmates?

Begin by tracing the hands of your classmates. Find out if there is a lot of variation in the size of your classmates' hands. Do boys and girls require the same size gloves? What variations are there in hand size among girls? What variations are there among boys' hand sizes?

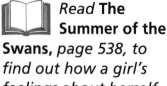
Read **The Summer of the Swans,** *page 538, to find out how a girl's feelings about herself change during adolescence.*

What changes happen during adolescence?

Think about how rapidly a fetus grows. An infant grows rapidly, too. There is one more stage in life in which very rapid growth takes place. It is **adolescence** (ad ul ES uns), the stage between childhood and adulthood. Most 12- to 13-year-olds have entered or are about to enter adolescence. Boys and girls change in size during infancy, childhood, and adolescence.

Adolescence begins with a stage called puberty (PYOO bur tee). Puberty is a time when the body begins to change rapidly. The body begins to develop male or female characteristics. For example, at puberty most girls and boys begin to grow taller. Boys' shoulders get broader. Their voices get lower.

Do any two people in your class look exactly alike? Probably not. Every person is different. And people are different in when and how they begin puberty. Some people reach puberty early, and some much later. There is no "right" time for everyone. Each person is different.

What happens in adulthood and old age?

The stage after adolescence is **adulthood.** During this time the body continues to change. But adults do not grow taller as they do in adolescence. The pictures here show a man as he was in adolescence and at two different times in adulthood. How has he changed?

Adults enter old age gradually. In the past, many people did not reach old age. But today, with

▼ Age 18   ▼ Age 37   ▼ Age 54

493

better health care, many people live long lives. Many older people now exercise often, eat properly, and are able to do most of the things younger people do. An age of 85 or 90 may sound very old to you. But the people shown here are that old. They lead happy, healthy lives. On pages 478–481 you read about how some older people are enjoying spending time with young people.

Lesson Review

1. List three things an infant needs to survive. Which of these things can it get for itself?

2. What activity might most people say shows that an infant has developed into a child?

3. Describe one change that occurs at puberty.

4. Why are people living longer than ever before?

Think! By the time you are an adult, most of the people living in the country now will be in old age. What special problems may be presented in the future if people live to older ages?

Skills

THINKING

Interpreting a kinship chart

You can look at a chart. You can see the words and symbols on the chart. You interpret the chart by learning what the words and symbols mean. Interpreting the chart can help you find information more quickly than reading the same information in words.

Practicing the skill

1. A kinship chart shows how people in a family are related. Look at the kinship chart. The males on the chart are shown with squares. The females are shown with circles. A double line connects two parents. A single line going up and down shows a child of those two parents.

2. The person who made the chart is indicated by the word *me*. Is that person male or female?

3. How many brothers and sisters does the person who made the chart have? Which grandparents are shown, the mother's parents or the father's parents?

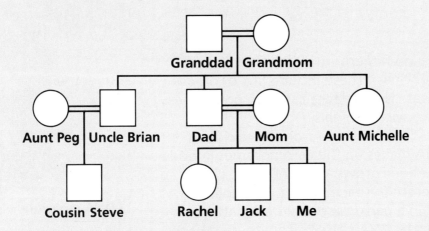

Thinking about the skill

What does the chart not show about the person who made it?

Applying the skill

Make up a family with ten members and list their names on a piece of paper. Make a kinship chart, using the names you wrote. Trade charts with another student. Interpret that student's kinship chart.

How do DNA fingerprints help to solve crimes?

How do detectives track criminals? One way is to use the fingerprints a criminal leaves behind. Each person has a different set of fingerprints. Those left at the scene of a crime can reveal the guilty person.

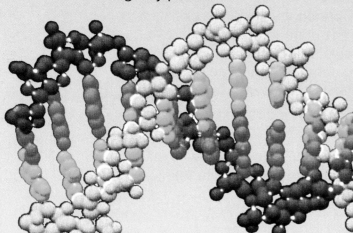

But what if there are no fingerprints left behind? Criminals may leave other clues. These include bits of blood, hair, skin, saliva, and sweat. Now science can help police use even these tiny clues to convict criminals.

The process used to identify people from these clues is DNA fingerprinting. DNA makes up the chromosomes in body cells. It controls how the body grows and functions. Like fingerprints, DNA is different for each person. The cells in hair, skin, or blood contain a person's special DNA pattern. Scientists can now match the DNA pattern from these cells to the pattern of DNA in a suspect's cells. A match can show that the suspect is the criminal.

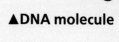

▲DNA molecule

Scientists discovered this kind of fingerprinting by breaking apart DNA. They used chemicals to split the huge DNA molecule. When split, it forms strands of different lengths. When the strands are lined up, they form a pattern of lines. The pattern looks something like the bar code on a food package.

STS

FORENSIC TEST

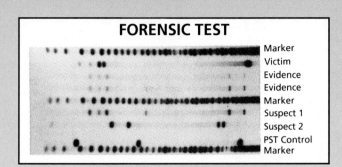

Marker
Victim
Evidence
Evidence
Marker
Suspect 1
Suspect 2
PST Control
Marker

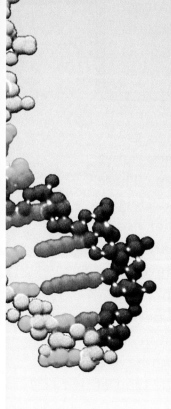

Each person's line pattern is different. That is because each person's DNA is different. Could two people ever show the same DNA fingerprints? Scientists say that the chances of that happening are 100 million to 1.

Police have used fingerprints to solve crimes for about 100 years. But DNA fingerprinting is new. It was first used to solve a murder case in 1987. Police in England hunted a killer for 4 years. A DNA match led police to the guilty man.

Soon after the English case, DNA fingerprinting was used to solve hundreds of crimes. Juries accepted DNA matches as proof of guilt. But that changed in 1989 when scientists questioned the DNA evidence in a murder case. They did not agree with the conclusions made by the DNA lab. This is because DNA matching is a complex task. Critics charged that some DNA fingerprinting labs may not be careful enough in their work. If police are to use DNA to solve crimes, the results must be reliable.

Critical thinking

Suppose you are a member of a jury at a trial. You are not a scientist. Experts show you DNA fingerprints that are supposed to match the suspect to the crime. How could a laboratory mistake cause serious problems?

Using what you learned

Make a model of DNA fingerprints. Cut out the UPC labels from several packages. You may wish to cut out two that are the same. Then ask a classmate to look at the labels and decide if any of them match. Discuss how important it is for people to be properly trained in reading DNA fingerprints.

4. Passing on Information

Getting Started Fold your hands in front of you. Which thumb is on top? Try to fold your hands the other way. Does this way feel strange? The way people fold their hands is a characteristic they received from their parents. What other such characteristics can you name?

Words to Know
trait
recessive trait
dominant trait
gene
genetics

What are traits?

You can probably name many characteristics that are passed from parents to children. These include the color of hair, eyes, and skin. Height, body size, and features of the face are other examples. Any characteristic passed from parents to children is called a **trait.** What traits have been passed on to members of the family shown?

You probably have noticed that a child may look like his or her parents in some ways but not in other ways. For example, brown-eyed parents can have a blue-eyed child. How does this happen? The trait of blue eyes comes from the parents. But in the parents, this trait is hidden. The trait that is hidden is called a **recessive trait.** The trait that hides another trait is called a **dominant trait.**

The pictures show some human traits. Notice which traits are dominant and which are recessive.

| ▼ Tongue rolling, dominant trait | ▼ Cleft chin, dominant trait | ▼ Red hair, recessive trait | ▼ Blue eyes, recessive trait |

What causes traits?

You have learned that chromosomes carry information about what a living thing is like. A **gene** is a section of a chromosome. You can think of a chromosome as being somewhat like a string of beads. Each "bead" is a gene.

You learned that genes are made of a chemical called DNA. The DNA in a gene is like a code that stores information for the cell. Each gene has the information for one trait. A gene that has the information for a dominant trait is called a dominant gene. A gene that has the information for a recessive trait is called a recessive gene.

The genes control what traits a living thing will have. Genes also control what traits a living thing can pass to its young.

How are traits passed on?

Remember that body cells have 46 chromosomes. Sex cells have only half that number. Half your genes came from your mother and half from your father. Every individual has a different combination of genes. That makes each person different.

Genetics (juh NET ihks) is a branch of science that deals with the way traits are passed from parents to children. The pictures show a trait that has been studied—unattached and attached ear lobes. Ear lobes that are unattached, or free, are the dominant trait. Attached ear lobes are completely attached to the side of the head. Ear lobes that are attached are the recessive trait.

As you can see, describing traits can take many words. So scientists use letters to stand for the genes that cause traits. If a trait is dominant, it is shown by a capital letter. If a trait is recessive, a small letter is used. For example, a capital **F** stands for free ear lobes. A small letter **f** stands for attached ear lobes.

Genes are in pairs in body cells. For example, someone with free ear lobes could have the genes **Ff.** Now suppose this person marries someone with the same kinds of genes for free ear lobes. What might

*Jenny had never thought about it before, but maybe she could learn something about herself in her uncle's garden. You can too in **The Inheritance** in Horizons Plus.*

▼ Free earlobe

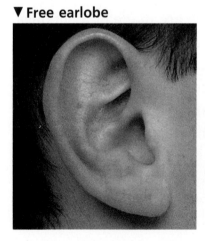

▼ Attached earlobe

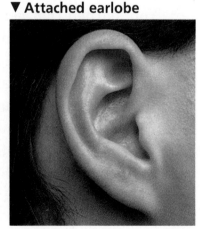

their children be like? To find out, follow the draw-ings. Remember that pairs of genes separate when sex cells form during meiosis. Fertilization brings new pairs together.

Look at drawing A. The father has free ear lobes. His genes are **Ff.** So half his sperm carry the dominant gene, **F.** The other half carry the recessive gene, **f.** The mother also has free ear lobes, and the genes **Ff.** So half her eggs carry the dominant gene, **F.** Half carry the recessive gene, **f.**

Now look at the colored lines in drawing B to see the possible ways these genes can combine during fertilization. First look at the blue line. This shows an **F** sperm joining with an **F** egg. This baby will have two dominant genes and will have free ear lobes. Now look at the red line. This shows an **F** sperm joining with an **f** egg. Look at the green line to see the result of an **f** sperm joining with an **F** egg. Both these babies would have free ear lobes. The purple line shows an **f** sperm joining with an **f** egg. This baby will have attached ear lobes. Remember, the recessive trait is seen only when there is no dominant trait to hide it.

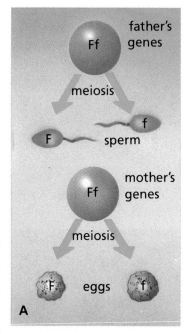

A

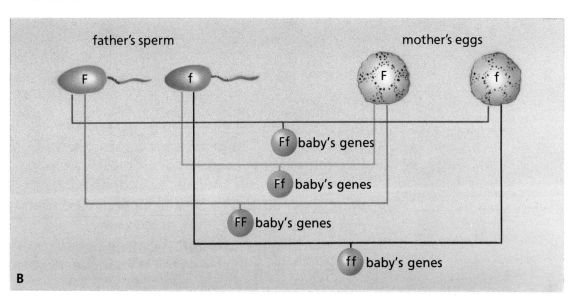

B

501

Sometimes a dominant trait does not completely hide another. Instead, there is a blending of the two. For example, in some flowers, red color is one trait and white is the other. But the red cannot completely hide the white. So a flower with both red and white traits is pink, not red. Other pairs of genes produce other colors, too. Many human traits, like skin color and height, are the result of blending.

Genetics is a much studied branch of science. But there is still a great deal to learn about the ways in which traits are passed on. Scientists are still studying DNA and how its code works. As new discoveries are made, you will probably hear more about DNA in the news.

▲ Red snapdragon

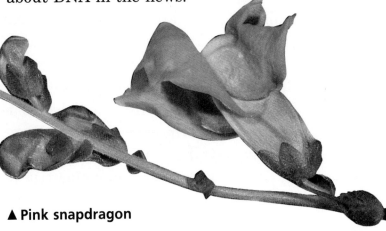

▲ Pink snapdragon

▲ White snapdragon

Lesson Review

1. What are genes?
2. Give two examples of inherited traits.
3. What percent of its genes does a baby receive from its mother? What percent does it receive from its father?
4. What is the difference between a dominant trait and a recessive trait?

Think! Two parents who can roll their tongues can have a child who is unable to roll the tongue. How is this possible?

502

Chapter Connections

Construct a different graphic organizer for this chapter.

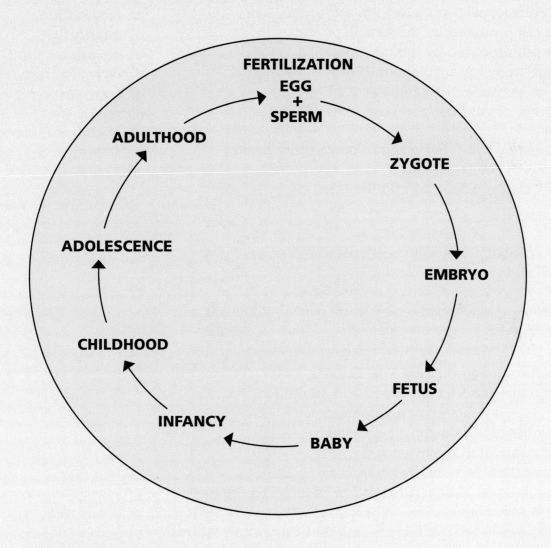

Writing About Science • Research

Much early research about dominant and recessive genes was conducted by Gregor Mendel. Read to find out about Mendel and his work. Write a paragraph about what you learned.

Science Terms

A. Write the letter of the term that best matches the definition.

1. Cell division that produces sex cells
2. Sex cell produced by the female parent
3. Sex cell produced by the male parent
4. Stage from 1 year to about 12 years of age
5. Stage between birth and 1 year of age
6. Process by which a sperm cell joins with an egg cell
7. Process by which living things make other living things of the same kind
8. Trait that is hidden by another trait

a. childhood
b. egg
c. fertilization
d. infancy
e. meiosis
f. recessive trait
g. reproduction
h. sperm

B. Copy the sentences below. Use the terms to complete the sentences.

adolescence   adulthood   chromosomes   dominant trait
embryo   fetus   gene   genetics   trait   zygote

1. A fertilized egg is called a _____.
2. The stage between childhood and adulthood is _____.
3. A _____ is a section of a chromosome.
4. An inherited characteristic is called a _____.
5. The stage after adolescence is _____.
6. A trait that hides another trait is a _____.
7. For 2 months after fertilization, a developing organism is called an _____.
8. Structures in the nucleus of a cell that carry information about what a living thing is like are _____.
9. The branch of science that deals with the way traits are passed from parents to children is _____.
10. A developing organism is called a _____ at the beginning of the third month of development.

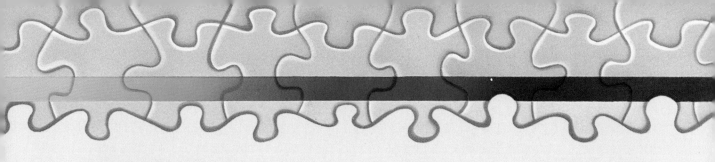

Science Ideas

Use complete sentences to answer the following.

1. How is sexual reproduction different from asexual reproduction?
2. What happens at fertilization?
3. List the three stages of development in order from fertilization to birth.
4. List three activities that a child can do but an infant cannot do.
5. What are some changes that take place at puberty?
6. In which stage of life does growth in height stop?
7. What are genes and where are they located?
8. Why does a child not look exactly like one parent?

Applying Science Ideas

1. Many sperm may reach an egg. But once one sperm enters the egg, the egg immediately develops a tough covering, which keeps out other sperm. Why is this covering important?
2. How is DNA fingerprinting helpful in solving crimes? What are some problems in using DNA fingerprinting as evidence in a trial?

Using Science Skills

Examine the kinship chart. Who are Maria's grandchildren? Who are Paul's cousins?

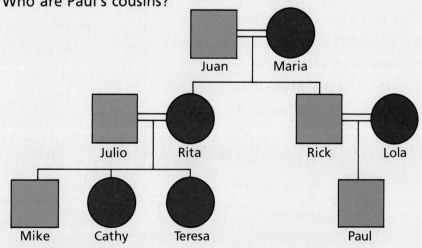

Chapter 15

Body Systems at Work

Cold Facts

What do skiers, mountain climbers, and ice skaters all have in common? They each face the threat of hypothermia (hye poh THUR mee uh). Hypothermia is the term for what happens when the body's temperature falls below 37° C (98.6° F), the normal body temperature for humans. Hypothermia usually comes from long periods of time spent in the cold.

Have you ever stayed outdoors in the cold for very long periods of time? Perhaps you started to shiver. Shivering is among the first signs of hypothermia.

Hypothermia is a sign that the body can no longer endure the cold. Hypothermia affects the body like a weak battery affects a toy. The activities of both the toy and the body are slowed. In the condition of hypothermia, the heart beats more slowly. The body uses less oxygen. The hands and feet receive less blood. The fingers and toes may begin to freeze.

In the early stages of hypothermia, the body temperature may drop only a few degrees. A person may simply move and speak slowly. In later stages the person may not know where he or she is. The person may slip into a coma. The result can be death.

The cure for hypothermia is slow, careful warming of the body. For first aid the person should be wrapped in a blanket and kept warm. In serious cases a doctor should examine the victim.

There are ways to avoid hypothermia. One is to wear warm clothes when you are outside in cold weather. Another is to wear layers of clothing instead of one heavy coat or jacket. Because most body heat escapes from the top of the head, another way to prevent hypothermia is to wear a hat. Finally do not stay outside if you begin to feel cold.

Who is most at risk of developing hypothermia? The answer is people who stay in the cold for a long time. They include skiers, hikers, and people who work outdoors in the winter. Young children and older adults need special protection against hypothermia. Their bodies are very sensitive to changes in temperature. They may get hypothermia in temperatures that feel just cool to other people.

As you have read, hypothermia can be life threatening. But it can also be a life saver. In some operations, doctors use hypothermia as a tool. In heart surgery, for example, they lower a patient's body temperature. This low temperature slows down body activity. As a result, an operation can be done safely.

Discover

Which type of fabric is the best insulator?

ACTIVITY

Materials   5 cans · 5 thermometers · 5 different pieces of fabric: cotton, wool, nylon, polyester, cotton/polyester blend

Procedure

Try to figure out which type of fabric is the best insulator. Work with four of your classmates. Wrap one piece of fabric around each can. Fill the cans about half-full with hot tap water. Place a thermometer in each can. Record the temperature of the water in each can. Record the water temperature every 10 minutes for half an hour. Which fabric was the best insulator? How could you tell? What do you think would happen if you wrapped two pieces of fabric around the same can? Design and try an experiment to test your prediction.

In this chapter you will find out about other ways in which your body works. You will also find out about ways to help keep your body working properly.

1. The Body Asleep

Words to Know
sleep
nervous system
respiratory
  system
circulatory
  system

Getting Started   Picture a tiger in your mind. Is it in color? When you sleep, your mind forms pictures called dreams. How does the brain's activity when one is awake differ from that when one is asleep?

What is sleep?

Perhaps you keep a diary or journal. Suppose one evening you decide to write a special entry. In it you will describe an entire day in your life. The entry will tell what you did, thought, and felt. Throughout this chapter are parts of such an entry.

The next morning you begin to write. You tell about falling asleep the evening before. Whenever you can, for the rest of the day, you will be busily writing. Here is the way the entry begins.

▼ The body during sleep

I turned out the light and flopped into bed. The street light shone directly into my eyes. I turned away from the light. I heard voices from the kitchen but could not make out the words. I tried to remember if I had fed the dog.

Still trying, I closed my eyes. The voices seemed much quieter.

I must have slept for a short time. Then I awoke with the thought, Did I give the dog fresh water? My eyelids felt heavy. Suddenly I seemed to be falling. I jumped. Half awake, I realized that I hadn't been falling at all. I rolled over and snuggled deeper into my pillow.

Perhaps those words describe the way you sometimes fall asleep. You probably spend from 7 to 10 hours sleeping. **Sleep** is a state of lowered mental and physical activity. During sleep you are much less aware of your environment than when you are awake. Perhaps someone covered you with a blanket as you slept last night. If so, you may have moved yet remained asleep. But such movement is a sign that the brain functions during sleep.

The activity of the brain can be shown as waves on a recording called an EEG. The waves recorded appear smaller and closer together as brain activity increases. Here is a picture of a person sleeping. Two EEGs are also shown. Notice that the two are different. Based on these EEGs, how would you compare brain activity when a person is asleep and when a person is awake?

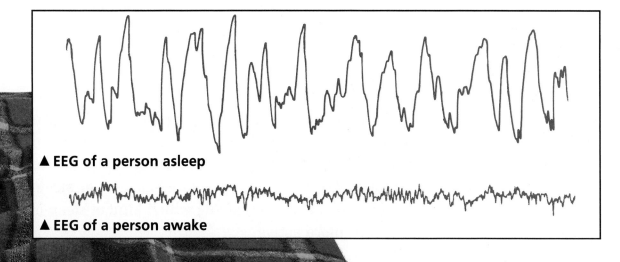

▲ **EEG of a person asleep**

▲ **EEG of a person awake**

brain

spinal cord

nerves

Whether a person is asleep or awake, the brain is always active. As you may remember, the brain is part of the nervous system. The **nervous system** is a control system made up of the brain, the spinal cord, and the nerves. In the nervous system, messages travel along nerve cells. These messages can be from the outside environment or from other body systems.

◀ **Nervous system**

How can you tell that the nervous system functions during sleep? The nervous system controls breathing and heartbeat. During sleep, breathing is constant, and the heart continues to beat.

Remember the decreased brain activity shown on the EEG. Then think of the journal entry. Voices seemed to become quieter. While falling asleep, you become less aware of things. You react more and more slowly. Even your eyes move more slowly. Your eyelids close. Finally, you are asleep.

▲ **EEG recorded during dream sleep**

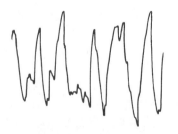

▲ **EEG recorded during nondream sleep**

What happens during sleep?

It may surprise you to learn that you dream every night. Scientists have found that there are two kinds of sleep—dream sleep and nondream sleep. You spend part of the night in each kind of sleep. Compare these EEGs. During which kind of sleep is the brain more active?

512

The person being tested is in a sleep lab. Instruments show that the eyes are moving rapidly back and forth. Such activity is called rapid eye movement, or REM. REM occurs during dream sleep. The person seems to be "watching" the dream.

Perhaps your sleep pattern is like that of most people. If so, upon falling asleep, you first go into nondream sleep. But after 1 to 2 hours, brain activity increases, and you begin dreaming. During dream sleep, muscles are contracted and the body is still. After 15 to 30 minutes, you again enter nondream sleep. This pattern continues all night. Unless awakened during or just after dream sleep, most people do not remember their dreams.

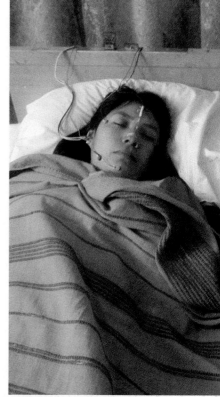
▲ **Person being tested in a sleep lab**

How do body systems function during sleep?

Experiments show that sleep is needed for the brain to function normally. A person who goes without sleep becomes tense. Mental ability, such as that for doing math problems, is reduced.

This graph shows a person's body temperatures for a 24-hour period. Notice the temperatures shown in degrees Celsius (°C). Normal body temperature is 37°C (98.6°F). What is a person most likely doing when body temperature is at its lowest? As body temperature falls during sleep, awareness decreases. And body systems become less active.

Changes in body temperature during 24 hours ▼

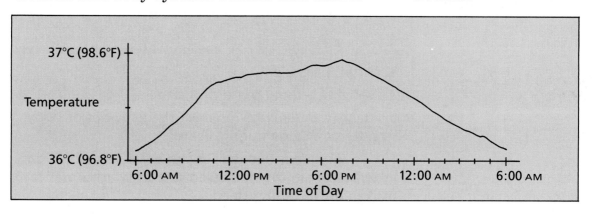

Temperature

37°C (98.6°F)

36°C (96.8°F)

6:00 AM 12:00 PM 6:00 PM 12:00 AM 6:00 AM

Time of Day

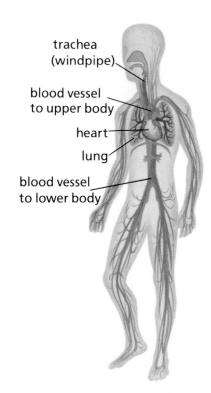

trachea
(windpipe)

blood vessel
to upper body

heart

lung

blood vessel
to lower body

You may remember studying two other body systems. One, the **respiratory** (RES pur uh tor ee) **system**, is a transport system that brings oxygen into the body. The other, the **circulatory** (SUR kyoo luh tor ee) **system**, is a transport system that carries food and oxygen to cells. Both systems are less active during sleep. Breathing rate slows. Less oxygen is used by cells. Heartbeat also slows. Blood pressure falls. Then food reaches cells at a slower rate.

Systems involved in movement are also less active during sleep. During REM periods, some muscles are even paralyzed. But the body does move during sleep. Look at the pictures of a person sleeping. Notice the changes in position. Although body movement occurs, it is decreased during sleep.

▲ **Respiratory and circulatory systems**

▲ **Position changes during sleep**

Lesson Review

1. What is sleep?
2. Describe a usual pattern of sleep.
3. Identify three ways in which the activities of body systems change during sleep.

Think! Oxygen is needed for the breakdown of sugar in cells. Explain the decreased rate at which sugar is broken down during sleep.

THINKING

Skills

Identifying observations that support an inference

Suppose two boys are talking. One boy says that he has felt very tired lately. He remarks that he has been getting up earlier than usual for the last week. The other boy makes an inference that his friend is tired because he is not getting enough sleep. An inference is an explanation for something that happens. People use their observations to make inferences.

Practicing the skill

1. Imagine that as you are walking a friend taps you on the back from behind. You turn and observe that she is wearing a blue jacket and tennis shoes. You also observe that she is breathing rapidly, is carrying a small backpack, and is perspiring.

2. From the observations, you make the inference that your friend ran to catch up with you. Write down each observation that supports the inference that your friend had been running.

3. Suppose your friend told you that she had not been running. With that information you make the new inference that your friend's backpack was heavy. Write each observation that supports this inference.

Thinking about the skill

You found observations that supported each inference. What did you think about to find those observations?

Applying the skill

The picture shows a baby in a crib. Observe the picture carefully. List as many observations as you can about the picture. Circle all observations that support the inference that the baby is asleep.

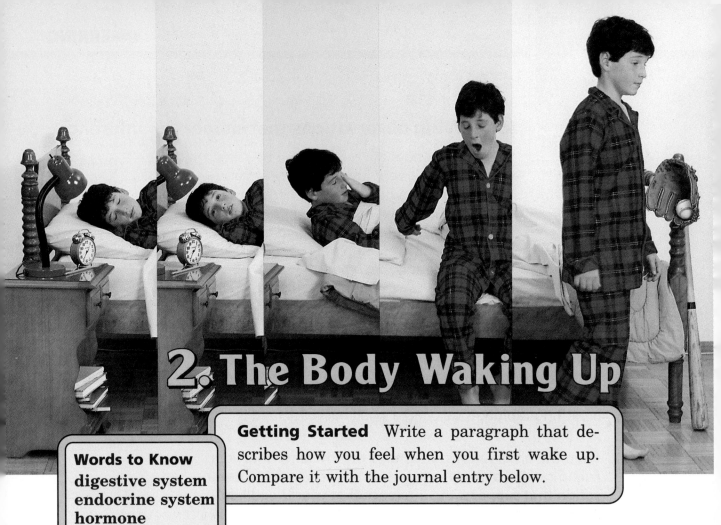

2. The Body Waking Up

Getting Started Write a paragraph that describes how you feel when you first wake up. Compare it with the journal entry below.

How do the body systems change when you wake up?

You might feel wide awake when you first wake up. Or you might feel half asleep for a while. This is the way the journal describes waking up.

The alarm clock jangled me awake. I fumbled around on the bedside table for the alarm's "off" button. Finally I found it and turned off the alarm. It cannot be time to get up already, I thought, and closed my eyes again. Then I heard the thump of bowls on the kitchen table. I looked at the clock again. Uh-oh—only half an hour before the school bus comes.

My feet hit the floor. I splashed cold water on my face, then shivered into my clothes. By the time I reached the kitchen, I was wide awake.

The nervous system becomes more active as you wake up. You become more aware of your environment. Your senses begin to receive more messages. Perhaps this morning you smelled food cooking or heard raindrops on your window. Maybe you felt the cold of the bathroom floor. As you may know, the nervous system helps you receive and interpret messages from the sense organs.

The nervous system works with other systems. Notice the boy in the pictures. Getting out of bed requires the activity of systems of muscles and bones. The brain controls such movement. As you know, the brain is part of the nervous system.

As body activity increases upon waking, the amount of energy the body uses also increases. The demand for food and oxygen then increases. Remember that the circulatory system and the respiratory system supply cells with food and oxygen. Both systems increase their activity when the body awakens. Study these graphs. How do your breathing rate and heart rate change when you get out of bed?

 Wanted: A detective who knows about human body systems. You can apply when you try **The Human Body: Circulation and Respiration.**

Changes in breathing and heart rate upon waking up ▼

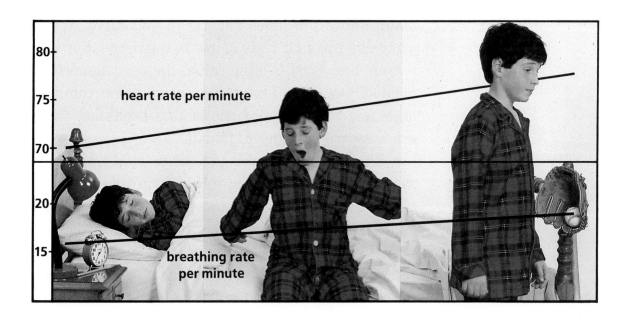

Why is breakfast an important meal?

When you wake up in the morning, you might be hungry. You may not have eaten for 12 or more hours. Like a campfire to which no wood has been added for a time, your body is low on fuel.

Food is the body's fuel. Cells get energy by breaking down the nutrient (NOO tree unt) sugar. A nutrient is a part of food that your body must have to stay healthy.

Some nutrients in breakfast foods ▼

Vitamins	Minerals	Carbohydrates	Fats	Proteins

fresh fruit
fruit juice
whole-grain
  bread
milk
eggs
cheese
	milk
	cheese
	oatmeal
	ready-to-eat
	  cereal
	fruit juice
	fresh fruit
		fruit juice
		apples
		bananas
		oatmeal
		ready-to-eat
		  cereal
			milk
			cheese
			eggs
				oatmeal
				milk
				cheese
				eggs

▼ Digestive system

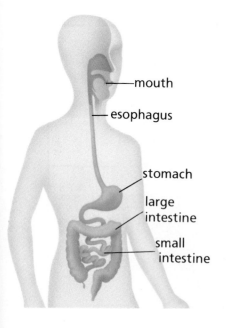

mouth

esophagus

stomach

large intestine

small intestine

Even as you sleep, your body uses nutrients. Nutrients are used for growth, repair of cells, and maintaining processes that keep you alive. When you wake up, your body is low in nutrients. For this reason, breakfast is often called the most important meal of the day. This table shows some common breakfast foods. It also shows that breakfast foods are a source of many nutrients.

The **digestive** (dih JES tihv) **system** is the system that changes food into a form that cells can use. This drawing shows the path that food follows as it is digested. A system of muscles is involved in chewing food and pushing it through the small intestine. What systems supply the oxygen needed for cells to release energy from digested food?

ACTIVITY

Explore Together

How can you compare the amount of vitamin C in fruit juices?

Organizer

Materials

safety goggles · grease pencil · 4 test tubes · test-tube rack · graduate · indophenol blue indicator · vitamin C tablet, dissolved in water · fruit juice samples · dropper

Procedure

Caution: *Wear safety goggles for this activity.*

Manager

A. Use a grease pencil to number four test tubes 1 to 4. Place them in a test-tube rack. Using a graduate to measure, add 5 mL of indophenol blue to each test tube. Indophenol blue turns colorless in the presence of vitamin C.

Investigator

B. Add vitamin C solution to test tube 1, one drop at a time. Shake after the addition of each drop. Count the drops needed to make the indicator colorless.

Recorder

C. Make a table like the one shown. Record the number of drops added to test tube 1.

Test Tube Number	Solution or Juice Tested	Number of Drops Added
1	vitamin C	
2		
3		
4		

Investigator, Recorder

D. Using a clean dropper, repeat step **B** for each sample of fruit juice. Record the number of drops added. The more vitamin C there is in a juice, the fewer the number of drops needed to turn the indicator colorless.

Group, Recorder

E. Rearrange the juice samples in order from the one with the most vitamin C to the one with the least.

Writing and Sharing Results and Conclusions

Group, Recorder

1. What is the purpose of testing the vitamin C solution?

2. Which juice tested has the most vitamin C?

Reporter

3. Compare your results with those of your classmates.

What are the body's chemical controllers?

Two systems, the nervous system and the endocrine (EN doh krihn) system, are the main controllers of body activity. The **endocrine system** is a control system made up of glands. Glands are organs and tissues that make and release chemicals.

Both the nervous system and the endocrine system send messages. You know the nervous system sends messages along nerves. The endocrine system sends chemical messages through the blood. A chemical made by an endocrine gland is called a **hormone** (HOR mohn). As you read about some of the organs of the endocrine system, find them in the drawing.

When you wake up, the cells begin to use more energy. How can the body increase the amount of energy it uses? Think about a car in which the engine is running. What happens when the driver presses the gas pedal of the car? More gasoline is released, and the rate at which the car uses energy increases. In a similar way, the thyroid (THYE roid) gland releases a hormone. This hormone increases the rate at which the body uses energy stored in food. Energy is released only from food that has been broken down by the digestive system.

▼ **Endocrine system**

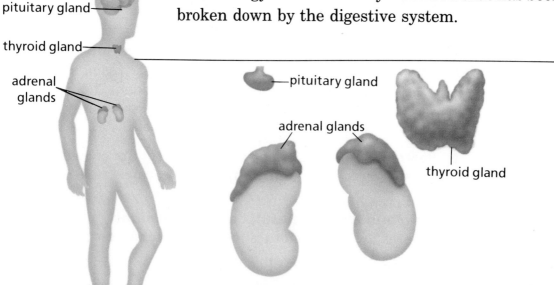

pituitary gland

thyroid gland

adrenal glands

pituitary gland

adrenal glands

thyroid gland

▲ A time when the activity of the endocrine system increases

Have you ever ridden a roller coaster? Perhaps your heart thumped and your palms became sweaty. These responses are caused by endocrine organs called the adrenal (uh DREE nul) glands, which release hormones. One of these hormones, adrenaline (uh DREN uh lihn), prepares the body to deal with danger and stress. In running away from danger, what systems are most affected?

Another endocrine gland, the pituitary (pih-TOO uh tair ee) gland, produces many hormones. One helps control growth. Some pituitary hormones control the activity of other endocrine organs. For example, one pituitary hormone controls the activity of the thyroid gland.

Lesson Review

1. What changes occur in the activity of the nervous system as you wake up?
2. Explain how three body systems work together to supply food and oxygen to cells.
3. What is the function of the thyroid gland?

Think! Suppose a sudden noise awakens you. Identify, in order, the body systems whose activity might increase.

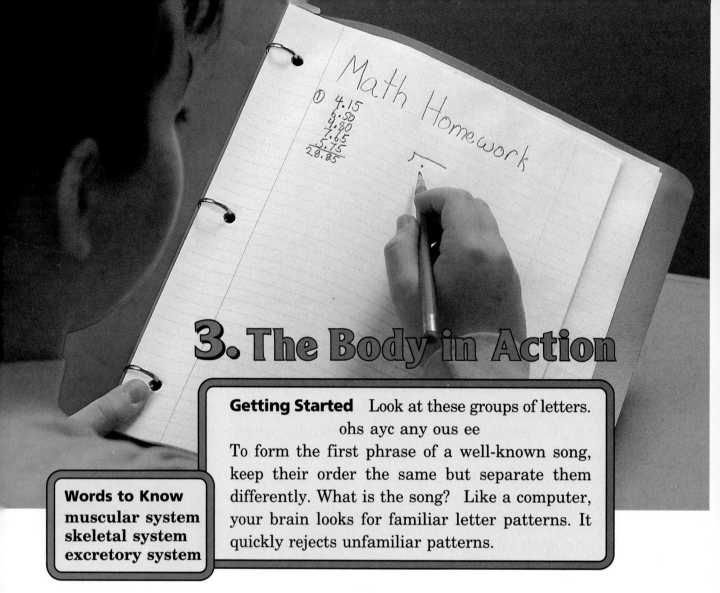

3. The Body in Action

Getting Started   Look at these groups of letters.

ohs ayc any ous ee

To form the first phrase of a well-known song, keep their order the same but separate them differently. What is the song? Like a computer, your brain looks for familiar letter patterns. It quickly rejects unfamiliar patterns.

Words to Know
muscular system
skeletal system
excretory system

What is the structure of the brain?

Did you ever want to use a computer to do math word problems? Here is how you might feel.

I crumpled up the paper and threw it. There was a soft thud as it landed in the wastebasket. At least I did that right, I thought.

I took out another sheet of paper and wrote the heading. That was easy. I read the problem again. I had trouble deciding which number to divide into which. My heart beat a little faster. I wondered if I had the numbers lined up the right way. Yea! The answer checked—only two more problems to go!

A title for this part of your journal might be "Using a Living Computer." The brain is much like a computer. Its functions are very organized. For example, one part of the brain, called the cerebellum (ser uh BEL um), helps the body's muscles work together smoothly. The cerebellum helps control body movements such as those of the swimmer shown here. Find the cerebellum in this drawing. It is the cerebellum that would help you bat a ball or throw a piece of paper into a wastebasket.

Below the cerebellum is the part of the brain called the brainstem. The brainstem controls many activities that are automatic. For example, the brainstem controls heartbeat, breathing, and the digestion of food. It also helps to control body temperature.

Body movements controlled by the cerebellum ▼

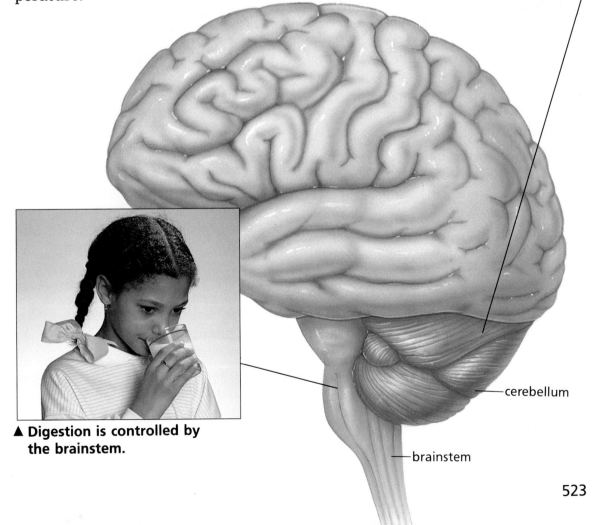

▲ **Digestion is controlled by the brainstem.**

cerebellum

brainstem

523

Explore

How is body temperature controlled?

ACTIVITY

Bang! And the marathon begins! The racers spring forward. Minute by minute the long, rugged course unfolds before them. On and on they run—up and down hills, around sharp turns, across endless stretches. Shapes of rigid muscles shine with sweat. The work of muscles produces heat. The body has a way to remove some of this heat.

Materials
safety goggles · water · 2 plastic cups · masking tape · marker · isopropyl alcohol · cotton balls · timer

Procedure
Caution: *Wear safety goggles for this activity.*

A. Pour a small amount of water into a cup. Use tape to label the cup *water*. Pour a small amount of alcohol into another cup. Label this cup *alcohol*.

B. Soak a cotton ball in the water. Squeeze the cotton ball to remove the excess water.

C. Rub the cotton ball on your wrist. Allow your wrist to dry.
   1. Describe how your skin feels as it dries.

D. Dip one cotton ball in water and another in alcohol. Hold one cotton ball in each hand and squeeze out the excess liquid.

E. Set a timer. Rub the cotton ball with water on one wrist. Quickly rub the cotton ball with alcohol on the other wrist. Record the

time required for each liquid to evaporate.

F. Repeat steps **D** and **E** two times. Use a calculator to average your results.
   2. Which liquid evaporates faster?
   3. Which wrist feels cooler?

Writing and Sharing Results and Conclusions
1. When is the body cooled by the evaporation of a liquid?
2. Explain which would lower a fever faster—a sponge bath with alcohol or with water.

524

The largest part of the brain is the cerebrum (se REE brum). One of its functions is memory, the ability to store and recall information. The cerebrum helps you remember how to do long division. It helps you recognize a friend's face in less than a second. Identify this picture. How long did it take you to recall the name?

This drawing shows some other functions of the cerebrum. Notice that some areas of the cerebrum control the movements of certain body parts. Some areas interpret messages from the sense organs. The cerebrum also controls all your thinking. It is the cerebrum that helps you solve math word problems.

▼ **Body parts and function controlled by the cerebrum**

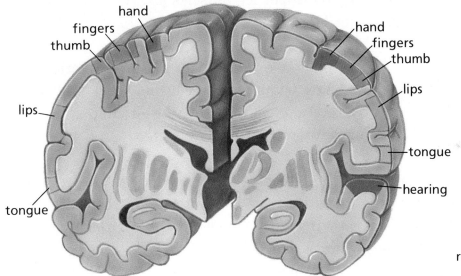

Skeletal and muscular systems ▼

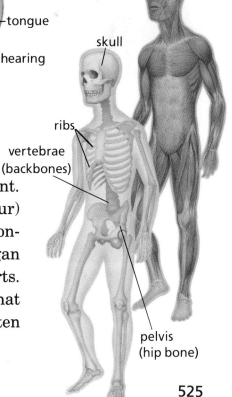

What systems are active during exercise?

The nervous system helps to control movement. But two other systems, the muscular (MUS kyoo lur) system and the skeletal system, more directly control movement. The **muscular system** is the organ system made up of muscles, which move body parts. The **skeletal system** is the frame of bones that supports the body. Both systems, shown here, often work together.

thigh bone

leg muscle

▲ **How muscles move bones**

Bones are moved when muscles that are attached to the bones contract, or get shorter. The drawing shows upper leg muscles attached to bones in the lower leg. What happens when these muscles contract?

As you play or exercise, you may have noticed that your heart beats faster. You may feel "out of breath." When you feel this way, the circulatory and respiratory systems are being affected.

How are wastes removed from the body?

You know that the circulatory and respiratory systems are involved when you play or exercise. These systems are also involved in removing wastes from body cells. Wastes, which result from chemical changes in the body, are harmful if allowed to build up. Therefore, the body must get rid of wastes. The system that removes wastes from the body is the **excretory** (EKS kruh tor ee) **system.**

One waste is carbon dioxide. It forms in cells when oxygen combines with food, releasing energy. Carbon dioxide is carried to the lungs and exhaled, or breathed out. What system picks up carbon dioxide from cells and carries it to the lungs?

Another waste is urea (yoo REE uh), a poison formed when proteins are broken down. The body gets rid of some urea through the skin when you perspire. The kidneys rid the body of most urea. Look at the drawings as you read about the kidneys.

The blood picks up urea and other wastes from the cells. As the blood passes through the kidneys, wastes are filtered out. Water also passes into the kidneys. The liquid waste that forms is urine (YOOR-ihn). Urine flows into a sac called the bladder. Here urine is stored until it leaves the body.

Some water that passes into the kidneys returns to the blood. A hormone from the pituitary gland controls the amount of water that is returned. What system is then helping to control kidney function?

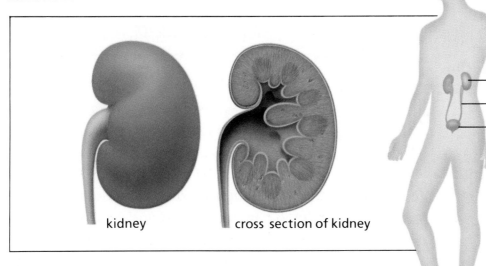

kidney

cross section of kidney

kidney
ureter
bladder

▲ **Excretory system**

Lesson Review

1. List three functions of the cerebrum.
2. Explain how muscles and bones work together.
3. How is urea removed from the body?

Think! A person whose left cerebrum is injured cannot move the right arm. What does this fact indicate about how the brain is connected to body parts that it controls?

4. The Body's Defenses

Getting Started Probably you have played a game in which two teams battle each other. This picture shows another kind of battle, as seen through a microscope. Study the picture and see if you can tell the two teams apart.

Words to Know
infection
immune system
drug abuse
drug addiction

What is an infection?

The battle shown in the picture above can take place in the human body. Here is what the journal might say about a similar battle.

The school bus bounced over a big bump in the road. My book bag slid forward and scraped across my skinned elbow. Ouch! That hurt! I grabbed my arm and twisted it to get a look at my elbow.

Yesterday it looked very different. After I fell off my bike, my elbow had stung. I brushed away the dirt. The skin was scraped and bleeding. But the stinging stopped after a while. I even forgot about it—until I took a shower. The soap and water made it sting all over again.

Today it is red around the edges. It feels hot. And that yellow stuff in the center looks awful!

Did you know that a break in the skin allows very small living things to get into the body? You probably know them as germs. The germs in a skinned elbow are bacteria (bak TIHR ee uh). Bacteria, shown below, are simple, one-celled organisms that can upset the normal functioning of the body.

A condition in which functions of the body are upset is called a disease. A disease that is caused by bacteria or viruses (VYE rus ihz) is called an **infection.** Bacteria may release poisons that injure and kill cells. Viruses reproduce inside cells and kill the cells. Some diseases, such as most kinds of heart disease, are not caused by infections.

When the body is infected, the number of white blood cells increases. Some white cells, like the one in the picture, eat bacteria. Some white blood cells are killed fighting an infection. The cell remains form a yellow material called pus. You might see pus in an infected wound, such as a skinned elbow.

Some kinds of white blood cells make chemicals called antibodies. These chemicals can destroy poisons made by bacteria and can kill bacteria. Cells and tissues that are involved in fighting disease make up the **immune** (ihm MYOON) **system.**

▼ **Bacteria**

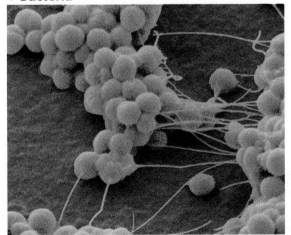

▼ **White blood cell eating bacteria**

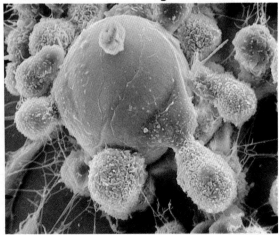

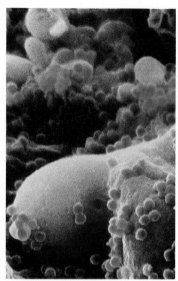

▲ Virus that causes AIDS

One serious infection that attacks the immune system is AIDS. It is caused by a virus, shown here. The immune system of a person with AIDS does not function properly. AIDS victims can die from other infections that their bodies cannot fight. Scientists are searching for ways to treat and cure this disease.

What is drug abuse?

Medicine sometimes helps the immune system fight disease. A medicine is a drug—a chemical taken into the body that affects how the body functions. But not all drugs are medicines.

The misuse of drugs is called **drug abuse.** Drug abuse harms the body. One abused drug is alcohol. Another abused drug, nicotine (NIHK uh teen), is found in tobacco. Tobacco is made into cigarettes. These tables show how drinking alcohol and smoking tobacco can affect the body. What body system is most affected by the use of tobacco?

Some Effects of Drinking Alcohol
Damage to the pancreas and liver Decrease of brain-cell activity Slowed rate of heartbeat Slowed rate of breathing Slowed reaction time Irritation of the lining of the stomach

Some Effects of Smoking Tobacco	
Substance in Tobacco	**Effect of Substance**
nicotine	narrowing of blood vessels and faster rate of heartbeat
carbon monoxide	reduced oxygen in the blood and shortness of breath
tars	damaged air passages in the lungs

Problem Solving
It All "Ads" Up

Scientists have found that cigarette advertisements can influence the number of people who smoke. These ads often show young, healthy people having a good time. The people in the ads are shown holding or smoking cigarettes. Perhaps different ads might convince people *not* to smoke.

What might discourage people from smoking?

Draw an ad that might convince people of your age not to smoke. How might you catch their attention? What facts can you give? Share the ad with your class.

People who misuse a drug can develop a strong need for that drug. The condition in which a person needs a drug is called **drug addiction** (uh DIHK-shun). A drug addiction can make a person who cannot get the drug feel very sick.

Other abused drugs, which are illegal, include crack, heroin (HER oh ihn), and marijuana (mar ih-WAH nuh). Crack is a form of cocaine (koh KAYN). The use of cocaine, which raises blood pressure and increases heart rate, can result in sudden death. Heroin lowers the activity of the nervous system. The use of heroin can also cause death.

Marijuana causes people to see and hear things that are only imagined. Marijuana can damage brain cells. What body system does brain-cell damage directly affect?

How can you keep the body systems healthy?

On page 506, you read about how to protect yourself from hypothermia. You cannot protect yourself against *all* injury and disease. But you can help to keep body systems working properly.

A person's habits can affect body systems in a healthy or an unhealthy way. Eating many foods with a high percentage of fat can lead to disorders of the circulatory system. Misusing drugs can damage the nervous system. A habit of regular exercise benefits the respiratory, circulatory, and muscular systems. Find in the table below some habits that are part of a healthy way of life.

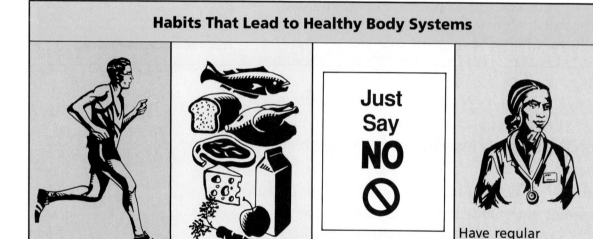

Habits That Lead to Healthy Body Systems

Exercise regularly. | Eat a balanced diet. | Never take harmful drugs. | Have regular medical and dental checkups.

Physical Science
CONNECTION

A person's body temperature rises when the person has an infection. Use reference books to find out why this happens.

Lesson Review

1. How does the immune system help the body fight infection?
2. Compare the effects of tobacco and alcohol on the body systems.
3. List some ways to stay healthy.

Think! How might a count of white blood cells tell a doctor if a patient has an infection?

Chapter Connections

Write an explanation of the differences between the body asleep and the body waking up. Use the graphic organizer to help you.

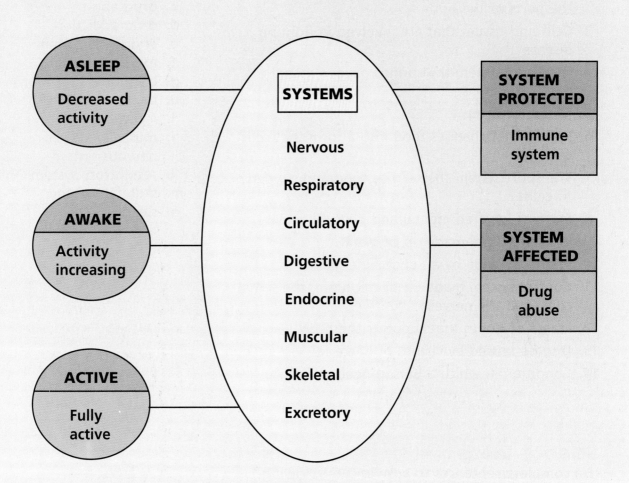

Writing About Science • Narrate

Keep a journal about your dreams. For several nights, keep paper and a pencil next to your bed. When you wake up in the morning, write down everything you remember about your dreams.

Science Terms

Write the letter of the term that best matches the definition.

1. System that removes wastes from the body
2. Organ system made up of muscles, which move the parts of the body
3. Cells and tissues that are involved in fighting disease
4. Transport system that brings oxygen into the body
5. Misuse of drugs
6. System that changes food into a form that cells can use
7. Transport system that carries food and oxygen to cells
8. State of lowered mental and physical activity
9. Control system made up of glands
10. Chemical made by an endocrine gland
11. Control system made up of the brain, the spinal cord, and the nerves
12. Frame of bones that supports the body
13. Disease caused by viruses or bacteria
14. Condition in which a person needs a drug

a. circulatory system
b. digestive system
c. drug abuse
d. drug addiction
e. endocrine system
f. excretory system
g. hormone
h. immune system
i. infection
j. muscular system
k. nervous system
l. respiratory system
m. skeletal system
n. sleep

Science Ideas

Use complete sentences to answer the following.

1. Name the system that controls breathing and keeps the heart beating during sleep.
2. Describe the dream and nondream pattern of sleep.
3. Compare the activity of body systems when one is asleep with that when one is awake.
4. What are the three systems that work together to supply food and oxygen to cells?

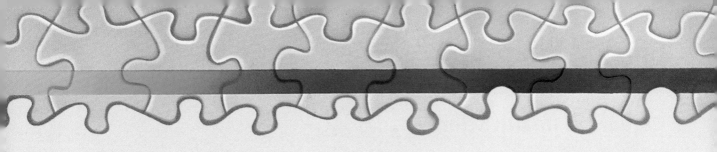

5. Name two endocrine organs and describe their functions.

6. This drawing shows the three parts of the brain. Identify each part by letter and give at least one function of each part.

7. Identify two body systems that are directly involved in causing movement. Describe how they work together.

8. What body waste is removed by both the skin and the kidney? What waste is removed by the lungs?

9. Which cells of the circulatory system are directly involved in fighting disease?

10. Describe the effects of nicotine on the body.

11. Name some ways to help keep body systems healthy.

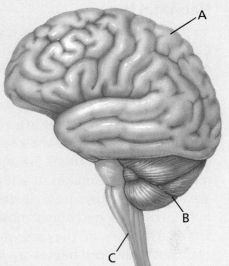

Applying Science Ideas

1. Muscle tone and muscle activity are low during dream sleep. What conclusions can you draw about the stage of sleep in which sleepwalking most likely occurs?

2. Predict how the activity of the thyroid gland changes over a 24-hour period. Explain your reasoning.

3. Explain how damage to the spinal cord might lead to the inability to move certain body parts.

Using Science Skills

Suppose at an outside ice hockey game you see a young boy who is shivering. He is wearing a thin blue jacket. A red hat is on his lap. You make the inference that he is not dressed warmly enough. What observations support your inference?

Careers in Health Science

Neonatal Nurse

Susana Perez has always loved babies. That is why she became a neonatal nurse. A **neonatal nurse** takes care of newborn babies.

Babies need a lot of care when they are born. While they are in the hospital, nurses like Susana keep a careful watch over them. Susana has many duties. She makes sure the babies are fed. She makes sure they have normal bladder and bowel movements. She also makes sure they are warm.

Most newborn babies are healthy. But some babies have problems. Susana must give these babies special care. For example, some babies are premature, or born too early. They are very small and their organs are not fully developed. These babies cannot maintain body heat. So Susana wraps them in blankets and places them on heated mattresses. She feeds them through tubes in their veins. She also keeps them away from bright lights and loud noises.

Susana shows new parents how to care for their babies, too. "Men and women are not born knowing how to be parents," Susana says. "They have to be taught." Susana shows them how to feed and bathe their babies. She tells them what to do if the babies get sick.

Neonatal nurses work with many other people in the hospital. They depend on **pharmacists,** who make the medicines for the babies. **Lab technicians** do tests on the blood of babies. The tests help the nurse determine if the babies are healthy.

Susana works at a hospital in Orange, California. She has been a neonatal nurse for ten years. Susana had to study hard to become a nurse. "I took lots of science in high school," Susana says. Susana went to a junior college for two years. Then she took a special exam to become a licensed registered nurse.

What does Susana like best about her job? "The babies," she says. "We become their second mothers. We are happy when babies are strong enough to go home. But we're a little sad to see them leave, too."

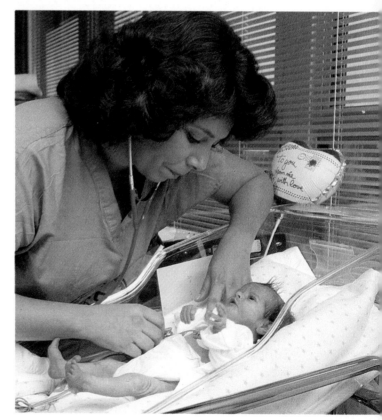

Connecting Science Ideas

1. A neonatal nurse helps to determine if a newborn baby's body systems are functioning properly. Make a list of the body systems. Next to each system, suggest how the nurse might observe its functioning.   **Careers; Chapter 15**

2. You read about hypothermia on pages 506–509. In what way are premature babies in danger of suffering from hypothermia?   **Chapter 15; Chapter 14**

3. You read that premature babies may be fed through tubes in their veins. What two systems of the body does this method of feeding replace? Why do you think this method of feeding is necessary?   **Careers; Chapter 15**

4. How does the function of the endocrine system change in relation to a person's stage of growth?   **Chapter 14; Chapter 15**

5. You have learned that a condition in which body functions are upset is called a disease. Is AIDS a disease that is caused by an infection or is it a trait that is passed through the genes? Explain your answer.   **Chapter 15; Chapter 14**

6. On pages 478–481 you read about a program called CLASP. What kind of advice might an older person give a child about the dangers of the use of alcohol and tobacco?
Chapter 14; Chapter 15

Unit Project

You have learned that your body changes from one stage of growth to the next. Obtain from a doctor some growth graphs that show height, weight, and head size data for infants, children, and adolescents. Learn to read the graphs. Compare the rate of growth from one stage to the next. Create a display to summarize what you learned.

from

The Summer of the Swans

Written by Betsy Byars
Illustrated by Ted CoConis

*Growing up is not always easy. During adolescence everything
seems to change. What was fine yesterday is all wrong today.
That's how Sara Godfrey feels. Have you ever felt that way?*

Sara Godfrey was lying on the bed tying a kerchief on the dog, Boysie. "Hold your chin up, Boysie, will you?" she said as she braced herself on one elbow. The dog was old, slept all the time, and he was lying on his side with his eyes closed while she lifted his head and tied the scarf.

Her sister Wanda was sitting at the dressing table combing her hair. Wanda said, "Why don't you leave Boysie alone?"

"There's nothing else to do," Sara answered without looking up. "You want to see a show?"

"Not particularly."

"It's called 'The Many Faces of Boysie.'"

"Now I know I don't want to see it."

Sara held up the dog with the kerchief neatly tied beneath his chin and said, "The first face of Boysie, proudly presented for your entertainment and amusement, is the Russian Peasant Woman. Taaaaaa-daaaaaa!"

"Leave the dog alone."

"He likes to be in shows, don't you, Boysie?" She untied the scarf, refolded it and set it carefully on top of the dog's head.

With a sigh Wanda turned and looked at the dog. "That's pathetic. In people's age that dog is eighty-four years old." She took a can of hair spray and sprayed her hair."And besides, that's my good scarf."

"Oh, all right." Sara fell back heavily against the pillow. "I can't do anything around here."

"Well, if it's going to make you that miserable, I'll watch the show."

"I don't want to do it any more. It's no fun now. This place smells like a perfume factory." She put the scarf over her face and stared up through the thin blue material. Beside her, Boysie lay back down and curled himself into a ball. They lay without moving for a moment and then Sara sat up on the bed and looked down at her long, lanky legs. She said, "I have the biggest feet in my school."

"Honestly, Sara, I hope you are not going to start listing all the millions of things wrong with you because I just don't want to hear it again."

"Well, it's the truth about my feet. One time in Phys Ed the boys started throwing the girls' sneakers around and Bull Durham got my sneakers and put them on and they fit perfectly! How do you think it feels to wear the same size shoe as Bull Durham?"

"People don't notice things like that."

"Huh!"

"No, they don't. I have perfectly terrible hands—look at my fingers—only I don't go around all the time saying, 'Everybody, look at my stubby fingers, I have stubby fingers, everybody,' to *make* people notice. You should just ignore things that are wrong with you. The truth is everyone else is so worried about what's wrong with *them* that—"

"It is very difficult to ignore the fact that you have huge feet when Bull Durham is dancing all over the gym in your shoes. They were not stretched the tiniest little bit when he took them off either."

"You wear the same size shoe as Jackie Kennedy Onassis if that makes you feel any better."

"How do you know?"

"Because one time when she was going into an Indian temple she had to leave her shoes outside and some reporter looked in them to see what size they were." She leaned close to the mirror and looked at her teeth.

"Her feet *look* littler."

"That's because she doesn't wear orange sneakers."

"I like my orange sneakers." Sara sat on the edge of the bed, slipped her feet into the shoes, and held them up. "What's wrong with them?"

"Nothing, except that when you want to hide something, you don't go painting it orange. I've got to go. Frank's coming."

She went out the door and Sara could hear her crossing into the kitchen. Sara lay back on the bed, her head next to Boysie. She looked at the sleeping dog, then covered her face with her hands and began to cry noisily.

"Oh, Boysie, Boysie, I'm crying," she wailed. Years ago, when Boysie was a young dog, he could not bear to hear anyone cry. Sara had only to pretend she was crying and Boysie would come running. He would whine and dig at her with his paws and lick her hands until she stopped. Now he lay with his eyes closed.

"Boysie, I'm crying," she said again. "I'm really crying this time. Boysie doesn't love me."

The dog shifted uneasily without opening his eyes.

"Boysie, Boysie, I'm crying, I'm so sad, Boysie," she wailed, then stopped and sat up abruptly. "You don't care about anybody, do you Boysie? A person could cry herself to death these days and you wouldn't care."

She got up and left the room. In the hall she heard the tapping noise of Boysie's feet behind her and she said without looking at him, "I don't want you now, Boysie.

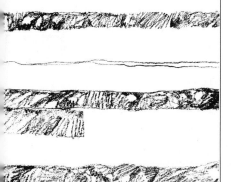

Go on back in the bedroom. Go on." She went a few steps farther and, when he continued to follow her, turned and looked at him. "In case you are confused, Boysie, a dog is supposed to comfort people and run up and nuzzle them and make them feel better. All you want to do is lie on soft things and hide bones in the house because you are too lazy to go outside. Just go on back in the bedroom."

She started into the kitchen, still followed by Boysie, who could not bear to be left alone, then heard her aunt and Wanda arguing, changed her mind, and went out onto the porch.

Behind her, Boysie scratched at the door and she let him out. "Now quit following me."

Her brother Charlie was sitting on the top step and Sara sat down beside him. She held out her feet, looked at them, and said, "I like my orange sneakers, don't you, Charlie?"

He did not answer. He had been eating a lollipop and the stick had come off and now he was trying to put it back into the red candy. He had been trying for so long that the stick was bent.

"Here," she said, "I'll do it for you." She put the stick in and handed it to him. "Now be careful with it."

She sat without speaking for a moment, then she looked down at her feet and said, "I hate these orange sneakers. I just *hate* them. She leaned back against the porch railing so she wouldn't have to see them and said, "Charlie, I'll tell you something. This has been the worst summer of my life."

She did not know exactly why this was true. She was doing the same things she had done last summer—walk to the Dairy Queen with her friend Mary, baby-sit for Mrs. Hodges, watch television—and yet everything was different. It was as if her life was a huge kaleidoscope, and the kaleidoscope had been turned and now everything was changed. The same stones, shaken, no longer made the same design.

But it was not only one different design, one change; it was a hundred. She could never be really sure of anything this summer. One moment she was happy, and the next, for no reason, she was miserable. An hour ago she had loved her sneakers; now she detested them.

"Charlie, I'll tell you what this awful summer's been like. You remember when that finky Jim Wilson got you on the seesaw, remember that? And he kept bouncing you up and down and then he'd keep you up in the air for a real long time and then he'd drop you down real sudden, and you couldn't get off and you thought you never would? Up and down, up and down, for the rest of your life? Well, that's what this summer's been like for me.

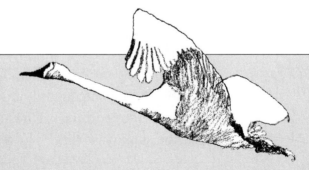

Reader's Response

If you could talk to Sara, what would you say to her to
help her feel better about herself?

Selection Follow-up

The Summer of the Swans

Responding to Literature

1. How are the changes Sara faces during adolescence affecting the way she feels abour herself?

2. When Sara complains about the size of her feet, Wanda gives her some advice. What does she tell her?

3. All people go through four stages of growth. At which stage of growth is Sara? Wanda? Charlie?

4. What does the author mean when she says about Sara, "It was as if her life was a huge kaleidoscope, and the kaleidoscope had been turned and now everything was changed"?

5. Write a letter to Sara explaining why you think she has had an "up and down summer."

Books to Enjoy

The Summer of the Swans by Betsy Byars
Read the book to learn how Sara's feelings about herself and others change.

Hatchet by Gary Paulsen
After a plane crash, a young boy survives fifty-four days in the wilderness with only the aid of the hatchet his mother gave him. During this time, he comes to terms with his parents' divorce.

Go For It! by Judy Zerafa
This book is a self-help manual for teenagers on how to set goals and reach their full potential. It also discusses positive self-image, problem solving, and setting achievable goals.

Glossary

Some words in this book may be new to you or difficult to pronounce. Those words have been spelled phonetically in parentheses. The syllable that receives stress in a word is shown in small capital letters.

For example: **Chicago** (shuh KAH goh)

Most phonetic spellings are easy to read. In the following Pronunciation Key, you can see how letters are used to show different sounds.

PRONUNCIATION KEY

a	after	(AF tur)
ah	father	(FAH thur)
ai	care	(kair)
aw	dog	(dawg)
ay	paper	(PAY pur)
e	letter	(LET ur)
ee	eat	(eet)
ih	trip	(trihp)
eye	idea	(eye DEE uh)
y	hide	(hyd)
ye	lie	(lye)
oh	flow	(floh)
oi	boy	(boi)
oo	rule	(rool)
or	horse	(hors)
ou	cow	(kou)
yoo	few	(fyoo)
u	taken	(TAY kun)
	matter	(MAT ur)
uh	ago	(uh GOH)

ch	chicken	(CHIHK un)
g	game	(gaym)
ing	coming	(KUM ing)
j	job	(jahb)
k	came	(kaym)
ng	long	(lawng)
s	city	(SIH tee)
sh	ship	(shihp)
th	thin	(thihn)
thh	feather	(FETHH ur)
y	yard	(yahrd)
z	size	(syz)
zh	division	(duh VIHZH un)

A

absorbed (ab SORBD) Light that is trapped by matter. p. 272

acid (AS ihd) A compound that turns blue litmus to red. p. 223

adaptation (ad up TAY shun) A trait that helps an organism survive in its environment. p. 177

adolescence (ad ul ES uns) The stage in human life between childhood and adulthood. p. 492

adulthood (uh DULT hood) The stage in human life after adolescence. p. 493

air mass (air mas) A large body of air that has about the same temperature and humidity throughout. p. 403

altitude (AL tuh tood) The distance above sea level. p. 421

amplitude (AM pluh tood) A measure of the amount of energy in a sound wave. p. 303

artificial satellite (ahrt uh FIHSH-ul SAT uh lyt) An object made by people that orbits another object in space. p. 412

astronomical unit (as truh NAHM ih-kul YOON iht) A unit used to measure distances in the solar system, equal to 149.6 million km (93 million miles). p. 438

atmosphere (AT mus feer) The mixture of gases that surround the earth. p. 368

atomic number (uh TAHM ihk NUM-bur) The number of protons in an atom of an element. p. 207

B

base (bays) A compound that turns red litmus to blue. p. 223

biodegradable matter (bye oh dih-GRAY duh bul MAT ur) Matter that can be broken down by living things. p. 149

black dwarf (blak dworf) The remains of a white dwarf star that has used up all its fuel. p. 451

black hole (blak hohl) A small region in space resulting from the collapse of a massive star. p. 453

Bohr model (bawr MAHD ul) A model of the atom, developed by Niels Bohr, that shows electrons moving in orbits around the nucleus of the atom. p. 203

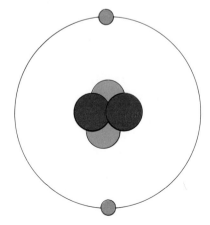

C

camouflage (KAM uh flahzh) An adaptation that helps an animal blend in with its environment. p. 141

carbon-oxygen cycle (KAHR bun-AHKS ih jun   SYE kul) The movement of carbon and oxygen through an eco-system. p. 108

carnivore (KAHR nuh vor) An organism that eats only animals. p. 98

cell (sel) The basic unit of all living things. p. 32

cell membrane (sel   MEM brayn) A structure that surrounds and protects the cell. p. 41

cell wall (sel   wawl) A rigid struc-ture that surrounds the cell membrane in some cells. p. 41

chemical bond (KEM ih kul   bahnd) The force that holds together the atoms in a compound. p. 213

chemical reaction (KEM ih kul   ree-AK shun) A reaction in which one or more substances change to form new substances. p. 235

childhood (CHYLD hood) The stage in human life from 1 year to about 12 years of age. p. 491

chlorophyll (KLOR uh fihl) The green pigment that absorbs energy from sunlight. p. 71

chloroplast (KLOR uh plast) A green structure in a plant cell where food is made. p. 71

chromosomes (KROH muh sohmz) Threadlike structures in the nucleus of a cell that carry information about the characteristics of the living thing. pp. 39, 483

circulatory system (SUR kyoo luh-tor ee   SIHS tum) A transport system that carries food and oxygen to cells. p. 514

climate (KLYE mut) The average of weather conditions for a region over a long period of time. p. 418

cloud seeding (kloud   SEED ing) A method used to cause clouds to release precipitation. p. 415

community (kuh MYOO nuh tee) All the populations living together in a region. p. 115

compound (KAHM pound) A sub-stance formed when two or more ele-ments combine chemically. p. 212

compression (kum PRESH un) The region of a sound wave in which the particles are crowded together. p. 301

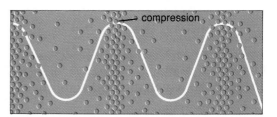

concave lens (kahn KAYV lenz) A lens that is thinner in the middle than it is at the edge. p. 279

concave mirror (kahn KAYV MIHR-ur) A mirror in which the reflecting surface curves inward. p. 277

constellation (kahn stuh LAY-shun) A group of stars that seem to form a picture. p. 442

consumer (kun SOOM ur) An organism that gets energy from other living things or the remains of once-living things. p. 97

convex lens (kahn VEKS lenz) A lens that is thicker in the middle than it is at the edge. p. 279

convex mirror (kahn VEKS MIHR-ur) A mirror in which the reflecting surface curves outward. p. 277

coral animal (KOR ul AN ih-mul) A stinging-cell animal that forms a limestone skeleton. p. 139

corrosion (kuh ROH zhun) A chemical change in which a metal combines with elements such as oxygen. p. 240

cytoplasm (SYT oh plaz um) The thick, jellylike substance that forms most of a cell. p. 40

D

decomposer (dee kum POHZ-ur) An organism that breaks down once-living things, releasing the energy stored in them. p. 97

diffusion (dih FYOO zhun) The process by which particles move from a region where there is a large amount of a substance to a region where there is a small amount. p. 43

digestive system (dih JES tihv SIHS tum) The system that changes food into a form that cells can use. p. 518

dome mountain (dohm MOUNT-un) A mountain formed when a large area of the earth's surface is slowly bent upward. p. 394

dominant trait (DAHM uh nunt trayt) A trait that hides another trait. p. 499

drug abuse (drug uh BYOOS) The misuse of drugs. p. 530

drug addiction (drug uh DIHK-shun) The condition in which a person needs a drug. p. 531

E

earthquake (URTH kwayk) A shaking and trembling of the earth's crust. p. 378

ecosystem　(EK oh sihs tum)　All the living and nonliving things in an environment and the ways they affect one another. p. 94

egg　(eg)　The sex cell produced by a female parent. p. 483

electric current　(ee LEK trihk KUR unt)　A continuous movement of electrons through a conductor. p. 328

electromagnetic spectrum　(ee lek-troh mag NET ihk SPEK trum)　The arrangement of waves of radiant energy in order of wavelengths and frequencies. p. 267

electron cloud model　(ee LEK trahn kloud MAHD ul)　The model of the atom that shows electrons forming a cloud as they move around the nucleus of the atom. p. 205

element　(EL uh munt)　Matter that is made of just one kind of atom. p. 206

elliptical galaxy　(ee LIHP tih kul GAL uk see)　A galaxy that is shaped like a football. p. 456

embryo　(EM bree oh)　**1.** The part of a seed that develops into a young plant. p. 83. **2.** A developing human for the first 2 months after fertilization. p. 487

endangered species　(en DAYN jurd SPEE sheez)　A species that is in danger of becoming extinct. p. 181

endocrine system　(EN doh krihn SIHS tum)　A control system made up of glands. p. 520

era　(IHR uh)　A main division of time in the history of the earth. p. 166

evolution　(ev uh LOO shun)　The process of change that can produce new species from existing species over time. p. 175

excretory system　(EKS kruh tor ee SIHS tum)　The system that removes wastes from the body. p. 526

extinct organism　(ek STINGKT OR guh nihz um)　A kind of organism that was once alive but no longer exists anywhere on the earth. p. 118

F
fault　(fawlt)　A break in the earth's crust. p. 378

fault-block mountain　(fawlt blahk MOUNT un)　A mountain formed when a block of rock is raised along a fault. p. 390

fertilization　(fur tul ih ZAY shun)　The process by which a sperm cell joins with an egg cell. pp. 79, 486

fetus　(FEET us)　A developing human at the beginning of the third month of development. p. 488

focus (FOH kus) A point underground where the vibrations of an earthquake begin. p. 379

folded mountain (FOHLD ed MOUNT un) A mountain formed when rock layers are squeezed together. p. 391

food chain (food chayn) The path by which energy is transferred from one organism to another. p. 101

food web (food web) Overlapping, or linking, food chains in an ecosystem. p. 103

formula (FOR myoo luh) A group of symbols that shows the elements in a compound. p. 216

fossil (FAHS ul) Any kind of evidence of something that was alive a long time ago. p. 161

frequency (FREE kwun see) The number of waves that pass by a point each second. p. 266

front (frunt) The boundary between two air masses. p. 406

fungi (FUN jye); *singular form,* fungus (FUNG gus) One-celled or many-celled organisms that look somewhat like plants but do not contain chlorophyll. p. 54

G
galaxy (GAL uk see) A huge rotating group of stars. p. 454

gene (jeen) A section of a chromosome. p. 499

generator (JEN ur ayt ur) A machine that changes mechanical energy into electrical energy. p. 333

genetics (juh NET ihks) The branch of science that deals with the way traits are passed from parents to children. p. 500

germination (jur muh NAY shun) The development of the embryo of a seed into a young plant. p. 83

glacier (GLAY shur) A large body of moving ice. p. 424

global winds (GLOH bul wihndz) The bands of moving air that circle the earth. p. 408

greenhouse effect (GREEN hous e FEKT) The trapping of heat by gases in the atmosphere. p. 426

H
herbivore (HUR buh vor) An organism that eats only plants. p. 97

high tide (hye tyd) The time when the water reaches the highest point on land. p. 132

hormone (HOR mohn) A chemical made by an endocrine gland. p. 520

hydrocarbon (hye droh KAHR-bun) A compound made of just the two elements hydrogen and carbon. p. 218

hydrosphere (HYE droh sfihr) All the parts of the earth that are water. p. 369

I

ice age A period when the earth's climate became cooler. p. 424

immune system (ihm MYOON SIHS-tum) Cells and tissues that are involved in fighting disease. p. 529

indicator (IHN dih kayt ur) A dye that changes color when mixed with an acid or a base. p. 222

infancy (IHN fun see) The stage in human life between birth and 1 year of age. p. 490

infection (ihn FEK shun) A disease caused by viruses or bacteria. p. 529

infrasonic sound (ihn fruh SAHN-ihk sound) Sound with a frequency below 20 hertz. p. 315

inherit (ihn HER iht) To receive a trait from a parent. p. 176

integrated circuit (IHN tuh grayt-ihd SUR kiht) A circuit in which all the parts and connections are on a tiny silicon chip. p. 345

intensity (ihn TEN suh tee) The brightness of a light. p. 266

intertidal zone (ihn tur TYD-ul zohn) The area of shoreline that is under water during some parts of the day and above water during other parts of the day. p. 128

ion (EYE un) An atom that has gained or lost electrons. p. 213

irregular galaxy (ihr REG yoo lur GAL uk see) A galaxy that has no specific shape. p. 456

J

jet stream (jet streem) A narrow band of very fast-moving air high in the troposphere. p. 410

K

kilowatt-hour (KIHL oh waht our) A unit equal to 1,000 watts of electrical energy used for 1 hour. p. 343

kingdom (KING dum) Largest unit of classification of living things. p. 52

L

latitude (LAT uh tood) The distance north or south of the equator measured in degrees. p. 418

lava (LAH vuh) Molten rock that reaches the earth's surface. p. 385

law of conservation of mass (law uv kahn sur VAY shun uv mas) The law that states that matter cannot be created or destroyed by any chemical reaction. p. 238

life processes (lyf PRAH ses-ihz) All the activities that enable organisms to survive. p. 33

light telescope (lyt TEL uh-skohp) A device that gathers light from stars and other objects in space. p. 444

light-year (lyt yihr) The distance light travels in one year, equal to 9.5 trillion km. p. 439

lithosphere (LIHTH oh sfihr) The earth's crust plus the rigid upper part of the mantle. p. 376

low tide (loh tyd) The time when the water is at its lowest point on land. p. 132

luminous (LOO muh nus) Producing light. p. 287

M

magma (MAG muh) Molten rock mixed with gases within the earth. p. 385

magnitude (MAG nuh tood) The brightness of a star. p. 448

meiosis (mye OH sihs) The kind of cell division that produces sex cells. p. 485

metabolism (muh TAB uh lihz-um) All the chemical changes that take place in a living thing. p. 34

microprocessor (mye kroh PRAHS-es ur) A computer on a chip. p. 346

mitosis (mye TOH sihs) The process by which one cell divides, forming two new cells. p. 47

molecule (MAHL ih kyool) A particle formed by sharing electrons. p. 214

moneran (moh NER un) A one-celled organism that lacks a nucleus but has nuclear material throughout the cytoplasm. p. 55

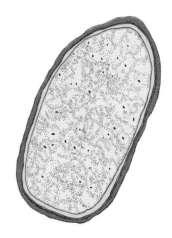

muscular system (MUS kyoo lur SIHS tum) The organ system made up of muscles, which move body parts. p. 525

N

natural selection (NACH ur ul suh-LEK shun) The process by which living things that are adapted to their environment survive. p. 178

nebula (NEB yuh luh) A huge cloud of dust and gases in space. p. 450

nervous system (NUR vus SIHS-tum) The control system made up of the brain, the spinal cord, and the nerves. p. 512

neutralization (noo truh luh ZAY-shun) A chemical reaction, or change, between an acid and a base. p. 225

neutron star (NOO trahn stahr) A very small, very dense star. p. 452

nitrogen cycle (NYE truh jun SYE-kul) The movement of nitrogen through an ecosystem. p. 110

nuclear fission (NOO klee ur FIHSH un) A nuclear reaction in which large nuclei are split apart. p. 248

nuclear fusion (NOO klee ur FYOO-zhun) A nuclear reaction in which small nuclei join to form a larger nucleus. p. 254

nuclear reaction (NOO klee ur ree AK shun) A reaction in which the nuclei of atoms change. p. 246

nuclear reactor (NOO klee ur ree AK tur) A device in which a nuclear chain reaction is controlled so that the energy is released slowly. p. 249

nucleus (NOO klee us) The control center of a cell. p. 39

O

ocean pollution (OH shun puh-LOO shun) The dumping of harmful materials into the ocean. p. 149

omnivore (AHM nih vor) An organism that eats both plants and animals. p. 98

opaque (oh PAYK) Not transmitting light. p. 273

open-ocean zone (OH pun OH-shun zohn) The area of the ocean with the greatest depth. p. 129

organic compounds (or GAN ihk KAHM poundz) Compounds that contain carbon. p. 218

ovary (OH vuh ree) The large base of the pistil of a flower. p. 77

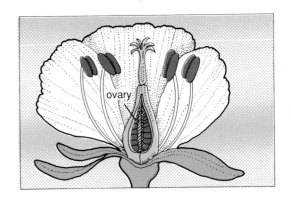

oxidation (ahks ih DAY shun) A chemical change in which oxygen reacts with other substances. p. 240

ozone (OH zohn) A gas in the upper atmosphere that absorbs most of the ultraviolet radiation from the sun. p. 429

P

parallel circuit (PAR uh lel SUR-kiht) A circuit in which the electrons have more than one path that they can follow. p. 331

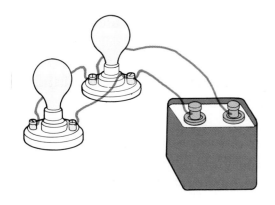

Periodic Table (pihr ee AHD-ihk TAY bul) A chart that contains many facts about the elements and their atoms. p. 207

petrified (PE trih fyd) Having turned to stone. p. 162

phloem (FLOH em) A kind of tissue made of tubes that carry food through a plant. p. 66

photosynthesis (foht oh SIHN thuh-sihs) The process by which plants make food. p. 70

pistil (PIHS tihl) The female reproductive part of a flower. p. 77

pitch (pihch) How high or low a sound seems. p. 303

plane mirror (playn MIHR ur) A mirror in which the reflecting surface is flat. p. 277

plankton (PLANGK tun) Tiny plants and animals that float in the ocean. p. 127

plate tectonics (playt tek TAHN-ihks) A theory that states that the lithosphere is made of plates that move very slowly. p. 377

polar climate (POH lur KLYE-mut) A climate that has an average temperature lower than 10°C (50°F) during the warmest month. p. 422

pollination (pahl uh NAY shun) The process by which pollen grains move from a stamen to a pistil. p. 77

polymer (PAHL uh mur) An organic compound that consists mainly of a long chain of carbon atoms. p. 220

population (pahp yoo LAY shun) A group of the same kind of organism living together in the same region. p. 115

predator (PRED uh tur) An animal that kills another animal for food. p. 102

prevailing winds (pree VAYL ing wihndz) Winds that blow from the same direction over long distances. p. 409

prey (pray) An animal that is hunted by another animal. p. 102

producer (proh DOOS ur) A living thing that can make its own food. p. 96

protist (PROHT ihst) A one-celled organism that lives in water. p. 54

R

radio telescope (RAY dee oh TEL-uh skohp) A device that gathers radio waves from objects in space. p. 445

radioactive dating (ray dee oh AK-tihv DAYT ing) A method of measuring the age of rocks and fossils. p. 165

radioactive elements (ray dee oh AK-tihv EL uh munts) Elements whose nuclei naturally break down into other nuclei. p. 246

rarefaction (rer uh FAK shun) The region of a sound wave in which particles are spread apart. p. 301

recessive trait (rih SES ihv trayt) A trait that is hidden by another trait. p. 499

red giant (red JYE unt) An old star that has greatly enlarged and is cool compared with a yellow star. p. 451

reflected (rih FLEK ted) Light that is bounced off the surface of an object. p. 272

refraction (rih FRAK shun) The change in direction of light when it passes from one kind of matter to another. p. 274

reproduction (ree pruh DUK shun) The process by which living things produce other living things of the same kind. pp. 35, 482

respiration (res puh RAY shun) A process in living things in which oxygen combines with food, releasing energy from the food. p. 74

respiratory system (RES pur uh tor-ee SIHS tum) The transport system that brings oxygen into the body. p. 514

rocket (RAHK iht) A spacecraft that contains a powerful engine. p. 458

root hair (root hair) One of the threadlike structures that grow from the surface of a root. p. 65

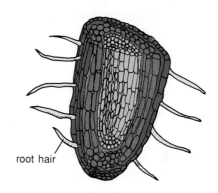

root hair

S

salt (sawlt) A compound that can be formed when an acid is mixed with a base. p. 225

scavenger (SKAV ihn jur) An animal that eats a dead or dying animal that it finds. p. 102

seed coat (seed koht) A tough covering that protects a seed. p. 83

seismograph (SYZ muh graf) An instrument that measures and records earthquake waves. p. 380

series circuit (SIHR eez SUR-kiht) A circuit in which the electrons have only one path on which to move. p. 331

shallow-ocean zone (SHAL oh OH-shun zohn) The area of the ocean that starts at the low-tide line and ends where the ocean bottom drops off sharply. p. 128

skeletal system (SKEL uh tul SIHS-tum) The frame of bones that supports the body. p. 525

sleep (sleep) A state of lowered mental and physical activity. p. 511

sonar (SOH nahr) A method of using ultrasonic sound to locate objects under water. p. 318

space shuttle (spays SHUT ul) A spacecraft that carries passengers and equipment into space. p. 459

space station (spays STAY shun) A spacecraft that stays in orbit for long periods. p. 462

species (SPEE sheez) The smallest group into which living things are classified. p. 167

spectroscope (SPEK troh skohp) A device that separates light into a band of colors. p. 447

sperm (spurm) The male reproductive cell; the sex cell produced by the male parent. pp. 77, 483

spiral galaxy (SPYE rul GAL uk-see) A galaxy that has arms extending from a central region. p. 456

stamen (STAY mun) The male reproductive part of a flower. p. 77

static electricity (STAT ihk ee lek-TRIHS ih tee) An electric charge that collects on the surface of an object. p. 327

stomate (STOH mayt) One of the small openings usually found on the bottom surface of leaves. p. 67

supernova (soo pur NOH vuh) The violent explosion of a star that has a high mass. p. 452

synfuel (SIHN fyoo ul) A fuel put together from other materials. p. 243

T

temperate climate (TEM pur iht KLYE mut) A climate that has an average summer temperature above 18°C (64°F) and an average winter temperature below 10°C (50°F). p. 422

theory (THEE uh ree) An idea that is supported by evidence. p. 170

tide pool (tyd pool) A depression in rock that is filled with ocean water. p. 137

trait (trayt) A characteristic passed from parents to children. p. 498

translucent (trans LOO sunt) Allowing some light through, but scattering the light. p. 273

transmitted (trans MIHT ted) Light that passes through matter. p. 272

transparent (trans PER unt) Allowing light to pass through without scattering the light. p. 273

tropical climate (TRAHP ih kul KLYE mut) A climate that has an average temperature higher than 18°C (64°F) during the coldest month. p. 422

U

ultrasonic sound (ul truh SAHN ihk sound) Sound with a frequency above 20,000 Hz. p. 315

universe (YOON uh vurs) Everything that exists, including space and all objects in it. p. 456

V

vacuole (VAK yoo ohl) A fluid-filled sac in a cell. p. 40

variation (ver ee AY shun) A slight difference between members of a species. p. 176

vibration (vye BRAY shun) The rapid back-and-forth movement of matter that may produce sound. p. 299

virus (VYE rus) Something that does not fit into any of the five kingdoms of living things. p. 56

visible spectrum (VIHZ uh bul SPEK trum) All the bands of visible light. p. 286

volcanic mountain (vahl KAN ihk MOUNT un) A cone-shaped mountain formed of layers of lava and ash. p. 393

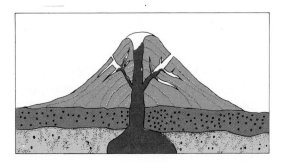

volcano (vahl KAY noh) An opening in the earth through which molten rock material reaches the earth's surface. p. 384

W

water cycle (WAWT ur SYE kul) The movement of water through an ecosystem. p. 106

wavelength (WAYV lengkth) The distance between the crest of one wave and the crest of the next wave. p. 265

white dwarf (hwyt dworf) An old, very dense star. p. 451

X–Z

xylem (ZYE lum) A kind of tissue made of tubes that carry water and minerals upward through a plant. p. 65

zygote (ZYE goht) A fertilized egg. p. 487

Index

Credits

Chapter 4 122–123: © P.M. David/Photo Researchers, Inc. 123: *inset* Larry Lipsky/TOM STACK & ASSOCIATES. 124–125: Michael A. Keller/The Stock Market. 124: *inset* Sea Studios, Inc./Peter Arnold, Inc. 125: *inset,* 127 *t.r.*: Animals Animals/Peter Parks/Oxford Scientific Films. 127: *t.m.* © D.P. Wilson-Davide Eric Hoskin/Science Source/Photo Researchers, Inc.; *b.m.* © Andrew Martinez/Photo Researchers, Inc.; *b.r.* Dave B. Fleetham/TOM STACK & ASSOCIATES; *b.* Animals Animals/Richard Kolar. 128: Ken Lax for SB&G. 130: © Andrew J. Martinez/Photo Researchers, Inc. 131: Tom Smoyer/Harbor Branch Oceanographic Institution. 132: *b.* Animals Animals/Doug Wechsler; *inset* Jeff Foott/Bruce Coleman. 133: *b.* Terry Domico/Earth Images; *inset* Robert E. Pelcham/Bruce Coleman. 135: *t.* © Tom McHugh/Photo Researchers, Inc.; *b.* Ken Lax for SB&G. 136: *t.l.* Ed Robinson/TOM STACK & ASSOCIATES; *b.l.* © D.P. Wilson/Science Source/Photo Researchers, Inc.; *b.r.* R.N. Mariscal/Bruce Coleman. 137: *t.l.* Animals Animals/Anne Wertheim; *b.r.* Animals Animals/Breck P. Kent. 138: Woodward/TOM STACK & ASSOCIATES. 139: Denise Tackett/TOM STACK & ASSOCIATES. 140: *t.l.* Animals Animals/Tim Rock; *b.r.* Animals Animals/Zig Leszczynski. 141: Ron Taylor/Bruce Coleman. 142: *t.l., t.r.* Animals Animals/Zig Leszczynski; *b.l.* Bill Wood/Bruce Coleman. 144–145: *b.* © Photo Researchers, Inc. 146: Animals Animals/Peter Parks/Oxford Scientific Films. 147: Dudley Foster/Woods Hole Oceanographic Institute. 148: *t.* George Marler/Bruce Coleman; *b.* Animals Animals/Lewis Trusty. 149: *t.* Mike Mathers/Black Star; *b.r.* © Shirley Richards/Photo Researchers, Inc. 150: Animals Animals/C.C. Lockwood. 151: Ken Lax for SB&G. 155: *t.r.* © Carleton Ray/Photo Researchers, Inc.; *b.r.* © Nancy Sefton/Photo Researchers, Inc.; *b.m., b.l.* © Al Grotell.

Chapter 5 156–157: Grant Heilman/Grant Heilman Photography. 156: *l. inset* Philip Sharpe/Earth Scenes; *r. inset* Harry Taylor/Oxford Scientific Films/Earth Scenes. 158–159: © M. Clave Jacana/Photo Researchers, Inc. 158: *inset* G. Poinar/University of California, Berkeley. 159: *inset, t.r.* Dan DeWilde for SB&G. 160: *t.* © Photo Researchers, Inc.; *b.* Mark A. Philbrook. 161: *l.* John Canalosi/Peter Arnold, Inc.; *r.* Bruce Coleman; *inset, t.r.* © Russ Kinne/Comstock. 162: Tom Bean/The Stock Market. 164: © J. Koivula/Science Source/Photo Researchers, Inc. 171: *l.* Bruce Coleman; *t.r.* © Frans Lauting/Photo Researchers, Inc.; *b.r.* © Kenneth Fink/NAS/Photo Researchers, Inc. 173: Bruce Coleman. 174: Victoria Beller-Smith for SB&G. 178: © Gregory K. Scott/Photo Researchers, Inc. 179: *l., m.r.* Kim Taylor/Bruce Coleman; *t.r., b.r.* Animals Animals/Breck P. Kent. 182: *l.* © M. Frandreau/Photo Researchers, Inc.; *r.* © 1988 James Balog/Black Star. 186: Courtesy of Dr. Eugene Kaplan. 190: *TASS* from Sovfoto.

Unit 2 opener 197: T.J. Florian/Rainbow.

Chapter 6 198–199: © 1991 Chuck O'Rear/Woodfin Camp & Associates. 200–201: NASA/John F. Kennedy Space Center. 201: *b.* © Dick Luria/Photo Researchers, Inc.; *t., m.* Bill Kontzias for SB&G. 204: Victoria Beller-Smith for SB&G. 205: Ken Lax for SB&G. 206–207: *background* Todd Haiman for SB&G. 206 *m.l., b.r.* J. Cancalosi/Peter Arnold, Inc.; *b.l.* Richard Megna/Fundamental Photographs; *m.r.* © Russ Lappa/Photo Researchers, Inc. 207: *m.m.* F. & A. Michler/Peter Arnold, Inc.; *b.r.* E.R. Degginger/Color-Pic, Inc. 208–209: George Baquero. 212: E.R. Degginger/Color-Pic, Inc. 214: Kim Taylor/Bruce Coleman. 215: Gene Ahrens/Bruce Coleman. 217: Light Mechanics for SB&G. 218–219: Todd Haiman for SB&G. 220: *t.* Ken Lax for SB&G; *b.* Todd Haiman for SB&G. 221: Todd Haiman for SB&G. 222–223: Richard Megna/Fundamental Photographs. 224: Ken Lax for SB&G. 225: E.R. Degginger/Color-Pic, Inc. 226: Richard Megna/Fundamental Photographs.

Chapter 7 233: *inset* Ken Karp for SB&G. 234: Todd Haiman for SB&G. 235: FPG. 236: Richard Megna/Fundamental Photographs. 237: Ken Lax for SB&G. 240: *t.l.* Michael Markin/Bruce Coleman; *t.r.* Melinda Berg/Bruce Coleman; *b.l.* Todd Haiman for SB&G. 241: Keith Gunnar/Bruce Coleman. 242: *t.* Todd Haiman for SB&G; *b.* E.R. Degginger/Bruce Coleman. 243: Ken Lax for SB&G. 244: Peter Menzel. 247: *m.r.* © 1991 Jose Fernandez/Woodfin Camp & Associates; *b.r.* © Will & Deni McIntyre/Photo Researchers, Inc. 251: *t.* © Hank Morgan/Photo Researchers, Inc.; *m.* SIU Biomedical Communications/Bruce Coleman; *b.* © Philippe Plailly/Science Photo Library/Photo Researchers, Inc. 252–253: John Elk III/Bruce Coleman. 254–255: NASA. 256: Mark Sherman/Bruce Coleman.

Chapter 8 260–261: Ken Karp for SB&G. 262–263: Otto Done/SuperStock. 262, 263: *insets* Ken Karp for SB&G. 268 Daedalus Enterprises, Inc. 269: *l.* FourbyFive/Superstock, Inc.; *r.* Joe Sachs for SB&G. 270: Richard Megna/Fundamental Photographs. 272, 273: Ken Lax for SB&G. 274: Richard Megna/Fundamental Photographs. 275: The Image Bank. 276: Grant Heilman/Grant Heilman Photography. 277: *l.* E.R. Degginger/Color-Pic, Inc.; *r.* 1989 Stephen Feld. 280: Joe Sachs for SB&G. 281, 282: John Lei/OPC for SB&G. 283: Ken O'Donoghue for SB&G. 284: © Steve Percival/Science Photo Library/Photo Researchers, Inc. 287: *t.* Paul Silverman/Fundamental Photographs; *b.* © John Kaprielian/Photo Researchers, Inc. 289: *t.* Runk-Schoenberger/Grant Heilman Photography; *b.* General Motors, Chrysler Corporation.

Chapter 9 294–295: Billy Rose Theatre Collection, The New York Public Library at Lincoln Center, Lenox and Tilden Foundations. 296–297: Bill Kontzias for SB&G. 297: *inset* Elizabeth Hathon for SB&G. 298: *t.* Joe Sachs for SB&G; *b.* U.S. Sprint & J. Walter Thompson. 300: *t.* Ken Lax for SB&G; *b.* Richard Megna/Fundamental Photographs. 302: Kip Peticolas/Fundamental Photographs. 303: *b.* Animals Animals/B.G. Murray, Jr.; *m.m.r.* J.C. Carton/Bruce Coleman. 304: Victoria Beller-Smith for SB&G. 305: Ken Lax for SB&G. 306: Victoria Beller-Smith for SB&G. 307: © Bob Daemmrich Photography. 308, 309: Ken Lax for SB&G. 310: *inset* John Elk III/Stock, Boston. 311: *l.* Ken Sherman/Bruce Coleman; *r.* Banus March/FPG. 312: © Ralph Wetmore/Photo Researchers, Inc. 313: John Curtis/Offshoot for SB&G. 316: *t.l.* S.L. Craig, Jr./Bruce Coleman; *m.l.* © Krautkramer Branson; *r.* © S.I.U./Science Source/Photo Researchers, Inc. 317: Victoria Beller-Smith. 318: Woods Hole Oceanographic Institute.

Chapter 10 322–323: Robert E. Daemmrich/Tony Stone Worldwide; 322: *inset* IBM. 324–325: Susan T. McElhinney. 325: *b. inset* Martha Cooper; *t. inset* Bill Kontzias for SB&G. 326: Richard Megna/Fundamental Photographs. 327: John Lei/OPC for SB&G. 329: Richard Megna/Fundamental Photographs. 330: John Lei/OPC for SB&G. 331: Richard Megna/Fundamental Photographs. 332: © 1991 Terrence Moore/Woodfin Camp & Associates. 335: David Dempster/Offshoot for SB&G. 336: Richard Megna/Fundamental Photographs. 340: E.R. Degginger/Color-Pic, Inc. 341: John Lei/OPC for SB&G. 342: *t.* Sybil Shelton/Peter Arnold, Inc.; *b.* E.R. Degginger/Color-Pic, Inc. 343: E.R. Degginger/Color-Pic, Inc. 344: Kristen Brochmann/Fundamental Photographs. 345: *l.* © Dan McCoy/Rainbow; *inset* IBM. 346–347: Robert Mathena/Fundamental Photographs. 347: *inset* Courtesy of Motorola; *r.* Robert Mathena/Fundamental Photographs. 348: John Lei/OPC for SB&G. 352: Geoffrey King for SB&G.

Unit 3 opener 363: K. & M. Kraft/Peter Arnold, Inc.

Chapter 11 364–365: Pennington/Black Star. 366–367: David Hiser/Photographers, Aspen. 366: *inset* Enrico Ferorelli. 367: *inset* Ken Karp for SB&G. 369: *l.* Gene Ahrens/Bruce Coleman; *r.* © NASA/Photo Researchers, Inc. 371: Mickey Gibson/Earth Scenes. 378: © 1991 George Hall/Woodfin Camp & Associates. 380: *b.l.* © Vince Streano/The Stock Market; *inset, b.m.* © William E. Ferguson; *t.r.* © Ted Mahieu/The Stock Market. 382–383: Kent Reno. 383: *t.l.* University of California, Berkeley; *b.r.* Associated Press. 384–385: E.R. Degginger/Bruce Coleman. 388–389: Michael Lawton/Cirama. 388: *b.l.* Gary Braasch/U.S. Forest Service. 389: *inset* © Kelly W. Culpepper/Photo Researchers, Inc. 390: John M. Burnley/Bruce Coleman. 391: Lee Foster/Bruce Coleman. 392: Victoria Beller-Smith for SB&G. 393: © 1991 Mike Yamashita/Woodfin Camp & Associates. 394: Robert E. Pelham/Bruce Coleman. 397: © John Bova/Photo Researchers, Inc.

Chapter 12 398–399: Russell Lee/Standard Oil Collection/University of Louisville. 399: David J. Maenza/The Image Bank. 400–401: Enrico Ferorelli/DOA. 401: Dan DeWilde for SB&G. 402: *t.* Herman Kokojan/Black Star; *b.l.* Jeff Gnass. 405: John Lei/OPC for SB&G. 410: NOAA/NESDIS. 411: Herman Kokojan/Black Star. 412–414: NOAA/NESDIS. 415: © 1991 Jim Brandenberg/Woodfin Camp & Associates. 416–417: *b.l.* Gary David Gold; *t.r.* Keith Kent/Peter Arnold, Inc. 417: *inset* Lightning Location and Protection, Inc. 418: © Brett Palmer/The Stock Market. 421: © James W. Kay. 422: National Climatic Data Center, Asheville, NC. 423: *l.* Richard Steedman/The Stock Market; *m.* © 1991 Leo Touchet/Woodfin Camp & Associates; *r.* © Wynn Miller/After Image, Inc. 424: Charles Krebs/The Stock Market. 425: *r.* John Lei/OPC for SB&G; *l.* Wendell Metzer/Bruce Coleman. 426: Barry O'Rourke/The Stock Market. 428: Michael P. Gadomski/Bruce Coleman. 429: *t.* © NASA/Science Source/Photo Researchers, Inc.; *b.* Jack Swenson/TOM STACK & ASSOCIATES. 430: NASA/Goddard Institute for Space Studies.

Chapter 13 434–435: David A. Hardy/Science Photo Library/Photo Researchers, Inc. 435: Movie Still Archives. 436–437: The Picture Cube. 439: California Institute of Technology & Carnegie Institute of Washington. 441: NASA. 443: © Roger Ressmeyer/Starlight. 444: © Dan McCoy/Rainbow. 445: *l.* © Max Planck/Institut fur Radioastronomie/Science Photo Library/Photo Researchers, Inc.; *r.* © NRAD/AUI/Science Photo Library/Photo Researchers, Inc.; *b.r. inset* © T.J. Florian/Rainbow. 447: *t.l.* National Optical Astronomy Observatories; *b.r.* © Dept. of Physics/Imperial College/Science Photo Library/Photo Researchers, Inc. 450: U.S. Naval Observatory/Grant Heilman Photography. 454: *t.* © Dr. Jean Lorre/Science Photo Library/Photo Researchers, Inc.; *b.* National Optical Astronomy Observatories. 456: *l.* U.S. Naval Observatory/Tersch Enterprises; *r.* National Optical Astronomy Observatories. 458–459: © Roger Ressmeyer/Starlight. 460: Victoria Beller-Smith for SB&G. 461: Lockheed Missiles & Space Co., Inc. 466: Waverly Person/U.S. Dept. of Interior Geological Survey. 468: Smithsonian Institution. 470: Chip Clark. 472: Smithsonian Institution. 474: Chip Clark. 475: Smithsonian Institution.

Unit 4 opener 477: © Manfred Kage/Peter Arnold, Inc.

Chapter 14 478–481: Yoav Levy/PHOTOTAKE. 482: John Mais. 483: *t.r.* © BioPhoto Associates/Science Source/Photo Researchers, Inc.; *b.l.* © John Giannicchi/Science Source/Photo Researchers, Inc.; *b.m.* © Dr. G. Schatten/Science Photo Library/Photo Researchers, Inc. 488: Phil Degginger. 489: J.T. Miller/The Stock Market. 490: *t.* © A. Glauberman/Photo Researchers, Inc.; *inset* D.P. Herschkowitz/Bruce Coleman. 491: Richard Haynes for SB&G. 492: Ken Karp/OPC for SB&G. 493: © Myron Kanfer. 494: *l.* © Blair Seitz/Photo Researchers, Inc.; *r.* E.R. Degginger/Color-Pic, Inc. 496: *m.* © Chemical Design/LTD/Science Photo Library/Photo Researchers, Inc.; *t.l.* © Adam Hart-Davis/Science Photo Library/Photo Researchers, Inc.; 497: Lifecode. 498: © Richard Hutchings/Photo Researchers, Inc. 499: *m.l., r.* FourbyFive/Superstock, Inc.; *m.r.* Norman Owen Tomalin/Bruce Coleman. 502: *t.l.* © Richard Parker/Photo Researchers, Inc.; *b.l.* Linda Dufurrena/Grant Heilman Photography; *r.* Patti Murray/Earth Scenes.

Chapter 15 506–507: Larry Fischer/Masterfile. 508–509: © Dick Hanley/Photo Researchers, Inc. 509: Dan DeWilde for SB&G. 510: John Leo/OPC for SB&G. 511, 512: Courtesy of Upjohn Company, Kalamazoo, MI. 513: Michal Heron; 514: © Ted Spagna. 515: David Dempster for SB&G. 516, 517: John Lei/OPC for SB&G. 518: Todd Haiman for SB&G. 521: *t.* Bill Varie/The Image Bank; *b.* Julian Baum/Bruce Coleman. 522: Ken Lax for SB&G. 523: *t.r.* David Madison/Duomo; *b.l.* Zefa/The Stock Market. 524: Ken Lax for SB&G. 525: The Bettmann Archive. 526: Bruce Curtis/Peter Arnold, Inc. 528: © Manfred Kage/Peter Arnold, Inc. 529: *l.* © Manfred Kage/Peter Arnold, Inc.; *r.* David Scharf/Peter Arnold, Inc. 530: © Petit Format/Lennart Nilsson/Boerhinger Ingelheim/Photo Researchers, Inc. 531: Ken Lax for SB&G. 536: Tony Kawashima for SB&G.

ACKNOWLEDGMENTS

Grateful acknowledgment is made to the following publishers, authors, and agents for their permission to reprint copyrighted material. Any adaptations are noted in the individual acknowledgments and are made with the full knowledge and approval of the authors or their representatives. Every effort has been made to locate all copyright proprietors; any errors or omissions in copyright notice are inadvertent and will be corrected in future printings as they are discovered.

pp. 188–196: "A Mammoth Mummy" from *Tales Mummies Tell* by Patricia Lauber (Crowell). Copyright © 1985 by Patricia G. Lauber. Reprinted by permission of Harper & Row, Publishers, Inc., and of the author.

pp. 354–362: Excerpt from *The Green Book* by Jill Paton Walsh, illustrated by Lloyd Bloom. Text copyright © 1982 by Jill Paton Walsh. Illustrations copyright © 1982 by Lloyd Bloom. Reprinted by permission of Farrar, Straus and Giroux, Inc., and of David Higham Associates Limited.

pp. 468–476: "Antrodemus" from *Auks, Rocks and the Odd Dinosaur* by Peggy Thomson (Crowell). Copyright © 1985 by Peggy Thomson. Reprinted by permission of Harper & Row, Publishers, Inc.

pp. 511 and 512: EEG's Courtesy of The Upjohn Company, Kalamazoo, Michigan, Current Concepts, 1982, p. 7.

pp. 538–546: From *The Summer of the Swans* by Betsy Byars, illustrated by Ted CoConis. Copyright © 1970 by Betsy Byars. All rights reserved. Reprinted by permission of Viking Penguin, a division of Penguin Books USA, Inc.